D0976873

BODY IMAGES
Development, Deviance, and Change

BODY IMAGES
Development, Deviance, and Change

Edited by

THOMAS F. CASH
THOMAS PRUZINSKY

THE GUILFORD PRESS
New York   London

© 1990 The Guilford Press
A Division of Guilford Publications, Inc.
72 Spring Street, New York, NY 10012

Printed in the United States of America

This book is printed on acid-free paper.

Last digit is print number: 9 8 7 6 5 4 3 2

Library of Congress Cataloging-in-Publication Data

Body images : development, deviance, and change / edited by Thomas F.
Cash and Thomas Pruzinsky.
     p.   cm.
   Includes bibliographical references.
   Includes index.
   ISBN 0-89862-438-X
   1. Body image. I. Cash, Thomas F. II. Pruzinsky, Thomas.
   [DNLM: 1. Body Image. 2. Self-Concept.   BF 697.5.B63 B668]
BF697.5.B63B62   1990
155.2—dc20
for Library of Congress   90–3405
                                                                    CIP

Newbridge Book Clubs
For information about our audio products, write us at:
Newbridge Book Clubs, 3000 Cindel Drive, Delran, NJ 08370

Dedicated to our families, who put up with us and believe in us; they are the beauty in our lives.

To Diane, Thomas, and Ben
—T.F.C.

To Rhonda
—T.P.

Contributors

Madeline N. Altabe is a doctoral candidate in clinical psychology at the University of South Florida. She received her M.A. in 1989, and her research interests include cognitive approaches to body image, food categorization, and self–ideal discrepancies. Her thesis—"Menstrual Cycle, Body Image, and Eating Disturbance"—was recently accepted for publication by the *International Journal of Eating Disorders*.

Norman R. Bernstein, Ph.D. is a world-recognized expert on the emotional care of the facially burned and disfigured. He is currently Professor of Psychiatry at Harvard Medical School, a consultant to the Shriner's Institute in Boston, and a Visiting Professor of Psychiatry at the University of Chicago, where he also was previously affiliated with the University of Chicago Burn Center. Dr. Bernstein has published numerous books and articles in the areas of facial deformity and disfigurement, and is a leader in the development of programs for integrated medical and psychosocial care of individuals with facial disfigurement. Among his books are the classic *Emotional Care of the Burned and the Facially Disfigured* (Little, Brown & Co., 1976) and the more recent *Coping Strategies for Burn Survivors and Their Families* (Praeger Scientific, 1988).

Thomas F. Cash, Ph.D. is Professor of Psychology at Old Dominion University in Norfolk, Virginia. For the 15 years that have passed since receiving his doctorate in clinical psychology, he has conducted a research program principally concerned with the psychology of physical appearance—including numerous scientific publications on physical attractiveness, body image and body–image therapy, grooming behaviors such as cosmetics use, and aesthetic surgeries, as well as articles on other aspects of psychology. In addition to the present volume, Dr. Cash has produced a self-help audiotape series, *Body Image Therapy: A Program for Self-Directed Change* (Guilford). He serves on the editorial boards of the *Journal of Social and Clinical Psychology* and the *Journal of Applied Social Psychology,* is active in numerous professional associations, and has served as consultant to various national corporations and organizations. Dr. Cash also maintains a private psychotherapy practice.

Milton T. Edgerton, M.D. is an internationally known surgeon for his development of techniques in elective and reconstructive surgery. He has authored over 400 scholarly publications, including seminal work on the psychological aspects of plastic surgery and a recent book called *The Art of Surgical Technique* (Williams & Wilkins, 1988). He is

Professor and Chairman of the Department of Plastic and Maxillofacial Surgery at the University of Virginia Medical School. He is a past president of the American Society of Plastic and Reconstructive Surgery.

April Fallon, Ph.D. is Assistant Professor of Psychology in the Department of Psychiatry at the Medical College of Pennsylvania. She teaches and supervises psychiatric residents and psychology interns in individual and group psychotherapy. Her research interests include group psychotherapy, sociocultural aspects of psychopathology, body image, and eating disorders.

Seymour Fisher, Ph.D. is Professor of Psychology, Department of Psychiatry and Behavioral Science, State University of New York Health Science Center (Syracuse). His research program focuses on the behavioral and psychosomatic consequences of the meanings individuals assign to various parts of their bodies. His work also concerns the differential effectiveness of biological as compared to psychological treatments for particular forms of psychological distress. Dr. Fisher wrote *Development and Structure of the Body Image* (Lawrence Erlbaum Associates, 1986).

Rita Freedman, Ph.D. maintains a private practice in Scarsdale, New York. She was formerly Professor of Psychology and Women's Studies at the State University of New York at New Paltz and at the College of New Rochelle. She is the author of *Beauty Bound* (Lexington Books, 1986) and *Bodylove* (Harper & Row, 1988), and her work has been featured in both scholarly and popular publications. She lectures extensively on topics related to body image and the psychology of women.

Jasna Jovanovic is a Ph.D. candidate in the Department of Human Development and Family Studies at The Pennsylvania State University. A student member of the Society for Research on Adolescence and the Society for Research in Child Development, her research has focused on early adolescent/social context interactions. She received fellowships from the International Research and Exchanges Board and from the Department of Education Fulbright–Hays Division to collect data in Yugoslavia on culture as a contextual influence on adolescent development.

David W. Krueger, M.D. is Clinical Professor of Psychiatry at the Baylor College of Medicine, and is Director of the Eating Disorders Treatment Program at Spring Shadows Glen Hospital in Houston, Texas. He maintains a private practice of psychiatry and psychoanalysis in Houston. Among his scholarly works, Dr. Krueger is the editor of a volume entitled *Emotional Rehabilitation of Physical Trauma and Disability* (Spectrum Publications, 1984) and is the author of *Body Self and Psychological Self: A Developmental and Clinical Integration of Disorders of the Self* (Norton, 1989).

Richard M. Lerner, Ph.D. is Professor of Child and Adolescent Development at The Pennsylvania State University. He is a Fellow of the American Psychological Society, of the American Psychological Association (Divisions 2, 7, and 9), and of the American Association for the Advancement of Science. He has been a Fellow at the Center for Advanced Study in the Behavioral Sciences, and a Visiting Scientist at the Max Planck Institute for Human Development and Education in Berlin. He is the author or editor of 20 books and over 125 articles and chapters. His research interests include the study of the role of organismic individuality in personality and social development, especially during the transition from childhood to adolescence.

Michael J. Mahoney, Ph.D. is Director of Clinical Psychology at the University of North Texas. The author of 12 books and numerous scientific articles, Dr. Mahoney helped pioneer the "cognitive revolution" in psychology. Chosen to be a Master Lecturer on Psychotherapy Process in 1981 and a G. Stanley Hall Lecturer in 1988, Dr. Mahoney has received several professional awards, including a 1984 Fulbright Award and a 1985 Citation Classic from Science Citation Index in recognition of the influence of his 1974 book *Cognition and Behavior Modification* (Ballinger, 1984). Dr. Mahoney has served on the Editorial Boards of twelve scientific journals and has worked with the U.S. Olympic Committee since 1978 in the area of sports psychology. His research interests include basic processes in psychological development and psychotherapy, theoretical and philosophical issues, psychology of science, and health and sports psychology. His forthcoming book, *Human Change Processes: The Scientific Bases of Psychotherapy* (Basic Books, 1990), attempts to integrate the research literatures from several disciplines as they bear on the conceptualization and facilitation of psychological change.

Louis A. Penner, Ph.D. is a Professor and Chair of the Psychology Department at the University of South Florida. His research interests include helping behavior, individual differences in social behavior, and methodological issues in social and clinical psychology. In line with the last interest, he has conducted several studies on psychometric issues related to the measurement of body image. He is currently on the editorial boards of the *Journal of Social and Clincal Psychology* and the *Review of Personality and Social Psychology*.

Michael J. Pertschuk, M.D. is Clinical Associate Professor of Psychiatry at the University of Pennsylvania Medical School. He heads the Psychiatry Section of the Center for Human Appearance at the University of Pennsylvania Medical Center, and is Chairman of the Department of Psychiatry at The Graduate Hospital in Philadelphia. His research has focused on psychosocial studies of craniofacial malformations and appearance change. He has also published research in the area of eating disorders.

Thomas Pruzinsky, Ph.D. is Assistant Professor of Plastic and Maxillofacial Surgery, as well as Assistant Professor of Behavioral Medicine and Psychiatry, at the University of Virginia School of Medicine. Dr. Pruzinsky has published work concerning the role of the psychologist in treating individuals undergoing cosmetic and reconstructive surgery. He is a consulting reviewer for the journal *Plastic and Reconstructive Surgery* and is on the editorial board of *Medical Psychotherapy: An International Journal*. His clinical expertise includes the assessment and treatment of children, adolescents, and adults seeking elective cosmetic surgery or surgical reconstruction after disease or trauma. He is the coordinator of psychosocial services for the University of Virginia Burn Center.

James C. Rosen, Ph.D. is Associate Professor of Psychology and Director of the Clinical Psychology program at the University of Vermont in Burlington. Dr. Rosen has conducted and published extensive research in the areas of behavior therapy, bulimia nervosa, weight reduction, and body image.

Franklin C. Shontz, Ph.D. is Professor of Psychology at the University of Kansas. For the past 20 years, he has been active in research and writing on the nature of body image in general and bodily experience in disability in particular. He has published numerous papers on these topics and his books in the area include *Perceptual and Cognitive Aspects of Body Experience* (Academic Press, 1969) and *The Psychological Aspects of Physical Illness and Disability* (MacMillan, 1975).

J. Kevin Thompson, Ph.D. is Associate Professor of Psychology at the University of South Florida. His research interests include body image, eating disorders, and psychotherapy integration. He has edited special issues of *Behavior Modification* and the *Journal of Cognitive Psychotherapy,* and is on the editorial board of the *International Journal of Eating Disorders.* He has recently completed *Body Image Disturbance: Assessment and Treatment* (Pergamon Press, 1990).

Preface

The past 2 decades have witnessed the emergence of significant scholarly thought and research in the construction of a psychology of physical appearance. The extant scholarship, both basic and applied, transcends the academic discipline of psychology. The field has become multidisciplinary in scope—involving scientific and practitioner elements from both the behavioral sciences and the biomedical sciences. Unfortunately, however, its multiprofessional nature also serves to segment the field. The advancement and implications of knowledge from one professional domain do not necessarily reach those in other disciplines. In order for the field to become productively interdisciplinary, there must be active collaboration in the acquisition, dissemination, and application of this knowledge. A principal aim of this book is to bring together prominent scientist-practitioners whose ideas, research, and clinical work represent this interface of the professions concerned with human physical appearance.

The psychology of physical appearance may be conveniently divided into two foci: (1) the concern with *external, objective* attributes of physical appearance and their personal and social implications for human development and experience; and (2) the concern with *internal, subjective* representations of physical appearance and bodily experience. This latter perspective is often termed "body image." Far from a single entity, the body-image construct is multidimensional, with diverse theoretical and empirical meanings. The most productive psychology of physical appearance requires an integrative emphasis on both the objective and the subjective foci. And it must capture the rich diversity of what body image entails. Thus, *body image is body images*.

This volume reviews and elucidates diverse concepts of body image, body-image development, psychosocially dysfunctional deviations from normal appearance, and methods of facilitating body-image change. Body-image concepts are frequently employed to explain a range of psychological phenomena including personality development, psychopathology (e.g., eating disorders, body dysmorphic disorder, etc.), and adjustment of individuals to deformity, disfigurement, disability, and disease. Moreover, people expend considerable time, money, and behavioral effort to overcome both objective and perceived defects in their appearance and to maintain and enhance their physical aesthetics. The pursuit of beauty (or, for that matter, a "normal" appearance) is often actually a search for psychosocially satisfying body images.

The major questions addressed by the book are these: What are the meaningful parameters or components of the body-image construct and how are they best measured? What are the physical, developmental, social, and cultural determinants of the unfolding of these facets of body image? How do gender and objective attributes of appearance influence the subjective experience of the body? What are the roles of body images in the development and change of personality and psychopathology? How do deleterious changes in physical appearance and physical competence affect body images? How can one promote adaptive body-image change through the self-management of physical aesthetics, through medical–surgical procedures, and through various psychotherapeutic and somatopsychic interventions?

This volume consists of 6 sections that provide coherent topical organization of 16 chapters. Each chapter is authored by a nationally or internationally prominent expert on that specific topic. Overviews of the six sections follow:

PART I: CONCEPTS AND ASSESSMENT OF BODY IMAGES

This introductory section places body image into theoretical, historical, and methodological contexts. In Chapter 1, Seymour Fisher, a psychologist who has devoted over 30 years of his career to the topic, provides an insightful historical overview of the body-image concept and articulates its complex multidimensional nature. In Chapter 2, Kevin Thompson, Louis Penner, and Madeline Altabe focus on the critical psychometric and methodological considerations in the measurement of various body-image concepts. Their chapter has much practical utility for researchers and clinicians who wish to accurately assess body-image parameters in various clinical and nonclinical populations. Both chapters offer valuable reflections upon the longstanding controversies about the core nature of "body image."

PART II: BODY, SELF, AND SOCIETY: DEVELOPMENT OF BODY IMAGES

This section considers the multiple determinants of body experience, placing body images into a life-span developmental context. All three chapters take a transactional/ecological perspective on the unfolding and changing of body images. Thomas Cash's initial chapter, Chapter 3, introduces the psychology of physical appearance and focuses on the interface between subjective body images and objective physical attributes along a continuum of normal physical appearance and attractiveness. Breaking with the traditional paradigm that regards appearance and body images largely as static traits, Cash explores the dynamic self-creation of appearance and body experience. In Chapter 4, psychologist April Fallon offers a thought-provoking examination of body attributes and images from a sociocultural perspective, emphasizing similarities and differences in gender-linked, cross-cultural definitions and representations of standards of beauty and aesthetic deviance. Finally, building upon the earlier chapters, Chapter 5 contains Richard Lerner and Jasna Jovanovic's careful analysis of body-image development across the life span from their well-researched developmental contextual framework.

PART III: DIVERGENCE AND DYSFUNCTION OF BODY IMAGES

This section considers personally distressing body-image difficulties—first, from the aforementioned "objective" perspective, and, then, from the more "subjective" perspective. The first two chapters of this section offer sensitive and thoughtful observations on the psychosocial impact of conditions of objectively defined negative deviations from the continuum normal appearance. Psychiatrist Norman Bernstein, in Chapter 6, captures the nature of body experience and self-image among individuals with congenital deformities or disfiguring injuries or diseases. Then, in Chapter 7, psychologist Franklin Shontz considers objective deviations of body competence—"physical disabilities." He delineates his well-established model of body experience, draws upon the important "insider–outsider" distinction, and articulates the impact of disability on individuals' subjective experiences of body and self.

Chapters 8 and 9 concern subjective deviance and focus on those individuals with an objectively "normal" appearance but who have a subjective perception of themselves as aesthetically deviant. Thomas Pruzinsky's Chapter 8 capitalizes on his clinical experience in a plastic surgical setting and offers insights into specific psychopathologies of body experience (e.g., persons with hypochondriacal, body dysmorphic, somatic delusional, or gender identity disorders), as well as the relation of body-image dysfunction to such disorders as depression, schizophrenia, and sexual dysfunction. Finally, in Chapter 9, psychologist James Rosen provides a thorough, critical, and scholarly review of the literature on body-image distortion and dissatisfaction among persons with eating disorders (bulimia and anorexia nervosa).

PART IV: BODY-IMAGE CHANGE THROUGH BODILY CHANGE

Parts IV and V focus on the professional interventions through which persons seek to alter negative, dysfunctional body images defined and discussed in the previous section. The emphasis of the chapters in this and the subsequent section is on the nature of the psychosocial change process brought about through physical or psychological interventions, the integration of the changes into the "personality" and the sense of self, as well as the maintenance of the changes in self-concept that result from these interventions. The chapters in Part IV deal with body-image change by bodily change—through cosmetic and reconstructive surgeries. In Chapter 10, Pruzinsky collaborates with Milton Edgerton, a renowned plastic surgeon, to delineate the psychosocial issues and outcomes associated with elective cosmetic surgery for "correcting" objectively minor, yet psychologally salient, deviations in normal appearance. These authors take the strong stance that such surgery is inextricably a body-image intervention. Then, in Chapter 11, psychiatrist Michael Pertschuk continues this theme and considers reconstructive surgery for changes in major deviations (deformities and disfigurements) of appearance.

PART V: BODY-IMAGE CHANGE THROUGH PSYCHOLOGICAL CHANGE

Next we turn from medical-surgical methods for body-image enhancement to consider formal psychotherapeutic interventions. What types of specific psychotherapeutic procedures can be employed to promote body-image change? Are these approaches effective? These are the basic questions addressed by the four chapters in this section of the book. From quite diverse perspectives, each author details the conceptual basis of his or her approach to body image and, often illustrated with case material, describes the therapeutic procedures for promoting body-image improvement. In the lead chapter, Chapter 12, psychiatrist David Krueger offers insights and interventions derived from his integrated understanding of various psychodynamic theories. In Chapter 13, clinical psychologist Rita Freedman presents a cognitive–behavioral approach to body-image therapy, accompanied by considerable procedural detail and review of its empirical support. Pruzinsky's Chapter 14 examines strategies that, while certainly less mainstream than psychodynamic or cognitive–behavioral approaches, may hold promise. He elucidates various somatopsychic interventions, or "body therapies," that range from dance or movement therapy to Rolfing and that are employed alone or within a verbal psychotherapeutic context. Finally, in Chapter 15, prominent theorist-researcher-clinician Michael Mahoney offers his wisdom in an integrative, forward-looking discourse on "embodiment" and the processes of human change.

PART VI: SYNTHESIS OF BODY IMAGES

This section consists of a concise concluding chapter that summarizes and integrates the principal themes interwoven throughout the book. Thus, it is our editorial opportunity to attempt to "pull it all together." These emergent themes, we believe, reflect not only the current status of research, theory, and clinical work in the body-image field but will serve, we hope, to articulate goals for the future development of the field.

Having conveyed what our book is about, allow us a moment to mention how it came about. Just a few years ago, at a professional conference, we (the editors) met for the first time. We had been aware of one another's involvements in our shared area of interest, but living in our respective professional niches, we never got around to "picking each other's brain" about physical appearance and body image. Though we are both scientists and clinical practitioners, one of us (Cash) works largely as a researcher in an academic department of psychology, and the other (Pruzinsky) works largely as a clinician in a medical school department of plastic surgery. Standing in the hotel lobby, we launched into lively conversation for hours. In addition to our emergent friendship, this book is one of the fruits of our encounter.

Over the course of several months and numerous telephone meetings, we developed a detailed prospectus for this volume. We constructed our rank-ordered "wish list" of the best scholars to contribute chapters in each specific facet of body-image development, deviance, and change. Fortunately for us and for the reader, we received an enthusiastic commitment from our top-choice candidate for every chapter. Their cooperation and collaboration during the ensuing year of writing, editing, and revising greatly enhanced the pleasure as well as the productivity of this scholarly enterprise.

We are also grateful to the many others who have contributed, directly and indirectly, to this work. The experts at Guilford, especially Sharon Panulla, Sarah Kennedy, and Seymour Weingarten, have been enthusiastic, patient, and exacting—at just the right times. For his skill and diligence in the initial editing of all chapter drafts, we extend special thanks to Thomas F. Cash, Jr. As our contributing authors know, that phase was the responsibility of the "Three Tom Team." In addition, Dr. Cash extends his sincere gratitude to the fine faculty and students of the Department of Psychology at Old Dominion University, especially to its chair Dr. Peter J. Mikulka, and to a good friend and colleague Dr. Tim Brown. Dr. Pruzinsky greatly appreciates the support of the University of Virginia Department of Plastic and Maxillofacial Surgery, with special thanks to Dr. Milton Edgerton for his mentorship and to Drs. Ray Morgan, John Persing, Richard Edlich, and John Kenney.

Contents

P A R T   I

CONCEPTS AND ASSESSMENT
OF BODY IMAGES

C H A P T E R 1

The Evolution of Psychological Concepts about the Body

Seymour Fisher

Interest in the body as a psychological phenomenon has dramatically effloresced. As one scans the current scientific literature dealing with the psychological experience of one's own body, the quantity and diversity of studies are impressive. Research dealing with this topic has gone off in all directions. Investigators are actively exploring such areas as perception of one's own body attractiveness (e.g., Cash, Cash, & Butters, 1983), phantom limb experiences (e.g., Cofer, 1980), body-size distortions associated with anorexia nervosa (e.g., Casper, Halmi, Goldberg, Eckert, & Davis, 1979), the body boundary (Fisher, 1986), responses to plastic surgery (e.g., Goin & Goin, 1981), accuracy of perception of body sensations (e.g., Katkin, Blascovich, & Koenigsberg, 1984), distortions in body feelings associated with psychopathology (Fisher, 1986), and so forth. Concepts pertaining to body perception are also being tentatively applied to the understanding of the effects of drugs, exercise regimens, psychotherapy, surgery, subliminal stimuli, rolfing, and an apparently endless series of other variables (Fisher, 1986). It should be added that such concepts are surreptitiously infusing certain areas of research under the guise of terms like *self-awareness*, *sex-role definition*, and *somatic anxiety* (Fisher, 1986). In any case, what particularly impresses me about the multiple branches of the current work dealing with body attitudes and feelings is how disconnected they are. These branches often thrive in "splendid isolation," as if the others did not exist. Cross-references by researchers in the different areas are, at best, sparse. I am focusing on this point because it duplicates a pattern typifying the developmental history of this line of research. Looking back at the early pioneering *body-image* enterprises, one sees that they rarely acknowledged each other. They often targeted different classes of behavior and used divergent nomenclatures. Terms like *body image, body concept, body schema,* and *body percept* were employed without serious attempts to integrate them. More will be said shortly about such matters of nomenclature.

Let us examine the major derivative sources of the scientific study of the body as a psychological object. We will look at the themes characterizing each and consider some of their interactions.

NEUROLOGICAL ROOTS

The examining room of the neurologist was one of the earliest contexts in which body experiences were highlighted. The sheer dramatic uniqueness of the distortions in body perception triggered by brain damage could not help but capture the attention of neurologists. Brain-damaged patients often displayed spectacular symptoms that variously included denial of the existence of body parts, inability to distinguish the right and left sides of the body, refusal to acknowledge the incapacitation of paralyzed body regions, and even attributing new or supernumary body parts to themselves. Patients verbalized bizarre beliefs, such as saying an area of the body seemed to belong to someone else or one side of the body was "lined with iron" (Critchley, 1953). Neurologists who witnessed such phenomena became aware that the normal modes of body perception are not immutable and that they represent an organized process that can go awry. This, in turn, piqued their curiosity as to the nature of the organizing process. Also, as might be expected, they focused particularly on which structures of the brain might be central to maintaining a normal pattern of body experience. Their fascination with locating the central controls for body experience in a delimited brain region has persisted and still finds expression in the work of some contemporary neurologists.

Around the turn of the century, detailed reports were already appearing concerning apparent links between certain forms of distorted body perception and brain damage. For example, Bonnier (1905) described instances in which brain-damaged individuals felt that their whole body had completely disappeared (aschematia). Pick (1922) introduced the term *autotopagnosia* to refer to patients who were disturbed in orientation to their body surface (e.g., not being able to differentiate the right from the left side). He was led by his work in this area to theorize that each individual evolves "a spatial image of the body." This image was said to be an inner representation of one's own body as it appears consciously from information provided by sensory input. Interestingly, Pick also became fascinated with phantom-limb phenomena and speculated that phantom-limb sensations derived from discrepancies between the previous body configuration and the new altered configuration resulting from the amputation. Other observers, such as Poetzl (see Schilder, 1950) and Pineas (see Critchley, 1966), were also compiling a dossier of the body perception distortions found in neurological patients. Incidentally, one of the first laboratory experiments in this area was carried out by Hoff and Poetzl (1931), who reported that if areas of the brain are chilled through openings resulting from skull defects, patients state they cannot perceive their limbs on the side opposite to the chilling. As one scans the writings of the early neurologists interested in distorted body perceptions, one is impressed with their zeal in inventorying the full range of such distortions and assigning them to categories with esoteric names. There was a pseudo-exactness about the categorizations and their presumed ties to localized brain defects. Note that it was presumed that psychological factors, as such, play little part in the distortions, and no real thought was given to the possibility that the experience of being brain damaged may trigger alterations in body experience that reflect defensive strategies at a time of stress rather than the impact of damage to specific brain areas.

Particularly prominent among the neurologists drawn into the realm of distorted body experiences was a British investigator, Henry Head. He examined a number of neurological syndromes (e.g., hemiasomatognosia and anosognosia) in body-image terms and contributed rich clinical material. He originated the term *body schema* and was the first to construct a theory with some detailed elaboration concerning how body perceptions are integrated and unified. He proposed that each individual builds a model or picture of self that constitutes a standard against which postures and body movements are judged. Such a model, he said, would be a basic requirement if persons were to have the capability of shifting from one position to another in a coherent fashion. He referred to this model as a "schema." The following is his own description of it:

> Every recognizable change enters into consciousness already charged with its relation to something that has gone before, just as on a taximeter the distance is presented to us already transformed into shillings and pence. So the final products of the tests for the appreciation of posture or passive movement rise into consciousness as a measured postural change.
>
> For this combined standard, against which all subsequent changes of posture are measured before they enter consciousness, we propose the word "schema." By means of perpetual alterations in position we are always building up a postural model of ourselves which constantly changes. Every new posture of movement is recorded on this plastic schema, and the activity of the cortex brings every fresh group of sensations evoked by altered posture into relation with it. Immediate postural recognition follows as soon as the relation is complete. (1926, p. 605)

It is interesting that he considered the functioning of the body schema to be largely unconscious. Although he emphasized the role of the schema in orienting posture and body movement, his speculations suggest that he entertained the view that it also served as a frame of reference for interpreting other kinds of experiences. Head is often accorded accolades for originating the idea of a "body schema," but questions have been raised (e.g., Bartlett, 1926; Oldfield & Zangwill, 1942) as to how much of a contribution it actually represented. There was, in fact, little specificity provided as to how a schema is organized or how it mediates judgments. However, the term *body schema* proved to be a catchy one, and it became widely used in neurological and other circles as an explanatory mode.

Another major figure in the stream of neurologists concerned with distorted body perception was Josef Gerstmann. Working in Vienna around 1924, he came upon a brain-injured woman who was unable to recognize her own fingers (nor those of the examiner), had great difficulty in writing, could not perform even simple arithmetical calculations, and was incapable of distinguishing right from left on her own body. This cluster of symptoms was later reported to exist in other patients (e.g., Critchley, 1953) and became known as the Gerstmann syndrome. It was described as being due to a brain lesion in the parieto–occipital region of the left, or the dominant, hemisphere. This syndrome attracted much interest because Gerstmann put it forward as an instance of a well-organized defect in the ''body image'' that could be linked to the dysfunction of a circumscribed brain sector. The apparent clustering of the four types of symptoms (finger agnosia, right–left disorientation, agraphia, dyscalculia) was intriguing because on the surface they seem to have little in common. The possibility was raised that the finger agnosia was particularly central because the fingers are important in counting and arithmetical operations and also obviously in writing. In turn, this could suggest that the integrity of many of our skills may depend upon the proper functioning of certain basic aspects of the ''body image.'' The Gerstmann formulation proved to be a stimulant to theorizing and research about the organization of body experience (e.g., Benton, Hutcheon, & Seymour, 1951; Critchley, 1953; Strauss & Werner, 1938; Teitelbaum, 1941). However, it has been the target of increasing criticism. In 1971, Poeck and Orgass reviewed the available literature and concluded that the Gerstmann syndrome is a fiction. Not only did they point out that the four supposed components of the syndrome show low interrelations, but they argued that most reports of specific body-schema disturbances in neurological patients are reflections of more generalized brain defects rather than a specific species of body-schema defect. They did, in fact, disagree with the idea favored by many preceding neurologists that the parietal lobes are a site for a body-image center.

It should be noted that a recurrent interest among neurological observers was the phantom-limb phenomenon. Extensive discussions concerning this matter can be found in the writings of such individuals as Head, Pick, Lhermitte, and Schilder. Basically, they regarded the phantom experience as the expression of a central body-image process. They speculated that when persons continue to experience an amputated body part as if it were still there, this was due to the persistence of a central body image that had not yet adapted to the body loss and distorted the meaning of stimuli in order to negate the loss. Head and Holmes (1911–1912) sought to document the central body-image origin of the phantom by describing a case in which injury to the parietal cortex by cerebral hemorrhage blocked previously reported contralateral phantom sensations. They reasoned that the stroke the patient suffered altered a brain area with significant body-image functions and, in so doing, abolished the phantom-limb illusion. Many case reports were published by others who argued pro and con concerning a central explanation for phantom sensations and also the specific brain areas most likely to control such sensations. Later research that stemmed in part from these early speculations was largely concerned with the relative importance of central versus peripheral factors in the origin of phantom sensations (e.g., Haber, 1956; Teuber, Krieger, & Bender, 1949) and the influences upon phantom experiences of such variables as developmental maturity and psychodynamic defenses (Simmel, 1956).

An account of the neurological roots of the study of body experience would be grossly incomplete without a discussion of the work of Paul Schilder, who was one of the outstanding thinkers in this area. Before reviewing Schilder's contributions, let us consider for a moment what the neurologists were assuming, learning, and thinking as they witnessed the impact of brain damage and loss of body parts upon body experience. First, they were able to inventory and classify the curious array of distorted body perceptions reported by their patients (Critchley, 1965). Second, they made the study of body-image phenomena scientifically acceptable. Third, they conjured up the notion of a central body-image schema or controlling monitor that registers body perceptions and integrates them. Fourth, they proposed linear relationships between specific classes of distorted body perceptions and injuries to specific compartments of the brain. Fifth, and finally, they kept the psychological side of their formulations simple and gave little or no consideration as to how body experience may be tied to personality and psychodynamic variables.

PAUL SCHILDER'S CONTRIBUTIONS

Paul Schilder almost single-handedly upgraded the study of body experience, taking it beyond a parochial focus on the distorted perceptions induced by brain damage. It is true that his own interest in this area was originally stimulated by his observations of neurological patients. He began his professional life as a neurologist, and he was indeed fascinated with the variety of unusual body-image events he encountered. In his writings, we find him diversely commenting on such phenomena as depersonalization, the Gerstmann syndrome, anosognosia, problems brain-damaged persons have in "crossing" their own midline, and their difficulties in differentiating right and left. But even in his early work, he was already going beyond neurological perspectives in his analysis of body experience. As far back as 1914, he published a monograph that looked not only at depersonalization but at the whole basic issue of self-awareness itself. In 1923, he published a treatise, *Das Koerperschema*, that examined a number of general issues relating to the body image that were to preoccupy him until his death in 1940.

The fact is that he quickly decided that the distortions in body experience linked to brain pathology need to be analyzed not only in relation to brain physiology but also with respect to a larger psychological framework. When in 1935 he wrote his major volume *The Image and Appearance of the Human Body*, he specifically noted in the preface that the study of body image should include at one extreme the data from organic pathology and at the other extreme the findings of psychoanalysis. He turned out to be uniquely qualified for instituting a multifaceted approach to body-image phenomena. He was well versed in neurology, philosophy, psychodynamic ideas, and the general psychology of his day. Also, by way of his theoretical orientation, he was inclined to cross the boundaries of disciplines and seek the integration of concepts. In *The Image and Appearance of the Human Body*, his viewpoint was apparent in the fact that he analyzed body image not only within the context of the "organic" but also psychoanalysis and sociology. Thus, there are three separate sections to the book: (1) "The Physiological Basis of the Body-Image," (2) "The Libidinous Structure of the Body-Image," and (3) "The Sociology of the Body-Image."

It might be well to digress for a moment and look at Schilder's (1950) definition of "body image":

> The image of the human body means the picture of our own body which we form in our mind, that is to say, the way in which the body appears to ourselves. There are sensations which are given to us. We see parts of the body-surface. We have tactile, thermal, pain impressions. There are sensations which come from the muscles and their sheaths—sensations coming from the innervation of the muscles—and sensations from the viscera. Beyond that there is the immediate experience that there is a unity of the body. This unity is perceived, yet it is more than a perception. We call it a schema of our body or bodily schema, or, following Head, who emphasizes the importance of the knowledge of the position of the body, postural model of the body. The body schema is the tri-dimensional image everybody has about himself. We may call it "body image." (p. 11)

Schilder went on to indicate that significant parts of the body image could remain outside of central awareness in largely unconscious ("schemata") forms but still exert potent influence. This definition is widely eclectic. Schilder includes conscious and unconscious elements, all varieties of body sensations, and a Gestalt-like "perceived unity" that is "more than a perception," and in other contexts he emphasized that the body image is not only a cognitive construction but also a reflection of wishes, emotional attitudes, and interactions with others. This rather loose definition contrasts with the views of other body-image theorists who want to make the term more precise and who urge the use of specific nomenclature that differentiates between the cognitive and emotional aspects of body-image organization. Shontz (1969) has been in the forefront of those who urge that such eclectic definitions are so imprecise that they impede research. He particularly suggests that distinctions be made between perception of one's body as an object in space (involving postural adjustment and stimulus localization), concepts about one's body ("ideas about. . . somatic structures and processes," p. 204) and body values ("a set of emotionally charged attitudes, or values about the body," p. 203). Correspondingly, he would favor the use of such specific terms as *body schemata*, *body concepts*, and *body values*. I have taken the position elsewhere (Fisher, 1986) that while one may theoretically distinguish among such dimensions, there is considerable evidence that even the simplest of spatial schemata or body concepts are measurably influenced by emotional and personality parameters. The work of Witkin, Lewis, Hertzman, Machover, Meissner, and Wapner (1954) and Witkin, Dyk, Faterson, Goodenough, and Karp (1962) supports this view insofar as it demonstrates that elementary judgments concerning the position of one's body in space are significantly mediated by numerous personality factors.

But returning again to the specifics of Schilder's work, one would have to say that his most unique contribution was that he introduced the idea that body-image variables have central pertinence not only for the pathological but also the everyday events of life. Note that he described the life space as comprised of "a world partly animate, partly inanimate, there is our body, and finally there is a personality which has this close and specific relation to the body" (1950, pp. 283–284). He was curious about practically every aspect of body experience, including the "feel" of the usual sensory inputs, fluctuations in perceived body size, feelings of lightness versus heaviness, and awareness of "surface" versus "interior" regions of the body. He raised questions about the impact upon the body image of socializing with others, of being touched, of feeling angry, of being unattractive, of laughing or crying, of sexual intimacy, of wearing certain types of clothing, of relating to one's parents in specific ways, and so forth. The flavor of some of his speculations, which often focused on the fluidity of body experience, is conveyed by the following:

> Every emotion therefore changes the body-image. The body contracts when we hate, it becomes firmer, and its outlines toward the world are more strongly marked. . . We expand the body when we feel friendly and loving. We open our arms, we would like to enclose humanity in them. We expand, and the borderlines of the body-image lose their distinct character. . . .We expand and we contract the postural model of the body; we take parts away and we add parts; we rebuild it; we melt the details in; we create new details; we do this with our body and with the expressions of the body itself. We experiment continually with it. When the experimentation with the movement is not sufficient, then we add the influence of the vestibular apparatus and of intoxicants to the picture. When even so the body is not sufficient for the expression of the playful changes and the destructive changes in the body, then we add clothes, masks, jewelry, which again expand, contract, disfigure, or emphasize the body-image and its particular parts. (1950, pp. 210–211)

Incidentally, Schilder often introduced his own introspections to illustrate points. For example, in discussing phantom-limb sensations, he described such sensations that he experienced after loss of two of his fingers in an automobile accident.

Many of Schilder's formulations about the body image were strongly colored by psychoanalytic ideas. While he was not a psychoanalyst, he was well-versed in psychoanalytic theory. Before coming to the United States, he actually had a good deal of contact with the Vienna Psychoanalytic Society and apparently some degree of exchange with Freud. Congruent with Freud's formulations, he assigned central importance to the oral, anal, and genital "erogenic zones." These zones were said to be the major landmarks of the body image, and each was assumed to take on prominence developmentally in accordance with Freud's timetable. Wishes or desires pertinent to a zone were said to intensify awareness of, and also produce physiological changes in, it. Schilder suggested: "It is as if energy were amassed on these particular points. There will be lines of energy connecting the different erogenic points, and we shall have a variation in the structure of the body-image according to the psychosexual tendencies of the individual" (1950, pp. 124–125). He, like Freud, attributed much importance to feelings about the primary body openings, since "it is by these openings that we come in closest contact with the world" (p. 124). He also attributed special symbolic meanings to areas that mimic body openings. For example, he depicted the eyes as a "receptive organ" and a "symbolic opening through which the world wanders into ourselves." (p. 125). He gave a good deal of attention to what he considered the potentiality of any body part to take on an arbitrary symbolic meaning; elaborated particularly on the ways in which "genitalized" protruding parts of the body may be equated with each other, as might be likewise true of invaginated body areas. He notes:

> What goes on in one part of the body may be transfused to another part of the body. The role of the female genital organs may appear as a cavity in another part of the body, the penis as a stiffness or a piece of wood somewhere else. . . The nose may take the significance of the phallus. The protruding parts of the body may become symbols of the male sex organ. Cavities and entrances of the body are largely interchangeable. Vagina, anus, mouth, ears, and even the entrance of the nose and ears belongs to the same group. (p. 171)

As might be expected, he ascribed basic significance to the role of Oedipal conflicts in body-image matters. Indeed, he concluded that the "emotional unity of the body is dependent on the development of full object relations in the Oedipus complex" (p. 172). His translation of psychoanalytic theory into body image terms was pretty straightforward and largely within the guidelines spelled out by Freud. He did differ from Freud on two points. First, he rejected the idea of a death instinct that aimed at dissolution of the body. Second, he placed more emphasis than did Freud on the body image as a changing and shifting entity. Although he assumed the centrality of the major "erogenic zones," he felt that as new stimuli and relationships impinged on people the relative prominence of these zones changed—as did the meanings, sizes, and experiential intensities of many other body areas (e.g., musculature, viscera) that he portrayed as also being influential in the body image.

A considerable part of his book, *The Image and Appearance of the Human Body*, explores the role of the body image in psychopathological syndromes. He had a good deal of experience with a range of neurotic and schizophrenic patients and was intrigued with the body-image distortions they apparently manifested. He was especially interested in hypochondriasis, conversion hysteria, and depersonalization, probably because they so directly involve symptomatology defined in somatic terms. In theorizing about "hypochondria," he constructed a model (in largely conventional psychoanalytic terms) that pictures the site of complaint as the target of increased "narcissistic libido." This increase presumably reflects a process whereby the organ in question comes to symbolically represent a forbidden wish, usually of a sexual nature. Schilder says: "An important psychological quality of the hypochondriac organ has to be emphasized. It is genitalized and it very often symbolizes genitals" (p. 142). Schilder attributed an analogous process of symbolization to the development of conversion hysterical symptoms. But he proposed a distinction between the mechanisms involved in the hysterical versus hypochondriacal conditions. He stated that in the case of hypochondria the symptom represents a simple transposition or transfer of sensation or libido from the genitals to the symptomatic organ. However, he saw the hysterical symptom as "not only the product of transposition" but also "innumerable condensations which lead to this transposition" (p. 170). Thus, by way of illustration, he suggests that in the instance of Freud's case of Dora, her hysterical coughing was not simply a transfer of genitalized sensations, but also an "expression of identification" with certain attributes of her mother. Obviously, this distinction is vague, and Schilder offered little to which to anchor it. In discussing depersonalization (experiencing one's own body as strange and alien), which he thought "almost every neurosis has in some phases of its development" (p. 139), he said that it was "beyond doubt" due to a condition "where the individual does not dare to place his libido either in the outside world or his own body. The change in the body-image results from the withdrawal of libido from the body-image" (p. 140).

His discussions of psychopathology abound with accounts of the dramatic and bizarre body-image distortions he tells us he witnessed in his schizophrenic patients. He describes individuals who feel their entire body is destroyed, coming apart, transformed into the opposite sex, and so forth. He considered that the distortions shown by schizophrenics were on a continuum with those displayed by patients with organic brain pathology and could not be sharply distinguished. Etiologically, he traced the schizophrenic body-image difficulties to poor socialization and a past history of poor object relations. He specified that feelings of body disintegration reflect the turning of hostility against the self. Indeed, he assigned much importance to sadomasochistic attitudes as an explanation for many of the sensations of organ loss and deficiency he observed in the general psychiatric population. While he was at Bellevue in New York City, he inspired a series of studies (e.g., Bromberg & Schilder, 1932; Machover,

1949; Bender & Keeler, 1952) of body-image phenomena in both neurotic and schizophrenic individuals. Following his death, when his influence ebbed, research investment in the body-image experiences of schizophrenics declined sharply and has been reinstated only sporadically.

Overall, what has been the impact of Schilder's work? Obviously, one of the prime things he accomplished was to highlight the general importance of body attitudes and feelings in explaining behavior. He was the first to devote entire volumes to the topic of body image, and he showed that it was reasonable to apply body-image concepts not only to mysterious distortions associated with organic brain pathology but also to almost all facets of normal, everyday living. He could see the mediating role of body image in everything from one's clothing choices to aesthetic preferences to ability to empathize with the emotions of others. One should mention too his introduction of psychoanalytic concepts into explicit body-image theorizing. Freud had priority in applying psychoanalytic ideas to aspects of body perception and more will be said about this shortly, but he did not focus on the body-image aspects of psychoanalytic theory in the detailed and systematic ways that Schilder did. Basically, one can say that Schilder foresaw most of the major modern lines of research dealing with body experience. He anticipated the importance of body-size perception that is now so prominent in studies of anorexia nervosa and that was, until recently, central to attempts to distinguish the schizophrenic's body perceptions from those of normal controls. Also, early on, he devoted serious attention to the dimension embracing beauty, appearance, and attractiveness that was taken up by Jourard and Secord (1955) and eventually stimulated a sizeable percentage of the current publications concerned with body perception in normal individuals. His speculations about the differences in perception of body interior versus surface areas and his observations concerning fantasies about body intrusion anticipated the later stream of research concerned with body-image boundaries (e.g., Fisher & Cleveland, 1968; Fisher, 1986). One could extend this recitation even further. For example, consider that the recent surge of studies dealing with the effects of exercise on body perception was anticipated by Schilder's thoughtful exploration of how exercise and dancing register on body experience.

PSYCHOANALYTIC INFLUENCES

Since Freud, there has rarely been a time that psychoanalysts have not been impressed with the centrality of body feelings and fantasies. This is true, first of all, because Freud's libido theory, with its oral, anal, and genital stages, is fundamentally a statement of how attention and behavior are presumably mediated by signals linked to certain major body areas infused with symbolic meanings. As already noted, this libido model served as the framework for Schilder's theorizing. A second reason psychoanalysts have been drawn to body experience derives from the fact that their investigatory approach relies almost entirely on patients' close scrutiny of their own stream of thoughts and feelings; and such scrutiny inevitably reveals all kinds of preoccupations and distortions pertaining to one's own body. As is well known, Freud himself commented in *The Ego and the Id* (1927) that "The ego is first and foremost a body ego" (p. 31). If one looks at the details of his major theoretical formulations, one finds body-image concepts and mechanisms repeatedly put forward. Just to take a few at random, "castration anxiety" was said to be the agent for resolving the Oedipus complex in males, and the "penis-baby equation" was depicted as serving in parallel fashion for the female. Paranoia was said to represent the projection of anal (homosexual) impulses; hysteria involved the symbolic genitalization of nongenital body areas; and so forth. The original Freud, in contrast to the neo-Freudians, constantly portrayed things in the language of body imagery.

A number of the outstanding followers and apostates of Freud constructed body-image addenda to the theory. Thus, many of Alfred Adler's descriptions of personality dynamics teem with implicit references to body experience. Clearly, his theory that neurosis and other aspects of maladjustment are strategems to compensate for organ inferiority has strong body-image connotations. Apropos of this point, Cleveland and I (Fisher & Cleveland, 1968) noted:

> He [Adler] indicated that when an individual has a morphologically inferior organ or an organ which is below par for functional reasons the individual develops generalized feelings of inferiority and has to compensate for the "defect" by use of another organ or by intensified use of the inferior organ itself. Is Adler not really saying that when the individual perceives an aspect of his body as inferior, he generalized this inferiority to his total concept of himself? One organ in the total body scheme takes on exaggerated importance and size relative to the rest of the body scheme and exerts a generalized distortion effect. (pp. 46–47)

Whereas most other psychoanalytic theorists were not as body oriented as Adler, there were several who made thoughtful contributions about special aspects of body experience. Both Jung (1926, 1931) and some of his followers (Fordham, 1951; Perry, 1953; also Rank, 1929) elaborated on the notion that persons conceptualize their bodies as containers or protective enclosures within which they can find refuge and fend off attack. They implicitly underscored the potential importance of feelings about one's body boundaries. Much more elaborate treatments of body-boundary phenomena appeared in the writings of Federn (1926, 1952) and Reich (1949). Thus, Federn made the concept of "ego boundary" central to normal psychological functioning. He portrayed individuals as possessing a boundary that maintains a distinction between what is outside and inside the body and as a prerequisite for reality testing. He speculated in some detail about the fluctuations of this ego boundary during sleep, altered states of consciousness, and psychosis. Without a properly functioning boundary, individuals were said to experience the world as strange and depersonalized.

When schizophrenic regression occurred, the boundary was said to contract and to become more inflexible and in some ways more impermeable. Reich, too, was fascinated with boundary functioning, as he was with various other aspects of body experience. He proposed complex links between the individual's personality conflicts,the expression of these conflicts in patterns of muscle tonus, and the impact of these tonus patterns upon the individual's experiences of self and others. He hypothesized that certain conflicts result in persons "armoring" themselves and actually modeling their bodies after something with hard and rigid (defensive) surfaces. He indicated that the more one had had parents who emphasized inhibition and self-control, the more one would be inclined to convert one's boundary into a state of armored hardness. He felt that one of the main purposes of psychotherapy was to loosen and dissolve the "armor." The boundary dimension and other body-image notions showed up fairly strongly too in Erikson's (1950) theoretical constructs. He particularly portrayed males and females as distinguishable with respect to how closed off their body boundaries are. He described females as more open and receptive to forces coming in from the outside, and he actually collected experimental data that appeared to verify his view (1951).

These psychoanalytic theorists who highlighted boundary mechanisms significantly influenced Cleveland and myself in our initial explorations of body-boundary articulation (Fisher & Cleveland, 1968). When we first observed boundary differences in the inkblot perceptions of patients with different kinds of psychosomatic symptoms, we were primed by the previous psychoanalytic formulations to give weight to these observations and to construct more elaborate models of how body boundaries mediate various aspects of normal behavior. This led to a major new area of empirical research dealing with the organization of body experience and eventually produced detailed findings concerning the relationship of the body boundary to personality, psychosomatic symptomatology, psychopathology, patterns of autonomic response, and behavior in groups. The psychoanalytic precursors similarly influenced the research enterprises of Witkin et al. (1954, 1962). Their approach was based upon how accurately the true vertical is judged in the absence of any spatial cues except for those emanating from one's own body; and it produced a mine of information concerning how persons differentiate their bodies from the surrounding field (i.e., how they articulate their boundaries).

"CLASSIC" PHILOSOPHICAL AND PSYCHOLOGICAL CURRENTS

We have just completed an abbreviated survey of some of the major influences that set the stage for modern scientific studies of the organization of body experience. But nothing yet has been said about philosophical influences and forerunners. In fact, we know that for centuries philosophers have been concerned about the role of the body in being human, in the structure of ego, and the construction of reality. Spicker (1970) has thoroughly reviewed the major philosophical speculations about the world of the body. He points out that Aristotle, Plato, and Descartes wrestled with the dualism of soul (or mind) and body, and tried to come up with a reasonable account of how these two entities could interact. The concept of body, with its animal attributes, has forever been difficult to integrate with the image of the human person as distinct from the nonhuman. Speculations about the body as a philosophical construct have run through the writings of Spinoza, Kant, Dewey, Merleau-Ponty, Sartre, and others (Spicker, 1970). There is a distinctive modern sound to Kant's speculation that one possesses a body schema that acts as a mediating device in the process of integrating behavior and that the projection of self-features upon the object world is a basic way of establishing a linkage between self and world. One should also single out Merleau-Ponty's (1962) work because it was based on a wide knowledge of the scholarly literature dealing with body image up to the 1960s. He depicted the body as a basic experiential agent that introduces order and meaning into our interactions with other objects. For him, the body is a highly organized sector of space that is the only consistent framework for experience and the only anchor offering a persistent line of stability for perception. The body with its ability to sustain purposeful movement "super-imposes upon physical space a potential or human space" (p. 111). Merleau-Ponty emphasizes over and over that the body image is not a sum of perceptual inputs or an associational construction, but is rather Gestalt-like. Wapner and Werner (1965) say of Merleau-Ponty that he "probably more fully and profoundly than any other present-day philosopher has brought forth the significance of the body concept for the forming of the human world" (p. 4).

Until recent years, few psychologists within the main current of academic psychology were attracted to the topic of body experience. Psychology text-books rarely even mentioned it. However, looking back, one finds a number of instances in which concepts with body-image significance were indirectly invoked. Here are a few examples:

First, consider Lotze's well-known theory of spatial localization, which was based on the assumption that one experientially builds up a map of all points on one's body (also on the retina) such that each point has a "local label" defined by the unique sensory experiences associated with that locale. Basically, he proposed that it is necessary to build up an organized series of "body landmarks" that can provide reference points when interpreting spatial matters (Fisher & Cleveland, 1968).

Second, consider the early work based on introspection. Wundt discussed at length the role of kinesthetic sensations in defining the experience of spatial continuity. Indeed, the introspective method, with its search of the immediate stream of experience, almost inevitably leads to an awareness of the ever present background of body experiences. The role of body sensations and feelings in mediating behavior comes to the fore. Note that the Wurzberg group (Kulpe,

Marbe, Ach, and Watt) assigned major importance to kinesthetic sensations in modulating psychophysical judgments. The whole concept of "determining tendency" formulated by this group is anchored in body experience. Titchener theorized that body sensations were important modifiers of the process of perception. In discussing this point, Allport (1955) states: "In Titchener's view there is one special type of sensation that is paramount as a contextual, meaning-providing process, namely, kinesthesis. As the organism faces the situation it adopts an attitude toward it, and kinaesthetic sensations resulting from this attitude (assuming it to be a muscular tension or reaction) give the context and meaning to the object to which the organism is reacting" (pp. 78–79).

The body as a psychological object began to gain prominence in conventional psychological circles when it was introduced in the context of classical perceptual phenomena. There were two major influences in this respect. One is represented by the work of Witkin et al. (1954, 1962). This group demonstrated that relatively simple judgments concerning one's position in space are influenced by body attitudes. In essence they were led by their data to conclude that the ability to make spatial judgments and in general to separate an item from its context is somehow linked with a sense that one's body is a differentiated entity, a clearly bounded one. The fusion of perceptual and body-image notions reflected the fact that the participants in the Witkin research group represented a unique mix of persons adept in classical perceptual methodology and also persons with psychoanalytic backgrounds. One of the participants was Karen Machover who had been strongly influenced by Schilder. One of her primary interests was related to body image as expressed in the human figure drawing. Her book *Personality Projection in the Drawing of the Human Figure* (1949) became a prominent point of entree for body-image concepts into American as well as European clinical psychology. The sensori-tonic group at Clark, under the leadership of Wapner and Werner (1965), also legitimated the study of body perception by pointing out that it falls within the same realm as object perception. They published many studies in which they demonstrated how object perception is influenced by body attitudes and also how body perception is modified by the surrounding nonbody context. Their work provided detailed data concerning such issues as perception of body size, ability to separate one's body as a perceptual object from nonself objects, and the modes of body perception associated with developmental maturity.

Brief reference should be made to a few other avenues through which concepts concerned with the body as a psychological object have been introduced into the mainstream of psychology. A cluster of researchers (e.g., Harris, 1965; Kohler, 1962; Stratton, 1897; Wittreich, as described by Fisher, 1970) probed the effects of individuals' wearing lenses that distort their perceptions of both themselves and other objects. Such work particularly dramatized the plasticity of body perception. Another avenue has been represented in the research of diverse investigators who have looked at the developmental aspects of spatial perception—for example, right–left differentiation (e.g., Piaget, 1964), sex-role definition (e.g., Kohlberg, 1966), standards of attractiveness (e.g., Lerner, 1972), and body maturity (e.g., Koff, Rierdan, & Silverstone, 1978). Such research has made developmental psychologists familiar with, and largely accepting of, the part that body attitudes play over the course of normal developmental phases. One should add that still another important avenue is represented by a number of investigators (e.g., Shontz, 1977; Wright, 1960) who have tried to understand how persons adapt to body disablement, chronic disease, and persistent pain. Body-image attitudes as explanatory concepts have become acceptable coinage in the context of the growing discipline of rehabilitation psychology.

Note that there has been a long-standing and growing interest in body-experience phenomena among many social scientists outside of psychology. Intriguing ideas are to be found in the writings of observers like Foucault (1980), Douglas (1970), Hertz (1960), Polhemus (1975), Turner (1984), Birdwhistle (1970), and O'Neill (1985). Due to space limitations, I will not elaborate more about this realm.

OVERVIEW

Current research dealing with the body as a psychological object has branched into multiple domains. There are essentially nine primary topical areas of inquiry:

1. Perception and evaluation of one's own body appearance.
2. Accuracy of perception of one's body size.
3. Accuracy of perception of one's body sensations.
4. Ability to judge the spatial position of one's body.
5. Feelings about the definiteness and protective value of the body boundaries.
6. Distortions in body sensations and experiences associated with psychopathology and brain damage.
7. Responses to body damage, loss of parts, and surgery.
8. Responses to various procedures designed to camouflage the body cosmetically or somehow to "improve" it.
9. Attitudes and feelings pertinent to the sexual identity of one's body.

As I earlier indicated, there has been relatively little communication among these areas of research. Each has tended to develop its own theoretical mini-models and modes of measurement. The diversity of the origins of the whole enterprise concerned with body experience continues to be reflected in the diversity of the current scene. A greater exchange of ideas and methods among the domains of interest would likely be productive. However, one also needs to recognize that there are indeed quite different and perhaps largely independent dimensions represented in the conglomeration grouped under the rough rubric of "body image." It has become increasingly obvious that the early use of this term to represent a unidimensional construct is simplistic. Body experience is turning out to be an exceedingly complex affair. There is no such entity as "The Body Image." The research data unmistakably indicate that body experience is multidimensional. At any point in time, persons may be simultaneously monitoring such different aspects of their body as its apparent attractiveness, position in space, boundary security, relative prominence in the total perceptual field, variations in the size attributes of its different parts, and so forth. In addition, we know that some aspects of the body-image experience are easily available to conscious awareness, whereas others are concealed at unconscious levels. Some aspects of body experience involve areas of functioning relatively free of anxiety and others are highly linked with potential threat. Add to this complexity the fact that there are striking gender and developmental differences in how body experience is organized. One can no longer defend an approach to body image that seeks to compress it into a few narrow categories. It is not reasonable to quantify some limited feature of body experience and label it as "The Measure of Body Image." One can no more expect diverse measures of body experience to correlate indiscriminately with each other than one would anticipate such to hold true for a range of personality measures.

The inexhaustible list of behaviors that has turned out to be linked with measures in the body-experience domain documents the ubiquitous influence of body attitudes. Human identity cannot be separated from its somatic headquarters in the world. How persons feel about their somatic base takes on mediating significance in most situations. This may explain why each decade since Schilder's pioneering work has witnessed manifold multiplication of research publications concerned with the psychological organization of that base.

REFERENCES

Allport, F. H.(1955). *Theories of perception and the concept of structure*. New York: Wiley.

Bartlett, F. C. (1926). *Review of Henry Head's Aphasia and kindred disorders of speech. Brain, 49,* 581–587.

Bender, L., & Keeler, W. R. (1952). The body image of schizophrenic children following electric shock therapy. *American Journal of Orthopsychiatry, 49,* 581–587.

Benton, A. L., Hutcheon, J. F., & Seymour, E. (1951). Arithmetic ability, finger localization capacity and right–left discrimination in normal and defective children. *American Journal of Orthopsychiatry, 21,* 756–766.

Birdwhistle, R. (1970). *Kinesics and context*. Philadelphia: University of Pennsylvania Press.

Bonnier, P. L. (1905). L'aschematie. *Révue Neurologie, 54,* 605–621.

Bromberg, W., & Schilder, P. (1932). On tactile imagination and tactile after-effects. *Journal of Nervous and Mental Disease, 76,* 133.

Cash, T. F., Cash, D. W., & Butters, J. W., (1983). "Mirror, mirror, on the wall . . . ?": Contrast effects and self-evaluations of physical attractiveness. *Personality and Social Psychology Bulletin, 9,* 351–358.

Casper, R. C., Halmi, K. A., Goldberg, S. C., Eckert, E. D., & Davis, J. M. (1979). Disturbances in body image estimation as related to other characteristics and outcome in anorexia nervosa. *British Journal of Psychiatry, 134*, 60–66.

Cofer, J. B., (1980). *Phantom breast concomitants among mastectomy patients*. Unpublished doctoral dissertation, North Texas State University.

Critchley, M. (1953). *The parietal lobes*. London: Arnold.

Critchley, M. (1965). Disorders of corporeal awareness in parietal disease. In S. Wapner & H. Werner (Eds.), *The body percept* (pp. 68–81). New York: Random House.

Douglas, M. (1970). *Purity and danger: An analysis of pollution and taboo*. Harmondsworth, England: Penguin Book.

Erikson, E. H. (1950). *Childhood and society*. New York: Norton.

Erikson, E. H. (1951). Sex differences in the play of preadolescents. *Journal of Orthopsychiatry, 21*, 667–692.

Federn, P. (1926). Some variations in ego feeling. *International Journal of Psychoanalysis, 7*, 434–444.

Federn, P. (1952). *Ego psychology and the psychoses*. New York: Basic Books.

Fisher, S. (1970). *Body experience in fantasy and behavior*. New York: Appleton-Century-Crofts.

Fisher, S. (1986). *Development and structure of the body image* (Vols. 1 & 2). Hillsdale, NJ: Erlbaum.

Fisher, S., & Cleveland, S. E. 91968). *Body image and personality* (rev. ed.). New York: Dover Press.

Fordham, M. (1951). Some observations on the self in childhood. *British Journal of Medical Psychology, 24*, 83–96.

Foucault, M. (1980). *The history of sexuality*. New York: Vintage.

Freud, S. (1927). *The ego and the id*. London: Hogarth.

Goin, M. K., & Goin, J. M. (1981). *Changing the body: Psychological effects of plastic surgery*. Baltimore: Williams & Wilkins.

Gorman, W. (1969). *Body image and image of the brain*. St. Louis, MO: Warren H. Green.

Haber, W. B. (1956). Observations on phantom limb phenomena. *A.M.A. Archives of Neurology and Psychiatry, 75*, 624–636.

Harris, C. S. (1965). Perceptual adaptation to inverted, reversed, and displaced vision. *Psychological Review, 72*, 419–444.

Head, H. (1926). *Aphasia and kindred disorders of speech*. London: Cambridge University Press.

Head, H., & Holmes, G. (1911–1912). Sensory disturbances from cerebral lesions. *Brain, 34*, 102–254.

Hertz, R. (1960). *Death and the right hand*. New York: Free Press.

Hoff, H., & Poetzl, O. (1931). Experimentalle nachbildung von anosognosia. *Zeitschrift Gesamte Neurologie Psychiatrie, 137*, 722–734.

Jourard., S. M., & Secord, P. F. (1955). Body cathexis and the ideal female figure. *Journal of Abnormal and Social Psychology, 50*, 243–246.

Jung, C. G. (1926). *Psychological types*. London: Kegan Paul, Trench, Trubner.

Jung, C. G. (1931). *Psychology of the unconscious*. New York: Dodd, Mead.

Katkin, E. S., Blascovich, J., & Koenigsberg, M. R. (1984). Autonomic self-perception and emotion. In W. Waid (Ed.), *Sociophysiology* (pp. 117–138). New York: Springer-Verlag.

Koff, E., Rierdan, J., & Silverstone, E. (1978). Changes in representation of body image as a function of menarcheal status. *Developmental Psychology, 14*, 635–642.

Kohlberg, L. (1966). A cognitive–developmental analysis of children's sex-role concepts and attitudes. In E. E. Maccoby (Ed.), *The development of sex differences* (pp. 82–173). Stanford: Stanford University Press.

Kohler, I. (1962). Experiments with goggles. *Scientific American, 206*, 62–86.

Lerner, R. M. (1972). "Richness" analysis of body build stereotype development. *Developmental Psychology, 7*, 219.

Machover, K. (1949). *Personality projection in the drawing of the human figure*. Springfield, Illinois: Charles C. Thomas.

Merleau-Ponty, M. (1962). *Phenomenology of perception*. London: Routledge and Kegan Paul.

Oldfield, R. C., & Zangwill, O. L. (1942). I. Head's concept of schema and its application in contemporary British psychology. II. Critical analysis of Head's theory. III. Bartlett's theory of memory. *British Journal of Psychiatry, 33*, 58–64, 113–129.

O'Neill, J. (1985). *Five bodies*. Ithaca: Cornell University press.

Perry, J. W. (1953). *The self in psychotic process: Its symbolization in schizophrenia*. Berkeley: University of California Press.

Piaget, J. (1954). *The construction of reality in the child*. New York: Basic Books.

Pick, A. (1922). Storung der orientierung am eigenen korper. *Psychologische Forschung, 1*, 303–315.

Poeck, K., & Orgass, B. (1971). The concept of the body schema: A critical review and some experimental results. *Cortex, 77*, 254–277.

Polhemus, T. (1975). Social bodies. In J. Benthall & T. Polhemus (Eds.), *The body as a medium of expression* (pp. 13–35). New York: Dutton.

Rank, O. (1929). *The trauma of birth*. New York: Harcourt, Brace.

Reich, W. (1949). *Character analysis*. New York: Orgone Institute Press.

Schilder, P. (1914). *Selbstbewusstsein und personlichkeitbewusstsein*. Berlin: Springer.

Schilder, P. (1923). *Das koerperschema*. Berlin: Springer.

Schilder, P. (1950). *The image and appearance of the human body*. New York: International Universities Press.

Shaskan, D. A., & Roller, W. L. (Eds.). (1985). *Paul Schilder. Mind explorer*. New York: Human Sciences Press.

Shontz, F. C. (1969). *Perceptual and cognitive aspects of body experience*. New York: Academic Press.

Shontz, F. C. (1977). Physical disability and personality. In J. Stubbins (Ed.), *Social and psychological aspects of disability* (pp. 333–353). Baltimore: University Park Press.

Simmel, M. L. (1956). On phantom limbs. *Archives of Neurology and Psychiatry, 75*, 637–647.

Spicker, S. M. (Ed.). (1970). *The philosophy of the body*. Chicago: Quadrangle Books.

Stratton, G. M. (1897). Vision without inversion of the retinal image. *Psychological Review, 4*, 341–360.

Strauss, A., & Werner, H. (1938). Deficiency in the finger scheme in relation to arithmetic disability. *American Journal of Orthopsychiatry, 81*, 719–723.

Teitelbaum, H. A. (1941). Psychogenic body image disturbances associated with psychogenic aphasia and agnosia. *Journal of Nervous and Mental Disease, 93*, 581–612.

Teuber, H. L., Krieger, H. P., & Bender, M. B. (1949). Reorganization of sensory function in amputation stumps: Two-point discrimination. *Federation Proceedings, 88*, 156.

Turner, B. S. (1984). *The body and society*. New York: Basil Blackwell.

Wapner, S., & Werner, H. (Eds.). (1965). *The body precept*. New York: Random House.

Witkin, H. A., Dyk, R. B., Faterson, H. F., Goodenough, D. R., & Karp, S. A. (1962) *Psychological differentiation*. New York: Wiley.

Witkin, H. A., Lewis, H. B., Hertzman, M., Machover, K., Meissner, P., & Wapner, S. (1954). *Personality through perception*. New York: Harper & Brothers.

Wright, B. A. (1960). *Physical disability—a psychological approach*. New York: Harper & Brothers.

CHAPTER 2

Procedures, Problems, and Progress in the Assessment of Body Images

J. Kevin Thompson
Louis A. Penner
Madeline N. Altabe

In recent years, procedures for the assessment of multiple aspects of body image have proliferated. The great majority of measurement techniques have focused on the assessment of some facet of the physical appearance component of body image. Generally, researchers and clinicians have focused on two aspects of appearance-related body image: a perceptual component, commonly referred to as size-perception accuracy (i.e., estimation of body size) and a subjective component, which entails attitudes toward body size/weight, other body parts, or overall physical appearance (Cash & Brown, 1987). Although most assessment instruments that measure the subjective realm focus on the satisfaction component, instruments have recently been constructed that also assess subjective concerns, cognitions, anxiety, and anticipated avoidance of certain situations (actual behavioral observation rating protocols have not been developed).

Although this chapter will focus on the physical-appearance aspect of body image, other conceptualizations of body image (e.g., Fisher, 1986; Lacey & Birtchnell, 1986; Touyz & Beaumont, 1987) have also generated considerable research. In Chapter 1 of this volume, Seymour Fisher addresses these in greater detail. Yet, they deserve brief mention here as well. For instance, a perturbation of neurological functioning may lead to various body-image disturbances such as the failure to perceive that a part of the body belongs to the self. Another disturbance involves the actual removal of a part of the body with a coexisting lack of perceptual realization of the loss—the phantom-limb phenomena.

In addition, various theoretical schools, especially psychoanalytic psychology, have richly incorporated conceptions of body image into their frameworks. The body-boundary concept was introduced by Fischer (1986), who noted that people vary "with respect to the firmness or definiteness they ascribe to their body boundaries" (p. 329). At one extreme are individuals who clearly differentiate their bodies from other objects, while other individuals fail to make this important demarcation. Fisher's (1986) projective methodology for the measurement of the body boundary construct has produced a wealth of empirical and heuristic information.

Developmentalists have similarly included the assessment of body image as a crucial ingredient for accurate conceptualizations of the pubertal process, especially in females (Brooks-Gunn & Petersen, 1983). Generally, the issue of body image in this area is much broader in scope than a narrow focus on physical appearance aspects of puberty. For instance, Koff, Rierdan, and Silverstone (1978) evaluated human figure drawings in adolescent females but focused primarily on the greater sexual differentiation contained in the drawings of postmenarcheal as opposed to premenarcheal girls. It should be noted, however, that the appearance component is also studied in many investigations of the significance of puberty (Attie & Brooks-Gunn, 1989; Gargiulo, Attie, Brooks-Gunn, & Warren, 1987).

Thus, it quickly becomes apparent that the phrase *body image* has been used as an umbrella label with its specific meaning depending on an individual researcher's definition. Reflecting the current zeitgeist in body-image research, this chapter will emphasize the physical appearance facet of body image. During the past decade, much research in this area has focused on size overestimation in individuals with eating disorders (Cash & Brown, 1987). However, it is becoming apparent that many non-eating-disordered individuals have some level of appearance-related, body-image disturbance, such as general dissatisfaction, specific size/weight dissatisfaction, or size perception inaccuracy (especially overestimation of body sizes) (Cash, Winstead, & Janda, 1986; Thompson & Psaltis, 1988; Thompson & Spana, 1988).

In some cases, this disturbance may take the form of extreme disparagement, a phenomenon historically referred to as dysmorphophobia (Hay, 1970) and included in the recent DSM-III-R (American Psychiatric Association, 1987) as a somatoform disorder labelled *Body Dysmorphic Disorder*. As Pruzinsky articulates subsequently in this volume, the outstanding characteristic of this disorder is the aversion of a particular aspect of the body that appears normal to an observer. Of course, this issue must be clearly differentiated from someone with an extreme body-image dissatisfaction due to an objective physical deformity. Later chapters will deal selectively with the surgical treatment of subjective and objective deformity.

This chapter consists of three principal sections. First, we will briefly review and discuss the techniques used for the measurement of perceptual and subjective aspects of the physical appearance component of body image. The measures that are reviewed have been used with a variety of clinical and nonclinical populations. This section will also provide a table that contains a brief description, psychometric information, and an address of the individual to contact for further information about the particular instrument. Second, we will examine research that has attempted to measure convergence between the various procedures. Less applied in nature, this section will evaluate the relative independence versus overlap of various measures. Third, specific recommendations for the utilization of instruments in certain settings and with idiosyncratic populations will be offered.

ASSESSMENT OF THE PERCEPTUAL COMPONENT OF PHYSICAL APPEARANCE: SIZE-ESTIMATION ACCURACY

Accuracy of body-size perception has often been referred to as "body-image distortion"; however, we will use the term *size-estimation accuracy*. Interest in this aspect of body image can be traced to the seminal study by Slade and Russell (1973) that observed greater size overestimation in anorexics than among controls. These findings were extended and elaborated, using a variety of assessment procedures. In recent years, evidence has mounted, however, suggesting that size overestimation is not specific to the anorexic population (Cash & Brown, 1987; Slade, 1985; Thompson & Thompson, 1986). Therefore, these techniques are currently used in the investigation of diverse populations.

In general, there are two broad categories of devices used for the assessment of size-estimation accuracy. Cash and Brown (1987) labelled these two categories the body-part and distorting image (whole-body) procedures. Body-part or site procedures (we will use *site* because the estimation stimuli are generally not specific parts but are sites on the body) require that subjects match the width of the distance between two points to their own estimation of the width of a specific body site. For instance, Slade and Russell (1973) constructed the movable caliper technique (MCT), which consisted of a horizontal bar with two lights mounted onto a track. The subject could adjust the width between the two lights to match his/her estimate of the width of a given body site.

This body-site size-estimation procedure gave rise to a host of conceptually similar procedures. For instance, Askevold (1975) created the Image Marking Procedure (IMP), which involves subjects' marking their approximated body widths on a sheet of paper that is attached to a wall. Ruff and Barrios (1986) designed the Body Image Detection Device (BIDD), which projects a beam of light onto a wall that the subject matches to his/her estimate of a given site. Thompson and colleagues modified the BIDD to include a simultaneous presentation of four light beams (representing the cheeks, waist, hips, and thighs) and referred to the instrument as the Adjustable Light Beam Apparatus

(ALBA) (Thompson & Spana, 1988; Thompson & Thompson, 1986). An illustration of the ALBA procedure is presented in Figure 2.1.

For these and other site-estimation procedures, an assessment of a subject's actual widths (measured with body calipers) is compared with the subject's estimate; and a ratio of over- or underestimation of size is computed. Generally, the majority of subjects overestimate all body sites, and some data suggest that the waist is overestimated to the greatest degree (Thompson & Spana, 1988). Because the estimates of the sites are highly correlated, some researchers sum across sites, giving a composite index of overestimation. It may be advisable, depending upon the experimental or clinical purpose of the assessment, to evaluate each estimation site individually. (Specific descriptions, psychometric characteristics, and other information for these techniques are contained in Table 2.1.)

The second major category of size-estimation procedures consists of the whole-image adjustment methods. With this methodology, the individual is confronted with a real-life image, presented via videotape, photographic image, or mirror feedback that is modified to be objectively smaller or larger than reality. Subjects are allowed to select the stimulus image that matches their own conception of their size. Among the various whole-image procedures are the distorting mirror of Traub and Orbach (1964), distorting photograph technique

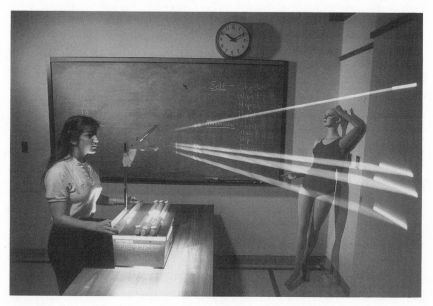

FIGURE 2.1.   A subject adjusts the width of light beams to match her own estimate of the width of her cheeks, waist, hips, and thighs. The instrument is the Adjustable Light Beam Apparatus (ALBA) (Thompson & Spana, 1988).

TABLE 2.1. FREQUENTLY USED MEASURES FOR THE ASSESSMENT OF PHYSICAL APPEARANCE-RELATED ASPECTS OF BODY IMAGE

Name	Author(s)	Description	Reliability[a,b,c]	Standardization Sample	Address
Body size-estimation procedures					
Adjustable Light Beam Apparatus (ALBA)	1. Thompson & Spana (1988)	Adjust width of light beam projected on wall to match perceived size	1. IC: .83 TR: immed. (.83–.92) 1 wk (.56–.86)	1. 159 female	J. Kevin Thompson Department of Psychology University of South Florida Tampa, FL 33620
Body Image Detection Device (BIDD)	1. Ruff & Barrios (1986) 2. Barrios, Ruff, & York (1989)	Adjust distance between two lights to match perceived size	1. IC: .91, .93 TR: 3 wk (bulimics: .82–.87; controls: .72–.85) 2. IC: .21–.82 TR: 3 wk (.34) 4 wk (.94) 7 wk (.37)	1. 20 normal and 20 bulimic undergraduates 2. College females	Billy A. Barrios College of Liberal Arts Department of Psychology University of Mississippi Oxford, MS 38677
Movable Caliper Technique (MCT)	1. Slade & Russell (1973) 2. Slade (1985)	Adjust distance between two lights to match perceived size	1. IC: anorexics (.72–.93) controls (.37–.79) 2. IC: anorexics (.72) controls (.63)	1. 14 female anorexics and 20 female postgraduates and secretaries 2. Anorexics	Peter Slade Department of Psychiatry & Dept. of Movement Science Liverpool University Medical Sch. P.O. Box 147 Liverpool, L69 3BX, England
Body-Size Estimation	1. Kreitler & Kreitler (1988)	Subjects, eyes closed, use the distance between their outstretched hands to indicate perceived size	1. IC: body (.75–.88) face (.79–.82) 2. TR: 2 wk (.93–.97)	1. 240 normal males and females ranging in age from 4–30 years	Shulamith Kreitler Department of Psychology Tel Aviv University Ramat Aviv Tel Aviv 69978, Israel
Kinesthetic Size Estimation Apparatus (KSEA)	1. Cited in Gleghorn, Penner, Powers, & Schulman (1987)	Blindfolded subjects adjust the distance between two calipers to match perceived size	1. IC: none given 2. TR: immed. (.45–.65)	1. 110 females aged 17–45 consisting of normal undergraduates and eating-disordered	Pauline Powers Department of Psychiatry University of South Florida Tampa, FL 33620

(continued)

TABLE 2.1 (Continued)

Name	Author(s)	Description	Reliability[a,b,c]	Standardization Sample	Address
Image Marking Procedure (IMP)	1. Askevold (1975) 2. Barrios et al. (1989)	Subjects indicate their perceived size by marking two endpoints on a life-size piece of paper	2. IC: .25–.62 TR: 3 wk (.17) 4 wk (.33) 7 wk (.14)	2. College females	Finn Askevold Psychosomatic Department Oslo University Hospital Oslo, Norway
Whole-image adjustment procedures					
TV-Video Method	1. Gardner, Martinex, & Sandoval (1987) 2. Gardner & Monteniof (1988) 3. Gardner, Martinez, Espinoza, & Gullegos (1988)	Subjects adjust the horizontal dimension of a TV image of themselves to match perceived size. Subsequent studies have also assessed ideal size and individual size estimation. Data are subject to signal detection analysis	IC: none given TR: none given	1. 38 Normal and obese adults 2. Normal and anorexic females	Rick M. Gardner Department of Psychology University of Southern Colorado Pueblo, Colorado 81001
None given	1. Alleback, Hallberg, & Espmark (1976)	Subjects adjust the horizontal dimension of a video image to match perceived size	1. IC: not applicable TR: none given	1. 69 male and female adults consisting of obese and control subgroups	Peter Alleback Furugatan SA 171 50 Solna, Sweden
None given	1. Freeman, Thomas, Solyom, & Hunter (1984)	Subjects tell the experimenter when a video image of themselves matches their perceived size	1. IC: front profile correlation (.62) TR: 7–22 days, frontal (bulimics and anorexics: .91; controls: .83)	1. 20 eating-disordered females (bulimics and anorexics) and 20 normal females	Richard J. Freeman Department of Psychology Simon Fraser University Burnaby, B.C. Canada V5A 1S6
Distorting Photograph Technique	1. Glucksman & Hirsch (1969) 2. Garner & Garfinkel (1981)	Subjects indicate size by adjusting a photograph that is distorted from 20% under to 20% over actual size	1. IC: not applicable 2. IC: not applicable TR: 1 wk (anorexics: .75; controls: .45) 1 yr (anorexics: .56; controls: .70)	2. Anorexics and controls	David Garner Department of Psychiatry Director of Research Eating Disorders Section Michigan State University West Fee Hall Lansing, MI 48824

Distorting Video Technique	1. Touyz et al. (1985)	Subjects indicate size by adjusting photograph that is distorted by 50% under to 50% over actual size	1. IC: not applicable TR: immed. (.82) 1 day (.63) 8 wk (.61)	1. Anorexics and bulimics	S.W. Touyz Dept. of Clinical Psychology Westmead Hospital Westmead 2145 New South Wales, Australia
None given	1. Huon & Brown (1986)	Concave, convex, ordinary mirrors; adjustable TV image	1. IC: not applicable TR: none given	1. Anorexics, bulimics, and controls	G. F. Huon or L.B. Brown School of Psychology University of New South Wales Box 1, Kensington, NSW 2033 Australia
Figures/silhouettes					
Figure Rating Scale	1. Fallon & Rozin (1985) 2. Thompson & Altabe (in press)	Subjects select from nine figures of various sizes	1. IC: not applicable TR: none given 2. TR: 2 wk; range for six different ratings (females: .55–.71; males: .60–.92)	1. 475 male and female undergraduates	April Fallon Department of Psychiatry Medical College of Pennsylvania at Eastern Penn. Psychiatric Institute 3200 Henry Avenue Philadelphia, PA 19129
None given	1. Buree, Papageorgis, & Solyom (1984)	Nineteen female silouettes, which vary in size	1. IC: not applicable TR: none given	1. 19 anorexics and 19 controls	Demetrios Papageorgis Department of Psychology 2136 West Mall University of British Columbia Vancouver, B.C. V6T 1Y7
None given	1. Counts & Adams (1985)	Silhouettes are drawn from subjects' photos, sizes increased and decreased by 2.55, 5.05, and 7.55	1. IC: not applicable TR: none given	1. Bulimics, dieting females, and formerly obese and nondieting females	H.E. Adams Department of Psychology University of Georgia Athens, CA 30602
Body Image Silhouette Scale	1. Powers & Erickson (1986)	Subjects select from seven figures of various sizes	1. IC: not applicable TR: none given	1. 164 female undergraduates	Pamela D. Powers Department of Psychology Academic Center Virginia Commonwealth University Richmond, VA 23284

(continued)

27

TABLE 2.1 (Continued)

Name	Author(s)	Description	Reliability[a,b,c]	Standardization Sample	Address
Body Image Assessment (BIA)	1. Williamson, Davis, Bennett, Goreczny, & Gleaves (in press)	Subjects select from nine figures of various sizes	1. IC: not applicable. TR: immed.–8 wk (.60–.93) (bulimics: .83 current, .74 ideal; obese: .88 current, n.s. ideal; binge-eaters: .81 current, .65 ideal)	659 females, including bulimics, binge-eaters, anorexics, normals, obese subjects, and atypical eating disordered subjects	Donald A. Williamson Department of Psychology Louisiana State University Baton Rouge, LA 70803-5501
Body Build Assessment Program	1. Dickson-Parnell, Jones & Braddy (1987)	A computer program allows subjects to create figures	1. IC: not applicable TR: results did not differ significantly between trials	197 male and female undergraduates	Barbara Dickson-Parnell Department of Psychology Clemson University Clemson, S.C. 29634-1511
Questionnaire Measures					
1. Cognitions					
Bulimia Cognitive Distortions Scale (BCDS); Physical Appearance Subscale	1. Schulman, Kinder, Powers, Prange, & Gleghorn (1986)	Subjects indicate degree of agreement with 25 statements	1. IC: .97; for entire scale TR: none given	55 female outpatient bulimics aged 17–45 and 55 normal females aged 18–40	Bill N. Kinder Department of Psychology University of South Florida Tampa, FL 33620
Body Image Automatic Thoughts Questionnaire (BIATQ)	1. Cash, Lewis, & Keeton (1987) 2. Brown, Johnson, Bergeron, Keeton, & Cash (1990) 3. Cash (personal communication, April 11, 1990)	Subjects indicate frequency with which they experience 37 negative and 15 positive body-image cognitions	1. IC: .90 for bulimic and normal subjects for both positive and negative subscales 3. TR: 2 wk; positive scale (male: .73; female: .71) negative scale (male: .84; female: .90)	33 female bulimic inpatients and 79 female undergraduates	Thomas F. Cash Department of Psychology Old Dominion University Norfolk, VA 23529-0267

28

2. Multi-Dimensional Scales

Scale	Reference	Description	Reliability	Sample	Source
Body–Self Relations Questionnaire (BSRQ)	1. Winstead & Cash (1984)	Subjects indicate degree of agreement with 140 statements. There are 9 subscales: cognitive, affective, and behavioral scales for each of 3 domains—appearance, fitness, and health	1. IC: 68–91 (males: .91; females: .87) for appearance evaluation subscale TR: .65–.91 TR: .65–.91	Undergraduates	Same as above
Multidimensional Body–Self Relations Questionnaire (MBSRQ)	1. Cash, Winstead, & Janda (1986) 2. Brown, Cash, & Mikulka (1990) 3. Cash (1990) 4. Cash (personal communication, April 11, 1990)	Factor analysis of 54 items from the above scale yielded 7 subscales; plus, Body Areas Satisfaction Scale and weight-related items	1. IC: .75–.91 4. TR: 2 wk; range (.78–.94)	2,000 adult respondents to a magazine survey	Same as above
Semantic Differential Body Image Scale	1. Leon, Lucas, Colligan, Ferdnande, & Kamp (1985)	Subjects rate their bodies along 16 different dimensions. Combinations of these dimensions form different constructs	1. IC: none given TR: 3 wk (.61–.86)	580 male and female 12th-grade students	Gloria Leon Department of Psychology University of Minnesota MJinneapolis, Minnesota 55455
Body Attitude Scale	1. Kurtz (1969)	Subjects rate 30 body concepts along 3 dimensions: evaluation, potency, and activity	1. Generalizability coefficients ranged from .86–.95 for the three dimensions	169 male and female undergraduates	Richard M. Kurtz Department of Psychology Washington University St. Louis, Missouri 63130

3. Body Satisfaction/Esteem Measures

Scale	Reference	Description	Reliability	Sample	Source
Body Cathexis Scale	1. Secord & Jourard (1953)	Subjects indicate degree of positive feeling toward various body parts/aspects	1. IC: split-half reliability (males: .78; females: .83) TR: none given	45 male and 43 female undergraduates	See Secord and Jourard (1953)
Revised Body Cathexis Scale	1. Ward, McKeown, Mayhew, Jackson, & Piper (1990)	Subjects indicate degree of satisfaction with 22 of the original Body Cathexis Scale items. The remaining items were factor analyzed and divided into 5 body region subscales	1. IC: .90 for entire scale TR: 2 wk (.73)	403 female undergraduates	Tom E. Ward Associate Professor P.O. Box 7604 Henderson State University Arkadelpha, AR 71923

(continued)

TABLE 2.1 (Continued)

Name	Author(s)	Description	Reliability[a,b,c]	Standardization Sample	Address
Colour the Body Task	1. Huon & Brown (1990)	Subjects color an outline of a body divided into 21 regions. Red indicates liking, black–disliking, both–mixed feelings, blank–neutral feelings	1. IC: none given TR: none given	67 female bulimics and 67 female matched controls	G. F. Huon University of Wollongong P.O. Box 1144 Wollongong, NSW2500 Australia
Body Mapping Questionnaire	1. Huon & Brown (1990)	Subjects indicate on a 5-point scale their degree of liking for the above 21 regions	1. IC: none given TR: none given	Same as above	Same as above
Eating Disorders Body Dissatisfaction (BD) Scale	1. Garner, Olmstead, & Polivy (1983)	Subjects indicate their degree of agreement with 9 statements about body parts being too fat	1. IC: anorexics (.90) controls (.91) TR: none given	113 female anorexics and 577 female controls	David Garner Department of Psychiatry Director of Research Eating Disorders Section Michigan State University West Fee Hall Lansing, MI 48824
Body Satisfaction Scale (BSS)	1. Slade, Dewey, Newton, Brodie, & Kiemle (in press)	Subjects indicate degree of satisfaction with 16 body parts. Instrument has been factor analyzed into 3 subscales: general, head, and body dissatisfaction	1. IC: general (.87, 89, .89) hand (.80, .82, .89) body (.79, .82, .79) TR: none given	All females: 452 undergraduates, 463 nursing students, 40 volunteers, 169 overweight subjects, 55 bulimics, and 29 anorexics	P.D. Slade Department of Psychiatry and Department of Movement Sciences Liverpool Univ. Medical School P.O. Box 147 Liverpool, L69 3BX, England
Body Esteem Scale	1. Franzoi & Shields (1984)	Modification of body cathexis scale with 16 new items. Factor analysis yielded 3 factors each for male and female samples	1. IC: .78–87 TR: none given	366 female and 257 male undergraduates	Stephen L. Franzoi Training Program in Social Psychology Indiana University Bloomington, IN 47405
Body Esteem Scale	1. Mendelson & White (1985)	Subjects report their degree of agreement with various statements about their bodies	1. IC: split-half reliability (.83) TR: none given	97 boys and girls aged 8.5–17.4 years; 48 were overweight, 49 were normal weight	Donna Romano White Department of Psychology Concordia University 1455 de Maisonneuve West Montreal, Quebec Canada H3G-1M8

Measure	Reference	Description	Reliability	Sample	Author/Address
Self-Image Questionnaire for Young Adolescents Body-Image subscale	1. Petersen, Schulenberg, Abramowitz, Offer, & Jarcho (1984)	Designed for 10–15 year olds. 11-item body image subscale assesses positive and negative feelings toward the body	1. IC: boys (.81) girls (.77) TR: stability coefficients for total questionnaire: 1 yr (.60); 2 yr (.44)	335 6th-grade students who were followed through the 8th grade	Anne C. Peterson, College of Health & Human Development, 101 Henderson Building, Penn State University, University Park, PA 16802

4. Anxiety/Concern Scales

Measure	Reference	Description	Reliability	Sample	Author/Address
Mirror Focus Procedure	1. Butters & Cash (1987) 2. Keeton, Cash, & Brown (1990)	Subjects look at themselves in a 3-way mirror and then rate their level of discomfort	1. IC: not applicable TR: none given	Undergraduates	Thomas F. Cash, Department of Psychology, Old Dominion University, Norfolk, Virginia 23529-0267
Body Shape Questionnaire (BSQ)	1. Cooper, Taylor, Cooper, & Fairburn (1987)	Subjects indicate the frequency with which they react in a particular way to events (e.g., worry about thighs when sitting)	1. IC: females (.93) TR: none given	1. Bulimics 2. Undergraduates 3. Family planning clinic attender 4. Occupational	Peter Cooper, University of Cambridge, Department of Psychiatry, Addenbrooke's Hospital, Hills Road, Cambridge, CB2 2QQ England
Body Image Anxiety Scale	1. Reed, Thompson, & Brannick (1990)	Subjects rate the anxiety associated with 16 body sites (8 weight relevant; 8 nonweight relevant); trait and state versions available	1. IC: trait (.88, .82) state (.82–.92) TR: 2 wk (.87)	Undergraduates and therapy students	J. Kevin Thompson, Department of Psychology, University of South Florida, Tampa, FL 33620

Miscellaneous

Measure	Reference	Description	Reliability	Sample	Author/Address
Body image behavior questionnaire	1. Rosen, Saltzberg, & Srebnik (1990)	Subjects indicate the frequence with which they engage in body-image-related behaviors	1. IC: .87 TR: 2 wk (.89)	145 female undergraduates	James C. Rosen, Department of Psychology, University of Vermont, Burlington, VT 05405
Subjective rating index	1. Ruff & Barrios (1986) 2. Barrios et al. (1989)	Subjects rate body width with respect to their conception of norm for their age, height, and sex (0 = much smaller; 50 = normal; 100 = much greater than normal	1. IC: .91 and .93 TR: 3 wk (.60–.93) 2. IC: none given TR: 3 wk (.94) 4 wk (.92) 7 wk (.58)	1. Bulimics and controls (college females) 2. Controls (college females)	Billy A. Barrios, Department of Psychology, College of Liberal Arts, University of Mississippi, Oxford, Mississippi 38677

[a]IC, internal consistency (unless otherwise stated, Cronbach's alpha).
[b]TR, test-retest.
[c]Nunnally (1970) suggests that .70 is a minimum acceptable internal consistency ratio for measures currently under initial development and validation.

developed by Glucksman and Hirsch (1969), and the video distortion procedure of Alleback, Hallberg, and Espmark (1976). Among these procedures, the distorting photograph technique has received the greatest amount of attention (Garner & Garfinkel, 1981; Garner, Garfinkel, & Bonato, 1987). The measure of perceptual inaccuracy obtained with these procedures is the degree of discrepancy between the actual real-life image and that selected by the subject. Recent innovations in technology have allowed researchers to create quite elaborate whole-image measurement techniques (Table 2.1).

There are several general considerations in the selection and utilization of a specific size-estimation procedure. First, as Table 2.1 illustrates, there is a broad range in the reliability of various instruments. Some measures do not have acceptable reliabilities and few instruments have been evaluated with different population groups. Second, the choice between a site-specific or a whole-image adjustment procedure is a major consideration. Body-site estimation procedures provide information regarding accuracy that is specific to individual sites, whereas, whole-image procedures produce a single index. This is a valid choice point because research indicates that overestimation may be very site specific and not constant across all sites, for a given individual (Thompson & Spana, 1988). It is also possible that confrontation with a real-life image that gradually increases in size may upset an individual sensitive to such an occurrence. In fact, we have heard of cases that involved individuals who refused to continue with the task given the disruptive, dysphoric experience of viewing a "larger" self. Therefore, it is possible that the demands of the testing situation, for the whole-image procedures, may interfere with the validity of the measurement. Finally, the cost and technical expertise that are required of the whole-image procedures may make these procedures prohibitive for some researchers or clinicians.

There are also pertinent methodological issues which should be considered when using the perceptual procedures. For instance, the specific instructional content given to subjects may affect their ratings. It has been found that subjects' estimates are larger if they are asked to rate based on how they feel as opposed to how they rationally view their body (Huon & Brown, 1986; Thompson & Dolce, 1989; Thompson, Dolce, Spana, & Register, 1987). Gardner and colleagues have developed an interesting slant on the instructional issue by using a signal-detection procedure (e.g., Gardner, Martinez, & Sandoval, 1987). Subjects are presented a video image that is distorted too large or too small by 6%. The subject must respond on each trial as to whether the image is normal or distorted. If the image is actually distorted and the subject states "yes," then a "hit" is recorded. If the body is not distorted and the subject reports that it is, then a "false alarm" is recorded. The hit and false alarm rates can be used to estimate sensory sensitivity and response bias. Gardner believes that this procedure allows the researcher to separate sensory and nonsensory (personality, attitudes, motivation) factors in size-estimation accuracy. If estimation inaccuracies are due to sensory deficits, responses would be independent of any response bias or tendency to state that the image is distorted (i.e., a lax response criterion).

Other contextual issues have also been shown to affect estimations. Button, Fransella, and Slade (1977) have demonstrated that available illumination in the laboratory may have an effect on size-estimation procedures. The researchers found that anorexics overestimated to a larger degree when the lights were brighter. Collins, Beumont, Touyz, Krass, Thompson, and Philips (1987) found that the presence of facial cues and type of clothing were two variables that affected size estimation.

Subject factors also seem to influence level of overestimation. For instance, actual body sizes are negatively correlated with level of size overestimation; smaller subjects overestimate to a larger degree (Cash & Green, 1986; Coovert, Thompson, & Kinder, 1988). In fact, when anorexics and normal subjects are matched on absolute size of body sites that are estimated, the groups have equivalent levels of overestimation (Penner, Thompson, & Coovert, in press). Williams, Davis, Goreczy, and Blouin (1989) also make a strong case for controlling for body size as a confounding variable with bulimic populations. Another subject factor that influences size estimation appears to be women's menstrual cycle. Altabe and Thompson (in press) found that the waist was overestimated to a larger degree during the perimenstrual stage (premenstrual and menstrual) than during the intermenstrual phase. Pasman and Thompson (1988) also found that individuals who engage in bodybuilding/weightlifting athletic activity are more accurate than runners or sedentary individuals.

Finally, in view of the fact that the great majority of subjects in body-image research are females, the gender of the experimenter is an experimental issue deserving consideration. Few studies report this information and only one investigation has experimentally manipulated experimenter gender (Thompson & Connelly, 1988). Although this study found no differences between estimations of female subjects made in the presence of a male versus a female experimenter, the issue is far from closed. Investigators should continue to evaluate characteristics of the experimenter such as gender and weight.

ASSESSMENT OF THE SUBJECTIVE COMPONENTS OF PHYSICAL APPEARANCE

The following measures vary greatly in the specific aspect of the subjective component of physical appearance that is measured. In some cases, the alteration of instructional content will determine whether the measure is addressing satisfaction, concerns, cognitions, anxiety, or some other appearance-related component. In many cases, it is also difficult to determine if the measure is tapping into an affective or cognitive component of body image. The specific way in which the instrument is used will often determine this differentiation.

The most widely used methods of determining an overall rating of size/weight satisfaction are the schematic figures or silhouettes of different body sizes, ranging from very small to very large (Fallon & Rozin, 1985; Keeton, Cash, & Brown, 1990; Thompson & Psaltis, 1988; Williamson, Davis, Bennett, Goreczny, & Gleaves, in press). Subjects are asked to choose the figure that they think reflects their current and ideal body size. The discrepancy between these two measures is taken as an indication of level of dissatisfaction. These silhouettes also can be employed in a manner to produce an index of whole-body size-estimation accuracy. One strategy entails conversion of subjects' "current self" silhouette selection to T scores from height/weight normative tables (Williamson et al., in press). Another approach involves raters' classification of subjects' body size with the same silhouettes (Keeton et al., 1990). As Table 2.1 indicates, researchers have created many different sets of these stimuli. Figure 2.2 is an illustration of one such figural rating procedure.

A potential technical improvement of the figural/schematic rating procedure involves the presentation of body figures on a computer screen (Dickson-Parnell, Jones, & Braddy, 1987). With this method, subjects can adjust the sizes of nine body sites to arrive at the exact image representation that they believe fits their own dimensions. Again, a measure of generic satisfaction with the body (i.e., self–ideal discrepancy) can be obtained by asking subjects to create an ideal and realistic image.

Cash and colleagues have pioneered the use of a mirror focus procedure, which they believe measures the affective component of dissatisfaction (Butters & Cash, 1987; Keeton et al., 1990). Subjects are asked to examine all of their body features as they gaze into a full-length, tri-fold mirror for 30 seconds at a

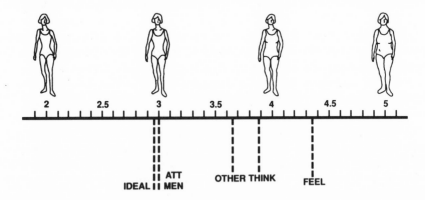

FIGURE 2.2.   Body-size ratings on the Figure Rating Scale. Mean ratings for women for ideal rating, how they *think* they look, how they *feel* they look, how others see their figure, and the figure they think is most attractive to men (sample: college females aged 17–25). From *Eating and Its Disorders* by A.J. Stunkard and E. Stellar (Eds.), 1984, New York: Raven Press. Copyright 1984 by Raven Press. Reprinted by permission.

distance of 3 feet (without being observed by the experimenter). They are then asked to rate their comfort–discomfort level on a subjective units of distress scale from 0 (absolute calm) to 100 (extreme discomfort). This measure appears to be very sensitive to momentary changes in dissatisfaction, thus making it ideal for laboratory work.

Ruff and Barrios (1986) developed a procedure that requires subjects to give a subjective rating for their estimated size width, presented onto a wall using the BIDD (discussed earlier as a site-estimation procedure). Subjects are asked to judge the width of their projected beam by comparing it to those of other individuals of their gender, age, and height. They rate their judgment of the width of the beam on a scale from grossly below the norm (0) to grossly above the norm (100).

Questionnaire measures generally focus on a broader conception of the subjective component; however, some scales focus fairly exclusively on weight/size dissatisfaction. For instance, probably the first widely used instrument was the Body Cathexis Scale (Secord & Jourard, 1953). Berscheid, Walster, and Bohrnstedt (1973) developed the Body Parts Satisfaction Scale (BPPS), which lists 24 body parts that are rated on a scale ranging from extremely dissatisfied to extremely satisfied. The BPPS yields several factor scores as well as a composite score (Bohrnstedt, 1977). Garner, Polivy, and Olmstead (1983) created the Eating Disorders Inventory, which has, as one of its seven scales, a subscale labelled Body Dissatisfaction, which largely measures weight-related dissatisfaction.

There are also many questionnaire measures that focus on the assessment of more complex representations of physical appearance. Kurtz (1969) used a semantic differential procedure (corresponding to Osgood's three dimensions of evaluation, potency, and activity) in the rating of 30 different body concepts (such as color of hair, facial complexion, weight, etc.). This scale has also been modified and used recently by other researchers (Table 2.1). Fisher (1970) developed the Body Distortion Questionnaire to assess peculiar experiences of the body and its functions.

Cash and colleagues (Butters & Cash, 1987; Cash & Green, 1986; Cash et al., 1986; Noles, Cash, & Winstead, 1984) developed the Body–Self Relations Questionnaire (BSRQ) which has three attitudinal subscales (evaluation, attention/importance, behavior) for each of three somatic domains (appearance, fitness, health). The physical appearance evaluation scale has been used extensively in research on body image (Pasman & Thompson, 1988; Thompson & Psaltis, 1988). Sample items include "I like my looks just the way they are" and "I am physically unattractive." A recent modification of the BSRQ, the Multidimensional BSRQ (MBSRQ) (Cash, 1990), combined the attention/importance and behavioral subscales into an orientation domain (Brown, Cash, & Mikulka, 1989) and added subscales that deal with body-areas satisfaction and weight attitudes (Brown, Cash, & Lewis, 1989; Cash, 1989).

This research group also recently developed the Body Image Automatic

Thoughts Questionnaire (BIATQ) which has subjects rate the frequency of 52 appearance related cognitions on a five-point scale (Brown, Johnson, Bergeron, Keeton, & Cash, 1988; Cash, Lewis, & Keeton, 1987). Thirty-seven of the items are negative, body-related self-statements and 15 are positive, body-related self-statements. In a similar vein, Schulman, Kinder, Powers, Prange, and Gleghorn (1986) developed a Bulimia Cognitive Distortions Scale (BCDS) that contains a subscale that primarily measures cognitive distortions related to physical appearance. Examples of items include "My value as a person is related to my weight" and "If my hair isn't perfect I'll look terrible."

Cooper, Taylor, Cooper, and Fairburn (1987) developed the Body Shape Questionnaire, which deals with concerns about body shape. Typical items from this measure include "Have you felt so bad about your shape that you have cried?" and "Has feeling bored made you brood about your shape?" This measure taps a somewhat different construct than appearance satisfaction or evaluation. For instance, items request subjects to rate (never to always) the following questions: "Has eating even a small amount of food made you feel fat?" "Have you worried about your flesh not being firm enough?"

Rosen, Saltzberg, and Srebnik (1990) offered the first measure aimed at the assessment of the behavioral aspects of body-image disturbance. Although some items in previous questionnaire measures (particularly, the Body Shape Questionnaire and the Body–Self Relations Questionnaire) included questions on behavioral activities relevant to body image, neither focused exclusively on this dimension. Rosen's measure is labelled the Body Image Behavior Questionnaire and requires subjects to rate 19 items with regard to the frequency with which they engage in certain behaviors that prompt concern with physical appearance (such as "I wear baggy clothes" or "I look at myself in the mirror"). There are four subscales—clothing, social activities, eating restraint, and grooming and weighing).

Finally, Reed, Thompson, and Brannick (1990) recently developed the Body Image Anxiety Scale (BIAS), which assesses state and trait components of individuals' anxiety regarding weight and non-weight-relevant body sites. Subjects' state anxiety is measured in three different situations that are constructed to produce low, medium, and high levels of appearance anxiety. The trait measure assesses generalized body-image anxiety, nonspecific to situational issues. Therefore, this measure could be used for survey work, to establish a measure of general level of disturbance (trait) or laboratory work, in the measurement of specific manipulations of immediate body-image anxiety level (state). In addition, the utilization of all three state situations, for a given individual, could provide a profile analysis of the cross-situational nature of that person's level of disturbance.

Several measures have been developed and validated on adolescent and child populations. For example, Offer, Ostrov, and Howard (1982) developed the Offer Self-Image Questionnaire for adolescents aged 14–18 years. It contains

130 items and 11 scales; the body and self-image subscale can be used as a measure of general appearance evaluation. This scale was subsequently modified and revalidated to make it useful with younger adolescents and the body and self-image scale was renamed simply "body image" (Petersen, Schulenberg, Abramowitz, Offer, & Jarcho, 1984).

Mendelson and White (1982) developed the Body Esteem Scale for use with children and adolescents (ages 7–11 years). These items generally reflect how a person values his/her appearance and looks and include items such as "I like what I look like in pictures" and "Kids my own age like my looks." The Body Dissatisfaction subscale of the Eating Disorders Inventory has also been validated on an adolescent sample (Williams, Schaefer, Shisslak, Gronwaldt, & Comerci, 1986) and has been used in the measurement of dissatisfaction with adolescents (Fabian & Thompson, 1989).

It is apparent that there are many subtle distinctions between various aspects of physical appearance, particularly with regard to assessment in the subjective realm. Scales vary in the degree to which they primarily measure satisfaction, evaluation, concern, thoughts, behaviors, and/or appearance anxiety. Some scales are fairly discrete at tapping into one of these aspects (because of specific instructional protocols or narrowly derived items); however, other scales probably measure some combination of the above concepts. The selection of a specific scale will generally depend on the needs of the researcher or clinician. If one is interested very narrowly in overall weight/size satisfaction, the use of figures or silhouettes would appear to provide a precise measure. Subjects' selection of current and ideal sizes could be used to arrive at a discrepancy score, yielding a single index of general dissatisfaction.

It might be argued that the subject's selection could be biased toward a larger than real figure, if, in fact, they also perceptually overestimate their size. For instance, the perceptual overestimation might lead them to choose a figure larger than they really are, thus accenting the difference between their chosen and ideal figure. This problem might be corrected by having trained raters pick the schematic figure that most closely approximates the real size figure of the subject. For example, as mentioned earlier, Keeton et al. (1990) had independent judges match photographs of subjects to silhouettes to provide an objective measure of actual size silhouette which could be compared to the subject's own silhouette selection. However, this procedure may only be necessary if the researcher wants to use the schematic figures to assess size-perception accuracy. If the figures are to be used to get at subjective dissatisfaction, the assessor would want the subject to pick the figure that most closely approximates his/her conception of actual size. The discrepancy between self-selected and ideal figure then becomes an index of body satisfaction. Ideally, the most information would be gained by the use of both procedures, along the lines of the Keeton et al. (1990) investigation.

With regard to figure ratings, it should also be noted that the specific instructional protocol may affect subjects' selection of current figure. For instance, Thompson and Psaltis (1988) found that figures chosen based on an emotional rating (subjects rated based on how they "felt" most of the time) are larger than those selected based on how subjects "think" they look (Figure 2.2). This difference between affective and cognitive figure selection may be theoretically and clinically important.

It would also seem advisable, when possible, to have subjects rate their own bodies on some measure of dissatisfaction (such as the Mirror Focus Procedure) rather than some indirect indice of their size (such as the self-rating of size-width normativeness represented by light beams—the Subjective Rating Index) (Ruff, & Barrios, 1986). Because self-adjusted light beams generally contain a degree of overestimation, on average about 21% (Thompson & Spana, 1988), subjects are not producing a subjective rating of their own body or its size, but of a stimulus which, in fact, may be larger than their own body. Hence, the subjective rating may be confounded by size-perception inaccuracy when this procedure is used.

An alternative strategy, which still allows the use of size-estimation procedures, has subjects estimate widths using instructions to rate current *and* ideal widths (as with the schematic figures). For instance, Thompson and Dolce (1989) found that ideal-size estimates using the adjustable light beam apparatus were significantly smaller than estimates of how subjects felt or thought they looked. When this procedure is used, as Keeton et al. (1990) have also urged, one may get a subjective measure of dissatisfaction and concurrently obtain a perceptual measure of size overestimation.

The choice of a particular body-image measure will be determined by the needs of the researcher or clinician. Because of the differences in the specific aspects of physical appearance that are assessed across instruments, the assessor should be cautious against overgeneralizing the meaningfulness of high scores on a unitary index. For instance, subjects may score high on general dissatisfaction, moderately on an index of automatic negative thoughts about appearance, and low on size/weight-related indices. Therefore, it may be prudent to use a wide variety of measures, especially in survey, laboratory, or clinical situations where little previous research exists. Also, from an individualized treatment philosophy, it is important to understand the exact nature of a given client's body-image disturbance. We will return to this issue in the last section on applications and recent developments.

It is obvious from the review thus far that there are a multitude of measures for an increasingly large number of ways of conceptualizing appearance-related body image. Interestingly, very little research has addressed the correspondence between various aspects of body image. Do measures of size perception all tap into the same construct? What is the relationship between subjective and perceptual measures? Are these indices related in a similar way to outcome measures that reflect general psychological distress? These issues will now be examined.

CONVERGENCE AND DIVERGENCE AMONG VARIOUS MEASURES

The extent to which some body-image measures converge while others diverge is of both theoretical and practical importance. With regard to the former, consider the distinction that is usually made between the perceptual and subjective components of body image. One rather obvious and direct test of this proposal would be whether the measures concerned with the perceptual and subjective components do, in fact, form two clusters or groups. That is, are the within-group correlations substantial (convergence), and are they, on average, greater than the correlations between the groups (divergence)? This important notion of using convergent and divergent correlations as a means of determining a measure's *construct validity* was proposed some 30 years ago by Campbell and Fiske (1959). From a practical perspective, the clinician who uses a particular body-image measure as part of the diagnosis of a problem and to help in developing a treatment plan should be reasonably confident that the index or measure assesses what the measure's author(s) claims it does. However, with regard to construct validity, it is of both theoretical and practical value to know the psychosocial correlates of a body-image measure.

Despite the potential theoretical and practical value of such data, in the body-image literature there is a relative dearth of studies that have provided information that would address the issues just presented. We could find only two studies that utilized Campbell and Fiske's (1959) classic multitrait–multi-method approach to determine the divergent and convergent validity of a set of body-image measures (Gleghorn, Penner, Powers, & Schulman, 1987; Keeton et al., 1990).

Convergence among Perceptual Measures

The perceptual measures of body image, as noted earlier, can be divided into single-site and whole-body estimation procedures. A few studies have considered how well the measures within each type correlate with one another and also how they relate across categories. Gleghorn et al. (1987) gave 110 women two measures of whole-body estimation procedures—the Open Door Technique (ODT) (Simonson, 1978) and the Distorting Photograph Technique (DPT) (Glucksman & Hirsch, 1969). Three single-site estimation procedures were also included: the IMP (Askevold, 1969), MCT (Slade & Russell, 1973), and the Kinesthetic Size Estimation Apparatus (KSEA) (see Table 2.1). With regard to the latter set of measures, Gleghorn et al. found substantial convergence between the estimates produced by the three site-estimation procedures, but there was also strong evidence of sizeable "method variance." That is, two different sites measured by the same device correlated more highly than the same site measured by two different devices. For example, shoulders and hips estimates with the IMP were more highly correlated than were two estimates of the shoulders using the IMP and the MCT. Thus, it appears that the methods one uses to obtain estimates of specific body sites does make a difference.

The two measures of overall body-size were not significantly correlated ($r = .03$) with one another, and only the ODT showed significant correlations with the estimates of the size of particular body sites, although as one would hope, these correlations were substantially lower than those among the site-estimation procedures. Keeton et al. (1990) obtained similar findings. For both male and female subjects, they found no relation between a whole-body procedure and a site measure of size estimation. Also, Brodie and Slade (1988) found a nonsignificant relation between a body-site estimation procedure and a whole-body measure.

Convergence among Subjective Measures

Very little work exists with subjective measures of body image that has investigated the convergence issue. Keeton et al. (1990) administered measures of satisfaction with body appearance, body-part sizes, and weight; all of the resulting correlations were significant and exceeded .51. Further, for females, but not males, responses to these measures correlated well with affective reactions to looking at oneself in a three-way mirror and subjects' estimates of how their body size compared to the size of their peers (a measure that Keeton et al. consider to be subjective rather than perceptual). Thompson and Psaltis (1988) found fairly high correlations (above .50) between a questionnaire measure of physical appearance evaluation (Body–Self Relations Questionnaire) and a figure selection of current body size, indicating that larger figures were associated with greater dissatisfaction. Interestingly, there was no relation between ideal figure and appearance evaluation. Gleghorn et al. (1987) found a high correlation (.66) between an attitudinal measure and a body dissatisfaction index. Cash (1989) found that overall (Gestalt) appearance evaluation is predictable from a weighted sum of satisfaction with discrete body parts.

Relation between Perceptual and Subjective Measures

The few studies that have evaluated how perceptual and subjective measures correlate with one another have produced somewhat conflicting results. Thompson and Spana (1988), in a sample of college females, found no relation between physical appearance evaluation and size overestimation. Also, Fabian and Thompson (1989), in a sample of adolescent females, found no relation between physical appearance evaluation and size overestimation. Keeton et al. (1990) and Cash and Green (1986) failed to find any significant relation between perceptual overestimation and subjective indices.

On the other hand, Gleghorn et al. (1987) found small, but significant relations between the two types of measures. Keeton et al. suggested that the difference in results between their study and Gleghorn et al. might be partially due to the inclusion of bulimics in the latter study's sample. However, the small, but significant correlations were roughly equivalent when Gleghorn et al. compared a sample of normal college women to bulimics. Brodie and Slade (1988) reported findings consistent with those of Gleghorn in a sample of English women (age range of 19–57 years). Rosen et al. (in press) found significant correlations between his behavioral avoidance scale and both size overestimation and body-shape concern. In sum, some data partially support the existence of weak, but significant correlations between perceptual and subjective measures of body image. Nevertheless, the magnitude of these relations appears to be less than the level of the "within component" correlations, supporting the distinction between perceptual and subjective components.

Relation between Body-Image Measures and Other Variables

Finally, we consider how the measures of perceptual and subjective aspects of body image correlate with scales that purport to assess constructs that theoretically should be related to body image (for a more extensive review of this issue, see Thompson, 1990). The constructs most commonly examined include eating disturbance, self-esteem, and depression. With regard to eating disturbance, findings are quite strong in suggesting that eating dysfunction is correlated with subjective body-image disturbance (Brodie & Slade, 1988; Brown, Cash, & Lewis, 1989; Cash & Brown, 1987; Fabian & Thompson, 1989; Keeton et al., 1990; Thompson & Psaltis, 1988). The association between perceptual accuracy and eating dysfunction is less clear (Cash & Brown, 1987). With few exceptions, little consistent connection has been observed between size overestimation and eating disturbance (Brodie & Slade, 1988; Coovert, Thompson, & Kinder, 1988; Fabian & Thompson, 1989; Keeton et al., 1990). Rosen examines these issues in considerable detail in a subsequent chapter in this volume.

Thompson and Thompson (1986) found a significant negative correlation between self-esteem and size overestimation, indicating that women with the greatest overestimation had the lowest self-esteem (there was an insignificant relation for men). Taylor and Cooper (1986) similarly found a strong association between depression and size overestimation—greater depression was paralleled by larger levels of inaccuracy. Thompson and Psaltis (1988) found that size of current figure (using figure rating scales) was positively correlated with depression and a history of being teased about physical appearance. Ideal figure rating was unrelated to these measures. Fabian and Thompson (1989) found that level of overestimation was uncorrelated with self-esteem, depression, and teasing history for premenarcheal adolescent females. However, for postmenarcheal subjects, teasing history and depression level were positively associated with size overestimation. Also, in their study, body satisfaction was significantly related to depression and teasing history, for both samples.

Keeton et al. (1990) found that most subjective but fewer perceptual measures correlated significantly with a measure of general psychological functioning (SCL-90-R). Brodie and Slade (1988) also found no reliable correlations between the perceptual measures and depression, whereas there was a significant relation between depression and body satisfaction. Similarly, Gleghorn and Penner (1989) found that size overestimation was unrelated to self-esteem, whereas a satisfaction measure was significantly related to self-esteem and self-regard. Finally, Noles et al. (1985) observed greater body-image dissatisfaction among depressed than nondepressed students and found that whereas depressed students were fairly accurate in appraising their physical attractiveness, nondepresed students exaggerated how attractive they were.

SUMMARY AND RECOMMENDATIONS

There now exists a multitude of assessment instruments for the assessment of many aspects of appearance-related body-image disturbance. The selection of a specific measure or measures depends highly on the clinician or researcher's specific purpose or the population under investigation. However, a few general recommendations may be offered. First, the measure should be psychometrically sound. Nunnally (1970) suggests that the internal consistency should be at least .70 for measures in a preliminary state of development and validation. Ideally, the reliability ratio should approach .90. We suggest that a similar standard should be adopted for test–retest reliability. It should be noted, however, that some of the procedures listed in Table 2.1 attempt to measure a *state* aspect of body-image; therefore, the test–retest reliability might not meet the requirements noted above.

It would also appear prudent to be as comprehensive as possible, utilizing, at the very least, a perceptual and subjective index. With regard to the choice of a specific perceptual measure, the site-estimation procedures may be more desirable for several reasons. They are less expensive and require less technical expertise to administer. Also, as discussed in detail earlier, some subjects have difficulty with the whole-body estimation task (viewing themselves increasing in size). In addition, excellent psychometric data and norms exist for some of these measures, particularly the ALBA (Thompson & Spana, 1988). Finally, as mentioned previously in the discussion of perceptual procedures, there are several methodological issues that should receive attention when these assessments are conducted, including instructional protocol, laboratory illumination level, clothing worn during measurement, and subject characteristics (actual size, menstrual phase, athletic involvement).

With regard to the selection of a subjective index, there are several available with adequate psychometric characteristics (Table 2.1). It is advisable to choose an instrument that might tap into several different aspects of body image, including affective, cognitive, and behavioral. In this regard, the MBSRQ (Cash, 1990) would appear to be the most comprehensive and widely validated. Currently, while there are no available behavioral coding systems, the Rosen et al. (1990) subjective rating of avoidance of situations does appear to measure this construct. Therefore, it would appear reasonable to include it in any comprehensive body-image assessment battery.

Other measures might be selected given certain idiosyncratic issues with specific clients. For instance, if anxiety regarding body image is relevant, especially if the anxiety appears to be situational and not generalized, the Body Image Anxiety Scale (Reed et al., 1990) might prove useful. The same logic would lead the clinician to a body-shape measure (Cooper et al., 1986) or dysfunctional cognitions index (Cash et al., 1988; Schulman et al., 1986).

In addition, given the recent focus on self-ideal discrepancy measures, some type of figure or schematic rating method should be utilized. In fact, along the lines of Thompson and Dolce (1989) and Keeton et al. (1990), it is possible to use a site-estimation procedure to assess both subjective and perceptual disturbance by requiring subjects to estimate their current and ideal widths. The discrepancy is used as a subjective index and the comparison of current with actual body-site sizes (measured with calipers, for example) yields an assessment of size-perception accuracy.

As Table 2.1 illustrates, some subjective measures are simply unacceptable at the current time because they lack reliability and remain psychometrically suspect. Therefore, widely used, psychometrically validated measures should be selected for research and clinical purposes. This is particularly a consideration if the subject population is composed of adolescents or males, as so few of the measures have been validated with these populations. Factor structures and reliabilities based on college female samples may not easily generalize to other subject groups.

In general, future research should also attempt to measure body image via a multiple response system assessment. For instance, Wiener, Seime, and Goetsch (1989) describe a procedure whereby the subject's subjective, physiological, and behavioral responses are recorded while she views a photograph of herself increasing in size (they use a video distortion technique) (Figure 2.3). These researchers believe that their tripartite assessment of *fear of weight gain* is a comprehensive analysis of one aspect of body-image disturbance. This type of laboratory manipulation, designed to provoke body-image dysfunction in certain populations, should serve as a model for future investigations.

Future research should also focus more efforts on the measurement of convergence/divergence among different body-image measures and the relation between these indices and other psychosocial variables. The data in this area are inconclusive and multimethod–multitrait methodologies should be considered. More extensive validation of various instruments with different subject samples, along the lines of Cash's (1990; Chapter 3, this volume) work with the

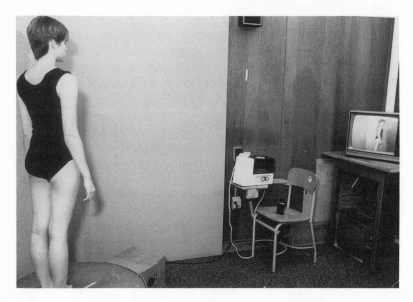

FIGURE 2.3. A subject observes her image on a distorting video monitor as it progressively increases in size. From the procedure outlined by Wiener et al. (1989). Photograph provided by R. Seime, University of West Virginia.

Multidimensional Body–Self Relations Questionnaire, should be undertaken. In sum, the pace of work in the assessment of body image appears to be accelerating in a number of areas and this development should have a salutary effect on research and clinical work in the field of body image.

REFERENCES

Alleback, P., Hallberg, D., & Espmark, S. (1976). Body image—An apparatus for measuring disturbances in estimation of size and shape. *Journal of Psychosomatic Research, 20,* 583–589.

Altabe, M., & Thompson, J. K. (in press). Menstrual cycle, body image, and eating disturbance. *International Journal of Eating Disorders.*

Altabe, M., Thompson, J. K., & Penner, L. (1990). *Clinical correlates of body image discrepancy indices.* Unpublished manuscript.

American Psychiatric Association (1987). *Diagnostic and statistical manual of mental disorders* (3rd ed., rev.). Washington: Author.

Askevold, R. (1975). Measuring body image: Preliminary report on a new method. *Psychotherapy and Psychosomatics, 26,* 71–77.

Attie, I., & Brooks-Gunn, J. (1989). Development of eating problems in adolescent girls: A longitudinal study. *Developmental Psychology, 25,* 70–79.

Barrios, B. A., Ruff, G. A., & York, C. I. (1989). Bulimia and body image: Assessment and explication of a promising construct. In W. G. Johnson (Ed.), *Advances in eating disorders* (Vol. 2, pp. 67–89). New York: JAI Press.

Berscheid, E., Walster, E., & Bohrnstedt, G. (1973, November). The happy American body: A survey report. *Psychology Today, 11,* 119–131.

Bohrnstedt, G. W. (1977). *On measuring body satisfaction*. Unpublished manuscript, Indiana University, Bloomington, Indiana.

Brodie, D. A., & Slade, P. D. (1988). The relationship between body-image and body-fat in adult women. *Psychological Medicine, 18*, 623–631.

Brooks-Gunn, J., & Petersen, A. C. (Eds.). (1983). *Girls at puberty*. New York: Plenum Press.

Brown, T. A., Cash, T. F., & Lewis, R. J. (1989). Body-image disturbances in adolescent female binge-purgers: A brief report of the results of a national survey in the U.S.A. *Journal of Child Psychiatry and Psychology, 30*, 605–613.

Brown, T. A., Cash, T. F., & Mikulka, P. J. (1990). *Attitudinal body image assessment: Factor analysis of the Body–Self Relations Questionnaire*. Unpublished manuscript.

Brown, T. A., Johnson, W. G., Bergeron, K. C., Keeton, W. P., & Cash, T. F. (1988, Nov.). *Assessment of body-related cognitions in bulimia: The Body Image Automatic Thoughts Questionnaire*. Paper presented at the Association for the Advancement of Behavior Therapy, New York.

Buree, B., Papageorgis, D., & Solyom, L. (1984). Body image perception and preference in anorexia nervosa. *Canadian Journal of Psychiatry, 29*, 557–563.

Butters, J. W., & Cash, T. F. (1987). Cognitive–behavioral treatment of women's body-image dissatisfaction. *Journal of Consulting and Clinical Psychology, 55*, 889–897.

Button, E. J., Fransella, F., & Slade, P. D. (1977). A reappraisal of body perception disturbance in anorexia nervosa. *Psychological Medicine, 7*, 235–242.

Campbell, D. T., & Fiske, D. W. (1959). Convergent and discriminant validation by the multitrait–multimethod matrix. *Psychological Bulletin, 56*, 81–105.

Cash, T. F. (1988, November). *Body image and beyond*. Presentation as invited discussant for the symposium "Body image or images? In search of the elusive intervening variable." Convention of the Association for the Advancement of Behavior Therapy, New York.

Cash, T. F. (1989). Body-image affect: Gestalt versus summing the parts. *Perceptual & Motor Skills, 69*, 17–18.

Cash, T. F. (1990). *The Multidimensional Body–Self Relations Questionnaire*. Unpublished manuscript and software.

Cash, T. F., & Brown, T. A. (1989). Gender and body images: Stereotypes and realities. *Sex Roles, 21*, 361–373.

Cash, T. F., & Brown, T. A. (1987). Body image in anorexia nervosa and bulimia nervosa: A review of the literature. *Behavior Modification, 11*, 487–521.

Cash, T. F., & Green, G. K. (1986). Body weight and body image among college women: Perception, cognition, and affect. *Journal of Personality Assessment, 50*, 290–301.

Cash, T. F., Lewis, R. J., & Keeton, P. (1987, March). *Development and validation of the Body-Image Automatic Thoughts Questionnaire: A measure of body-related cognitions*. Paper presented at the meeting of the Southeastern Psychological Association, Atlanta, GA.

Cash, T. F., Winstead, B. A., & Janda, L. H. (1986, April). Body image survey report: The great American shape-up. *Psychology Today, 20*, 30–44.

Cohn, L. D., Adler, N. E., Irwin, C. E., Millstein, S. G., Kegeles, S. M., & Stone, G. (1987). Body-figure preferences in male and female adolescents. *Journal of Abnormal Psychology, 96*, 276–279.

Collins, J. K. (1986). The objective measurement of body image using a video technique: Reliability and validity studies. *British Journal of Psychology, 77*, 199–205.

Collins, J. K. (1987). Methodology for the objective measurement of body image. *International Journal of Eating Disorders, 6*, 393–399.

Collins, J. K., Beumont, P. J. V., Touyz, S. W., Krass, J. L., Thompson, P., & Philips, T. (1987). Accuracy of body image with varying degrees of information about the face and body contours. *International Journal of Eating Disorders, 6*, 67–73.

Cooper, P. J., Taylor, M. J., Cooper, Z., & Fairburn, C. G., (1987). The development and validation of the Body Shape Questionnaire. *International Journal of Eating Disorders, 6*, 485–494.

Coovert, D. L., Thompson, J. K., & Kinder, B. N. (1988). Interrelationships among multiple aspects of body image and eating disturbance. *International Journal of Eating Disorders, 7*, 495–502.

Dickson-Parnell, B., Jones, M., & Braddy, D. (1987). Assessment of body image perceptions using a computer program. *Behavior Research Methods, Instruments, & Computers, 19*, 353–354.

Fabian, L. J., & Thompson, J. K. (1989). Body image and eating disturbance in young females. *International Journal of Eating Disorders, 8*, 63–74.

Fallon, A. E., & Rozin, P. (1985). Sex differences in perceptions of desirable body shape. *Journal of Abnormal Psychology, 94*, 102–105.

Fisher, S. (1970). *Body experience in fantasy and behavior.* New York: Appleton-Century-Crofts.

Fisher, S. (1986). *Development and structure of the body image.* Hillsdale, NJ: Erlbaum.

Franzoi, S. L., & Shields, S. A. (1984). The body-esteem scale: Multidimensional structure and sex differences in a college population. *Journal of Personality Assessment, 48*, 173–178.

Freeman, R. J., Thomas, C. D., Solyom, L., & Miles, J. E. (1983). Body-image disturbances in anorexia nervosa: A reexamination and a new technique. In P. L. Darby, P. E. Garfinkel, & D. M. Garner (Eds.), *Anorexia nervosa: New developments in research* (pp. 117–127). New York: Alan R. Liss.

Freeman, R. J., Thomas, C. D., Solyom, L., & Hunter, M. A. (1984). A modified video camera for measuring body image distortion: Technical description and reliability. *Psychological Medicine, 14*, 411–416.

Gardner, R. M., Martinez, R., Espinoza, T., & Gallegos, V. (1988). Distortion of body image in the obese: A sensory phenomenon. *Psychological Medicine, 18*, 633–641.

Gardner, R. M., Martinez, R., & Sandoval, Y. (1987). Obesity and body image: An evaluation of sensory and non-sensory components. *Psychological Medicine, 17*, 927–932.

Gardner, R. M., & Moncrieff, C. (1988). Body image distortion in anorexics as a non-sensory phenomenon: A signal detection approach. *Journal of Clinical Psychology, 44*, 101–107.

Gargiulo, J., Brooks-Gunn, J., Attie, I., & Warren, M. P. (1987). Girls' dating behavior as a function of social context and maturation. *Developmental Psychology, 23*, 730–737.

Garner, D. M. (1981). Body image in anorexia nervosa. *Canadian Journal of Psychiatry, 26*, 224–227.

Garner, D. M., & Garfinkel, P. E. (1981). Body image in anorexia nervosa: Measurement, theory, and clinical implications. *International Journal of Psychiatry in Medicine, 11*, 263–284.

Garner, D. M., Garfinkel, P. E., & Bonato, D. P. (1987). Body image measurement in eating disorders. *Advances in Psychosomatic Medicine, 17*, 119–133.

Garner, D. M., Olmstead, M. A., & Polivy, J. (1983). Development and validation of a multidimensional eating disorder inventory for anorexia nervosa and bulimia. *International Journal of Eating Disorders, 2*, 15–34.

Gleghorn, A. A., & Penner, L. A. (1989, August). *Body image and self-esteem in normal weight women.* Paper presented at the annual meeting of the American Psychological Association, New Orleans.

Gleghorn, A. A., Penner, L. A., Powers, P. S., & Schulman, R. (1987). The psychometric properties of several measures of body image. *Journal or Psychopathology and Behavioral Assessment, 9*, 203–218.

Glucksman, M., & Hirsch, J. (1969). The response of obese patients to weight reduction. III: The perception of body size. *Psychosomatic Medicine, 31*, 1–17.

Hay, G. G. (1970). Dysmorphophobia. *British Journal of Psychiatry, 116*, 399–406.

Huon, G. F., & Brown, L. B. (1986). Body images in anorexia nervosa and bulimia nervosa. *International Journal of Eating Disorders, 5*, 421–439.

Huon, G. F., & Brown, L. B. (in press). Assessing bulimics' dissatisfaction with their body. *British Journal of Clinical Psychology.*

Keeton, W. P., Cash, T. F., & Brown, T. A. (1990). Body image or body images? Comparative, multidimensional assessment among college students. *Journal of Personality Assessment, 54,* 213–230.

Koff, E., Rierdan, J., & Silverstone, E. (1978). Changes in representation of body image as a function of menarcheal status. *Developmental Psychology, 14,* 635–642.

Kreitler, S., & Kreitler, H. (1988). Body image: The dimension of size. *Genetic, Social, and General Psychology Monographs, 114,* 7–32.

Kurtz, R. M. (1969). Sex differences and variations in body attitudes. *Journal of Consulting and Clinical Psychology, 33,* 625–629.

Lacey, J. H., & Birtchnell, S. A. (1986). Body image and its disturbances. *Journal of Psychosomatic Research, 30,* 623–631.

Leon, G. R., Lucas, A. R., Colligan, R. C., Ferdinande, R. J., & Kamp, J. (1985). Sexual, body-image, and personality attitudes in anorexia nervosa. *Journal of Abnormal Child Psychology, 13,* 245–258.

Leon, G. R., & Mangelsdorf, C. (1989). *The semantic-differential body image scale.* Unpublished manuscript.

Mendelson, B. K., & White, D. R. (1982). Relation between body-esteem and self-esteem of obese and normal children. *Perceptual and Motor Skills, 54,* 899–905.

Mendelson, B. K., & White, D. R. (1985). Development of self-body-esteem in overweight youngsters. *Developmental Psychology, 21,* 90–96.

Noles, S. W., Cash, T. F., & Winstead, B. A. (1985). Body image, physical attractiveness, and depression. *Journal of Consulting and Clinical Psychology, 53,* 88–94.

Nunnally, J. (1970). *Psychometric theory.* New York: McGraw-Hill.

Offer, D., Ostrov, E., & Howard, K., I. (1982). *The Offer Self-Image Questionnaire for Adolescents: A Manual* (3rd ed.). Michael Reese Hospital, Chicago.

Pasman, L., & Thompson, J. K. (1988). Body image and eating disturbance in obligatory runners, obligatory weight lifters, and sedentary individuals. *International Journal of Eating Disorders, 7,* 759–769.

Penner, L., Thompson, J. K., & Coovert, D. L. (in press). Size overestimation among anorexics: Much ado about very little. *Journal of Abnormal Psychology.*

Petersen, A. C., Schulenberg, J. E., Abramowitz, R. H., Offer, D., & Jarcho, H. D. (1984). A self-image questionnaire for young adolescents (SIQYA): Reliability and validity studies. *Journal of Youth and Adolescence, 13,* 93–111.

Powers, P. D., & Erickson, M. T. (1986). Body-image in women and its relationship to self-image and body satisfaction. *The Journal of Obesity and Weight Regulation, 5,* 37–50.

Reed, D., Thompson, J. K., & Brannick, M. (1990). *Development and validation of the Body Image Anxiety Scale (BIAS).* Unpublished manuscript.

Rosen, J. C., Saltzberg, E., & Srebnik, D. (1990). *Development of a body image behavior questionnaire.* Unpublished manuscript.

Ruff, G. A., & Barrios, B. A. (1986). Realistic assessment of body image. *Behavioral Assessment, 8,* 237–252.

Schulman, R. G., Kinder, B. N., Powers, P. S., Prange, M., & Gleghorn, A. A. (1986). The development of a scale to measure cognitive distortions in bulimia. *Journal of Personality Assessment, 50,* 630–639.

Secord, P. F., & Jourard, S. M. (1953). The appraisal of body-cathexis: Body-cathexis and the self. *Journal of Consulting Psychology, 17,* 343–347.

Simonson, M., (1978, February). *The management of obesity.* Paper presented at Johns Hopkins Medical Institution, Baltimore.

Slade, P. D., Dewey, M. E., Newton, T., Brodie, D., & Kiemle, G. (in press). Development and preliminary validation of the body satisfaction scale (BSS). *Psychology and Health.*

Slade, P. D., & Russell, G. F. M. (1973). Awareness of body dimensions in anorexia nervosa: Cross-sectional and longitudinal studies. *Psychological Medicine, 3,* 188–199.

Stunkard, A. J., Sorenson, T., & Schlusinger, F. (1983). Use of the Danish adoption register for the study of obesity and thinness. In S. Kety, L. P. Rowland, R. L. Sidman, & S W. Matthysse (Eds.), *The genetics of neurological and psychiatric disorders* (pp. 115–120). New York: Raven Press.

Taylor, M. J., & Cooper, P. J. (1986). Body size overestimation and depressed mood. *British Journal of Clinical Psychology, 25,* 153–154.

Thompson, J. K. (1987). Body size distortion in anorexia nervosa: Reanalysis and reconceptualization. *International Journal of Eating Disorders, 6,* 379–384.

Thompson, J. K. (1990). *Body image disturbance: Assessment and treatment.* Elmsford, NY: Pergamon.

Thompson, J. K., & Altabe, M. (in press). Psychometric qualities of the Figure Rating Scale. *International Journal of Eating Disorders.*

Thompson, J. K., & Connelly, J. J. (1988). Experimenter gender and size estimation accuracy. *International Journal of Eating Disorders, 7,* 723–725.

Thompson, J. K., & Dolce, J. J. (1989). The discrepancy between emotional vs. rational estimates of body size, actual size, and ideal body ratings: Theoretical and clinical implications. *Journal of Clinical Psychology, 45,* 473–478.

Thompson, J. K., Dolce, J. J., Spana, R. E., & Register, A. (1987). Emotionally versus intellectually based estimates of body size. *International Journal of Eating Disorders, 6,* 507–514.

Thompson, J. K., & Psaltis, K. (1988). Multiple aspects and correlates of body figure ratings: A replication and extension of Fallon and Rozin (1985). *International Journal of Eating Disorders, 7,* 813–818.

Thompson, J. K., & Spana, R. E. (1988). The adjustable light beam method for the assessment of size estimation accuracy: Description, psychometrics, and normative data. *International Journal of Eating Disorders, 7,* 521–526.

Thompson, J. K., & Thompson, C. M. (1986). Body size distortion and self-esteem in asymptomatic, normal weight males and females. *International Journal of Eating Disorders, 5,* 1061–1068.

Touyz, S. W., & Beumont, P. J. V. (1987). Body image and its disturbance. In P. J. V. Beumont, G. D. Burrows, & R. C. Casper (Eds.), *Handbook of eating disorders* (pp. 171–187). New York: Elsevier Science Publishers.

Traub, A. C., & Orbach, J. (1964). Psychophysical studies of body-image. I. The adjusting body-distorting mirror. *Archives of General Psychiatry, 11,* 53–66.

Ward, T. E., McKeown, B. C., Mayhew, J. L., Jackson, A. W., & Piper, F. C. (1990). *Body Cathexis Scale: Reliability and validity in an exercise setting.* Unpublished manuscript.

Wiener, A., Seime, R., & Goetsch, V. (1989, March). *A multimethod assessment of fear of weight gain in bulimic and low risk females.* Paper presented at the meeting of the Southeastern Psychological Association, Washington, DC.

Williams, R. L., Schaefer, C. A., Shisslak, C. M., Gronwaldt, V. H., & Comerci, G. D. (1986). Eating attitudes and behaviors in adolescent women: Discrimination of normals, dieters, and suspected bulimics using the Eating Attitudes Test and Eating Disorder Inventory. *International Journal of Eating Disorders, 5,* 879–894.

Williamson, D. A., Davis, C. J., Goreczny, A. J., & Blouin, D. C. (1989). Body-image disturbances in bulimia nervosa: Influences of actual body size. *Journal of Abnormal Psychology, 98,* 97–99.

Williamson, D. A., Davis, C. J., Bennett, S. M., Goreczny, A. J., & Gleaves, D. H. (in press). Development of a simple procedure for assessing body image disturbances. *Behavioral Assessment.*

Winstead, B. A., & Cash, T. F. (1984, March). *Reliability and validity of the Body–Self Relationship Questionnaire: A new measure of body image.* Paper presented at the Southeastern Psychological Association, New Orleans.

BODY, SELF, AND SOCIETY: DEVELOPMENT OF BODY IMAGES

CHAPTER 3

The Psychology of Physical Appearance: Aesthetics, Attributes, and Images

Thomas F. Cash

This chapter provides an overview of the psychology of physical appearance—the scientific study of how our physical aesthetics and our bodily attributes, including our somatic self-perceptions, affect our lives. In recent years, psychological studies of physical appearance have proliferated dramatically. This review examines some of our knowledge (and our ignorance) concerning physical appearance. The chapter focuses largely upon physical attributes that fall within the *normal range* of appearance. Subsequent chapters in this volume describe significant deviations, deformities, or disfigurements that fall outside the realm of normal physical aesthetics.

PERSPECTIVES ON APPEARANCE: "OUTSIDE AND INSIDE VIEWS"

From womb to tomb, what we look like is an important part of who we are—both to others, as well as to ourselves. The psychology of physical appearance may be neatly divided into two perspectives (Cash, 1985a): The first perspective is the "view from the outside"—the view of persons as social objects. This social-image perspective has traditionally examined the influences of *physical attractiveness* on social perceptions, interpersonal interactions, and human development. The second perspective in the psychology of physical appearance concerns the individual's subjective experience of his/her own physical aesthetics and attributes. This "view from the inside" entails studies of physical self-concept or body-image variables. Unfortunately, many researchers often adopt one perspective and ignore all others; they sometimes even discuss the perspectives as if they are equivalent. However, a comprehensive psychology of physical appearance must consider both views—especially because measures of self-perceived aesthetics or body image often have a modest-at-best empirical correspondence with socially perceived reality (Berscheid & Walster, 1974; Butters & Cash, 1987; Cash, 1981, 1985a; Cash & Soloway, 1975). In other words, beauty is no guarantee of a favorable body image, nor is homeliness a decree for a negative body image.

Another useful delineation in research literatures on physical appearance concerns whether investigators view appearance in its entirety (as a gestalt) or focus on more discrete facets or attributes of appearance. These distinctions of outer versus inner views and global appearance versus the appearance of specific features provide the organization for this chapter. I begin by reviewing our extant knowledge concerning overall physical appearance—first, how others perceive and react to physical attractiveness and, then, how we perceive and react to our own physical aesthetics. Next, I examine the importance of selected, specific bodily attributes, first in terms of social-image, then in terms of self-image. Finally, contrary to the prevailing paradigm, which regards appearance as a rather fixed and immutable characteristic of the person, I explore the important ways in which we *create* our own physical appearance. This topic concerns the relatively novel area of the self-management of physical aesthetics.

OVERALL APPEARANCE: SOCIAL IMAGES

Physical appearance is often the most readily available information about a person and conveys basic information about that person—most obviously, for example, the person's gender, race, approximate age, and possibly even socioeconomic status or occupation. Physical-appearance factors can determine who, among the many people we encounter in our daily lives, will remain strangers or mere acquaintances and who will become our close friends and loved ones. These observations underscore the importance of person perceptions during initial impression formation and represent a salient aspect of social psychological inquiry (Kleinke, 1975; Schneider, Hastorf, & Ellsworth, 1979).

Human beings maintain assumptions and attitudes about physical aesthetics and physical attributes and, often unconsciously, sort people into a variety of cognitive categories or prototypes. These implicit assumptions often mediate interpersonal attraction (and apathy or hostility), as well as the perceiver's overt responses to the "stimulus person." Behavioral scientists have conducted hundreds of studies verifying that physical-appearance variables—such as physical attractiveness, weight, height, facial characteristics, and grooming factors—are reliably perceived (not wholly idiosyncratic to the eyes of the beholder) and systematically affect social attitudes, attributions, and actions. During the 1980s, several detailed volumes have reviewed the psychological literature concerning appearance-based stereotyping (see Alley, 1988; Bull & Rumsey, 1988; Cash, 1981; Freedman, 1986; Hatfield & Sprecher, 1986; Patzer, 1985).

Appearance-Cued Stereotyping

The lion's share of the research literature on appearance stereotyping concerns a particular social goodness stereotype of beauty. In their now classic, seminal investigation of physical attractiveness, Dion, Berscheid, and Walster (1982) documented the existence of the stereotype "what is beautiful is good" (and conversely, "what is ugly is bad"). Relative to their less attractive counterparts, attractive males and females are viewed as being happier, more successful, smarter, more interesting, warmer, more poised, more sociable, and so forth. A recent meta-analytic review of the numerous studies of appearance and person perception confirms the beauty-is-good stereotype (Eagly, Ashmore, Makhijani, & Kennedy, in press). Regardless of the gender of the perceiver or the perceived, the strongest components of the beauty-is-good (ugly-is-bad) stereotype concern assumed social confidence (socially skillful, outgoing, popular, likable) and adjustment (happy, confident, well-adjusted).

At first glance, the ubiquity of the what-is-beautiful-is-good stereotype seems largely uncontested. Hatfield and Sprecher (1986) asserted that "people *believe* good-looking people possess all the virtues known to humankind" (p. xix). However, the aforementioned meta-analysis (Eagly et al., in press) suggested that the social goodness stereotype of attractiveness may be neither as strong nor as encompassing as we have perhaps come to think. Persons are not equally biased by others' looks; for example, sex-typed individuals (see Andersen & Bem, 1981; Cash & Kilcullen, 1985; Moore, Graziano, & Millar, 1987) and those sensitive to social impressions (i.e., high self-monitors; Snyder, Berscheid, & Glick, 1985) are especially influenced by the physical appearance of others. Furthermore, the implicit assumptions about physically attractive individuals may not always be positive (Cash & Duncan, 1984; Cash & Janda, 1984). Evidence confirms the operation of two additional stereotypes concerning beauty: (1) what is beautiful is self-centered, and (2) what is beautiful is sex-typed. Let's take a closer look at these stereotypes.

If people assume that good-looking people possess socially desirable personalities and have social advantages not afforded to plainer persons, it is not illogical or cognitively inconsistent that perceivers would also assume that attractive persons are cognizant of their social goodness. To consider oneself as attractive, socially advantaged, likable, popular, and so forth, suggests, in the eye of the beholder, that the beheld must be vain, egotistical, and self-centered. This represents a case of blaming the victims for our own stereotyping of them. A few studies have verified the operation of this self-centeredness stereotype of beauty (Cash & Duncan, 1984; Dermer & Thiel, 1975; Wilson & Cash, 1978). Imagine for a moment that you initiate conversation with a stranger at a party, and the stranger offers little eye contact, seldom nods or smiles at you, fails to reciprocate your personal self-disclosures, and exits abruptly. If this stranger were strikingly good-looking, I suspect you would be more apt to infer that the person is "stuck up"—as opposed to reasonable alternatives, such as shyness, social anxiety, or the lack of social competencies. The latter inferences are apt to be reserved for homely "nerds." Somewhat relatedly, the socially advantaged status of good-looking persons in our society may sometimes elicit envy and the assumption that these individuals would be less dutiful in the mundane chores of parenthood and less faithful as romantic partners (Cash & Duncan, 1984; Dermer & Thiel, 1975).

The third appearance stereotype takes into account the gender-specific meaning of physical attractiveness. Research has demonstrated that attractive persons are perceived to be more sex-typed than their less attractive same-sex peers (Bar-Tal & Saxe, 1976; Cash & Duncan, 1984; Deaux & Lewis, 1984; Gillen, 1981; Major & Deaux, 1981; Nakdimen, 1984). That is, attractive males are regarded as more masculine and attractive females as more feminine in their personalities; after all, they represent the prototypic ideal of their gender. As will be subsequently considered in more detail, these data carry the important implication that attractive persons could elicit sexist reactions to a greater extent than average-looking or unattractive persons.

Social Consequences of Appearance Stereotyping

While people certainly possess differential schemata about others based on their looks, to what extent do these assumptions translate behaviorally into the differential social treatment of attractive and unattractive individuals? The data here confirm that beauty makes a behavioral difference, beginning as early as infancy and continuing throughout the lifespan. For example, Hildebrandt and Fitzgerald (1983) and Langlois (1986) found that infant cuteness is positively related to maternal (or caregivers') social-bonding behaviors (e.g., liking, looking, kissing, cooing, smiling, etc.). Fathers also exhibit more antipathy toward unattractive than attractive offspring (Elder, Nguyen, & Caspi, 1985). Myriad studies further document that teachers attend and react more positively to good-looking than unattractive children (e.g., Adams, 1977; Clifford & Walster, 1973; Martinek, 1981). Homelier children also may be at greater risk for blame, punishment, and physical maltreatment (e.g., Berkowitz & Frodi, 1979; Dion, 1972, 1974; McCabe, 1988). In addition to their effects on adults, less attractive children are often less popular with their peers who, by the age of 6, differentiate and stereotype on the basis of physical aesthetics (see Bull & Rumsey, 1988; Langlois & Stephan, 1981).

As adolescence ensues, dating and mating are influenced by one's attractiveness rating. In their initial romantic attraction to potential dates, although males and females are equally affected by the physical attractiveness of the other-sex person, males surpass females in the degree to which they *believe* that, they have been influenced by the other's appearance (Sprecher, 1989). The association between physical attractiveness and dating popularity is moderate and significant (e.g., Berscheid, Dion, Walster, & Walster, 1971; Curran & Lippold, 1975; Reis, Nezlek, & Wheeler, 1980; Walster, Aronson, Abrahams, & Rottman, 1976). A recent meta-analysis of sex differences in the role of physical attractiveness and actual (behavioral) dating popularity (Feingold, 1990) has affirmed the popular assumption that males are more responsive to females' appearance than vice versa. Moreover, interesting research by Reis and his colleagues (1980, 1982) indicated that the quantity of other-sex interactions was greater for attractive males than for their less attractive male peers. For both males and females, physical attractiveness was predictive of greater intimacy and satisfaction in one's heterosexual interactions. Such findings may be understood in terms of the operation of cultural prescriptions that assign males the role of initiating date requests and assign females the role of accepting or rejecting the offers. As popular targets for such overtures, attractive females may become more selective "gatekeepers" of their intimate relations (Cash & Smith, 1982). Like the lyrics of Janis Ian's popular song, *At Seventeen*, about "valentines that never came for ugly duckling girls like me," unattractive females are often familiar with heterosocial apathy and, therefore, may lower their romantic expectations if "the prince isn't interested" (Weinberger & Cash, 1982).

Fortunately for those with less aesthetic appeal, the principle of *homogamy*, or "matching," also operates in dating and marital choices. In other words, persons form intimate relationships with those who are similar in attractiveness level. While this phenomenon also operates in same-sex friendships (Cash & Derlega, 1978), matching is clearly stronger in heterosocial, romantic dyads (for meta-analysis, see Feingold, 1988).

Researchers have sought to ascertain the influences of attractiveness in other important social contexts. For example, Barocas and Karoly (1972) experimentally confirmed that physically attractive persons receive more social reinforcement for the same behaviors than do their less attractive counterparts. Attractive individuals elicit greater behavioral compliance and efforts to please (Sigall, Page, & Brown, 1971), more honesty (Sroufe, Chaikin, Cook, & Freeman, 1977), greater personal self-disclosures (Brundage, Derlega, & Cash, 1977; Cash, 1978; Cash & Soloway, 1975; Kunin & Rodin, 1982), and the receipt of more help from others (Benson, Karabenick, & Lerner, 1976; West & Brown, 1975). Conversely, such findings point to the interpersonal adversities that are faced by physically unattractive persons.

In the workplace, several investigations indicate that physical unattractiveness may invite discrimination. Comparing equally qualified applicants, decision-makers often favor hiring attractive men and women in various employment contexts (Cash, Gillen, & Burns, 1977; Cash & Kilcullen, 1985; Dipboye, Arvey, & Terpstra, 1977; Dipboye, Fromkin, & Wiback, 1975). The evaluation of work itself can be affected by a worker's appearance. For example, research comparing the grades assigned to essays presumably written by either attractive or unattractive authors indicated that less attractive persons frequently received poorer evaluations (Cash & Trimer, 1984; Landy & Sigall, 1974). In her book *Too Old, Too Ugly, and Not Deferential to Men* (1988), anchorwoman Christine Craft tells of her personal and legal struggles in the beauty-biased world of television.

In our criminal justice system, the process of criminal apprehension and juridic judgment may be harsher for unattractive defendants, unless the crime is somehow beauty-related or suggests social arrogance (Efran, 1974; Friend & Vinson, 1974; Mace, 1972; Sigall & Ostrove, 1975; Solomon & Schopler, 1978). In the latter instances, beauty may foster attributions that tip the scales of injustice in the other direction.

In sum, in the service of our democratic ideals or our need to believe in a just world, we may wish that people not "judge books by their covers" and not react to others based upon physical appearance. Nevertheless, the social world clearly discriminates, especially against unattractive people, in a variety of important everyday situations—a phenomenon I call "beautyism." As is depicted graphically in Figure 3.1, Hatfield and Sprecher (1986) have argued that, all tolled, beautyism may be more detrimental to homely persons than it is beneficial to comely individuals.

As suggested above, though often ignored by many behavioral scientists, beauty does not always lead to positive social treatment. The operation of the beauty-is-sex-typed stereotype can yield interesting twists on the way in which appearance affects social judgment and behavior. Indeed, beauty may backfire, especially for women, in certain social-evaluative contexts. Cash, Gillen, and Burns (1977) found that when good-looking women apply for jobs typically

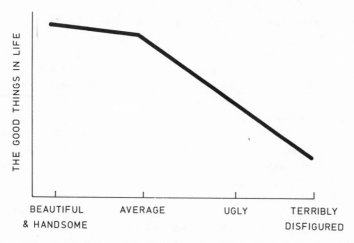

FIGURE 3.1. The psychosocial effects of physical appearance. From *Mirror, Mirror . . . : The Importance of Looks in Everyday Life* (p. 362) by E. Hatfield and S. Sprecher, 1986. Copyright 1986 by the State University of New York Press. Adapted by permission.

held by men (i.e., jobs construed as requiring masculine traits for success), good-looking female applicants may lose their advantage or even be discriminated against relative to their plainer peers (see also Cash & Janda, 1984; Heilman & Saruwatari, 1978). Furthermore, in work performance evaluations, Cash and Trimer (1984) and Heilman and Stopeck (1985a) observed that attractive women can also lose their favored positions when performing tasks regarded as masculine. Perhaps pretty women are assumed too feminine in their personalities and skills to be competent on masculine tasks. In addition, attractive women may elicit more unwanted sexual advances, comments, and inferences from others. Sometimes others may attribute the successes of attractive women to luck or to their good looks (including Machiavellian manipulation of their looks and sexuality) rather than to their skill or hard work (Cash & Janda, 1984; Cash & Trimer, 1984; Heilman & Stopeck, 1985b; Spencer & Taylor, 1988; Wilson et al., 1985). Similarly, good-looking persons themselves may have difficulty knowing whether persons who show interest in or reward them are really responding contingently to their behavior and not simply to their looks (Major, Carrington, & Carnavale, 1984; Sigall & Michela, 1976).

DEVELOPMENTAL CONSEQUENCES OF APPEARANCE FOR PSYCHOSOCIAL ADJUSTMENT

Human appearance decidedly affects the assumptions and reactions from our social environments. However, a crucial question remains: Do persons who differ in attractiveness come to differ, as a result of social treatment, in their personality characteristics and behavioral functioning? Thus, with respect to the influences of appearance on human development and experience, does a "self-fulfilling prophecy," evolve or behavioral confirmation of attractiveness stereotyping?

Social-developmental and transactional perspectives emphasize dynamic, reciprocal, organism–environment interactions within which physical appearance exerts interdependent effects on both interpersonal and intrapersonal processes (Adams, 1977; Langlois & Stephan, 1981; Lerner & Jovanovic, Chapter 5, this volume; Sorell & Nowak, 1981). Snyder, Tanke, and Berscheid (1977) conducted a creative experiment to examine this dynamic interplay. Specifically, the researchers told male college students that they would have a telephone conversation with a female student who was *either* physically attractive or physically unattractive (using a photographic manipulation). Assessments of the male subjects' initial expectations for the interactions did confirm a beauty-is-good assumption about their future interactant; men expected more interesting and positive social behaviors from attractive than from unattractive females. Did these expectations, in turn, lead the males themselves to behave differently in their interactions with the females? Absolutely. Judges, who were unaware of the nature of the experiment and rated only the males' portion of the taped conversations, observed more positive, outgoing, and socially interested behaviors among those males who believed they were interacting with an attractive partner than among males who believed their partner to be homely.

And now for the key question: Did this differential treatment by the males influence the self-perceptions and social behaviors of the actual women with whom they interacted? Judges who were blind to experimental conditions and rated only the womens' voices from the taped conversations confirmed differences. Those women interacting with men who assumed them to be attractive differed from the women interacting with men who believed them to be unattractive. The former exuded greater confidence and experienced their partner as liking them more than did the women who interacted with men in the "unattractive assumption" condition. These striking results, taken collectively with the aforementioned evidence, indicate that attractive persons receive greater support and encouragement to develop socially confident and competent behavioral repertoires. In contrast, unattractive people are more apt to encounter social environments that range from nonresponsive to rejecting and that discourage the development of social skills and a favorable self-concept. In Chapter 5 of this volume on appearance and psychosocial development, Lerner and Jovanovic further delineate and discuss these processes.

Psychologists have compared physically attractive and unattractive individuals on numerous personality characteristics, including clinically relevant measures of adjustment (see Burns & Farina, 1990; Cash, 1981, 1985a; Hatfield & Sprecher, 1986; Noles, Cash, & Winstead, 1985). Indeed, social anxiety and fear of social rejection as well as an external locus of control are more commonly experienced by less attractive individuals (e.g., Abbott & Sebastian, 1981; Cash & Begley, 1976; Cash & Burns, 1977; Cash & Smith, 1982; Goldman & Lewis, 1977; Reis et al., 1982). In 1978, Hobfoll and Penner conducted an informative experiment in which psychotherapists evaluated the self-concepts of attractive and unattractive persons on the basis of either videotaped or the audiotaped portion of interviews with them. The investigators found that attractive interviewees were *judged* to have a better self-concept than unattractive persons, regardless of the audiotaped versus videotaped source of information (consistent with evidence from Cash, Kehr, Polyson, & Freeman, 1977). Although the effects of attractiveness were significantly smaller when the judges were unaware of the person's appearance (in the audio condition), the effects nevertheless were present.

Therefore, not only can social stereotyping exaggerate differences between attractive and unattractive persons, valid individual differences do seem to exist as well. O'Grady (1982) asked 240 randomly selected persons of varying levels of physical attractiveness to indicate how vulnerable each felt to the future development of specific psychological problems. O'Grady found that physically unattractive subjects reported experiencing greater vulnerability to future psychological disturbance. A closer look at his data (cf. Cash, 1985a) indicated that unattractive persons felt at greatest risk for psychological disorders involving interpersonal conflict and anxiety.

Recently, Burns and Farina (1990) have conducted an impressively extensive review of the literature on physical attractiveness and adjustment. These researchers believe, as I do (Archer & Cash, 1985; Cash, 1985a), that physical unattractiveness represents a risk factor (i.e., a diathesis) in the development of psychopathology in general. In particular, the evidence is reasonably compelling that physical unattractiveness is among the diatheses for schizophrenia of already biogenetically vulnerable individuals. Not only are schizophrenics, especially more severely disturbed schizophrenics, premorbidly less attractive than a variety of matched controls (e.g., equating for socioeconomic status and age), but the social liability of their unattractiveness may continue to affect their treatment both in and out of the hospital (e.g., see also Archer & Cash, 1985; Farina et al., 1977, 1986; Napoleon, Chassin, & Young, 1980). Such far-reaching implications of physical appearance for human development cannot be ignored. Physical attractiveness is, by no means, a superficial and unimportant variable.

BODY-SELF RELATIONS: "THE INSIDE VIEW"

My realization of the substantial empirical independence of the social-image and self-image perspectives on physical appearance has led me, in recent years, to shift much of my research away from the psychological study of physical attractiveness to body-image investigations. In 1985, my colleagues and I had the valuable opportunity to conduct a body-image survey in *Psychology Today* magazine. The survey itself consisted of a special version of our attitudinal body-image measure, the Multidimensional Body-Self Relations Questionnaire (MBSRQ). Thompson and co-authors discuss this instrument in Chapter 2, dealing with body-image assessment, of this volume.

Our conceptual framework for the MBSRQ was largely derived from social-psychological perspectives on attitudes. In this case, we were interested in individuals' attitudes toward their own bodies. We conceived of the body as possessing *three* "somatic domains" and assessed attitudinal dimensions toward each domain. These somatic domains are physical appearance, physical fitness, and physical health/illness. The MBSRQ consists of individuals' affective evaluations of and cognitive/behavioral orientations toward each domain; a recent cross-validated factor analysis of the MBSRQ confirms this conceptual framework (Brown, Cash, & Mikulka, in press). The MBSRQ evaluation scales reflect how positively or negatively one feels about each of the domains. The orientation scales assess how personally important the various aspects of body image are, how much attention is focused on each aspect, and how behaviorally active a person is in maintaining or enhancing his/her bodily appearance, fitness, or health. In our survey (Cash, Winstead, & Janda, 1985, 1986) of nearly 30,000 respondents, we conducted an elaborate analysis of a stratified, random sample of 2,000 persons selected to represent the United States populations' sex by age distribution.

Table 3.1 captures the body-image evaluations and body-image orientations of survey respondents. With respect to evaluations of overall appearance, nearly a fourth of the men and a third of the women reported generally negative feelings about their appearance. A substantial minority of persons experienced negative affect about their physical fitness as well. Evaluation of health, it seems, is generally more favorable. Moreover, reflective perhaps of our appearance-conscious culture, fully 82% of men and 93% of women had strong appearance orientations—valuing, thinking about, paying attention to, and being behaviorally active in appearance management. Most respondents also had strong orientations toward fitness and health, albeit to lesser degrees than their orientations vis-á-vis appearance. Incidentally, when we examined age cohort effects, we found that adolescents (especially females) reported the strongest appearance orientations and the most negative appearance evaluations. Thus, the social, psychological, and appearance changes of adolescence bring, for many, intensely self-conscious and dysphoric body-image concerns (Pruzinsky & Cash, 1990).

TABLE 3.1. BODY-IMAGE EVALUATIONS AND ORIENTATIONS

MBSRQ dimension	Men	Women
Appearance evaluation		
Positive	76%	69%
Negative	24%	31%
Fitness evaluation		
Positive	81%	71%
Negative	19%	29%
Health evaluation		
Positive	91%	86%
Negative	9%	14%
Appearance orientation		
High	82%	93%
Low	18%	7%
Fitness orientation		
High	67%	57%
Low	33%	43%
Health orientation		
High	74%	78%
Low	26%	22%

Note. From "The Great American Shape-Up: Body Image Survey Report" by T.F. Cash, B.A. Winstead, & L.H. Janda, 1986, *Psychology Today, 20*(4), p.34. Copyright 1986 by *Psychology Today*. Adapted by permission.

Turning briefly to specific facets of appearance, Table 3.2 presents information from the Body Area Satisfaction Scales of the MBSRQ. These data are compared with the results of data collected in 1972 in a similar *Psychology Today* survey (Berscheid, Walster, & Bohrnstedt, 1973). Considering overall appearance satisfaction, we found in our 1985 survey that 34% of the men and 38% of the women were generally dissatisfied with their looks—percentages higher than were collected in 1972. Examining the extent of dissatisfaction with discrete areas of appearance confirms that weight-related concerns are substantial, possibly having even increased since 1972. The majority of both men and women reported dissatisfactions with their mid-torsos. A near majority of the men and over half of the women reported weight dissatisfaction; half of the women were dissatisfied with their lower torsos as well. If weight concerns are the bad news, then perhaps the good news is the extent to which persons of both sexes are satisfied with their height and with their facial characteristics.

Table 3.3 compares how men and women with positive and negative evaluations of appearance, fitness, and health scored on a scale of psychosocial adjustment that we included in our survey. Clearly, body-image evaluations have implications for evaluations of self. The vast majority, consistently over 90%, of persons with positive feelings about appearance, fitness, or health reported favorable psychological adjustment (i.e., a positive self-concept, life satisfaction, and the absence of loneliness and depression). In contrast, negative evaluations of appearance, fitness, and health were associated with lower levels of psychosocial adjustment. Obviously, if one dislikes the body one "lives in," it's difficult to be satisfied with "the self who lives there." As reviewed elsewhere (Archer & Cash, 1985; Cash, 1985a; Fisher, 1986; Thompson, 1990), negative body-image affect is associated with various indices of dysfunc-

TABLE 3.2. PERCENTAGE OF PEOPLE DISSATISFIED WITH BODY ATTRIBUTES

Body attributes	1972 Survey		1985 Survey	
	Men	Women	Men	Women
Height	13%	13%	20%	17%
Weight	35%	48%	41%	55%
Muscle tone	25%	30%	32%	45%
Face	8%	11%	20%	20%
Upper torso	18%	27%	28%	32%
Mid torso	36%	50%	50%	57%
Lower torso	12%	49%	21%	50%
Overall appearance	15%	23%	34%	38%

Note. From "The Great American Shape-Up: Body Image Survey Report" by T.F. Cash, B.A. Winstead, & L.H. Janda, 1986, *Psychology Today, 20*(4), p.32. Copyright 1986 by *Psychology Today*. Adapted by permission.

TABLE 3.3. PERCENTAGE OF WELL-ADJUSTED PERSONS AMONG THOSE WITH POSITIVE AND NEGATIVE BODY-IMAGE EVALUATIONS

MBSRQ dimension	Men	Women
Appearance evaluation		
Positive	95%	97%
Negative	62%	73%
Fitness evaluation		
Positive	92%	94%
Negative	63%	79%
Health evaluation		
Positive	92%	94%
Negative	63%	64%

Note. From "The Great American Shap-Up: Body Image Survey Report" by T.F. Cash, B.A. Winstead, & L.H. Janda, 1986, *Psychology Today, 20*(4), p.36. Copyright 1986 by *Psychology Today.* Adapted by permission.

tional psychosocial functioning among nonclinical samples and psychiatric patients. In another chapter of this book, Pruzinsky pursues the topic of body-image dysfunctions in a range of clinical populations.

Tables 3.1 and 3.2 also provide evidence of possible sex differences in body-image attitudes. Indeed, women have greater difficulty experiencing their bodies positively than do men. What is apparent, however, is that the sex differences are perhaps less extensive than many people think (Jackson, Sullivan, & Rostker, 1988; Keeton, Cash, & Brown, 1990; Silberstein, Striegel-Moore, Timko, & Rodin, 1988). In a recent experiment (Cash & Brown, 1989), men and women completed the MBSRQ in response to three instructional sets—for themselves, for the "typical male," and for the "typical female." As compared with the modest *real* sex differences found on several body-image indices (especially those dealing with weight-related concerns), the sexes were *believed* to differ substantially on every measured aspect of body image. Moreover, we found that the stereotypical misperception of the sexes entailed a more disparaging distortion of the body images of women than of men.

BODILY ATTRIBUTES: SOCIAL IMAGES AND SELF-IMAGES

Much of the earlier discussion concerning the impact and implications of physical attractiveness and attitudinal body images considered these variables as global percepts. A number of investigators have attempted to define attractiveness in relation to its physiognomic components (e.g., Berry & McArthur, 1988; Brown, Cash, & Noles, 1986; Franzoi & Herzog, 1987; Lucker, 1980;

Mueser, Grau, Sussman, & Rosen, 1984; Nakdimen, 1984). Brown et al. (1986), for example, found that ratings of overall physical attractiveness are additively influenced by judgments of facial attractiveness and below-the-neck body attractiveness. Similarly, with respect to body-image attitudes, feelings about discrete body parts often contribute uniquely and additively (though not equally) to the affective body-image gestalt (Cash, 1989a).

Certainly, various physiognomic facets of physical appearance deserve study in their own right. A number of interesting published works examine, from diverse vantage points, the psychosocial meanings of body parts from head to toe (see Brownmiller, 1984; Morris, 1985). Specialized writings also exist that focus on selected body areas—for example, on height or stature (Keyes, 1980; Roberts & Herman, 1986) and on facial attributes (Alley, 1988; Landau, 1989; Liggett, 1974). In a later chapter, Fallon takes a close cross-cultural look at specific body attributes. Here, I briefly highlight two facets of appearance from both the "outside view" and the "inside view"—thereby considering their influences on interpersonal perceptions and behaviors and their relationships with self-conceptions and body images. The chosen physical characteristics include (1) body weight, with special emphasis on the social and personal implications of obesity, and (2) hair, with particular focus on male pattern balding. I selected these two bodily foci, in part, because of their salience for females and males, respectively.

Body Weight: Obesity, Social Stigma, and Self-Stigma

Social Images of Obesity

Being overweight or obese is a highly stigmatizing condition in our society throughout the lifespan. When children were asked who they liked best among pictures of peers with physical handicaps and an obese child, the obese child was chosen last (Richardson, Goodman, Hastorf, & Dornbusch, 1961). Adjectives representing negative physical, personal, and social attributes are assigned by children and adults to individuals with endomorphic physiques (for review, see DeJong & Kleck, 1986). The stigmatic stereotyping of overweight persons may adversely affect their vocational (Larkin & Pines, 1979) and educational opportunities (Canning & Mayer, 1966). The stigma is lessened, though not eliminated, if social perceivers attribute the obesity to medical causes beyond the person's control; otherwise the person's weak character is regarded as responsible (DeJong, 1980). Obesity is associated with downward social mobility among women (Goldblatt, Moore, & Stunkard, 1965; Stunkard, 1975) and seems to affect women's social relationships more adversely than it does men's (Tiggemann & Rothblum, 1988). Stake and Lauer (1987) observed that overweight women dated less often, had less date or mate satisfaction, and experienced more peer criticism than overweight men or normal-weight men and women. The social prejudice and discrimination against overweight persons is so powerful that organizations such as the National Association to Advance Fat Acceptance have been established for social action and support on behalf of these individuals.

Self-Images and Obesity

The overweight condition, however, may be as much a state of mind as it is a state of body. One recent survey (see Seligman et al., 1987) queried nearly 500 children and found that over half of the girls regarded themselves as overweight, despite the fact that only 15% were actually overweight, and that 31% of 10-year-olds reported "feeling fat." Among college students, Klesges (1983) found that 58% of females and 20% of males who were of normal weight classified themselves as overweight. In the previously discussed *Psychology Today* body-image survey (Cash et al., 1986), 47% of females and 29% of males who were actually normal weight classified themselves as overweight. In contrast, 40% of underweight women judged themselves to be normal weight, compared to only 10% of men. Furthermore, as shown in Table 3.2, this survey revealed that 55% of females and 41% of males expressed dissatisfaction with their body weight. Thus, although our culture directs most of its weight-related messages toward females, males are not immune to the effects of such messages (Cash & Hicks, 1990; Drewnowski & Yee, 1987). The difference is that the second assertion in the maxim "You can't be too rich or too thin" applies more to females (e.g., Cash & Green, 1986) than to males in our society. Men are equally divided in their weight-related dissatisfactions between those who feel they are too heavy and those who feel they are too thin (Silberstein et al., 1988). Furthermore, in one investigation of the *distribution* of body fat (Radke-Sharpe, Whitney-Saltiel, & Rodin, 1990), overweight women with greater distributions of fat in the hips and buttocks, relative to waist and abdomen, reported stronger weight concerns and more disordered eating behaviors.

In a recent controlled study (Cash & Hicks, 1990), we discovered that how a normal-weight person classifies his/her weight has a strong bearing on the person's attitudinal body image, eating behaviors, and psychosocial well-being. Among objectively normal-weight individuals, those of either sex who proclaimed themselves overweight evaluated their bodies more negatively, having greater dissatisfaction not only with appearance but also with their bodily fitness and health. This investigation produced two additional key conclusions:

First, underscoring the importance of cognitive factors in the body-image construct, there were greater psychological differences among persons as a function of *self-classified* weight among truly normal-weight persons than there were between *actual* weight groups (i.e., normal-weight versus overweight persons) who thought of themselves as overweight. Thus, the label a person assigns to his/her weight has strong implications for the person's body-image affect and self-esteem (see also DelRosario, Brines, & Coleman, 1984; Tucker, 1982). Once this label has been self-assigned, the veridical presence of the overweight condition exerts only a few additional group differences. Secondly, Cash and Hicks's (1990) results did confirm that being overweight, whether in distorted self-perception or in reality, is more detrimental to the well-being of females than to males.

Unfortunately, weight loss carries no guarantee that the associated body-image dysphoria is lost as well. Consistent with Stunkard's original proposition (Stunkard & Burt, 1967; Stunkard & Mendelson, 1967), Cash, Counts, and Huffine (in press) observed that formerly overweight women (relative to never-overweight controls) may persist in their negative "vestigial" body-image thoughts, feelings, and concerns about weight. As Fallon, Rosen, and Freedman convey in Chapters 4, 9, 13, respectively, of this volume, these beliefs and self-images vis-à-vis body weight have important implications for emotional well-being and for the development of eating disturbances and disorders.

Male Pattern Hair Loss

Social Images

Although behavioral scientists have focused on numerous specific physiognomic attributes, one neglected area of inquiry has been that of hair loss. Among males hair loss occurs normally and progressively with age, usually as the result of androgenetic alopecia, or male pattern baldness (MPB). In the United States, over 30 million men, including the majority of men over the age of 50, have noticeable MPB. That researchers have largely ignored this characteristic is quite curious in view of the fact that human history confirms the existence of longstanding cultural symbolism associated with men's hair, its length, as well as its loss (Klenhard, 1986; Morris, 1985).

In a recent experiment (Cash, 1990), I investigated the initial impact of visible MPB on the social perceptions of men by perceivers of both sexes. Pairs of slides of balding and nonbalding controls were matched across age, race, and other physical characteristics. Subjects rated these stimulus persons on several important first-impression dimensions. The results revealed that generally less favorable initial impressions were created by balding than nonbalding men— including lower ratings of physical attractiveness, assumptions of less desirable personal and interpersonal characteristics, and overestimations of age. Perceivers' sex and age and stimulus persons' age were largely without consequence. Moreover, when perceived physical attractiveness was controlled statistically, the other negative attributions of the baldness stereotype were substantially diminished. Thus, the social-image effects of MPB appear to be a special instance of the operation of the beauty-is-good stereotype discussed earlier.

Self-Images

While social judgments can be adversely affected by the presence of visible hair loss among men, perhaps the more important question concerns how men with varying degrees of MPB experience their own hair loss. Based upon a reliable pictorial classification system of the degree of MPB, I studied the self-perceptions of 145 men—63 with some visible MPB, 40 with considerable MPB, and 42 nonbalding controls (Cash, 1987b, 1989b). Let me target several of the most striking findings in this extensive self-image investigation of hair loss:

First, when nonbalding controls were asked to imagine their personal reactions should they begin to experience gradual MPB, the vast majority expected significant increases in negative social and emotional events, greater mental preoccupation with their hair loss, as well as substantial behavioral efforts to conceal, compensate, and cope with the loss. Contrary to macho stereotypes, only 8% of these men indicated they would not be bothered at all should they begin to lose hair. Among those men with actual MPB, both the initial and cumulative effects of hair loss entailed substantial levels of reported stress, distress, and coping efforts. For example, 60% of our subjects with extensive hair loss attributed significant and continuing negative socioemotional effects to their hair loss. These stressful effects were greater for men with more noticeable hair loss, for those with an earlier onset of balding, for men who expected continued hair loss in the future, and for younger men, especially those who were single and uninvolved in intimate relationships. Table 3.4 summarizes some of the specific socioemotional events reported by men with modest and extensive MPB.

Our investigation further indicated that it would be inappropriate to

TABLE 3.4. PERCENTAGE OF BALDING MEN ATTRIBUTING SPECIFIC EXPERIENCES TO HAIR LOSS

Reported event	Modest MPB	Extensive MPB
Wish for more hair	52%	84%
Get teased by peers	45%	79%
Feel self-conscious	42%	78%
Worry about looks	49%	68%
Worry about more balding	44%	59%
Look older then age	40%	55%
Feel helpless about hair loss	37%	56%
Worry about aging	37%	46%
Envy good-looking men	33%	34%
Feel sensitive to criticism	33%	33%

Adapted from Cash (1987b).

conclude dramatic personality changes in men as a result of MPB. Except for more negative body-image attitudes, including dissatisfaction with their hair and with their overall appearance, balding men did not differ from controls on basic self-concept and personality functioning. Correlationally, however, among balding men, the more socioemotional stress they attributed to the experience of hair loss, the less satisfactory was their current level of psychosocial functioning. Perhaps in instances when hair loss exerts considerable distress, individuals' adjustment may suffer. Alternatively, of course, these data may suggest that men with the poorest premorbid adjustment may be most vulnerable to the adverse psychological effects of hair loss.

The collective results of the social-image and self-image studies confirm the hypothesis that balding has an essentially negative impact on the lives of men. This research, while only an initial step in understanding the effects of balding, attests to the importance of hair loss in the psychology of physical appearance. Future scientific inquiry is needed to ascertain the psychosocial effects of female androgenetic alopecia—the normal, diffuse hair loss that occurs for about 20 million American women.

AESTHETIC SELF-MANAGEMENT OF PHYSICAL APPEARANCE

Unfortunately, I believe, the dominant paradigm in the psychology of physical appearance is the "trait perspective"—the view that physical attractiveness is a static, fixed attribute of persons and that body images are essentially invariant. To the contrary, however, body-image percepts and attitudes also function as "state" variables, which fluctuate around some modal level in response to a variety of social environmental events—for example, weight-related cues (Cash & Brown, 1987; DelRosario et al., 1984) or the presence of social-comparison persons with certain physical characteristics (Cash, Cash, & Butters, 1983). The trait perspective further ignores the fact that people frequently and actively alter and control their physical aesthetics. At one extreme, people elect to receive cosmetic surgery (Cash & Horton, 1983; Pruzinsky & Edgerton, Chapter 10, this volume). People also achieve gradual physical changes by behavioral efforts to lose or gain weight. With time and a little help from their hormones, men grow facial hair. Yet everyday, with immediate results, men and women across the world engage in grooming behaviors to vary their physical appearance (Morris, 1985). As we saw in Table 3.1, the vast majority of American men and women are active in their orientations toward the development and maintenance of an attractive appearance. In my research on male pattern hair loss (Cash, 1987b, 1989b), the majority of balding men reported increases in various appearance-managing behaviors to compensate for or cope with their hair loss—dressing nicer, growing facial hair, improving hairstyle, working out to enhance physique, and so forth. Thus, in part, physical appearance is a self-creation—in response to general cultural and specific situational norms, self-presentational goals for social image and for body image, and varying mood states (Cash, 1981, 1987a, 1988).

Two aspects of aesthetic self-management have received the most scientific attention: (1) the use of facial cosmetics by women and (2) the use of clothing (see Figure 3.2 for an example of the ways in which a woman might use clothing to manage aesthetic appearance). Women's cosmetics use for aesthetic enhancement is a salient practice throughout the world, as has been true in many cultures for centuries (Cordwell, 1985; Liggett, 1974). Considering cosmetics from our two perspectives, social-image and self-image, produces two basic questions: What are the social-perceptual effects of cosmetics use? Do women feel differently about themselves, particularly in terms of body images, as a result of the application of facial makeup?

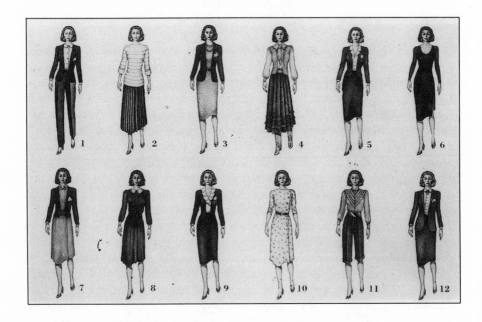

FIGURE 3.2.   A series of sketches of a woman varying her appearance by means of clothing. Sketches provided by Michael R. Solomon, Rutgers University.

In a recent review of the available research literature (Cash, 1987a, 1988), I have argued, from a self-presentational point of view (Leary & Kowalski, 1990; Schlenker, 1980), that cosmetics use in particular, and grooming behaviors in general, function to manage and control not only social impressions but also self-images (e.g., body-image affect, self-perceptions, and mood states). On the social perceptual side, Graham and Jouhar (1981) compared social judgments about women, preselected as average in attractiveness, who were photographed either without facial makeup or with professionally applied makeup. In the eyes of both male and female raters, the cosmetic makeover enhanced perceived physical aesthetics and generally produced more favorable personality attributions. Cox and Glick (1986) examined how several average-looking women were perceived when cosmetics-free versus following a professional makeover. The researchers found that raters' judgments of the amount of cosmetics did correlate positively with perceptions of attractiveness, femininity, and sexiness.

In a more recent investigation, social perceptions of women were compared under conditions in which the women were wearing their *customary* facial cosmetics versus following the removal of their makeup (Cash, Dawson, Davis, Bowen, & Galumbeck, 1989). Male social perceivers were more favorable in their judgments of attractiveness toward the women in the cosmetics-present than in the cosmetics-absent photograph. Surprisingly, female perceivers were not differentially affected by the presence or absence of makeup. Perhaps, as consumers of cosmetics, females are able to "see through" makeup to discern the person's natural appearance.

Turning to the self-image side of aesthetic self-management with cosmetics, several, mostly correlational, studies suggest a link between cosmetics use and a more positive body-image and feelings of social confidence and effectiveness (e.g., Cash & Cash, 1982; Cash, Rissi, & Chapman, 1985; Theberge & Kernaleguen, 1979; Wright, Martin, Flynn, & Gunter, 1970). In our afore-mentioned experiment on cosmetics (Cash et al., 1989), we also examined the subjects' body images in the customary cosmetics-present versus cosmetics-absent conditions. Results indicated more positive body-image cognitions and affect with cosmetics present than when subjects were cosmetics-free. A comparison of subjects' self-appraisals of physical attractiveness with observer ratings revealed that the women overestimated their attractiveness in the cosmetics-present condition and underestimated their attractiveness when without makeup. Moreover, the more makeup typically worn by the women, the greater the body-image differences between the two cosmetics conditions. In sum, "on the face of it," cosmetics appear to make a positive difference on self-image as well as on social-image.

Observed associations between specific individual-difference variables and cosmetics use also are in line with a self-presentational perspective. For example, high self-monitors, who are especially sensitive to impression management and are responsive to the physical appearance of others (Snyder et al., 1985), also report greater cosmetics use (Cash & Wunderle, 1987). Women with greater attentional self-focus and body-focus (i.e., public self-consciousness) are more apt to engage in aesthetic self-management with cosmetics (Cash & Cash, 1982; Miller & Cox, 1982). In another study (Cash, Rissi, & Chapman, 1985), greater cosmetics use was associated with less externality in locus of control; and women who were more situationally variable, or "strategic," in their pattern of cosmetics use were also more liberal in sex-role attitudes and more internal in locus of control for social outcomes. Finally, we found that women who were more feminine on a particular measure of sex-role identity (i.e., a measure reflecting histrionic emotionality and need for social approval and attention) used more facial cosmetics.

Let's now consider another universal tool of aesthetic self-management—clothing. Solomon (1985) and Kaiser (1985) have compiled interesting works concerning the social psychology of fashion and clothing. Many of the observations that these authors convey are congruent with self-presentational, impression-management perspectives. The popularity of Molloy's *Dress for Success* books (1975, 1977) attests to the importance of clothing and impression management in our society. One national field experiment (Cash, 1985b) manipulated grooming style, largely through the manipulation of clothing, to evaluate its influence on decisions about women in management. In short, this experiment involved "makeover" conditions that were equal in physical attractiveness but differed in the extent to which the image was socially perceived as "managerial" or "nonmanagerial." The nonmanagerial appearance was largely that of aesthetic feminization. The more androgynous, managerial appearance was generally successful in fostering more favorable professional personnel decisions about women applying for managerial positions at several U. S. corporate data-collection sites. Akin to the earlier discussion of the sex-typing of beauty, this study indicated that sex-typed attributions may be conveyed by the grooming style of the wearer.

In a similar experiment on women's attire and personnel selection decisions, Forsythe, Drake, and Cox (1985) found the masculinity–femininity of professional dress to influence interviewers' perceptions and recommendations regarding job applicants. A moderately masculine style was more advantageous than either feminine or masculine extremes. Perhaps the motives, the femininity, or the individuality of women are deemed suspect if women go so far as to become "clones" or "women in men's clothes." What's good for the gander may not always work for the goose. The meanings of specific types of attire should interact with situational contexts; "uniforms" are not uniform. For instance, a man or woman in a conservative (masculinized) suit is apt to be regarded differently if applying for a "financial district" position than for a job in a creative art department. Other investigations included in Solomon's (1985) *Psychology of Fashion* further reinforce the proposition that clothing communicates messages about its wearer to social audiences.

Though the literature is unfortunately sparse, grooming behaviors may be studied from the point of view of the characteristics of their intended audiences.

In an interesting study by Daly, Hogg, Sacks, Smith, and Zimring (1983), preening or self-grooming was unobtrusively observed among young adults in the restrooms of restaurants and bars. Females were found to preen more than males. And consistent with impression management theory, people preened more when they were about to join someone with whom they were having a new relationship as opposed to someone they knew very well. In other words, people are more motivated to manage their physical self-presentations early on in potentially meaningful or consequential relationships—such as new romances or a crucial job interview. Alas, as spouses know, sometimes "familiarity breeds unkempt."

Audiences are not always anticipated accurately by persons constructing their own physical self-presentations. In an experiment on job interviewing, von Baeyer, Sherk, and Zanna (1981) discovered that when female applicants *believed* their interviewer would be a "male chauvinist" (as opposed to a male with less traditional gender-role values), the interviewed women actually presented themselves in a more traditionally "feminine" manner. They did so not only in their verbal and nonverbal communications but also by grooming in a more physically attractive and traditionally feminine style. Because, as was discussed above, prettiness and feminine attire may elicit sexist assumptions and discrimination, especially by sex-typed perceivers (see Cash, 1985b; Cash & Kilcullen, 1985), such self-presentations may backfire and confirm interviewers' biases.

As was the case with women's cosmetics use, individual differences relevant to self-presentational processes have been associated with the strategic use of clothing as well—for example, public self-consciousness (Miller, Davis, & Rowold, 1982; Solomon & Schopler, 1982) and self-monitoring (Davis & Lennon, 1985; Zaidman & Snyder, as cited by Snyder, 1987). What is quite surprising, however, is the lack of scientific study concerning the effects of clothing on body-image affective states. From the "power tie" to one's comfy, well-worn jeans, I believe that clothing, along with other accoutrements of appearance, are "mood-altering substances." Surely some individuals engage in appearance-managing behaviors to create desired self-perceptions and emotional experiences. Here, good research is greatly needed.

We must begin to think creatively about the clinical applications of these findings and perspectives. An area of significant promise is the incorporation of "physical appearance training" into the treatment regimens for such diverse groups as socially anxious and inept youth, socially withdrawn and depressed elderly, severely obese persons, disheveled schizophrenics, cancer patients undergoing appearance-altering chemotherapy, to name but a few (Graham & Kligman, 1985a, 1985b; Mulready & Lamb, 1985; Pertschuk, 1985; Roberts, 1985).

CONCLUSIONS

Behavioral scientists have amassed considerable knowledge concerning the psychology of physical appearance. For better or worse, throughout our lives, the aesthetic appeal of our bodies and our bodily attributes affects how others view us and treat us. Our psychological development and unique self-experiences reflect not only our physically aesthetic impact on the social world around us, but also how we think, feel, and react to our own self-perceived physical attributes. Social images of appearance are not identical to personal body images; yet these phenomena converge in complicated ways to meaningfully influence human development, social relations, and personal experiences. Far from passive reservoirs, people interact with their own physical aesthetics to control and create its contextual meanings, whether those of the social context or those of the more private world of body-self relations.

REFERENCES

Abbott, A. R., & Sebastian, R. J. (1981). Physical attractiveness and expectations of success. *Personality and Social Psychology Bulletin 7*, 481–486.

Adams, G. R. (1977). Physical attractiveness research: Toward a developmental social psychology of beauty. *Human Development, 20*, 217–239.

Alley, T. R. (Ed.). (1988). *Social and applied aspects of perceiving faces*. Hillsdale, NJ: Erlbaum.

Andersen, S. M., & Bem, S. L. (1981). Sex typing and androgyny in dyadic interaction: Individual differences in responsiveness to physical attractiveness. *Journal of Personality and Social Psychology, 41*, 74–86.

Archer, R., & Cash, T. F. (1985). Physical attractiveness and maladjustment among psychiatric inpatients. *Journal of Social and Clinical Psychology, 3*(2), 170–180.

Barocas, R., & Karoly, P. (1972). Effects of physical appearance on social responsiveness. *Psychological Reports, 31*, 495–500.

Bar-Tal, D., & Saxe, L. (1976). Physical attractiveness and its relationship to sex-role stereotyping. *Sex Roles, 2*, 123–133.

Benson, P. L., Karabenick, S. A., & Lerner, R. M. (1976). Pretty pleases: The effects of physical attractiveness, race, and sex on receiving help. *Journal of Experimental Social Psychology, 12*, 409–415.

Berkowitz, L., & Frodi, A. (1979). Reactions to a child's mistakes as affected by his/her looks and speech. *Social Psychology Quarterly, 42*, 420–425.

Berry, D. S., & McArthur, L. Z. (1988). The impact of age-related craniofacial changes on social perception. In T. R. Alley (Ed.), *Social and applied aspects of perceiving faces* (pp. 63–87). Hillsdale, NJ: Erlbaum.

Berscheid, E., Dion, K., Walster, E., & Walster, G. W. (1971). Physical attractiveness and dating choice: A test of the matching hypothesis. *Journal of Experimental Social Psychology, 7*, 173–189.

Berscheid, E., & Walster (Hatfield), E. (1974). Physical attractiveness. In L. Berkowitz (Ed.), *Advances in Experimental Social Psychology* (Vol. 7, pp. 157–215). New York: Academic Press.

Berscheid, E., Walster, E., & Bohrnstedt, G. (1973, November). The happy American body: A survey report. *Psychology Today, 7*, 119–131.

Brown, T. A., Cash, T. F., & Mikulka, P. J. (in press). Attitudinal body-image assessment: Factor analysis of the Body-Self Relations Questionnaire. *Journal of Personality Assessment*.

Brown, T., Cash, T. F., & Noles, S. W. (1986). Perceptions of physical attractiveness among college students: Selected determinants and methodological matters. *Journal of Social Psychology, 126*, 305–316.

Brownmiller, S. (1984). *Femininity*. New York: Linden Press.

Brundage, L., Derlega, V., & Cash, T. F. (1977). The effects of physical attractiveness and need for approval on self-disclosure. *Personality and Social Psychology Bulletin, 3*, 63–66.

Bull, R., & Rumsey, N. (1988). *The social psychology of facial appearance*. New York: Springer-Verlag.

Burns, G. L., & Farina, A. (1990). *Physical attractiveness and adjustment*. Unpublished manuscript, Washington State University, Pullman, WA.

Butters, J. W., & Cash, T. F. (1987). Cognitive–behavioral treatment of women's body-image dissatisfaction. *Journal of Consulting and Clinical Psychology, 55*, 889–897.

Canning, H., & Mayer, J. (1966). Obesity—its possible effect on college acceptance. *New England Journal of Medicine, 275*, 1172–1174.

Cash, T. F. (1978). Self-disclosure in initial acquaintanceship: Effects of sex, approval motivation, and physical attractiveness. *Social & Behavioral Sciences Documents, 8*, 11. (Ms. No. 1642).

Cash, T. F. (1981). Physical attractiveness: An annotated bibliography of theory and research in the behavioral sciences. *Social & Behavioral Sciences Documents, 11*, 83. (Ms. No. 2370).

Cash, T. F. (1985a). Physical appearance and mental health. In J. A. Graham & A. Kligman (Eds.), *Psychology of cosmetic treatments* (pp. 196–216). New York: Praeger Scientific.

Cash, T. F. (1985b). The impact of grooming style on the evaluation of women in management. In M. Solomon (Ed.), *The psychology of fashion* (pp. 343–355). Lexington, MA: Lexington Press.

Cash, T. F. (1987a). The psychology of cosmetics: A review of the scientific literature. *Social and Behavioral Sciences Documents, 17*, 1. (Ms. No. 2800).

Cash, T. F. (1987b). *The psychosocial effects of male pattern balding: A scientific study*. Technical report for The Upjohn Company submitted to Manning, Selvage, and Lee, New York.

Cash, T. F. (1988). The psychology of cosmetics: A research bibliography. *Perceptual and Motor Skills, 66*, 455–460.

Cash, T. F. (1989a). Body-image affect: Gestalt versus summing the parts. *Perceptual and Motor Skills, 69*, 17–18.

Cash, T. F. (1989b). The psychosocial effects of male pattern balding. *Patient Care, 1* (1), 18–23.

Cash, T. F. (1990). Losing hair, losing points?: The effects of male pattern baldness on social impression formation. *Journal of Applied Social Psychology, 20*, 154–167

Cash, T. F., & Begley, P. J. (1976). Internal–external control, achievement orientation, and physical attractiveness among college students. *Psychological Reports, 38*, 1205–1206.

Cash, T. F., & Brown, T. A. (1987). Body image in anorexia nervosa and bulimia nervosa: A review of the literature. *Behavior Modification, 11*, 487–521.

Cash, T. F., & Brown, T. A. (1989). Gender and body images: Stereotypes and realities. *Sex Roles, 21*, 357–369.

Cash, T. F., & Burns, D. S. (1977). The occurrence of reinforcing activities in relation to locus of control, success–failure expectancies, and physical attractiveness. *Journal of Personality Assessment, 41*, 387–391.

Cash, T. F., & Cash, D. W. (1982). Women's use of cosmetics: Psychosocial correlates and consequences. *International Journal of Cosmetic Science, 4*, 1–14.

Cash, T. F., Cash, D. W., & Butters, J. (1983). "Mirror, mirror, on the wall. . . ?": Contrast effects and self-evaluations of physical attractiveness. *Personality and Social Psychology Bulletin, 9*, 351–358.

Cash, T. F., Counts, B., & Huffine, C. E. (in press). Current and vestigial effects of overweight among women: Fear of fat, attitudinal body image, and eating behaviors. *Journal of Psychopathology and Behavioral Assessment*.

Cash, T. F., Dawson, K., Davis, P., Bowen, M., & Galumbeck, C. (1989). The effects of cosmetics use on the physical attractiveness and body image of college women. *Journal of Social Psychology, 129*, 349–356.

Cash, T. F., & Derlega, V. J. (1978). The matching hypothesis: Physical attractiveness among same-sexed friends. *Personality and Social Psychology Bulletin, 4,* 240–243.

Cash, T. F., & Duncan, N. C. (1984). Physical attractiveness stereotyping among Black American college students. *Journal of Social Psychology, 122,* 71–77.

Cash, T. F., Gillen, B., & Burns, D. S. (1977). Sexism and "beautyism" in personnel consultant decision making. *Journal of Applied Psychology, 62,* 301–310.

Cash, T. F., & Green, G. K. (1986). Body weight and body image among college women: Perception, cognition, and affect. *Journal of Personality Assessment, 50,* 290–301.

Cash, T. F., & Hicks, K. L. (1990). Being fat versus thinking fat: Relationships with body image, eating behaviors, and well-being. *Cognitive Therapy and Research, 14,* 327–341.

Cash, T. F., & Horton, C. E. (1983). Aesthetic surgery: Effects of rhinoplasty on the social perception of patients by others. *Plastic and Reconstructive Surgery, 72,* 543–548.

Cash, T. F., & Janda, L. H. (1984). Eye of the beholder. *Psychology Today, 18*(12), 46–52.

Cash, T. F., Kehr, J., Polyson, J., & Freeman, V. (1977). The role of physical attractiveness in peer attribution of psychological disturbance. *Journal of Consulting and Clinical Psychology, 45,* 987–993.

Cash, T. F., & Kilcullen, R. (1985). The eye of the beholder: Susceptibility to sexism and beautyism in evaluation of managerial applicants. *Journal of Applied Social Psychology, 15,* 591–605.

Cash, T. F., Rissi, J., & Chapman, R. (1985). Not just another pretty face: Sex roles, locus of control, and cosmetics use. *Personality and Social Psychology Bulletin, 11,* 246–257.

Cash, T. F., & Smith, E. (1982). Physical attractiveness and personality among American college students. *Journal of Psychology, 111,* 183–191.

Cash, T. F., & Soloway, D. (1975). Self-disclosure correlates of physical attractiveness: An exploratory study. *Psychological Reports, 36,* 579–586.

Cash, T. F., & Trimer, C. (1984). Sexism and beautyism in women's evaluations of peer performance. *Sex Roles, 10,* 87–98.

Cash, T. F., Winstead, B. A., & Janda, L. H. (1985). Your body, yourself: A Psychology Today reader survey. *Psychology Today, 19*(7), 22–26.

Cash, T. F., Winstead, B. A., & Janda, L. H. (1986). The great American shape-up: Body image survey report. *Psychology Today, 20*(4), 30–37.

Cash, T. F., & Wunderle, J. M. (1987). Self-monitoring and cosmetics use among college women. *Journal of Social Behavior and Personality, 4,* 563–566.

Clifford, M. M., & Walster, E. (1973). The effect of physical attractiveness on teacher expectations. *Sociology of Education, 46,* 248–258.

Cordwell, J. M. (1985). Ancient beginnings and modern diversity of the use of cosmetics. In J. A. Graham & A. Kligman (Eds.), *Psychology of cosmetic treatments* (pp. 37–44). New York: Praeger Scientific.

Cox, C. L., & Glick, W. H. (1986). Resume evaluations and cosmetics use: When more is not better. *Sex Roles, 14,* 51–58.

Craft, C. (1988). *Too old, too ugly, and not deferential to men.* Rocklin, CA: Prima.

Curran, J. P., & Lippold, S. (1975). The effects of physical attractiveness and attitude similarity on attraction in dating dyads. *Journal of Personality, 43,* 528–538.

Daly, J. A., Hogg, E., Sacks, D., Smith, M., & Zimring, L. (1983). Sex and relationship affect social self-grooming. *Journal of Nonverbal Behavior, 7* (3), 183–189.

Davis, L. L., & Lennon, S. J. (1985). Self-monitoring, fashion opinion leadership, and attitudes toward clothing. In M. Solomon (Ed.), *The psychology of fashion* (pp. 177–182). Lexington, MA: Lexington Press.

Deaux, K., & Lewis, L. L. (1984). Structure of gender stereotypes: Interrelationships among components and gender label. *Journal of Personality and Social Psychology, 46,* 991–1004.

DeJong, W. (1980). The stigma of obesity: The consequences of naive assumptions concerning the causes of physical deviance. *Journal of Health and Social Behavior, 21,* 75–87.

DeJong, W., & Kleck, R. E. (1986). The social psychological effects of overweight. In C. P.

Herman, M. P. Zanna, & E. T. Higgins (Eds.), *Physical Appearance, Stigma, and Social Behavior: The Ontario Symposium, Vol. 3*. Hillsdale, NJ: Erlbaum.

DelRosario, M. W., Brines, J. L., & Coleman, W. R. (1984). Emotional response patterns to body-weight related cues: Influence of body weight image. *Personality and Social Psychology Bulletin, 10*, 369–375.

Dermer, M., & Thiel, D. I. (1975). When beauty may fail. *Journal of Personality and Social Psychology, 31*, 1168–1176.

Dion, K. K. (1972). Physical attractiveness and evaluations of children's transgressions. *Journal of Personality and Social Psychology, 24*, 207–213.

Dion, K. K. (1974). Children's physical attractiveness and sex as determinants of adult punitiveness. *Developmental Psychology, 10*, 772–778.

Dion, K., Berscheid, E., & Walster, E. (1972). What is beautiful is good. *Journal of Personality and Social Psychology, 24*, 285–290.

Dipboye, R. L., Arvey,R. D., & Terpstra, D. E. (1977). Sex and physical attractiveness of raters and applicants as determinants of resume evaluations. *Journal of Applied Psychology, 62*, 288–294.

Dipboye, R. L., Fromkin, H. L., & Wiback, K. (1975). Relative importance of applicant sex, attractiveness, and scholastic standing in evaluation of job applicant resumes. *Journal of Applied Psychology, 62*, 39–43.

Drewnowski, A., & Yee, D. K. (1987). Men and body image: Are males satisfied with their body weight? *Psychosomatic Medicine, 49*, 626–634.

Eagly, A. H., Ashmore, R. D. Makhijani, M. G., & Kennedy, L. C. (in press). What is beautiful is good, but. . . : A meta-analytic review of research on the physical attractiveness stereotype. *Psychological Bulletin*.

Efran, M. G. (1974). The effect of physical appearance on the judgment of guilt, interpersonal attraction, and severity of recommended punishment in a simulated jury task. *Journal of Research in Personality, 8*, 45–54.

Elder, G. H., Jr., Nguyen, T. V., & Caspi, A. (1985). Linking family hardship to children's lives. *Child Development, 56*, 361–375.

Farina, A., Burns, G. L., Austad, C., Bugglin, C., & Fischer, E. H. (1986). The role of physical attractiveness in the readjustment of discharged psychiatric patients. *Journal of Abnormal Psychology, 95*, 139–143.

Farina, A., Fisher, E., Sherman, S., Smith, W., Groh, T., & Mermin, P. (1977). Physical attractiveness and mental illness. *Journal of Abnormal Psychology, 86*, 510–517.

Feingold, A. (1988). Matching for attractiveness in romantic partners and same-sex friends: A meta-analysis and theoretical critique. *Psychological Bulletin, 104*, 226–235.

Feingold, A. (1990). *Gender differences in the effects of physical attractiveness: Testing evolutionary theory with three independent research domains*. Unpublished manuscript, Yale University, New Haven.

Fisher, S. (1986). *Development and structure of the body image*. Hillsdale, NJ: Erlbaum.

Forsythe, S., Drake, M. F., & Cox, C. E. (1985). Influence of applicant's dress on interviewer's selection decisions. *Journal of Applied Psychology, 70*, 374–378.

Franzoi, S. L., & Herzog, M. E. (1987). Judging physical attractivness: What body aspects do we use? *Personality and Social Psychology Bulletin, 13*, 19–33.

Freedman, R. (1986). *Beauty bound*. Lexington, MA: Lexington Books.

Friend, R. M., & Vinson, M. (1974). Leaning over backwards: Jurors' responses to defendants' attractiveness. *Journal of Communication, 24*, 1124–1129.

Gillen, H. B. (1981). Physical attractiveness: A determinant of two types of goodness. *Personality and Social Psychology Bulletin, 7*, 277–281.

Goldblatt, P. B., Moore, M. E., & Stunkard, A. J. (1965). Social factors in obesity. *Journal of the American Medical Association, 192*, 97–102.

Goldman, W., & Lewis, P. (1977). Beautiful is good: Evidence that the physically attractive are more socially skillful. *Journal of Experimental and Social Psychology, 13*, 125–130.

Graham, J. A., & Jouhar, A. J. (1981). The effects of cosmetics on person perception. *International Journal of Cosmetic Science, 3,* 199–210.

Graham, J. A., & Kligman, A. M. (1985a). Physical attractiveness, cosmetic use and self-perception in the elderly. *International Journal of Cosmetic Science, 7,* 85–97.

Graham, J. A., & Kligman, A. M. (Eds.). (1985b). *The psychology of cosmetic treatments.* New York: Praeger Scientific.

Hatfield, E., & Sprecher, S. (1986). *Mirror, mirror. . . The importance of looks in everyday life.* Albany, NY: SUNY Press.

Heilman, M. E., & Saruwatari, L. R. (1979). When beauty is beastly: The effects of appearance and sex on evaluation of job applicants for managerial and nonmanagerial jobs. *Organizational Behavior and Human Performance, 23,* 360–372.

Heilman, M., & Stopeck, M. (1985a). Being attractive, advantage or disadvantage? Performance-based evaluations and recommended personnel actions as a function of appearance, sex, and job type. *Organizational Behaviors and Human Decision Processes, 35,* 202–215.

Heilman, M., & Stopeck, M. (1985b). Attractiveness and corporate success: Differential causal attribution for males and females. *Journal of Applied Psychology, 70,* 379–388.

Hildebrandt, K. A., & Fitzgerald, H. E. (1983). The infant's physical attractiveness: Its effect on bonding and attachment. *Infant Mental Health Journal, 4,* 3–12.

Hobfoll, S. E., & Penner, L. A. (1978). Effects of physical attractiveness on therapists' initial judgments of a person's self-concept. *Journal of Consulting and Clinical Psychology, 46,* 200–201.

Jackson, L. A., Sullivan, L. A., & Rostker, R. (1988). Gender, gender role, and body image. *Sex Roles, 19,* 429–443.

Kaiser, S. B. (1985). *Social psychology of clothing.* New York: Macmillan.

Keeton, W. P., Cash, T. F., & Brown, T. A. (1990). Body image or body images?: Comparative, multidimensional assessment among college students. *Journal of Personality Assessment, 54,* 213–230.

Keyes, R. (1980). *The height of your life.* Boston: Little, Brown.

Kleinke, C. L. (1975). *First impressions: The psychology of encountering others.* Englewood Cliffs, NJ: Prentice-Hall.

Klenhard, W. (1986). *The bald book.* Santa Monica, CA: Science-Med Press.

Klesges, R. C. (1983). An analysis of body-image distortions in a nonpatient population. *International Journal of Eating Disorders, 2,* 35–41.

Kunin, C. C., & Rodin, M. J. (1982). The interactive effects of counselor gender, physical attractiveness, and status on client self-disclosure. *Journal of Clinical Psychology, 38,* 84–90.

Landau, T. (1989). *About faces.* New York: Anchor Books.

Landy, D., & Sigall, H. (1974). Beauty is talent: Task evaluation as a function of the performer's physical attractiveness. *Journal of Personality and Social Psychology, 29,* 299–304.

Langlois, J. H. (1986). From the eye of the beholder to behavioral reality: Development of social behavior and social relations as a function of physical attractiveness. In C. P. Herman, M. P. Zanna, & E. T. Higgins (Eds.), *Physical Appearance, Stigma, and Social Behavior: The Ontario Symposium, Vol. 3* (pp. 23–51). Hillsdale, NJ: Erlbaum.

Langlois, J. H., & Stephan, C. W. (1981). Beauty and the beast: The role of physical attractiveness in the development of peer relations and social behavior. In Brehm, Kassin, & Gibbons (Eds.), *Developmental social psychology* (pp. 152–168). New York: Oxford University Press.

Larkin, J. C., & Pines, H. A. (1979). No fat persons need apply. Experimental studies of the overweight stereotype and hiring preferences. *Sociology of Work and Occupations, 6,* 312–327.

Leary, M. R., & Kowalski, R. M. (1990). Impression management: A literature review and two-component model. *Psychological Bulletin, 107,* 34–47.

Liggett, J. (1974). *The human face*. New York: Stein & Day.

Lucker, G. W. (1980). Esthetics and a quantitative analysis of facial appearance. In G. W. Lucker, K. A. Ribbins, & J. A. McNamara (Eds.), *Psychological aspects of facial form* (pp. 49–79). Ann Arbor, MI: The University of Michigan Center for Human Growth and Development.

Mace, K. C. (1972). The "overt-bluff" shoplifter: Who gets caught? *Journal of Forensic Psychology, 4*, 26–30.

Major, B., Carrington, P. I., & Carnavale, P. J. (1984). Physical attractiveness and self-esteem: Attributions for praise from an other-sex evaluator. *Personality and Social Psychology Bulletin, 10*, 43–50.

Major, B., & Deaux, K. (1981). Physical attractiveness and masculinity and femininity. *Personality and Social Psychology Bulletin, 7*, 24–28.

Martinek. T. (1981). Physical attractiveness: Effects on teacher expectations and dyadic interactions in elementary age children. *Journal of Sport Psychology, 3*, 196–205.

McCabe, V. (1988). Facial proportions, perceived age, and caregiving. In T. R. Alley (Ed.), *Social and applied aspects of perceiving faces* (pp. 89–95). Hillsdale, NJ: Erlbaum.

Miller, F. G., Davis, L. L., & Rowold, K. L. (1982). Public self-consciousness, social anxiety, and attitudes toward the use of clothing. *Home Economics Research Journal, 10*, 363–368.

Miller, L. C., & Cox, C. L. (1982). For appearances' sake: Public self-consciousness and makeup use. *Personality and Social Psychology Bulletin, 8*, 748–751.

Molloy, J. T. (1975). *Dress for success*. New York: Warner.

Molloy, J. T. (1977). *The women's dress for success book*. New York: Warner.

Moore, J. S., Graziano, W. G., & Millar, M. G. (1987). Physical attractiveness, sex role orientation, and the evaluation of adults and children. *Personality and Social Psychology Bulletin, 13*, 95–102.

Morris, D. (1985). *Bodywatching: A field guide to the human species*. New York: Crown.

Mueser, K. T., Grau, B. W., Sussman, S., & Rosen, A. J. (1984). You're only as pretty as you feel: Facial expression as a determinant of physical attractiveness. *Journal of Personality and Social Psychology, 46*, 469–478.

Mulready, P. M., & Lamb, J. M. (1985). Cosmetics therapy for female chemotherapy patients (pp. 255–263). In M. Solomon (Ed.), *The psychology of fashion*. Lexington, MA: Lexington Press.

Nakdimen, K. A. (1984). The physiognomic basis of sexual stereotyping. *American Journal of Psychiatry, 141* (4), 499–503.

Napoleon, T., Chassin, L., & Young, R. D. (1980). A replication and extension of "physical attractiveness and mental illness." *Journal of Abnormal Psychology, 89*, 250–253.

Noles, S. W., Cash, T. F., & Winstead, B. A. (1985). Body image, physical attractiveness, and depression. *Journal of Consulting and Clinical Psychology, 53*, 88–94.

O'Grady, K. E. (1982). Sex, physical attractiveness, and perceived risk for mental illness. *Journal of Personality and Social Psychology, 43*, 1064–1071.

Patzer, G. L. (1985). *The physical attractiveness phenomena*. New York: Plenum.

Pertschuk, M. J. (1985). Appearance in psychiatric disorder. In J. A. Graham & A. Kligman (Eds.), *Psychology of cosmetic treatments* (pp. 217–226). New York: Praeger.

Pruzinsky, T., & Cash, T. F. (1990). Medical interventions for the enhancement of adolescents' physical appearance: Implications for social competence. In T. P. Gullotta (Ed.), *The Promotion of Social Competence in Adolescence*. Beverly Hills, CA: Sage.

Radke-Sharpe, N., Whitney-Saltiel, D., & Rodin, J. (1990). Fat distribution as a risk factor for weight and eating concerns. *International Journal of Eating Disorders, 9*, 27–36.

Reis, H. T., Nezlek, J., & Wheeler, L. (1980). Physical attractiveness in social interaction. *Journal of Personality and Social Psychology, 38*, 604–617.

Reis, H. T., Wheeler, L., Spiegel, N., Kernis, M., Nezlek, J., & Perri, M. (1982). Physical attractiveness in social interaction, II: Why does appearance affect social experience? *Journal of Personality and Social Psychology, 43*, 979–996.

Richardson, S. A., Goodman, N., Hastorf., & Dornbusch, S. M. (1961). Cultural uniformity in reaction to physical disabilities. *American Sociological Review, 90*, 44–51.

Roberts, J. V., & Herman, C. P. (1986). The psychology of height: An empirical review. In C. P. Herman, M. P. Zanna, & E. T. Higgins (Eds.), *Physical Appearance, Stigma, and Social Behavior: The Ontario Symposium, Vol. 3* (pp. 113–140). Hillsdale, NJ: Erlbaum.

Roberts, R. (1985). The British Red Cross beauty care and camouflage service in hospitals. In J. A. Graham & A. Kligman (Eds.), *Psychology of cosmetic treatments* (pp. 191–195). New York: Praeger Scientific.

Schlenker, B. R. (1980). *Impression management: The self-concept, social identity, and interpersonal relations.* Monterey, CA: Brooks/Cole.

Schneider, D. J., Hastorf, A. H., & Ellsworth, P. C. (1979). *Person perception* (2nd ed.). Reading, MA: Addison-Wesley.

Seligman, J., Joseph, N., Donovan, J., & Gosnell, M. (1987, July). The littlest dieters. *Newsweek*, 48.

Sigall, H., & Michela, J. (1976). I'll bet you say that to all the girls: Physical attractiveness and reactions to praise. *Journal of Personality, 44*, 611–626.

Sigall, H., & Ostrove, N. (1975). Beautiful but dangerous: Effects of offender attractiveness and nature of the crime on juridic judgment. *Journal of Personality and Social Psychology, 31*, 410–414.

Sigall, H., Page, R., & Brown, A. (1971). The effects of physical attraction and evaluation on effort expenditure and work output. *Representative Research in Social Psychology, 2*, 19–25.

Silberstein, L. R., Striegel-Moore, R. H., Timko, C., & Rodin, J. (1988). Behavioral and psychological implications of body dissatisfaction: Do men and women differ? *Sex Roles, 19*, 219–232.

Snyder, M. (1987). *Public appearances—Private realities: The psychology of self-monitoring.* New York: Freeman.

Snyder, M., Berscheid, E., & Glick, P. (1985). Focusing on the exterior and the interior: Two investigations of the initiation of personal relationships. *Journal of Personality and Social Psychology, 48*, 1427–1439.

Snyder, M., Tanke, E. D., & Berscheid, E. (1977). Social perception and interpersonal behavior: On the self-fulfilling nature of social stereotypes. *Journal of Personality and Social Psychology, 43*, 656–666.

Solomon, M. R. (Ed.). (1985). *The psychology of fashion.* Lexington, MA: Lexington Books.

Solomon, M. R., & Schopler, J. (1978). The relationship of physical attractiveness and punitiveness: Is the linearity assumption out of line? *Personality and Social Psychology Bulletin, 4*, 483–486.

Solomon, M. R., & Schopler, J. (1982). Self-consciousness and clothing. *Personality and Social Psychology Bulletin, 8*, 508–514.

Sorell, G. T., & Nowak, C. G. (1981). The role of physical attractiveness as a contributor to individual development. In R. M. Lerner & N. A. Bush-Rossnagel (Eds.), *Individuals as producers of their development: A life-span perspective* (pp. 389–446). New York: Academic Press.

Spencer, B. A., & Taylor, G. S. (1988). Effects of facial attractiveness and gender on causal attributions of managerial performance. *Sex Roles, 19*, 273–285.

Sprecher, S. (1989). The importance to males and females of physical attractiveness, earning potential, and expressiveness in initial attraction. *Sex Roles, 21*, 591–607.

Sroufe, R., Chaikin, A., Cook, R., & Freeman, V. (1977). The effects of physical attractiveness on honesty: A socially desirable response. *Personality and Social Psychology Bulletin, 3*, 59–62.

Stake, J., & Lauer, M. L. (1987). The consequences of being overweight: A controlled study of gender differences. *Sex Roles, 17*, 31–47.

Stunkard, A. J. (1975). Presidential address–1974: From explanation to action in psychosomatic medicine: The case of obesity. *Psychosomatic Medicine, 37*, 1975.

Stunkard, A. J., & Burt, V. (1967). Obesity and body image II. Age at onset of disturbances in the body image. *American Journal of Psychiatry, 123*, 1443–1447.

Stunkard, A. J., & Mendelson, M. (1967). Obesity and body image I. Characteristics of disturbances in the body image of some obese persons. *American Journal of Psychiatry, 123*, 1296–1300.

Theberge, L., & Kernaleguen, A. (1979). Importance of cosmetics related to aspects of the self. *Perceptual and Motor Skills, 48*, 827–830.

Thompson, J. K. (1990). *Body image disturbance: Assessment and treatment.* Elmsford, NY: Pergamon Press.

Tiggemann, M., & Rothblum, E. D. (1988). Gender differences in social consequences of perceived overweight in the United States and Australia. *Sex Roles, 18*, 75–86.

Tucker, L. A. (1982). Relationship between perceived somatotype and body cathexis of college males. *Psychological Reports, 50*, 983–989.

von Baeyer, C. L., Sherk, D. L., & Zanna, M. P. (1981). Impression management in the job interview: When the female applicant meets the male (chauvinist) interviewer. *Personality and Social Psychology Bulletin, 7*, 45–51.

Walster, E., Aronson, V., Abrahams, D., & Rottman, L. (1966). Importance of physical attractiveness in dating behavior. *Journal of Personality and Social Psychology, 4*, 508–516.

Weinberger, H. L., & Cash, T. F. (1982). The relationship of attributional style to learned helplessness in an interpersonal context. *Basic and Applied Social Psychology, 3*, 141–154.

West, S. G., & Brown, T. J. (1975). Physical attractiveness, the severity of the emergency, and helping: A field experiment and interpersonal simulation. *Journal of Experimental Social Psychology, 11*, 531–538.

Wilson, M., & Cash, T. F. (1978, April). *Divergent effects of physical attractiveness on impression formation as a function of the situational context.* Paper presented at Eastern Psychological Association, Washington, D.C.

Wilson, M., Crocker, J., Brown, C., Johnson, D., Liotta, R., & Konat, J. (1985). The attractive executive: Effects of sex of business associates on attributions of competence and social skills. *Basic and Applied Social Psychology, 6*, 13–23.

Wright, E. T., Martin, R., Flynn, C., & Gunter, R. (1970). Some psychological effects of cosmetics. *Perceptual and Motor Skills, 30*, 12–14.

CHAPTER 4

Culture in the Mirror: Sociocultural Determinants of Body Image

April Fallon

Of all the ways people think of themselves, none is so essentially immediate and central as the image of their own bodies: The body is experienced as a reflection of the self. Body image is the way people perceive themselves and, equally important, the way they think others see them. Body image is constantly changing, continuously modified by biological growth, trauma, or decline; it is significantly influenced and molded by life circumstances—accentuated by pleasure or pain.

Culturally bound and consensually validated definitions of what is desirable and attractive play an important part in the development of body image. One's body image includes his/her perception of the cultural standards,[1] his/her perception of the extent to which he/she matches the standard, and the perception of the relative importance that members of the cultural group and the individual place on that match.[2]

For example, a woman's perception of the ideal female body shape is a thin one (most likely thinner than the average weight of the population). Her perception is that she is heavier than that ideal (Fallon & Rozin, 1985). A review of the literature indicates that the influence of body image on self-concept is

---

[1] *Perception* of the ideal rather than the *actual* ideal held by the rest of the cultural group is important. Research has shown that an individual or a subgroup of individuals can have different perceptions as to what is ideal (Fallon & Rozin, 1985).

[2] Although body image includes one's perception of physical appearance, it can also include less concrete attributes such as intelligence, style of movement, and social skills, as well as some "personality" traits such as cleanliness/neatness. For the present purpose, I will be concentrating on perceptions of appearance only.

greater for females than for males (Lerner, Karabenick, & Stuart, 1973; Lerner & Sorell, 1981; Lerner & Brackney, 1978; Lerner & Karabenick, 1974). Women are more likely than men to equate self-worth with what they think they look like and what they believe other people think they look like. Women's self-concepts are correlated with their own perceptions of their attractiveness, whereas men's self-concepts relate more closely to perceptions of their physical fitness or effectiveness (Lerner, Karabenick, & Stuart, 1973). Therefore, even if men and women draw the same conclusion that they are too heavy, it is potentially more distressing to a woman; she is more likely to make efforts to alter her shape (Rozin & Fallon, 1988). Furthermore, men are often more realistic and accurate in seeing themselves as others see them than are women (Fallon & Rozin, 1985).

Here we can see culture setting the standard (a thin ideal), individual biology providing a backdrop for inadequacy or falling short (i.e., a heavier body), culture providing the acceptable avenue for alteration (dieting), and one's membership status (i.e., being female and having one's self-worth be dependent on one's physical attributes) within the cultural group influencing the vigor with which one pursues the avenue for alteration.

This chapter discusses some of the sociocultural aspects of body image. In order to understand some of the influences of culture on the formation and maintenance of body image, a discussion of attractiveness is essential.[3] First, I review similarities and differences in standards of attractiveness for different cultures and trace Western cultural ideas through time. Then, I compare how various sociocultural subgroups such as sex, cultural group, and social class differ in and are affected by their perceptions of the cultural ideal. Finally, I offer examples profoundly illustrating the extent to which individuals within a group will endure pain to achieve this "unnatural" cultural ideal.

CROSS-CULTURAL IDEALS OF BEAUTY: IS THERE A UNIVERSAL STANDARD?

In much of the animal kingdom (at least fish, fowl, and some primates), the male carries the bright colors and fancy feathers; he courts through attraction. In contrast, among *homo sapiens,* at least through most of civilization, the female has had this decorative role. Ford and Beach (1951) studied men and women in 190 tribal societies and found that the physical attractiveness of the female receives more explicit consideration than does the physical attributes of the

---

[3]Beauty, the cultural ideal, and attractiveness will all be used interchangeably throughout this chapter. Even though some think of beauty as being aesthetically beyond the ordinary (Freedman, 1986), this may or may not represent the cultural ideal.

male. The desirability of the male depends predominantly upon his skills of prowess.

Why is it more important for women to suit the culture's image of a beautiful body? Although both women and men can be sexually aroused by visual stimuli, men are more likely than women to seek out and report appreciation of erotic images of the other sex (Mazur, 1986). They are more visually interested in the opposite sex than are women. Some have suggested this is because of genetic differences (Symons, 1979), others point to persistent bias in socialization (Hesse-Biber, Clayton-Mathews, & Downey, 1987).

In trying to understand what men find attractive about the female body, Charles Darwin (1874) conducted a rudimentary cross-cultural survey and concluded that men judge the attractiveness of women by widely varying criteria and that there is no single standard of beauty with respect to the human body.

In cultures with changing clothing fashion (Europe, in particular), definitions of beauty often follow styles of dress (Hollander, 1978). Clothes hide certain parts of the body while exposing others. Until this century, women's fashions in the West totally concealed the lower body (Laver, 1963). Certain styles exposed shoulders, while corseting and fitted bodices revealed the forms of waists and busts. The body below the waist was completely covered so the shapes of hips and legs were irrelevant to fashion. People had no opportunity to compare the hips and legs, making it difficult to form consensual standards of beauty. As a result, Mazur (1986) suggests individual taste in the beauty of the lower body varied widely, even within the same culture. For example, the fleshy nudes of the Renaissance artist Titian (1477–1576) were drawn at nearly the same time as the slender erotic women of Lucas Cranach (1472–1553); the delightfully modern curves of Diego Velasquez's (1599–1660) "Venus" were depicted only slightly later than Peter Paul Rubens's (1577–1640) corpulent nymphs (Mazur, 1986).

In spite of great variability in notions of attractiveness, Kalick (1978) notes that within a given culture, a consensus prevails regardless of age, socioeconomic status, and ethnic differences, or changing standards. In addition, there are a few commonalities that hold across cultures. These include the secondary sexual characteristics of young women—not only firm breasts and hips, but general roundness rather than angularity, fleshiness rather than flabbiness, unblemished and smooth rather than saggy skin, and symmetry. These basic features are attractive in almost all societies and are illustrated in the ancient erotic art, though preferences differ for particular body parts, sizes, and shapes (Clark, 1980; Ford & Beach, 1951; Symons, 1979). Ford and Beach (1951) note that the familiar, well-known, and well-understood girls were judged to be the most beautiful by men in a particular culture. Mazur (1986) suggests that whatever geographic variability in beauty standards may have existed in earlier times, the rise of mass media in the 20th century is more likely to impose more uniform standards of both beauty and fashion throughout the world than has existed previously.

DETERMINANTS OF BEAUTY: NATURE
VERSUS CULTURE

There are two opposing views about what determines the body ideal in a particular culture. The first involved *biological determinism*. This view posits that during the course of evolution there was an increasing division of labor, with males specializing in hunting and females in food-gathering and child-rearing. As they adapted to these distinct roles, natural selection selected for the male and female bodies that most efficiently performed these functions. Men became more muscular and women developed more fat layers. Male respiration improved and the chest region became larger to house the larger lungs. In connection with giving birth, female hips widened. These and other biological sex differences were then amplified by cultural means—making females super-feminine and males super-masculine. This process reached a peak in earlier centuries, when the demands of breeding were still very heavy for most women (Morris, 1985). Consistent with this model, but with a slightly different emphasis, the psychoanalytic writers suggest that the experience of beauty has its origins in the unconscious mind. The experience of beauty comes from feelings of sensual excitement, which become transformed into aesthetic feelings when the primary sexual aim is wholly or partially inhibited.

This perspective argues that a woman is beautiful not because of the symmetry or proportioned body parts of her form but because of the potential sexual functions suggested by this form. This kind of theory explains at least the almost universal valuation of youth and health; "youth and health tend to exaggerate the differences between sexes and to heighten the performances in which the sexes respectively excel—strength and vigour in the male and child-bearing in the female" (Liggett, 1974, p. 150).

Yet some of the characteristics that are most closely associated with reproduction such as menstruation, pregnancy, and lactation are not highly valued in terms of aesthetic beauty. The swollen belly of pregnancy and the smells of menstruation are not considered very attractive. Similarly, the ethological perspective on male attractiveness emphasizes physiognomic features conveying maturity and social dominance (Keating, Mazur, & Segall, 1981); yet mature male attributes (e.g., baldness) are not always viewed as attractive (Cash, 1990).

This brings us to the second view—that culture is responsible for ideals of beauty. It is not dimorphism per se, but whether and how the cultural group values it. This view accounts for the tremendous variety of decorative rituals found throughout the world. Culture not nature decides that the Chinese "Golden Lotus" is lovelier than the unbound "goosefoot." It is culture that first covers parts of the female body and then worships them.

This view proposes that none of the practices of beautification are inherently more pleasing than others. Their aesthetic value depends on the meaning given to it by the particular culture. Black teeth, red lips, or a stark white face appear attractive to someone conditioned to appreciate them. For example, in the 19th century, in fashionable Paris or in decadent Venice where the Renaissance spirit prevailed, powder and rouge were acceptable cosmetic decorations. But in Protestant England and in America wearing powder and rouge connoted moral looseness. Such cultural relativity is also true of more major alterations. For example, there is no inherent physical value to a neck stretched by brass rings or a small nose designed by a plastic surgeon. Who can say whether scarring one's face is elegant or hideous or whether stretching one's lips with discs or implanting one's breasts with silicone is an aesthetic improvement or a horrific mutilation?

Another interesting example of cultural differences regarding the ideal standard is that of hair length and baldness. There is no evidence that baldness is relevant to reproduction and evolution, yet there are tenacious beliefs, at least in Western culture, that long hair is feminine and that men should wear their hair short (Brownmiller, 1984). In the East and in Africa (where men seldom go bald), this preference was either reversed or irrelevant. Egyptian pharaohs and their families had their natural hair removed. They covered their heads with wigs that were sexually distinct, while their slaves were required to wear their own hair. Other African and Indian tribes still decorate their long hair with shells, feathers, or beads, while the women go without ornamentation and with heads covered or shaved. This example of how culture has incorporated the genetics of the group suggests that genetics and biology can provide constraints upon which cultural preferences are built.

Cultural preferences for body shape make this nature–culture merger even more apparent. In many societies attractiveness equals a good shape and body size. Societies that admire body shape and size, however, do not agree on what constitutes an attractive body. Aesthetic preferences for body shape and size have varied widely over time and across cultures. Ford and Beach (1951) observed that in most of the societies they studied, robust women are thought to possess greater sex appeal and to be more sexually satisfying than thin women. In those societies, past and present, in which people are on the edge of survival, a plump wife is a status symbol. She graphically illustrates her husband's status and ability to provide to excess—a sign of wealth and survival where food is scarce (Ford & Beach, 1951; Rudofsky, 1972). In developing countries, obesity is more prevalent in higher social classes for men, women, and children (Sobal & Stunkard, 1987).

These examples illustrate that "Biology is not destiny . . . but a fact of nature which enters into the logic of every social system and every cultural ideology" (S. Whyle, cited in Freedman, 1986, p. 188).

BEAUTY IDEAL THROUGH TIME

The concept of beauty has never been static. In this section, I trace the popularity of various Western cultural ideals through time. In the interests of space, I concentrate on body shape and weight, although a similar presentation could be made for the face, skin, cosmetics, and clothing.

As previously mentioned, attractiveness and active efforts to attain the cultural ideal have been more a female than a male tradition, with the exception of the Greeks. Unlike the early Christian teaching that challenged the idea of beauty as a mind–body unit, the Greek conception of beauty included the outer form of the person as well as his/her inner qualities. The male body was revered and considered more attractive than the female body; in part because beauty included fitness. Although little is known about the actual preferences of the Greeks, philosophers presented the "Golden Mean" as the basic universal standard of beauty (Hambidge, 1920; Plato, 1925). The "Golden Mean" represented a balance. To be extreme or rare was to be imperfect. The perfect female torso was one in which the distance between the breast nipples, the distance from the lower edge of the breast to the navel, and the distance from the navel to the crotch were all of equal lengths.

The Romans on the other hand were more interested in the rarities of particular faces and persons. We know that the Romans valued thinness and hated obesity. They also loved to feast and used regurgitation to keep their weight down; in other words, bulimic behavior was a legitimate and socially accepted practice.

In the late middle ages, the "reproductive figure" was the ideal—corpulent, with emphasis on the stomach's "fullness" as a symbol of fertility (Garner, Garfinkel, & Olmstead, 1983). Between 1400 and 1700, fat was considered both erotic and fashionable. The maternal role was elevated in importance; woman-hood and motherhood were synonymous. Women were desired for their procreative value and were often either pregnant or nursing. The beautiful woman was portrayed as a plump matron with full, nurturant breasts. Art reveals how a particular culture has portrayed ideal male and female body shapes. For example, in Botticelli's "The Birth of Venus" (1485) the goddess of beauty was "drawn in the guise of an endomorph," moon-faced, pear-shaped, and well fleshed out.

In the 19th century, the idealized female included two polar opposites, which Banner (1983) called the "steel engraving lady" and the "voluptuous woman." Both shared corseted waistlines (down to an 18-inch circumference, if possible), but otherwise differed in physique and personality—one being delicate and frail, the other heavy and sexy. The steel engraving lady (named for the lithographic process that companies such as Currier and Ives used to illustrate her) was a fragile lady who was admired for her moral values, social status, and beauty. However, by the mid-19th century she was being "challenged" by a bigger, bustier, hippier, heavy-legged woman found among the lower classes, and actresses and prostitutes. In the United States, the popularity of the theater increased and voluptuous performers like Lillian Russell came into vogue. This full figure had also been traditionally portrayed in European art (see Figure 4.1), so that it gained sufficient visibility and stature to become briefly fashionable

FIGURE 4.1.   Art showing the 19th-century bustle (George Seurat's *Sunday Afternoon on the Island of La Grande Jatte)*. Photo provided by The Art Institute of Chicago.

among the upper classes (Mazur, 1986). At its height in the 1880s, young women in the United States worried about being too thin. Bottoms were broadened with bustles, and women used padding. They ate and weighed themselves frequently (Banner, 1983). Doctors encouraged a plump shape as a sign of health. Huge sculptures like the Statue of Liberty displayed large boned, sensually rounded figures. Painters, like Renoir, were portraying their women in much the same way (e.g., the "Blonde Bather I" in 1881) (Figure 4.2).

The buxom Venus did not survive into the 20th century. In the pre-World War I years, although the heavy-bodied woman was a favorite in burlesque and on the pages of the *National Police Gazette,* she was beginning to lose her popularity with the upper class (Mazur, 1986). The Gibson Girl appeared about 1890. This ideal combined elements of the older beauties with a few new features. From the steel engraving lady, she took a basic slender body line and sense of properness, though not frail delicateness. From the voluptuous woman, she took a large bust and hips. She appeared tall, partly because she piled her long hair on the top of her head. She stood erect (though back swayed) with corseting that shaped her chest into a "monobosom." Occasionally she wore swim and sports clothes (when she bicycled and exercised), which showed her graceful slender legs, rounded calves, and narrow ankles (Garbor, 1972). Until this time, respectable American women never showed their legs in public.

FIGURE 4.2. Art conveying "full-bodied beauty" (Pierre Auguste Renoir's *Blonde Bather I*). Photo provided by the Sterling and Francine Clark Art Institute, Williamstown, MA.

When World War I ended, waistlines were let out and hemlines rose (Laver, 1963). The curvy ideal was replaced by the flat-chested flappers. Dresses of the 1920s were curveless and the ideal body was almost boylike. Women removed the padding from their bodices, abandoned the corset, and began binding their breasts with foundation garments to flatten their silhouette (Caldwell, 1981). The brassiere was originally invented to hide breasts (Hatfield & Sprecher, 1984). Miss America contest winners of the 1920s had mean bust–waist–hip measurements of 32–25–35, and no winner had a bust larger than her hips (Mazur, 1986). Margaret Gorman, the first Miss America winner, had measurements of 30–25–32 (Deford, 1971). A woman's beauty was now judged by her cosmetically decorated face and exposed legs (Rudofsky, 1972). Beauty of the flapper era was notable for the near absence of female secondary sexual characteristics. Women were using rolling machines, iodine, starvation diets, and strenuous exercise to reduce their weight (Silverstein, Peterson, & Purdue, 1986). In 1926, the New York Times (2/24/26) reported that the New York Academy of Science convened a 2-day conference to study the "outbreak" of eating disorders.

The rise of mass media in the 20th century probably imposed more uniform standards of beauty and fashion in the West (Mazur, 1986). Beginning in the 1920s, cultural beauties, like actress Kay Francis who stood 5' 5" and weighed 112 pounds, flickered on the movie screen. Motion pictures and the now widely distributed *Ladies Home Journal* provided information on beauty standards to a larger number of men and women from the upper and middle classes.

"Flapper beauty" ended with the onset of the depression. In 1931, the New York Times (9/26/31) reported, "In the coming ampler silhouette, decreed to go with the Empress Eugenie hats, the Bureau of Home Economics sees hope for the wheat surplus. Milady of Fashion these experts say, will eat a lot of that wheat to bring back the curves lost by reducing diets" (p. 1). Hemlines fell and the narrow waist returned; female secondary sexual characteristics were reasserted as the desire for bustiness. Actresses like Kay Francis lost popularity compared to busty cinema stars like Jean Harlow, Mae West, and Greta Garbo, who reigned in the 1930s. In the 1930s the mean measurements of Miss America winners were 34–25–35; the average bust size increased by 2 inches from the past decade (Mazur, 1986). According to Mazur (1986), during the 1940s the leg came to equal, perhaps surpass, the breast as an erotic symbol. Hemmed stockings, with garters and high heels, became the national desired ideal. Betty Grable, in an one-piece bathing suit, posed for one of the most popular pinups of World War II; as she looked back over her shoulder, the camera showed her "million dollar legs" and rear end. Bustiness also increased. Miss America contestants' mean measurements in the 1940s were 35–25–35, with nearly all winners having larger busts than hips. Hollywood introduced the "sweater girl" (e.g., Lana Turner and Jane Russell).

During the 1950s, Hollywood and the fashion industry "promoted large-cleaved bustlines (and falsies), tiny cinch waists (and girdle), and wiggly-hipped walks (with high heels)" (Mazur, 1986, p. 291). It was a period of "bosom mania," as exemplified by *Playboy* magazine, which glorified large-breasted women (Weyr, 1978). Marilyn Monroe was the first Playboy centerfold. She and Jane Mansfield were the leading Hollywood screen queens. Like the 19th century, the 1950s had a thin as well as a voluptuous ideal of beauty; Grace Kelly and Audrey Hepburn are examples of the former. They symbolized a muted but classy sensuality, associated with the aristocracy rather than the "earthy" sexuality of Monroe (Mazur, 1986). Since 1950, almost all Miss America winners have had bust–hip symmetry. During this period waist size declined so that the body exhibited conspicuous curves (36–23–36) with fat redistributed away from the waist to hips and breasts.

This trend continued into the 1960s. Then in 1966, a 17-year-old, 97-pounder from England, Leslie Hornby Armstrong, nicknamed "Twiggy," burst onto the American fashion scene and draped her thin 31–22–32 skeleton over the pages of *Seventeen* and *Vogue* magazines. According to Mazur (1986), men in the United States never adjusted to the upper skinniness of Twiggy, though a compromise was struck when figures such as those of Farrah Fawcett and Cherly Tiegs became the new ideal. Today many feminists connect Twiggy's entrance onto the fashion scene with the appalling increase in eating disorders. However, from a different front, the curvy look, associated with motherhood, may have lost much of its value in a world striving for zero population growth (Freedman, 1986). In medical circles, obstetricians of the 1960s routinely placed pregnant women on strict diets that permitted a weight gain of only twenty pounds (a procedure that was later rejected because it threatened fetal growth).

Brownmiller (1984) argued that the French bikini also deserves special credit for "thinning" the female body in the 1960s. Although European women of all shapes felt free to sun themselves in tiny amounts of cloth, "puritanical American sensibility" viewed the body inside the bikini more critically. Fleshy curves that spilled out over the edges were considered gross. A slender figure was deemed more aesthetically pleasing in a bikini.

In the late 1960s, while movies and magazines continued to bulge with bosoms, measurements of pristine beauties, Miss America and Miss USA, were no longer reported. Shortly after 1969, when reporting of the measurements were resumed, the "voluptuous" figures of the Miss America and Miss USA began to recede; bust and hips were still symmetrical, contestants' height rose (by an average of 1 inch), and their weight fell (by an average of 5 pounds) (Mazur, 1986). Garner, Garkinkel, Schwartz, and Thompson (1980) collected data on Miss America winners from 1959 through 1978 and found that, over 2 decades, there was a significant decrease in weight per height of Miss America winners (see Figure 4.3). A similar phenomenon was happening in European countries. In 1951, Miss Sweden was 5′ 7″ and 151 lbs., in 1983 she was 5′ 9″ and 109 lbs. (Dryenforth, Wooely, & Wooley, 1984).

Madame Tussand's London Wax Museum polls its annual visitors as to

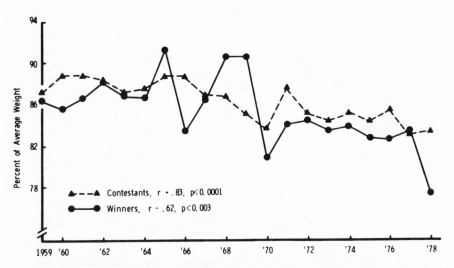

FIGURE 4.3. Percentage of average weight (based on the 1959 Build and Blood Pressure study of the Association of Life Insurance Medical Directors and Society of Actuaries) for Miss America Pagaent contestants and winners. From *Anorexia Nervosa: A Multidimensional Perspective* (p. 109) by P. E. Garfinkel and D. M. Garner, 1982, New York: Brunner/Mazel. Copyright 1982 by Brunner/Mazel. Reprinted by permission.

which figures in the museum are the most beautiful. Until 1970, Elizabeth Taylor was the most admired figure (Garkinkel & Garner, 1982). But then Ms. Taylor gained weight, in addition to a change in style. A *Women's Wear Daily* picture of her with husband John Warner had a caption that reads, "All our lives we have wanted to look like Elizabeth Taylor, and now—God help us—we do." While Ms. Taylor was gaining weight, Twiggy was busy losing weight, and in 1976 all 91 pounds of her (surely the most idealized anorectic—hipless, flat-chested, 20th-century Venus) had reached status of number one.

The sexy, sultry, voluptuous ideals followed the same decreasing trend. Data collected from *Playboy* magazine centerfolds over the same 20-year period (1958–1979) like that of the Miss America contestants, revealed decreasing bust and hip measurements and an increasing waist size; indeed they had "changed shape" over the 20 years (Garner et al., 1980) (see Figure 4.4). Playmates became taller during the 1970s. Bust and hips became generally smaller, and the waist larger (probably due to taller models). This trend continued into the 80s as the average weight of the playmates continued to drop (Mazur, 1986). In fact, *Playboy* centerfolds have grown slimmer every year since the magazine began (Freedman, 1986). Mazur (1986) reported that although their breasts remained large, Playmates have become increasingly linear—taller, leaner, and nearly hipless.

Several studies have empirically examined heterosexual reactions to different body shapes. Wiggins, Wiggins, and Congdon, (1968) conducted a careful study

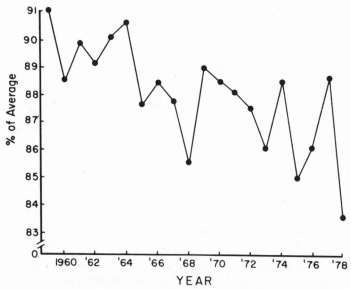

FIGURE 4.4. Changes in percentage of average weight in *Playboy* centerfolds over 20 years. From *Anorexia Nervosa: A Multidimensional Perspective* (p. 109) by P. E. Garfinkel and D. M. Garner, 1982, New York: Brunner/Mazel. Copyright 1982 by Brunner/Mazel. Reprinted by permission.

of what men think is beautiful in women by preparing 105 nude silhouettes in which they systematically varied shape of legs, breasts, and buttocks. In general, men in the 1960s thought the women with medium-size features were more attractive than those with unusually small or large features. The men's ideal, however, was a woman with slightly oversized breasts, medium to slightly small buttocks, and medium-sized legs. Similar results have been reported by others (see Hatfield & Sprecher, 1986, for a review).

By the early 1970s the idealized large bosom had given way to interest in small buttocks. Women, judging the attractiveness of female bodies, usually preferred slender figures, small buttocks, and middle- to small-size busts (Beck, Ward-Hull, & McLear, 1976; Horvath, 1979, 1981). When asked to comment on their bodies, diverse samples of women usually complained that they felt that they themselves were too heavy and that their hips and buttocks were too big, but not that their busts were too small (Mazur, 1986). Just a few years later, *Glamour* magazine asked a nonrandom sample of 100 men ("Men Tell," 1983) to name their favorite female body area, and the men chose buttocks over breasts by more than two to one.

Lavrakas (1975) interviewed women aged 18 to 30 to find out what they found most appealing in men. He found women preferred men with a tapered "V–look" medium-sized shoulders, a medium-thick waist and hips, and thin legs. The build they most disliked was "pear-shaped"—small shoulders and wide hips. Similar results were obtained by others (Horvath, 1979).

Commercial images both reflect and influence the social ideals of body shape and size. In 1894, a 5' 4 ", 140-pound model with a 37 bust and 38 hips represented the ideal. In 1947, she was down to 125 pounds. By 1975, she was reduced to 118 pounds, despite having grown to 5' 8 " (Freedman, 1986). Silverstein et al. (1986) sampled figures in ads from *Vogue* and *Ladies Home Journal* from 1890 to 1981. The slight curvaceousness of 1925 was replaced by more curvaceousness in 1930–1950, followed thereafter by a gradual decline in curvaceousness.

In the 1980s, a more muscular, healthy ideal of the female body has begun to emerge. *Time* magazine (Corliss, 1982) devoted a cover story to this entitled "New Ideal of Beauty." *Time* argued that this new woman is graceful and slim but stronger than previously portrayed. Examples include Jane Fonda and Victoria Principal. Female actresses in films of the 1980s no longer mince and wiggle; they stride. Females with naturally wide shoulders are given opportunities that would have been denied them earlier (Morris, 1985). A trend of greater acceptance of female body-building has surfaced. Fashions have accentuated this trend with the use of shoulder pads.

This section has traced the changes in aesthetic body-shape preferences over many centuries. Clearly such preferences do change. As the issue of survival of the species becomes a less salient concern, society adopts an ideal with regard to shape and weight that may even be at odds with biology.

Changes in preferences for skin tone have likewise occurred over the centuries. For many centuries in Japan, India, and Western societies (France, England, Italy, and the United States), pale or lighter skin has been associated with higher rank and greater beauty for both men and women. Peasants and laborers in the field were at a distinct disadvantage with regard to achieving such an ideal. Since nature could not always reliably respect these class distinctions, face and body powders were used as early as Cleopatra's time. In the 20th century, at least in the Western caucasian world, ideal preferences have changed to a year-round darkened look, a look that represents the group that can afford to sunbathe in the islands while the rest of society works indoors. By the end of World War I, cosmetics and artificial tanning agents were sold to achieve this look without having to leave one's house. Cosmetics, which had been too expensive for all but upper-class women, had become considerably cheaper as well. Their overuse became a sign of a worker rather than an upper-class woman. Today rich women use cosmetics, but in more limited ways. Often professionals are paid to apply them. Class is also distinguished by products of "refined quality" and high cost (Brownmiller, 1984). Among blacks in the United States, skin tone (as well as racial physiogmony) possesses considerable if not controversial meaning. Despite the "Black is Beautiful" movement, darker Blacks may experience more discrimination and lighter Blacks more favoritism, intraracially as well as interracially (Neal & Wilson, 1989).

It is my thesis that shape/weight and skin tone are but two examples of many that can be found. It seems, at least in western culture, that changes in preference for shape and skin are deviations from the average or natural state and only can be attempted and possibly achieved by the rich classes and castes due to the availability of resources (time, money, and supporting lifestyle). These "fashions" visually distinguish an individual's social class. As advances in society and technology enable the lower class to achieve these standards, a distaste for the "ideal" develops.

THE INFLUENCES OF GENDER, CLASS, AND CULTURE

Membership in or identification with a particular group can have a powerful influence on one's perceptions of one's own attributes. With respect to body image and attractiveness at least three types of groupings deserve special attention: sex, culture or subcultures, and social class. In this section, differences and similarities in each of these groups' conceptions of attractiveness and body image will be explored. Research where available will be presented.

Gender

We have already seen that for females in our society an increasingly thin standard has emerged. For men, the standard is one of moderate mesomorphy. Differences in each sex's perceptions of the cultural ideal, the extent to which they match it, and the importance of the match is quite remarkable. Because of the extensive coverage of gender, appearance standards, and body image elsewhere in this volume (see Chapters 3, 9, and 13 by Cash, Rosen, and Freedman, respectively), the reader is referred there for more detailed discussion. Here I will offer a summary of key points. Interpersonally, cognitively and professionally, attractive adults (men and women) are thought of more positively than unattractive adults (see Hatfield & Sprecher, 1986, for a review). It seems that this relationship between goodness and attractiveness is stronger for women than for men. Surprisingly, when directly questioned men and women are relatively satisfied with their overall appearance (Bersheid, Walster, & Bohrn-stedt, 1972; Cash, Winstead, & Janda, 1986), except about weight and shape.

Many studies have replicated the finding that females are more dissatisfied (Gray, 1977; Fallon & Rozin, 1985; Rozin & Fallon, 1988; Thompson & Psaltis, 1988) with their weight and shape than males, although the degree of dissatisfaction is somewhat a function of age. Adolescent boys are more interested in gaining or maintaining weight whereas girls' desire to lose weight begins to mount at puberty, increasing through adolescence (Nylander, 1971). College females judge their current figure to be significantly heavier than their ideal figure. In contrast, male college students (as a group) feel themselves to be close to their ideal in weight. Both men and women in their 40s and 50s share a similar dissatisfaction with body shape; both judge their ideal to be significantly thinner than their current shape (Rozin & Fallon, 1988). The change in men's attitudes appears to result from ideals that remain almost identical to that of their younger counterparts, while their actual figure becomes heavier with age. However, despite this discrepancy between current and ideal weights, these older men are similar in behavior to younger men with regard to their weight (e.g., they are less concerned than women about dieting and weight).

The female body has more fat than the male body. Women, therefore, naturally deviate from a lean and toned norm. If this is the ideal, females of normal weight are misjudged and also misjudge themselves as overweight. Men are more accurate than woman in assessing their proper weight; women feel overweight when they are not. In a study of college students' perceptions of ideal body shape, women more often overestimated their relative weight and rated their bodies as heavier than they thought men preferred as an ideal. In contrast, men judged their relative weight more accurately and generally felt that their current body shape was very close to what women wanted in an ideal man. Thus, men's perceptions help to keep them satisfied with their bodies, whereas women's perceptions motivate them toward weight obsession and dieting (Fallon & Rozin, 1985). We also found that 67% of the college women surveyed were dieting at least some of the time where as only 25% of the men were dieting (Rozin & Fallon, 1988). If dieting behavior indicates the degree of concern for achieving the cultural ideal, women are far more concerned about matching that ideal than are men. Our culture has provided women with a thin ideal that they seldom match. Women may distort further the extent of the overall lack of congruence between their shape and ideal (Fallon & Rozin, 1985). The culture has provided the method and the dictum that this can easily change—that nature needs only a gentle prod. Women are told directly and indirectly that if they cared and were responsible, they owe it to themselves and to their families to make the effort. Those who ignore their "potential" are depicted as lazy and loathesome and as having only themselves to blame. Even physicians share this belief; for example, a majority of physicians at a public outpatient medical clinic described their obese patients as "ugly" and "weak-willed" (Maddox & Liederman, 1969).

While the pursuit of and preoccupation with beauty are central features of the female sex-role stereotype (Rodin, Silberstein, & Striegel-Moore, 1985), some suggest that the extent of male body dissatisfaction is underestimated. Ninety-five percent of the men express dissatisfaction with some aspect of their bodies, and seventy percent of undergraduate men see a discrepancy between their own body and their ideal body type (Mishkind, Rodin, Silberstein, & Striegel-Moore, 1986; Calden, Lundy, & Schlafer, 1959; Tucker, 1982), with their greatest dissatisfaction toward chest, weight, waist, and height. Recently, several studies have found that men and women did not differ on several *global* measures of body dissatisfaction yet sometimes differed on the specific focus of their discontent: Females generally wanted to be thinner, whereas males were as likely to desire to be heavier (Cash & Brown, 1989; Silberstein, Striegel-Moore, Timko, & Rodin, 1988).

One implication of the emphasis on this most recent research is to study separately those subcultures of men and women in which appearance and weight are important. With respect to shape and weight, for example, Garner and Garfinkel (1978, 1980) found that those occupations in which there are intense pressures to maintain low body weight, for example dance and modelling, produce a higher rate of students with eating disorders and their milder variants than students of music. There are subgroups of men, as well, that place relatively greater emphasis on physical appearance and engage in excessive weight control behaviors. For example, gay males place an elevated importance on the physical self—body build, grooming, dress, and handsomeness (Kleinberg, 1980; Lakoff & Scherr, 1984). In a sample of heterosexual and homosexual college men, gay men expressed greater dissatisfaction with body build, waist, biceps, arms, and stomach than did heterosexual men. Homosexual men also indicated a greater discrepancy between their actual and ideal body shapes than did heterosexual men and showed higher scores on measures of eating disregulation and food and weight preoccupation (Mishkind, Rodin, Silberstein, & Streigel-Moore, 1986).

Class

Beauty and wealth have been associated with each other throughout history and in various cultures. The most powerful members of the group are able to obtain that which is most valued by the particular group. In addition, their power and wealth make them targets for emulation. In this way they have the power to dictate trends in fashion. Trends tend to filter down from the "haves" to the "have nots" and end when they become attainable by the "have nots." The link between beauty and wealth can clearly be seen in the following example: In the Orient in ancient times, a visibly well-fed woman brought honor to her husband to such an extreme that sometimes a powerful chieftain force-fed his wife as a testimony to his wealth. A complimentary greeting for the Punjab Indians translates into "You look fresh and fat today" (reported in Garner, Garfinkel, & Olmstead, 1983). A century ago in Western culture a curvy busomed woman signified luxury. The male's potbelly was worn proudly as a badge of success and well-being, indicating that he could afford to gorge himself on huge meals. When resources are scarce, weight is associated with prosperity and plump women are admired. However, when resources are plentiful, the weight ideal is in reverse. The Duchess of Windsor reportedly was to have said, "A woman can never be too rich or too thin." Today, in countries where there is no fear of starvation, the potbelly has lost its ostentatious grandness and has become a symbol of self-indulgence.

Upper class aristocratic women were formerly fat and well fed, then became thin and delicate. Now they strive to be firm and fit. It is still mainly upper-middle-class women who have the resources (time and money) to pursue the current fashion. Both the pursuit of thinness and the firm, fit look of 20th-century Western society (in which food is plentiful) may have begun as a visible upper class renunciation of the "common" shape. The connection between thinness and upper-class membership may even be responsible for a favorable stereotyping being applied to anorexia nervosa. As the rich become thin and fit, the body becomes a way to conspicuously distinguish the upper classes from the lower classes. The use of cosmetics, fashionable clothing, and plastic surgery are less deceptive; they are essentially only available to those that have considerable resources and can perhaps more reliably distinguish the classes than can shape and weight.

Culture

As we have said previously, each cultural group has its own unique definition of beauty. Because methodology in measuring body image is so diverse, unless the study makes a direct comparison of two different cultures, it is difficult to draw cross-cultural conclusions. In one study that has made the comparison, Tiggemann and Rothblum (1988) investigated attitudes about body weight and appearance among undergraduates at the Flinders University of South Australia and at the University of Vermont. Half of the subjects thought themselves to be overweight to some degree, although only one fifth of the sample was actually overweight. Weight was a much greater issue for all women, who felt more overweight, dieted more, expressed more body consciousness, and reported that weight had interfered more with social activities than did men. Vermont studies reported greater frequency of dieting, more concern about weight, and more body consciousness than did Australian students. Men and women in both cultures stereotyped obese people significantly more negatively, as being more self-indulgent, less self-disciplined, lazier, and less attractive, than they did nonobese targets. The negative stereotypes were more prevalent for the fat female body, and women tended to rate thin and fat bodies more discrepantly than did the men. The results indicate excessive and maladaptive concerns with weight among women and U.S. students in particular.

Little systematic work has been conducted on historical or current aspects of body image in non-Western countries. To date, the only published non-Western cross-cultural study compared preferences of Kenyan Asians, Kenyan British, and British females for various body shapes. There was relatively little disagreement between the groups with regard to the most attractive figures. What was different was the judgment of the obese figures. The British females judged and described the obese figures more negatively than did the Kenyan British females, and the Kenyan British females judged them more negatively than did the Kenyan Asians (Furnham & Alibhai, 1983).

This study is of interest for two reasons. First, there is no difference in what any of the three groups find most attractive. What does separate the groups is how negatively they view the heavier figures. This finding potentially contradicts the view expressed earlier that Third World countries prefer a plump figure. Second, it suggests that although the foundation of the formation of ideal body image may be one's intrapsychic life or one's native culture, residence in another culture can cause a change in one's perception of what is ideal in the direction of the "adopted" culture. A recent unpublished study asked students in India and in America to indicate their perceptions of their current and ideal shape. The study found that Indian women rated their ideal as being about what their current shape was. Indian and American men regarded their ideal as being somewhat heavier than their current figure. For American women there is a significant discrepancy between their current shape and the thin ideal they possess (Fallon, Rozin, Gogineni, & Desai, 1990).

Identification with one's cultural group (whether it be native or adopted) is important in the individual's perception of what is ideal. It also plays a role in the importance that the individual places on the match of his/her own body with the ideal. It follows that the more pressure an individual feels to conform to a shape that is different from his/her own, the more steps he/she will take to reduce this difference, whether it be by dieting, purging, or surgery.

PURSUIT OF BEAUTY AT A PAINFUL PRICE

The striving for beauty by individuals within a cultural group is a powerful determinant of behavior and the discontinuation of that behavior can sometimes reflect serious psychopathology (e.g., depression or a lack of will to live). Whether the goal is to increase sexual attractiveness or social appearance, the pursuit of this cultural ideal can occur even if the process or result of obtaining it is impractical, painful, or life-threatening. Such beauty practices take place almost without any regard for the amount of scientific warning. They have occurred in "developed" as well as "developing" groups from the beginning of recorded civilization. In this final section, I present cross-cultural examples of such problematic practices, undertaken in the service of striving for a cultural ideal.

Impractical Beauty Practices

It is an understatement to say that most cultures have a significant number of beauty practices that include the use of cosmetics (see Liggett, 1974, for more detailed descriptions of the various uses of paints and colors on the face), hair styling, and body painting. Most of these are temporary alterations of appearance and require an investment of time, but do not seriously hamper mobility or function, and are not life-threatening. For example, it is the custom in many Indian castes for brides to have intricate designs painted on their hands with a deep blue mixture of clay and Henna, which lasts for weeks before wearing away.

Even more impractical are long fingernails that decrease the competence of the hand, preclude making a fist, and can impose a minor hazard to others. Such nails convey the idea that their owner does not need to undertake manual work. In the U.S., only women are "permitted" to grow long nails; in some other cultures, males are allowed to grow nails (Morris, 1985).

Similarly, many clothing styles seriously hamper mobility. As Freedman (1986) put it, "in one way or other women's skirts have hemmed them in or tripped them up" (p. 89). The dress of the 1840s had a long train that draped in the mud. The bustle-back of 1890 made sitting an activity to be concentrated upon. The straight skirt of the 1950s hampered walking. The miniskirt of the 1970s made sitting difficult and bending impossible. Though in the 1970s women were permitted to wear pants in the classroom and office, the fashionable skin-tight, designer jeans allow for casual standing only, and with any movement the wearer runs the risk of restricting blood flow.

While countless examples of alterations causing inconvenience could be cited, a discussion of some painful alterations of the body will make it clear that peoples of both industrialized and nonindustrialized cultures are prepared to undergo an unbelievable amount of pain in the pursuit of the beauty ideals of their reference group.

Skin and Makeup

Throughout Western civilizations and in parts of the Eastern world such as India, there is the belief that a woman's skin should be lighter and more perfectly smooth than a man's skin (Liggett, 1974). For example, in many castes in India a woman is considered more desirable if she has lighter skin (R. R. Gogineni, May 1, 1988, personal communication). This difference has been depicted clearly throughout history in works of art. In ancient Egyptian wall paintings, yellow pigment was applied to female bodies, whereas reddish brown was the standard color for males. A light, shell-pink body was the convention for female nudes in Western art, whereas earthier flesh tones portrayed the masculine complexion. Today in the Western world, theatrical makeup remains divided into one range of shades for females, another for males. Biologically there is no natural difference in skin color between men and women. Darker skin has a greater concentration of the pigment melanin in the epidermis. While melanin has an obvious genetic correlation with race, a connection with gender does not exist.

Throughout history, men to some degree (as in England between 1790 and 1840) but mostly women have used cosmetics in an attempt to attain idealized beauty. The ancient Egyptians wore colored eye-shadows made from pounded green malachite, as well as a strong mercuric sulphide on the lips. Sublimate of mercury was popular for centuries for removing freckles. It not only removed freckles but stripped away the outer layer of skin and corroded the flesh underneath (Liggett, 1974). Ceruse, a cosmetic containing white lead used for whitening which was popular from Egyptian times until the 19th century, was actually composed of lead oxide, hydroxide, and carbonate. Lavish applications to the scalp of such noxious substances as sulphuric acid, turmeric, and alum water made some women bald. Kohl, the eye-shadow of the ancient Egyptians and Middle Ages, was largely composed of lead and antiomony sulphides. Many of these substances were highly dangerous because they were absorbed and stored in the body. Often women who used these substances died prematurely (see Liggett, 1974; Morris, 1985, for a review of this literature). While these are certainly examples of the deadly nature of this quest for beauty, it is unclear the extent to which the victims recognized the danger of the substances, for the application of these substances was immediately gratifying and generally not painful.

Skull Deformations

The softness of infants' skulls has enabled the horrific custom of deformation of the face and head most often practiced on girls to achieve beauty or to secure some magical protection against disease. The most common method was to apply pressure to the soft skull during the first weeks of life to make the head round, flat, or elongated, according to local taste. The forehead was then pressed with the hand and flattened. The nose, too, could be flattened (Liggett, 1974). Head deformation has ancient origins. Hippocrates and Pliny commented on its popularity among high-born Greek and Roman families. Until quite recently, it could be seen in Brittany, Normandy, and the region around Toulouse; in France it was achieved by the use of a very tight cap secured by strings. It can still be seen among some African peoples, in Greenland, and in Peru. Amazingly, it appears possible to make these changes without extensive brain damage.

Scarification of Cheeks

Many societies use powder, rouge, and paint to smooth away any unevenness on the cheek. Hence, permanent scarification or mutilation would not exist since they not only destroy this smoothness but also limit facial expression. Still, decorating the cheeks can include a variety of tattooing, excising, and hole boring. During their religious ceremonies, the Qadiri Dervishes of the Middle East press skewers through their cheeks when they have attained states of ecstasy (Morris, 1985).

Liggett (1974) reports that peoples of central Africa use cheek scarification to indicate tribal affiliation or to mark an important event. Brutal methods for cutting patterns on the face have included using a skull fragment to produce deep wounds into which black paint or wood ashes were placed. Repeated cutting and scratching of the same scars could be undertaken, leading to the formation of raised "hypertrophic" scar tissue. The Abipone people of South America used sharp thorns to cut. A mixture of blood and ashes was then placed into the wounds located on their faces, breasts, and arms. Liggett (1974) tells us that these markings were valued proclamations of clan membership and proof of passage through initiation rites. Both males and females would gladly acquire these scars and continue to enlarge their cicatrices; any person who wished to be considered fashionable had to manipulate his/her scars every week or so, cutting them deeper and putting wads into the cuts to cause the flesh to stand up. Special markings were sometimes made on the girls' faces at the time of marriage. If a girl unexpectedly received a desirable offer of marriage and the usual time to acquire the elaborate scarification could not be taken, the operation was speeded up with relentless vigour, amounting almost to torture (Liggett, 1974).

Aside from the use of cosmetics, the Western world is relatively free of these "facial adornments," though there was a brief resurgence of them in the 1970s with the commencement of the punk rock movement in London. Adolescents of both sexes could be seen with safety pins inserted in the flesh of their cheeks, usually close to the mouth. These mutilations were gradually softened and eventually replaced by fake safety pins to give the impression of being skewered through the flesh without actually harming it.

Alterations of Mouth and Teeth

Many groups encourage and even consider beautiful alterations in teeth and lips. These can make the process of eating a difficult and precarious chore. One such alteration that seems particularly remarkable is the insertion of woodenlike saucers into the lips. The procedure begins by inserting coin-sized discs; gradually, these are replaced by larger ones. In adulthood, the wearers display massive, plate-sized ornaments from their drooping lower lips (see Figure 4.5). Among African peoples, these discs (labrets) were even worn in pairs, which rattled together as the person tried to speak. The circumference of the distorted lips might be as great as 29 inches. One explanation given for these practices in Africa and Brazil was that they made the females of the tribes look unattractive to the Arab slave traders (Morris, 1985). Liggett (1974) tells us that the practice was a desirable thing to achieve, a mark of honor, that it was vigorously pursued, and its attainment lavishly celebrated. Whatever the true function may have been, it was completely disfiguring, and rendered ordinary facial expressions, eating, and speaking extremely difficult.

The teeth, necessary instruments for food intake, have been subject to all sorts of alterations—painting, blackening, removal, filling, and drilling holes. Peoples in Africa, Asia, and North America have been known to remove the central incisors to emphasize the canines and make the mouth look menacing (Morris, 1985). The natives of Australia and New Guinea celebrate the achievement of adulthood by having their two top front teeth knocked out. The Ibans drill holes through the six front teeth, insert star-shaped plugs of brass, and file the teeth to sharp points. In Bali, young adults are subjected to painful tooth-filing, to flatten out the points of the canines. With each of these alterations in the teeth, the tooth's structure is seriously compromised and invites infection, decay, and greater difficulty in eating. In the East Indies, the teeth were even filed off down to the gums as part of wedding, puberty, or mourning ceremonies.

Alterations of the Nose

Nose ornaments are worn in many different parts of the world, in tribal societies as well as among American and English groups of motorcycle riders. The nose is

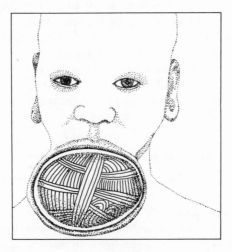

FIGURE 4.5. An example of an Ugandi lip plate.

prepared by having a hole or holes pierced in either the lower part of the septum or the fleshly nostril wings. This permanent mutilation labels him/her a member of a particular group or society.

As Pruzinsky and Edgerton discuss in Chapter 10 of this volume, rhinoplasty is a surgical solution sought by persons (including males) whose noses do not meet internalized standards. For some minorities (e.g., blacks, Jewish persons), this desire for transformation reflects an assimilation of white majority ideals and the rejection of features associated with ethnic identity.

Deformations of the Neck

The Karen women of upland Burma are known in Europe as "giraffe-necked" women. The females of this group are required by local fashion to start wearing brass neck rings from an early age (see Figure 4.6). Initially, five brass rings are fixed around the neck, then this number is increased gradually each year to a total of 24 rings. Brass rings are also put on the arms and legs, so that a woman might carry between 50 to 60 pounds of brass while walking long distances and working in the fields. This custom artifically lengthens the woman's neck. The record neck length recorded was $15\frac{3}{4}$ inches (Morris, 1985). The cervical muscles are stretched and the neck vertebrae pulled apart so severely that if such a woman

FIGURE 4.6.   An example of Burmese neck rings. From *The Virginian Pilot,* November 24, 1989, p. A20. Copyright 1989 by the Associated Press. Reprinted by permission.

had her heavy brass rings removed her neck would be unable to support her head. Europeans, fascinated by this cultural distortion of the human body, paraded a number of these long-necked women in circus side shows (Morris, 1985).

Modifications of Bodily Shape and Size

The fat content of a woman's body is usually 25%, whereas for males 15% is normal; this difference is not the result of exercise or strenuous labor. It seems to be a natural tendency of the female body to acquire a certain adipose mass. Of interest here are those practices, followed especially by women, that force the shape of the body into an unnatural form either by drastically reducing the waist (via the corset) or the entire body (via dieting and surgical liposuction).

Regarding the first practice, in past centuries a woman of status was required to endure a painful device of immobilization, the corset, which shortened her breath by tightly constricting her. Catherine de Médici of France and Elizabeth of England were among the first to wear the steel-ribbed corset—a compressing cage that pushed the soft flesh and rib cage inward. The corset induced a regal posture and smaller, feminized motions. An estimated pressure of up to 80 pounds might be exerted by the corset's squeeze, depending on the season's style and the determination of the wearer. The corset encouraged the idea that the female body was structurally unsound and needed to be supported by artificial contraptions at strategic points. A woman of the 19th century believed she was born with an imperfect, grossly shapeless, natural figure. A stiff foundation would compensate for the inability of her spine and musculature to support her breasts and stomach. Since her stomach and back muscles were atrophied from disuse and binding, she had reason to be grateful to her supporting stays, and without them she feared she might collapse into a degenerative heap, both physically and spiritually. Her erect, formal posture was identified with moral rectitude and social prosperity. Loosening the stays or leaving the house without them was interpreted as a sign of "loose" behavior. Indeed, the term "straitlaced" owes its origin to the corset. The second practice involves reducing overall weight to produce a shape more in line with a thin ideal. A cultural ideal of thinness below the average weight of women in that culture seems to increase their risk of anorexia and bulimia nervosa and other body-image disorders (Garfinkel and Garner, 1982). All cultures that have reported numbers of eating disorders have a thin ideal. Cultures that do not have the thin ideal have few reported cases of anorexia and bulimia (McCarthy, 1989). Thus, these disorders are, in part, an overcommittment or "overadaption" to the cultural ideal that is in vogue (Mazur, 1986).

Finally, a third practice for alteration of body size and shape due to adiposity involves the relatively new surgical technique of liposuction. Especially for women, this is the most frequently used cosmetic surgery, despite associated medical risks and side effects (Pruzinsky, 1988). Liposuction may be sought for "spot reducing" fat areas that do not conform to personal or societal ideas—again assuming one has the time and money to do so.

Breast Alterations

An alteration in breast size can be desired because of a wish to change the proportions of one's body or a wish to change the absolute size of the breasts. In the 20th-century U.S., while the desired uptilted cup shape with high-rounded breasts (usually associated with youth) has remained the desired form as depicted in art, fashion, and pornography, the ideal size has changed. In the 1930s and 1950s, when American women were encouraged to stay at home, large breasts were celebrated as the feminine ideal. In decades of spirited feminist activity such as the 1920s and the present, streamlined breasts are in fashion. While clothing styles and other props such as padded bras can change the appearance of breast size, surgery is required for a permanent alteration. In 1962 the introduction of silicone implants greatly improved the breast augmentation operation and facilitated its rapid spread. By the late 1970s, the demand for breast augmentation had leveled off (Mazur, 1986). Currently, plastic surgeons report that the trend on the east coast (where the pace is fast and businesslike) is toward breast reduction, whereas California movie stars and housewives on the Hollywood fringe still request augmentations, as did many Asian prostitutes during the Vietnam war in order to appeal to American GIs (Brownmiller, 1984). It should be noted however that, unlike augmentations, which have a purely aesthetic purpose, breast reduction is also requested for amelioration of physical discomforts caused by overly large breasts.

Other breast alterations, particularly in tribal societies, are rare, for the obvious reason of interference with breast feeding. Breast alteration is, therefore, usually restricted to decorative painting and to having ornamental objects hang over and around them. This aesthetic is shared by urban societies, although recently some Western females have started to break this rule by having their nipples pierced for the attachment of rings, chains, and other jewelry (Morris, 1985). In some instances, even males have followed suit. These developments, although comparatively minor, are probably a variant of punk rock fashion noted before.

Male Circumcision and Female Clitoredectomy

According to Morris (1985), male circumcision and female clitoredectomy probably were already well established in the Stone Age. For males, the removal of the foreskin has little effect on sexual performance, pleasure, or health. Female circumcision is a more serious mutilation; removal of the clitoris and the labia does drastically reduce sexual responsiveness. In the worst cases, girls have their labia and clitoris cut away and their vaginal openings stitched with silk, catgut, or thorns, leaving only a small opening for urine and menstrual blood.

The girl's legs are bound together to ensure that scar tissue forms. Later, when they marry, these females suffer the severe pain of having their artifically reduced orifices broken by their husbands. One result of this procedure, if performed in unhygenic conditions, is a high number of deaths and serious illnesses—especially in such countries as Oman, South Yemen, Domalia, Djibouti, Sudan, Southern Egypt, Ethiopia, and northern Kenya (Morris, 1985). More than 74 million or more of females alive today in parts of Africa, Indonesia, Malaysia, and the Middle East have had to endure this mutilation, which is practiced in more than 20 countries.

Male circumcision, however, still continues to be practiced in the West for religious and, until recently, health reasons. Recently, the American Academy of Pediatrics issued a statement indicating that circumcisions no longer were needed for health reasons (Committee on the Fetus and Newborn, 1975). It is interesting to note that after Britain introduced the National Health Plan less than 1% of the male babies were receiving the operation (Morris, 1985). However, in the United States more than 80% of male babies are still being circumcised. Since the America Academy of Pediatrics' decision, pediatricians and obstetricians have been debating heatedly the legitimacy of the procedure (Herzog & Alverez, 1986; Lincoln, 1986; Harkavy, 1987).

Foot Binding

Given the importance of the feet in everyday functioning, it seems remarkable that throughout history cultures have idealized the mutilated foot (see Fig. 4.7 for an example). Perhaps the most striking example is the 3-inch "Golden Lotus," a Chinese woman's foot reduced to one-third of its normal size by a foot-binding practice. Foot binding dates back to the late Tang dynasty, circa 900 A.D. Emperor Li Yu demanded that court dancers bind their feet into an arch

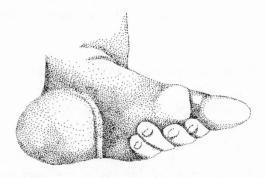

FIGURE 4.7.   An example of a foot that has been bound.

so they would walk on tiptoes with a seductive sway. The practice continued through the Sung and Ming dynasties for the daughters of the aristocracy. The art of foot binding and the striving for lily feet was practiced in China for nearly a thousand years, until the passing of Mandarin society in the 20th century. Chinese foot binding proceeded in this manner. When a girl was usually between the ages of 6 and 8, she was subjected to the agony of having her toes tied to her sole. A wide bandage was wrapped over the four small toes, bending them back on themselves; the bandage was then wound tightly around the heel, pulling the heel and toes closer together. Girls who cried or unwrapped their bandages were beaten. Despite the pain, they were required to walk in order to force the feet into accepting their new, buckled shape. Every couple of days, a new pair of shoes was put on, always one tenth of an inch shorter than before. The flesh petrified, the toenails fell out, and the bone–muscle structure was completely deformed. By the time these girls were adults they were permanently crippled, unable to walk normally; to move, they had to crawl or be carried.

Bound feet were considered the *sine qua non* of beauty and sexuality. They provided a permanent display of high status, since the women could do no manual labor; becoming a symbol of luxury and refinement. Moreover, the tiny foot had erotic significance in several ways. According to Taylor (1983), unbinding the foot and fondling it was part of lovemaking. The girls' husbands were said to enjoy not merely kissing their feet during sexual foreplay but actually taking the whole foot into their mouth and sucking it avidly. The erotic power of the foot was enhanced by concealment; only a husband could see or handle it. Men believed the tilt of the pelvis caused by the bound feet created folds in the vagina that intensified a woman's sexual desires. In addition, such a woman was unable to stray from her husband and had to totally depend on him for care. As Dworkin (1974) remarked, "Chinese men, it is clear, stood tall and strong on women's tiny feet." No man of high rank would marry a "goosefoot" woman. A woman's desirability was in direct proportion to her inability to walk. A woman whose feet had not been bound was doomed to be unmarried.

According to Brownmiller (1984), the bound foot illustrates several aspects of feminine aesthetics. It originated in a decadent upper class and became an enviable symbol of leisure. It cruelly exaggerated the small difference between a male and female body for the sake of artistic beauty. This "beautiful foot" imposed a serious handicap upon the foot's ability to function and reduced the females' competence to deal with the world around her, thus making the world a more dangerous place. It romanticized, and thereby justified, this reduced competence by turning it into a sexual attraction: It elevated her tiny, useless foot, to the level of "ornamental beauty." And it furthered the belief that this natural part of a woman was not attractive and required some extreme corrective measure.

The Chinese practice of mutilating the feet for beauty and fashion seems foreign to us. But every American child by the age of 5 years is familiar with the Disneyfied version of it, the fairy tale *Cinderella*. A prince was searching for a wife with very small feet. A tiny fur slipper was used to test prospective brides. The premise that a high-ranking male will find a tiny-footed female desirable regardless of her other qualities seems to be overlooked by modern audiences. Perhaps this is because in the modern version, Cinderella is very pretty. Remember though, in his search, the prince makes only one demand of his bride—that her foot should fit into the slipper. The latent message is that without beauty, virtue will not be noticed and, at the same time, that a girl's appearance can be quickly made over. When Cinderella's stepsisters struggle unsuccessfully to fit into the shoe, their mother gives them a knife, urging one to cut off a toe and the other to slice down a heel. She consoles them: "Once you are Queen you won't have to walk anymore."

In Western culture, the passion for small feet reached such intensity in earlier centuries that some ladies of fashion had their small toes amputated so that their feet would fit into even-more-pointed footwear. And today, by adulthood, most adult feet have been molded by shoes designed for attractiveness rather than comfort. Both men and women risk calluses, corns, bunions, and deformity. However, adulthood poses an additional hazard for the woman: the high-heeled pointed-toe shoe. Brownmiller (1984) notes even "emancipated" women still cramp their toes into shoes that give their feet and legs an illusory delicate seductive charm, despite the risks of twisted ankles, strained backs, shortened tendons, and torn ligaments, and the increased energy required to avoid the pitfalls, escalator grids, pavement cracks, and sidewalk gratings. The bound foot and a high-heeled, pointed shoe imposed problems of grace and self-consciousness "on what would otherwise be a simple art of locomotion, and in this artful handicap lies its subjugation and supposed charm" (p. 186).

CONCLUSION

While it is true that nature and biology influence and even constrain what gets defined as the ideal, it is clear that culture greatly affects what becomes the ideal. Against the backdrop of cultural ideals each individual must make assessments about his/her own attributes. The extent to which perceptions of self and the cultural ideal are discordant strongly influence body image and self-concept. Lerner and Jovanovic, in Chapter 5 of this volume, clearly show the developmental processes inherent in such "goodness" or "badness" of fit. Furthermore, one's motivation to reject and alter one's features is a function of the societal pressure one experiences to place body attributes in line with one's perception of the ideal. We have seen in this last section the degree to which people are willing to alter the body and reduce its effectiveness as well as threaten its existence in order to achieve this ideal. Such practices make obvious the extent to which the development and maintenance of body image is dependent upon reference group and status within that group.

REFERENCES

Banner, L. (1983). *American beauty*. New York: William Morrow.

Beck, S.B., Ward-Hull, C.I., & McLear, P.M. (1976). Variables related to women's somatic preferences of the male and female body. *Journal of Personality and Social Psychology, 34,* 1200–1210.

Berscheid, E., Walster, E., & Bohrnstedt, G. (1973, November). The happy American body: A survey report. *Psychology Today, 1,* 119–131.

Brownmiller, S. (1984). *Femininity*. New York: Ballentine Books.

Calden, G., Lundy, R.M., & Schlafer, R.J. (1959). Sex differences in body concepts. *Journal of Consulting Psychology, 23,* 278.

Caldwell, D. (1981). *And all was revealed: Ladies underwear. 1907–1980*. New York: St. Martin's Press.

Cash, T.F. (1990). Losing hair, losing points? The effects of male pattern baldness on social impression formation. *Journal of Applied Social Psychology, 20,* 154–167.

Cash, T.F., Winstead, B.A., & Janda, L.H. (1986). The great American shape-up. *Psychology Today, 20,* 30–37.

Cash, T.F., & Brown, T.A. (1989). Gender and body images: Stereotypes and realities. *Sex Roles, 21,* 357–369.

Clark, K. (1980). *Feminine beauty*. New York: Rizzoli.

Committee on the Fetus and Newborn. (1975). Report of the ad hoc task force on circumcision. *Pediatrics, 55,* 610–611.

Corliss, R. (1982, August 30). Sexes: The new ideal of beauty. *Time,* 72–73.

Darwin, C. (1874). *The descent of man*. London: John Murray.

Deford, F. (1971). *There she is: The life and times of Miss America*. New York: Viking Press.

Dworkin, A. (1974). *Women hating*. New York: Dutton.

Dyrenforth, S.R., Wooley, O.W., & Wooley, S.C. (1980). A woman's body in a man's world: Review of findings on body image and weight control. In J.R. Kaplan (Ed.), *A woman's conflict: The special relationship between women and food*. NJ: Prentice Hall.

Fallon, A., & Rozin, P. (1985). Sex differences in perception of desirable body shape. *Journal of Abnormal Psychology, 94,* 102–105.

Fallon, A., Rozin, P., Gogineni, R., & Desai, K. (1990). *Body image and eating disorders: A cross-cultural comparison between Indians and Americans*. Unpublished manuscript.

Ford, C., & Beach, R. (1951). *Patterns of sexual behavior*. New Haven: Harper & Brothers, and Paul B. Hoeber Medical Books.

Freedman, R. (1986). *Beauty bound*. Massachusetts: Lexington Books.

Furham, A., & Alibhai, N. (1983). Cross-cultural differences in the perception of female body shapes. *Psychological Medicine, 13,* 829–837.

Garbor, M. (1972). *The pinup*. New York: Bell.

Garfinkel, P.E., & Garner, D.M. (1982). *Anorexia nervosa: A multidimensional perspective*. New York: Brunnel/Mazel.

Garner, D.M., & Garfinkel, P.E. (1978). Sociocultural factors in anorexia nervosa. *Lancet, 2,* 674.

Garner, D.M., & Garfinkel, P.E. (1980). Socio-cultural factors in the development of anorexia nervosa. *Psychological Medicine, 10,* 647–656.

Garner, D.M., Garfinkel, P.E., & Olmsted, M. (1983). An overview of sociocultural factors in the development of anorexia nervosa. In P.L. Darby, P.E. Garfinkel, D.M. Garner, & D.V. Coscina (Eds.), *Anorexia nervosa: Recent developments* (pp. 65–82). New York: Allan R. Liss.

Garner, D.M., Garfinkel, P.E., Schwartz, D., & Thompson, M. (1980). Cultural expectations of thinness in women. *Psychological Reports, 47,* 483–491.

Hambidge, J. (1920). *Dynamic symmetry*. New Haven: Yale University Press.

Hatfield, E., & Sprecher, S. (1988). *Mirror, mirror: The importance of looks in everyday life*. New York: SUNY Press.

Harkavy, K.L. (1987). The circumcision debate [Letter]. *Pediatrics, 79*, 649–650.

Herzog, L.W. (1986). The frequency of foreskin problems in uncircumcised children. *American Journal of Diseased Child, 140*(3), 254–256.

Hesse-Biber, S., Clayton-Matthews, A., & Downey, J.A. (1987). The differential importance of weight and body image among college men and women. *Genetic, Social, and General Psychology Monographs, 113*, 509–528.

Hollander, A. (1978). *Seeing through clothes*. New York: Viking.

Horvath, T. (1979). Correlates of physical beauty in men and women. *Social Behavior and Personality, 7*, 145–151.

Horvath, T. (1981). Physical attractiveness: The influence of selected torso parameter. *Archives of Sexual Behavior, 10*, 21–24.

Kalik, S. (1978). Toward an interdisciplinary psychology of appearance. *Psychiatry, 41*, 243–253.

Keating, C.F., Mazur, A., & Segal, M.H. (1981). A cross-cultural exploration of physiognomic traits of dominance and happiness. *Ethology and Sociobiology, 2*, 41–48.

Kleinberg, S. (1980). *Alienated affections: Being Gay in America*. New York: St. Martin's Press.

Lakoff, R.T., & Scherr, R.L. (1984). *Face value, the politics of beauty*. Boston: Routledge & Kegan Paul.

Laver, J. (1963). *Costume through the ages*. New York: Simon & Schuster.

Lavrakas, P. (1975). Female preferences for male physiques. *Journal of Research in Personality, 9*, 324–334.

Lerner, R.M., & Brackney, B.E. (1978). The importance of inner and outer body parts: Attitudes in the self-concept of late adolescents. *Sex Roles, 4*, 225–238.

Lerner, R.M., & Karabenick, S.A. (1974). Physical attractiveness, body attitudes, and self-concept in late adolescents. *Journal of Youth and Adolescence, 3*, 307–316.

Lerner, R.M., Karabenick, S.A., & Stuart, J.L. (1973). Relations among physical attractiveness, body attitudes, and self concept in male and female college students. *Journal of Psychology, 85*, 119–129.

Lerner, R.M., & Sorell, G. (1981). Sex differences in self-concept and self-esteem of late adolescents: A time-lag analysis. *Sex Roles, 7*, 709–722.

Liggett, J. (1974). *The human face*. New York: Stein and Day.

Lincoln, G.A. (1986). Neonatal circumcision: Is it needed? *Journal of Obstetrical and Gynecological Neonatal Nursing, 15*, 463–466.

Maddox, G.L., & Liederman, U. (1969). Overweight as a social disability with medical implications. *Psychological Reports, 43*, 277–278.

Mazur, A. (1986). U.S. trends in feminine beauty and overadaptation. *Journal of Sex Research, 22*, 281–303.

McCarthy, M. (1989). *The thin ideal, depression and eating disorders in women: Is there a causal relationship?* Unpublished manuscript.

Men tell what they love. (1983, April). *Glamour*, pp. 238–241.

Mishkind, M.E., Rodin, J., Silberstein, L.R., & Striegel-Moore, R.H. (1986). The embodiment of masculinity. *American Behavioral Scientist, 29*, 545–562.

Morris, D. (1985). *Bodywatching, a field guide to the human species*. New York: Crown.

Neal, A.M., & Wilson, M.L. (1989). The role of skin color and features in the Black community: Implications for Black women and therapy. *Clinical Psychology Review, 9*(3), 323–334.

Nylander, I. (1971). The feeling of being fat and dieting in a school population. *Acta Socio-Medica Scandinavia, 1*, 17–26.

Plato, (1925). *Plato: Philebus*. (N.H. Fowler, Trans.). Cambridge: Harvard University Press.

Pruzinsky, T. (1988, May). *The changing face of plastic surgery: Developments and trends in requests for elective cosmetic surgery*. Paper presented at the annual meeting of the American Board of Medical Psychotherapists, Hilton Head, SC.

Rodin, J., Silberstein, L.R., & Striegel-Moore, R. (1985). Women and weight: A normative discontent. In T.B. Sonderegger (Ed.), *Nebraska Symposium on motivation, 1984: Psychology and gender*. Lincoln: University of Nebraska Press.

Rozin, P., & Fallon, A.E. (1988). Body image, attitudes to weight and misperceptions of figure preferences of the opposite sex: A comparison of men and women in two generations. *Journal of Abnormal Psychology, 97*(3), 342–345.

Rudofsky, B. (1972). *The unfashionable human body*. New York: Doubleday.

Silverstein, B., Peterson, B., & Perdue, L. (1986). Some correlates of the thin standard of bodily attractiveness for women. *International Journal of Eating Disorders, 5*, 895–905.

Sobal, J., & Stunkard, A.J. (1987). Socioeconomic status and obesity: A review of the literature. *Psychological Bulletin, 105*, 260–275.

Symons, D. (1979). *The evolution of human sexuality*. New York: Oxford University Press.

Taylor, L. (1983, July 24). Sunday today: The finest of the east. *The Sunday Star-Bulletin and Advertiser*, C1.

Tiggemann, M., & Rothblum, E.D. (1988). Gender differences in social consequences of perceived overweight in the United States and Australia. *Sex Roles, 18*, 75–86.

Thompson, R.S. (1987). Circumcision [Letter]. *Pediatrics, 80*, 303–350.

Tucker, L.A. (1982). Relationship between perceived somatotype and body cathexis of college males. *Psychology Reports, 50*, 983–989.

Weyr, T. (1978). *Reaching for paradise*. New York: Time Books.

Wiggins, J., Wiggins, N., & Conger, J. (1968). Correlates of heterosexual somatic preference. *Journal of Personality and Social Psychology, 10*, 82–90.

CHAPTER 5

The Role of Body Image in Psychosocial Development across the Life Span: A Developmental Contextual Perspective

Richard M. Lerner
Jasna Jovanovic

The physical (bodily) constitution of the developing organism and the organism's own cognitive and emotional appraisals of its constitution have been variables of central importance in developmental theory. For instance, within psychoanalytic theory (Freud, 1923, 1949), the stages of psychosexual development involve bodily (erogenous) zones; the person's emotional development hinges on external and internal means through which appropriate stimulation is provided to these bodily areas. Indeed, both Freud (1923) and Erikson (1968) see the body as so central to personality and social development as to claim that "anatomy is destiny." For example, Erikson (1968) states: "Am I saying, then, that 'anatomy is destiny?' Yes, it is destiny, insofar as it determines not only the range and configuration of physiological functioning and its limitation but also, to an extent, personality configurations" (p. 285).

In Piaget's (1950, 1970) developmental stage theory of cognition, the body also plays a central role in the person's development. In each of the six phases within the sensorimotor stage of development, circular reactions involving the body are elaborated in an increasingly more cognitively complex manner. These circular reactions primarily involve the infant's knowledge of actions on his/her own body, and thus initial cognitions about body functions. Secondarily, these reactions pertain to the infant's knowledge of the body's ability to act on a single external object. Finally, these reactions involve the infant's knowledge that he/she can act on one external object to influence still another one.

Thus, in both the psychoanalytic and Piagetian developmental theories the body—as a physical entity *and* as an object of one's emotions and knowledge— plays a central role in the development of the person's affective and cognitive processes. The role of the body in the person's psychological development has been stressed also in developmental perspectives that emphasize person–social context interactions as central in processes of change across ontogeny (e.g., Lerner, 1987). A key example of this latter theoretical orientation is termed *developmental contextualism* (Lerner, 1986; Lerner & Kauffman, 1985).

In developmental contextualism the body is seen as a key component of the person's organismic individuality, one evoking differential reactions from social-izing others, and thus promoting distinct feedback to the person. In addition, the person's appraisal of his/her own body—that is, cognitions and feelings about his/her body—are reactions which (1) derive in part from socializing others' reactions to the person (Cooley, 1902; Mead, 1934), and (2) from the person's cognitive and emotional developments involving the body, such as those noted by Piaget (1950). We refer to these cognitions and feelings about the body as "body image."

In the view of developmental contextualism, body image not only derives from person–social context relations and the individual's cognitive and emo-tional developments, but also contributes to both of these processes. In other words, how one thinks and feels about one's body will influence one's social relations and one's other psychological characteristics. This dual role of body image—as a product of social interactions and psychological developments *and* as a "producer" of (i.e., an influence on) these interactions and developments— is a key feature of the developmental contextual perspective. By focusing on this dual role we may gain understanding of the known and possible contributions of body image across the life span. That is, the processes of which the body and body image are a part should be involved continuously in psychosocial development.

In this chapter we discuss literature pertinent to this dual role of body image in psychosocial development. In addition, we point to areas of inquiry wherein research evaluating this role would be of further theoretical and substantive use. To accomplish these tasks we turn first to a discussion of the developmental contextual perspective and consider the central role played by an organism's individuality, as exemplified by its bodily attributes' effects on person-context relationships.

FEATURES OF THE DEVELOPMENTAL
CONTEXTUAL PERSPECTIVE

Since its inception as a specialization within the discipline, developmental psychology—or, as it was initially termed, *genetic psychology* (Hall, 1904)—has been dominated by a biological model of change. Indeed, the concept of development is biological in its scientific origin (Harris, 1957). Although the particular version of biological change that has influenced developmental psychology has been and remains Darwinian in character (White, 1968), this common heritage nevertheless has led to the formation of quite distinct models of development (Dixon & Lerner, 1988). For instance, mechanistic–behavioral conceptions of developmental change (Bijou, 1976), organismic–dynamic (Freud, 1949), and organismic–structural (Piaget, 1950) theories may be interpreted as having derived from this Darwinian heritage (Dixon & Lerner, 1988).

Despite this range of interpretations of the contribution of biology to psychological development, the organismic versions have predominated in developmental psychology and in fact have been termed "strong" developmental models (Reese & Overton, 1970). Thus, in the field of psychology in general, and perhaps in the scholarly community as a whole, the organismic theories of Freud, Erikson, and Piaget are typically held to be the classic, prototypic, or exemplary theories within developmental psychology (Lerner, 1986). Especially the organismic theories of Freud and Erikson have been labeled "predetermined epigenetic" (Gottlieb, 1983), where biology is seen as the prime mover of development. Intrinsic (e.g., maturational) changes are seen to essentially unfold. Although environmental or experiential variables may speed up or slow down these progressions, they can do nothing to alter the sequence or quality (e.g., the structure) of these hereditarily predetermined changes (Hamburger, 1957). In other words,

> [This view] as it applies to behavior, means that the development of behavior in larvae, embryos, fetuses, and neonates can be explained entirely in terms of neuromotor and neurosensory maturation [that is,] in terms of proliferation, migration, differentiation, and growth of neurons and their axonal and dendritic processes. In this view, factors such as the use or exercise of muscles, sensory stimulation, mechanical agitation, environmental heat, gravity, and so on, play only a passive role in the development of the nervous system. Thus, according to predetermined epigenesis. . . structural maturation determines function, and not vice versa.(Gottlieb, 1983, p. 11)

Victor Hamburger's organismic position epitomizes this view. He notes that "the architecture of the nervous system and the concomitant behavior patterns result from self-generating growth and maturation processes that are determined entirely by inherited, intrinsic factors, to the exclusion of functional adjustment, exercise, or anything else akin to learning" (Hamburger, 1957, p. 56).

However, another view of biological functioning exists, one that sees biological and contextual factors as reciprocally interactive. As such, developmental changes are probabilistic with respect to normative outcomes due to variation in the timing of the biological, psychological, and social factors that provide interactive bases of ontogenetic progression (Schneirla, 1957). Gottlieb

(1970) labeled this view as "probabilistic epigenetic." He used the term *probabilistic epigenesis* to indicate that individual behavioral development is not invariant or inevitable. Instead,

> the sequence or outcome of individual behavioral development is probable (with respect to norms) rather than certain [because] probabilistic epigenesis necessitates a bidirectional structure-function hypothesis. The conventional version of the structure-function hypothesis is unidirectional in the sense that structure is supposed to determine function in an essentially nonreciprocal relationship. . . . The bidirectional version of the structure-function relationship is a logical consequence of the view that the course and outcome of behavioral epigenesis is probabilistic: It entails the assumption of reciprocal effects in the relationship between structure and function whereby function (exposure to stimulation and/or movement of musculoskeletal activity) can significantly modify the development of the peripheral and central structures that are involved in these events. (Gottlieb, 1970, p. 123)

This probabilistic–epigenetic view is termed, within the field of life-span developmental psychology, developmental contextualism (Lerner, 1986). Within this conception of development, variables from biological, psychological, and social-contextual levels of analysis bidirectionally interact to provide the bases of behavior and development. It is important to stress that, in this literature, levels are conceived of as integrative organizations, and equally essential for the purpose of scientific analysis are both the isolation of parts of a whole and their integration into the structure of the whole. If the course of human development is the product of the processes involved in the "dynamic interactions" (Lerner, 1984) among integrative levels, then the processes of development are more plastic than was often previously believed (Brim & Kagan, 1980).

This developmental–contextual view of development provides the theoretical underpinning of the life-span view of human development (Lerner, 1986). This particular organismic–contextual view constitutes a new intellectual agenda of developmental psychology because this conception of human development "differs from most Western contemporary thought on the subject" (Brim & Kagan, 1980, p. 1) and as such redirects "the burden of proof to those who hold more static, deterministic views" (Sherrod & Brim, 1986, p. 575)—that is, predetermined epigenetic conceptions.

Nevertheless, such redirection does not obviate the need to demonstrate the empirical utility of models or hypotheses derived from developmental–contextual views of biopsychosocial interactions. In point of fact, there *is* a quite extensive literature presenting such empirical support (for reviews of this literature, see Hetherington, Lerner, & Perlmutter, 1988; Sorensen, Weinert, & Sherrod, 1986). Review of this literature in general is not appropriate for this chapter. However, one area of supportive research is an appropriate focus— namely, research on the role of characteristics of bodily individuality (body build and physical attractiveness) and body image in psychosocial development. This research tests a model of person–context relations associated with the developmental–contextual perspective: The goodness-of-fit model. Tests of this model provide support for the dual role of body image stressed in developmental contextualism—that is, body image as a product *and* as a producer of the person's psychosocial development. We turn now to a discussion of this literature.

THE GOODNESS-OF-FIT MODEL

All people have significant characteristics of individuality (Lerner, 1984). Moreover, the context surrounding each person is unique as well (Bronfenbrenner, 1979; Lerner, 1987; Schneirla, 1957). In other words, each person and his/her context are individually distinct as a consequence of the unique combination of genotypic and phenotypic features of that person and of the specific attributes of his/her context. The presence of such individuality is central to understanding the goodness-of-fit model. As a consequence of characteristics of physical individuality (for example, body build or physical attractiveness) and of psychological individuality (for instance, behavioral style or temperament), people elicit differential reactions in their socializing with others. These reactions may feed back to people, increase the individuality of their developmental milieu, and provide a basis for their further development. Schneirla (1957) termed these relations "circular functions." It is through the establishment of such functions in ontogeny that people may be conceived of as producers of their own development (Lerner, 1982). However, this idea of circular functions needs to be extended. In and of itself, the notion is mute regarding the specific characteristics of the feedback, such as its positive or negative valence, that a person will receive as a consequence of his/her individuality. What may provide a basis for the feedback?

Just as a person brings his/her singular characteristics to a particular social setting, there are specific demands that are placed on the person by virtue of the physical and/or social (significant others) components in the setting (Lerner & Lerner, 1987). Such demands provide the functional significance for a given characteristic of individuality; if congruent with the demands of a significant other (such as a peer or parent), this characteristic should produce a positive adjustment or adaptation. If that same attribute is incongruent with such demands, a negative adjustment is expected.

To illustrate, consider the case of the child in his/her family context and of the psychosocial and physical climate promoted by the parents. Parents can vary in their cognitive and behavioral attributes (for example, in their child-rearing attitudes and parenting styles; Baumrind, 1971); they can vary, too, in the physical features of the home they provide. These parent-based psychosocial and physical characteristics constitute presses for, or demands on, the child for adaptation. Simply put, parental characteristics are "translated" or "transduced" into demands on the child.

First, these demands may take the form of attitudes, values, or expectations held by parents (or, in other contexts, by teachers or peers) regarding the person's physical or behavioral characteristics. Second, demands exist as a consequence of the behavioral attributes of parents (or, again, of teachers or peers); these people are significant others with whom the individual must coordinate, or fit, his/her behavioral attributes in order for adaptive interactions to exist. Third, the physical characteristics of a setting (such as the noise level of the home or the presence or absence of access ramps for people with motor disabilities) constitute contextual demands. Such physical presses require the person to possess certain behavioral attributes in order for the most efficient interaction within the setting to occur.

The person's individuality in differentially meeting these demands provides a basis for the feedback he/she gets from the socializing environment. For example, considering the demand "domain" of attitudes, values, and expectations, parents and peers may have relatively distinct ideas about the physical appearance desired of their children or friends, respectively. Parents may want their children to be dressed in one style of clothes and/or to wear their hair in a particular way. Parents' preferences may be quite distinct from those found among peers, however, who may maintain ideas about what is fashionable in clothes and attractive in hair style that differ dramatically from those of parents. Children whose dress and appearance meet with parental approval might be unable to obtain such evaluations from peers. Simply, problems of adjustment to peer demands or to those of parents might develop as a consequence of a child's lack of match, or "goodness of fit," in either or both settings.

TESTS OF THE GOODNESS-OF-FIT MODEL

Over 15 years ago the first author and his colleagues initiated a line of research pertinent to the circular-functions, goodness-of-fit ideas outlined earlier. The idea was to explore the role of children's and adolescents' characteristics of physical individuality and their body images in providing a basis of their psychosocial development.

To provide support for the goodness-of-fit model, several links between characteristics of physical individuality and the social context had to be established. First, we had to demonstrate that there existed distinct sets of expectations, demands, or evaluations pertinent to different characteristics of individuality. Second, we had to demonstrate that adolescents whose characteristics of physical individuality fulfilled these expectations (met these demands, or received favorable evaluations) were also accorded social feedback consistent with these appraisals. Of course, we also had to establish that adolescents whose characteristics did *not* match these social appraisals received feedback consistent with their mismatch. Finally, we had to establish that the different adolescents developed body images and had characteristics of psychosocial development consistent with their respective types of feedback. We have provided some support for all three of these elements.

Social Appraisals of Different Body Types

We initially operationalized our concern with the role of physical individuality by a focus on variations in body type, or somatotype. We used Sheldon's (1940, 1942) terms of *endomorph, mesomorph*, and *ectomorph* to denote body types that are essentially fat or chubby, muscular or average, and thin or linear, respectively. We conducted a series of studies to discover (1) whether general, stereotypic appraisals exist for children and adolescents possessing one of these body types; (2) whether the age of the target person possessing the body type moderates the attributions made about him/her; (3) whether characteristics of the person giving the attribution (e.g., age, sex, or own body type) significantly moderate the nature of the attributions made; and (d) whether membership in a different cultural or national context affects attributions.

A series of studies (Iwawaki & Lerner, 1974, 1976; Lerner 1969a, 1969b, 1971; Lerner & Iwawaki, 1975; Lerner & Korn, 1972; Lerner & Pool, 1972; Lerner & Schroeder, 1971a, 1971b) demonstrated that highly positive stereotypes exist for children and adolescents possessing a mesomorphic body type; that markedly negative stereotypes exist for endomorphic children and adolescents; and that somewhat less unfavorable but still essentially negative stereotypes exist in regard to those having an ectomorphic body build. Moreover, the nature and strength of these stereotypes do *not* vary substantially as a function of (1) age of the person possessing the body type (e.g., the same sets of attributions were made with respect to drawings representing 5- , 15- , and 20-year-old endomorphs, mesomorphs, and ectomorphs); (2) age of the person making the attributions (e.g., 5- through 20-year-olds have essentially the same stereotypes regarding the three body builds); (3) body type of the attributor (e.g., chubby early adolescents have the same negative stereotypes about endomorphs as do average-build or thin early adolescents); (4) sex of the attributor; and (5) cultural membership of the attributor (i.e., Mexican and Japanese male and female children and adolescents have body-build stereotypes that are essentially identical to those maintained by their American counterparts).

Social Interactions

Do male and female children and adolescents who possess different body types receive feedback from their male and female peers that is consistent with these stereotypes? Several data sets we have gathered suggest that the answer is "yes." Using sociometric procedures we have found that as early as in kindergarten chubby and thin children receive fewer positive peer nominations (e.g., "who would you choose as leader?") and more negative nominations (e.g., "who is left out of games?") than is the case with average-build children (Lerner & Geller, 1969; Lerner & Schroeder, 1971b). Moreover, it appears that from middle childhood through early adolescence, different degrees of interpersonal distance, or personal space, are shown toward fat, average, and thin male and female children and early adolescents by their male and female peers.

Differences in personal space usage (in laboratory analogs) among children and adolescents are indicative of differences in the type or quality of their social relationships. Children use most personal space toward drawings representing chubby male and female age peers, least space toward average-build peer stimuli, and a level of space intermediate between these two extremes toward ectomorphic peer stimuli (Lerner, 1973; Lerner, Karabenick, & Meisels, 1975a; Lerner, Venning, & Knapp, 1975). These differences in personal space use remain stable over the course of one year (Lerner, Karabenick, & Meisels, 1975b). In addition, they have been replicated among Japanese kindergarteners through sixth graders (Iwawaki, Lerner, & Chihara, 1977; Lerner, Iwawaki, & Chihara, 1976).

Variations in body type are related to individual differences in physical attractiveness, with endomorphic and ectomorphic physiques generally being regarded as less attractive than other body types (e.g., mesomorphy, for males, and mesoectomorphy, for females; e.g., Lerner, 1969a; Staffieri, 1967, 1972). The different social behaviors expressed toward persons varying in body type may be just an instance, then, of different social reactions toward people differing in physical attractiveness. For example, data presented by Benson, Karabenick, and Lerner (1976) support this idea. Studying the incidence of helping behavior given by travelers in a large, metropolitan airport to strangers in need of assistance, Benson et al. (1976) found that both male and female adult travelers were significantly more likely to help physically attractive males and females than physically unattractive males and females. Indeed, as Cash summarizes in Chapter 3 of this volume, physical attractiveness exerts a powerful influence on a variety of social behaviors.

In sum, individual differences in bodily appearance are linked both to differing social appraisals and to differing social behaviors. The above-described data indicate support for the presence of the social-stimulus and social-feedback components of the circular-function concept. Do data exist as well to support the third component of this concept? In other words, do children and adolescents with differing bodily appearances show evidence of differential body-image development and enduring psychosocial functioning consistent with such stereotype-based social feedback? Again, the answer seems to be "yes." Let us now turn to evidence on this question.

Body Image and Psychosocial Development

Lerner and Korn (1972) found that the body images and self-concepts of chubby 5- , 15- , and 20-year-old males were more negative than those of peers with average builds. Similarly, other studies have indicated that those male and female late adolescents who see their bodily characteristics as less interpersonally attractive, or less instrumentally effective, have lower self-esteem than is the case for late-adolescent males and females whose body images are more favorable (i.e., self-perceived as more attractive and effective; Lerner & Brackney, 1978; Lerner & Karabenick, 1974; Lerner, Karabenick, & Stuart, 1973; Lerner, Orlos, & Knapp, 1976; Padin, Lerner, & Spiro, 1981). These relations among body image (i.e., specifically, self-perceived body attractiveness and body effectiveness) and self-esteem have been replicated among the Japanese ranging in grade level from seventh grade through the senior year of college (Lerner, Iwawaki, Chihara, & Sorell, 1980).

Moreover, these data linking body image and self-esteem are consistent with the idea noted above that findings relating individual differences in body type to social-context appraisal and feedback are just instances of a more general relation between individual differences in physical attractiveness and the social context. Indeed, Berscheid and Walster (1974) have suggested such a correspondence and, in addition, have demonstrated that there exists in American society a "what is beautiful is good" stereotype. Their research, as well as that of others (e.g., Dion, 1973; Langlois & Stephan, 1981; Mussen & Jones, 1957; Richardson, 1971), also documents that, consistent with such a physical attractiveness stereotype, children and adolescents receive differential feedback based on their characteristics of physical individuality—whether facial or somatotypic. Furthermore, such feedback is linked to differential psychological development (e.g., self-esteem) and social development (e.g., popularity, interpersonal aggression). Our own research also illustrates such relationships.

Lerner and Lerner (1977) studied two groups of early adolescents, fourth- and sixth-grade males and females. Each adolescent posed for a standard photographic slide, and from these slides a group of college students rated the fourth- and sixth-graders' facial physical attractiveness. The teachers of the early adolescents rated them in regard to their academic ability and school adjustment, and the adolescents' actual grades in that school year, as well as in the two preceding years, were obtained. In addition, the adolescents responded to a standard measure of personal and social adjustment, and their classroom peers provided sociometric ratings of each adolescent's negative and positive relationships. As compared to their physically attractive classmates, the physically unattractive male and female early adolescents had fewer positive peer relations, more negative peer relations, were judged by teachers as less able and adjusted, and actually scored lower on the standardized adjustment test. In addition, in both their present classes and in their classes of the two preceding years, the physically unattractive male and female early adolescents had lower grades than their physically attractive peers.

These results are consistent with those found with the students studied by Lerner and Lerner in the Pennsylvania Early Adolescent Transitions Study

(PEATS), a short-term longitudinal study of approximately 150 early adolescents, from the beginning of sixth grade across the transition to junior high school and the end of seventh grade (Lerner, 1987). In one study of the PEATS subjects, Lenerz and colleagues (1987) found that, as in past research, physically attractive males and females had more positive peer relations and fewer negative peer relations with both their male and female classmates than did physically unattractive males and females. In addition, parents of the physically unattractive early adolescent reported more problem behaviors in their children than did parents of the physically attractive early adolescents. Moreover, physically unattractive early adolescents perceived themselves to have more conduct and behavior problems than did physically attractive early adolescents. Finally, the classroom teachers of the early adolescents rated physically attractive students as more scholastically, socially, and athletically competent, and as more attractive, than physically unattractive students.

Similarly, Lerner, Delaney, Hess, Jovanovic, and von Eye (1990) found that the circular-functions component of the goodness-of-fit model was supported in regard to academic achievement. Based on the presence of a "what is beautiful is good" stereotype (Langlois, 1986), teachers were expected to differentially evaluate adolescents who differed in their physical attractiveness. These differential evaluations were expected to influence the achievements of adolescents as well as their self-evaluated academic competence. These self-perceptions, in turn, were expected to influence achievement. In both cases, however, it was expected that these indirect paths between attractiveness and achievement would be significant whereas the direct paths would not. The results of Lerner et al. (1990) confirm these expectations with respect to two indexes of achievement—grade point average (GPA) and scores on a standardized achievement test—at the beginning, middle, and end of sixth grade. Thus, these results underscore the importance of individual differences in physical attractiveness for social interactions and ensuing psychosocial developments.

Moreover, related data from the PEATS indicate further the importance of body image for these developments. Jovanovic, Lerner, and Lerner (1989) assessed how objective physical attractiveness (indexed by appraisals from others) and body image (operationalized by the adolescent's subjective view of his/her own appearance) related to each other *and* to the early adolescent's adjustment (indexed by self-esteem and anxiety). Results indicated that only low relations existed between either of two measures of objective attractiveness and body image. More importantly, however, self-appraised body image ratings of the adolescents were significantly associated with the two indices of adjustment. In essence then, within the PEATS, as in our prior research, the social appraisals and feedback linked to physical appearance are associated with linkages between body image and psychosocial functioning. Such relationships underscore the central role of physical appearance and body image in the person's development.

In sum, what this research literature suggests is consistent with the idea that, by "bringing" different physical characteristics to a situation, children and adolescents may affect how others react and provide feedback to them. This feedback may be linked to differential body-image development and psychosocial functioning. Indeed, the support for these relations found in our data may be derived as well from findings from other laboratories. For example, the well-documented links between differences in timing of maturation and psychosocial development (Jones & Bayley, 1950; Mussen & Jones, 1957; Tobin-Richards, Boxer, McNeill-Kavrell, & Petersen, 1984), and the sex differences found in regard to these links, may be accounted for in part by the fact that early, on-time, and late maturers "bring" to social situations body types that match, to differing degrees, desired male and female physiques. Early-maturing males tend to possess the positively stereotyped mesomorph physique, whereas late-maturing males tend to have less favorably stereotyped, primarily ectomorphic, physiques (Tanner, 1962). In contrast, the early-maturing female possesses, at least in early adolescence, the least favorably viewed body type (Lerner & Spanier, 1980; Staffieri, 1967), whereas the on-time maturing female has the most socially favored physique.

It is our view then, that when our data pertinent to the presence of this circular function between individual's physical characteristics and the social context are integrated with the longitudinal data from other laboratories (Brooks-Gunn & Ruble, 1980, 1982, 1983; Jones & Bayley, 1950; Mussen & Jones, 1957; Petersen, 1983; Tobin-Richards et al., 1983, 1984), the results collectively support the idea that people's physical characteristics may provide a source of their own body-image and psychosocial development by either matching or not matching the physicalistic stereotypes of their social context.

Moreover, physical characteristics other than body type, such as sex or race, may also be centrally involved in adolescents' contributions to their own development; these attributions may function in accordance with the goodness-of-fit model. For example, Kagan and Moss (1962) found that personality characteristics showing continuity from birth to maturity were those consistent with traditional sex-role stereotypes. Similarly, Jones and Haney (1981) indicated that race serves as a physical attribute channeling people along different developmental pathways. In addition, Busch-Rossnagel (1981) reviewed data indicating that physical disabilities lead to handicaps as a consequence of the poor fit between disabled persons and the demands of their social context. This evidence is consistent with Shontz's arguments in Chapter 7 of this volume—that contextual (social–environmental) factors are paramount in understanding adjustment to physical disability. Thus, there may be several physical organismic attributes that, alone and in interaction, serve to shape (through circular functions) a person's body image and act to challenge his/her development in a manner consistent with the goodness-of-fit model. This observation leads us to some more general conclusions.

CONCLUSIONS

Given the support for the developmental–contextual, goodness-of-fit model, as well as the support found in other studies from our laboratory (see J. Lerner, 1984; Lerner & Lerner, 1987), let us make some final statements regarding the developmental–contextual view of the role of body image in a person's psychosocial development across the life span. The concepts of biology, of context, and of the relations between the two found in a developmental–contextual perspective are, as a set, quite complex; they impose formidable challenges on those who seek to derive feasible research from this perspective. Nevertheless, this perspective leads to an integrated, multilevel concept of development in which the focus of inquiry is the person–environment dynamic interaction. Furthermore, such an orientation emphasizes the potential for intraindividual change in structure and function—that is, for plasticity across the life span.

The data reviewed here, as well as those derived from other laboratories (for reviews, see Hetherington, Lerner, & Perlmutter, 1988; Sorensen, Weinert, & Sherrod, 1986), underscore the current use of a life-span, developmental–contextual orientation. The future challenge for this perspective is the further derivation and empirical testing of models reflecting the nature of dynamic, interlevel interactions across time. Such tests will profit by triangulation of the constructs within each level of analysis thought to dynamically interact within a given model.

For instance, in regard to moving beyond our PEATS research and providing further tests of the goodness-of-fit model within early adolescence, bodily attributes could be simultaneously indexed both by molecular, hormonal variables, by anthropometric indices, and by more molar, bodily appearance measures. Not only would such triangulation provide convergent and discriminant validation information but also better insight into whether all modalities of functioning within a level of analysis are of similar import for adaptive functioning in particular person–context interactions. For example, perhaps because of the power of age-graded expectations regarding early adolescent social (and, particularly, heterosexual) behavior, hormonal changes are less important in the young person's interactions with peers and adults than are external, bodily appearance variables—variables that may make a person look older to significant others (Lerner, 1987). Indeed, Cash, Winstead, and Janda (1986) reported U.S. survey data that adolescents place more importance on appearance and have a more negative body image than persons in older groups.

Although there is some evidence to support this particular example of age-graded dating behavior in adolescence (Dornbusch et al., 1981), this particular data set is not developmental. Its existence—rather than obviating the need for further triangulation efforts—underscores the importance of such work. Moreover, the standard incorporation of multiple measures into future research is important, not only because of the new information it would provide about the developmental–contextual model but also because this information would provide insight into the most useful targets of interventions for enhancing the social behavior of the developing person.

One reasonably successful path we have taken in exploring the usefulness of a developmental–contextual perspective for understanding the role of body image in psychosocial development involves the testing of the goodness-of-fit model of person–context relations. Our own work would profit from the sort of triangulation that we call for. Furthermore, our work has focused primarily on the childhood and adolescent portions of the life span. In principle, the model we test can be deployed over the life course. Indeed, reviews of the literature extending into the adult years (e.g., Sorell & Nowak, 1981) suggest its usefulness across the life span. Future empirical work should directly test the use of the goodness-of-fit model in aiding understanding of the role of body image in the adult and aged years—especially in view of Harter's (in press) work that underscores the life-span importance of self-perceived appearance in feelings of self-worth. That is, Harter demonstrates that several domains of self-conceptions exist at successive portions of the life span. However, she finds that self-perceptions pertinent to physical appearance invariably account for the major proportion of the variance in feelings of general self-worth or self-esteem. Given that these self-perceptions may be regarded as integral to body-image, future research should investigate the functional significance of these perceptions across the adult and aged years. Representative issues to be addressed would be the covariants of body image in successive portions of these periods of life and the significance of individual differences in body image for continued physical and mental health and for social engagement and participation.

Of course the goodness-of-fit model is not the only conception of person–context relations that may be derived from a developmental–contextual orientation. There are perhaps an infinite number of possible interlevel relations that may occur and a potentially large array of ways to model them. Indeed, since current tests of other models derived from this orientation have found considerable empirical support (Baltes, 1987), we can expect that such extensions will be important additions to an already significant foundation.

In sum, the relative plasticity of human development across the life span—a plasticity deriving from the dynamic interactions between organism and context that characterize human functioning—is already well documented (Baltes, 1987; Brim & Kagan, 1980; Featherman, 1983; Hetherington, Lerner, & Perlmutter, 1988; R. Lerner, 1984; Sorensen, Weinert, & Sherrod, 1986). Given the present literature and the promise we see for tomorrow, we believe that there is reason for great optimism about the future scientific use of the developmental–contextual, goodness-of-fit model to understand the role of bodily attributes and body images in psychosocial development across the life span.

Acknowledgments.   The preparation of this manuscript was partially funded by grants to Richard M. Lerner and Jacqueline V. Lerner from the William T. Grant Foundation, from NIMH Grant MH3995, and from NICHD Grant HD23229.

REFERENCES

Baltes, P. B. (1987). Theoretical propositions of life-span developmental psychology: On the dynamics between growth and decline. *Developmental Psychology, 23*, 611–626.

Baumrind, D. (1971). Current patterns of parental authority. *Developmental Psychology Monographs, 4*, (No. 1, Part 2).

Benson, P. L., Karabenick, S. A., & Lerner, R. M. (1976). Pretty pleases: The effects of physical attractiveness, race, and sex on receiving help. *Journal of Experimental Social Psychology, 12*, 409–415.

Berscheid, E., & Walster, E. (1974). Physical attractiveness. In L. Berkowitz (Ed.), *Advances in experimental social psychology* (Vol. 7, pp. 157–215). New York: Academic Press.

Bijou, S. W. (1976). *Child development: The basic stage of early childhood.* Englewood Cliffs, NJ: Prentice-Hall.

Brim, O. J., Jr., & Kagan, J. (Eds.). (1980). *Constancy and change in human development.* Cambridge: Harvard University Press.

Bronfenbrenner, U. (1979). *The ecology of human development.* Cambridge: Harvard University Press.

Brooks-Gunn, J., & Ruble, D. N. (1980). Menarche: The interaction of physiology, cultural, and social factors. In A. J. Dan, E. A. Graham, & C. P. Beecher (Eds.), *The menstrual cycle: A synthesis of interdisciplinary research* (pp. 141–159). New York: Springer.

Brooks-Gunn, J., & Ruble, D. N. (1982). The development of menstrual-related beliefs and behaviors during early adolescence. *Child Development, 53*, 1567–1577.

Brooks-Gunn, J., & Ruble, D. N. (1983). The experience of menarche from a developmental perspective. In J. Brooks-Gunn & A. C. Petersen (Eds.), *Girls at puberty* (pp. 155–177). New York: Plenum Press.

Busch-Rossnagel, N. A. (1981). Where is the handicap in disability? The contextual impact of physical disability. In R. M. Lerner & N. A. Busch-Rossnagel (Eds.), *Individuals as producers of their development: A life-span perspective* (pp. 281–312). New York: Academic Press.

Cash, T. F., Winstead, B. A., & Janda, L. H. (1986). The great American shape-up. *Psychology Today, 20*, 30–37.

Cooley, C. H. (1902). *Human nature and the social order.* New York: Charles Schribner's Sons.

Dion, K. (1973). Young children's stereotyping of facial attractiveness. *Developmental Psychology, 9*, 183–188.

Dixon, R. A., & Lerner, R. M. (1988). A history of systems in developmental psychology. In M. H. Bornstein & M. E. Lamb (Eds.), *Developmental Psychology* (2nd ed., pp. 3–50). Hillsdale, NJ: Erlbaum.

Dornbusch, S. M., Carlsmith, J. M., Gross, R. T., Martin, J. A., Rosenberg, A., & Duke, P. (1981). Sexual development, age, and dating: A comparison of biological and social influences upon one set of behaviors. *Child Development, 52*, 179–185.

Erikson, E. H. (1959). Identity and the life-cycle. *Psychological Issues, 1*, 18–164.

Erikson, E. H. (1968). *Identity, youth and crisis.* New York: Norton.

Featherman, D. L. (1983). Life-span perspectives in social science research. In P. B. Baltes &

O. G. Brim, Jr. (Eds.), *Life-span development and behavior* (Vol. 5, pp. 1–57). New York: Academic Press.

Freud, S. (1923). *The ego and the id*. London: Hogarth.

Freud, S. (1949). *Outline of psychoanalysis*. New York: Norton.

Gottlieb, G. (1970). Conceptions of prenatal behavior. In R. Aronson, E. Tobach, D. S. Lehrman, & J. S. Rosenblatt (Eds.), *Development and evolution of behavior: Essays in memory of T. C. Schneirla* (pp. 111–137). San Francisco: Freeman.

Gottleib, G. (1983). The psychobiological approach to developmental issues. In M. M. Haith & J. J. Campos (Eds.), *Handbook of child psychology: Infancy and developmental psychobiology* (4th ed., pp. 1–26). New York: Wiley.

Hall, G. S. (1904). *Adolescence: Its psychology and its relations to physiology, anthropology, sociology, sex, crime, religion, and education* (Vols. 1 & 2). New York: Appleton.

Hamburger, V. (1957). The concept of development in biology. In D. B. Harris (Ed.), *The concept of development* (pp. 49–58). Minneapolis: University of Minnesota Press.

Harris, D. B. (Ed.). (1957). *The concept of development*. Minneapolis: University of Minnesota Press.

Harter, S. (in press). Causes, correlates and the functional role of global self-worth: A life-span perspective. In J. Kolligian & R. Sternberg (Eds.), *Perceptions of competence and incompetence across the life-span*. New Haven, CT: Yale University Press.

Hetherington, E. M., Lerner, R. M., & Perlmutter, M. (Eds.). (1988). *Child development in life span perspective*. Hillsdale, NJ: Erlbaum.

Iwawaki, S., & Lerner, R. M. (1974). Cross-cultural analyses of body-behavior relations: I. A. comparison of body build stereotypes of Japanese and American males and females. *Psychologia, 17,* 75–81.

Iwawaki, S., & Lerner, R. M. (1976). Cross-cultural analyses of body-behavior relations: III. Developmental intra- and inter-cultural factor congruence in the body build stereotypes of Japanese and American males and females. *Psychologia, 20,* 89–97.

Iwawaki, S., Lerner, R. M., & Chihara, T. (1977). Development of personal space schemata among Japanese in late childhood. *Psychologia, 2,* 89–97.

Jones, M. C., & Bayley, N. (1950). Physical maturing as related to behavior. *Journal of Educational Psychology, 41,* 293–313.

Jones, R. T., & Haney, J. I. (1981). A body-behavior conceptualization of a somatopsycho-logical problem: Race. In R. M. Lerner & N. A. Busch-Rossnagel (Eds.), *Individuals as producers of their development: A life-span perspective* (pp. 349–387). New York: Academic Press.

Jovanovic, J., Lerner, R. M., & Lerner, J. V. (1989). Objective and subjective attractiveness and early adolescent adjustment. *Journal of Adolescence, 12,* 225–229.

Kagan, J., & Moss, H. (1962). *Birth to maturity*. New York: Wiley.

Langlois, J. H. (1986). From the eye of the beholder to behavioral reality: The development of social behaviors and social relations as a function of physical attractiveness. In C. P. Herman (Ed.), *Physical appearance, stigma, and social behavior: The Ontario Symposium on Personality and Social Psychology* (pp. 23–51). Hillsdale, NJ: Erlbaum.

Langlois, J. H., & Stephan, C. W. (1981). Beauty and the beast: The role of physical attraction in peer relationships and social behavior. In S. S. Brehm, S. M. Kassin, & S. X. Gibbons (Eds.), *Developmental social psychology: Theory and research* (pp. 152–168). New York: Oxford University Press.

Lenerz, K., Kucher, J. S., East, P. L., Lerner, J. V., & Lerner, R. M. (1987). Early adolescents' organismic physical characteristics and psychosocial functioning: Findings from the Pennsylvania Early Adolescent Transitions Study (PEATS). In R. M. Lerner & T. T. Foch (Eds.), *Biological-psychosocial interaction in early adolescence: A life-span perspective* (pp. 225–247). Hillsdale, NJ: Erlbaum.

Lerner, J. V. (1984). The import of temperament for psychosocial functioning: Tests of a "goodness of fit" model. *Merrill-Palmer Quarterly, 30*, 177–188.

Lerner, R. M. (1969a). The development of stereotyped expectancies of body build-behavior relations. *Child Development, 40*, 137–141.

Lerner, R. M. (1969b). Some female stereotypes of male body build-behavior relations. *Perceptual and Motor Skills, 28*, 363–366.

Lerner, R. M. (1971). "Richness" analyses of body build stereotype development. *Developmental Psychology, 7*, 219.

Lerner, R. M. (1973). The development of personal space schemata toward body build. *Journal of Psychology, 84*, 229–235.

Lerner, R. M. (1982). Children and adolescents as producers of their own development. *Developmental Review, 2*, 342–370.

Lerner, R. M. (1984). *On the nature of human plasticity.* New York: Cambridge University Press.

Lerner, R. M. (1986). *Concepts and theories of human development* (2nd ed.). New York: Random House.

Lerner, R. M. (1987). A life-span perspective for early adolescence. In R. M. Lerner & T. T. Foch (Eds.), *Biological–psychosocial interactions in early adolescence: A life-span perspective* (pp. 1–6). Hillsdale, NJ: Erlbaum.

Lerner, R. M., & Brackney, B. (1978). The importance of inner and outer body parts attitudes in the self-concept of late adolescents. *Sex Roles, 4*, 225–238.

Lerner, R. M., Delaney, M., Hess, L. E., Jovanovic, J., & von Eye, A. (1990). Early adolescent physical attractiveness and academic competence. *Journal of Early Adolscence, 10*, 4–20.

Lerner, R. M., & Gellert, E. (1969). Body build identification, preference, and aversion in children. *Developmental Psychology, 1*, 456–462.

Lerner R. M., & Iwawaki, S. (1975). Cross-cultural analyses of body-behavior relations: II. Factor structure of body build stereotypes of Japanese and American adolescents. *Psychologia, 18*, 83–91.

Lerner, R. M., Iwawaki, S., & Chihara, T. (1976). Development of personal space schemata among Japanese children. *Developmental Psychology, 12*, 466–467.

Lerner, R. M., Iwawaki, S., Chihara, T., & Sorell, G. T. (1980). Self-concept, self-esteem, and body attitudes among Japanese male and female adolescents. *Child Development, 51*. 847–855.

Lerner, R. M., & Karabenick, S. A. (1974). Physical attractiveness, body attitudes, and self-concept in late adolescents. *Journal of Youth and Adolescence, 3*, 307–316.

Lerner, R. M., Karabenick, S. A., & Meisels, M. (1975a). Effects of age and sex on the development of personal space schemata towards body build. *Journal of Genetic Psychology, 127*, 151–152.

Lerner, R. M., Karabenick, S. A., & Meisels, M. (1975b). One-year stability of children's personal space schemata towards body build. *Journal of Genetic Psychology, 127*, 151–152.

Lerner, R. M., Karabenick, S. A., & Stuart, J. L. (1973). Relations among physical attractiveness, body attitudes, and self-concept in male and female college students. *Journal of Psychology, 85*, 119–129.

Lerner, R. M., & Kauffman, M. B. (1985). The concept of development in contextualism. *Developmental Review, 5*, 309–333.

Lerner, R. M., & Korn, S. J. (1972). The development of body build stereotypes in males. *Child Development, 43*, 912–920.

Lerner, R. M., & Lerner, J. V. (1977). Effects of age, sex, and physical attractiveness on child-peer relations, academic performance, and elementary school adjustment. *Developmental Psychology, 13*, 585–590.

Lerner, R. M., & Lerner, J. V. (1987). Children in their contexts: A goodness of fit model. In J. B. Lancaster, J. Altmann, A. S. Rossi, & L. R. Sherrod (Eds.), *Parenting across the life span: Biosocial dimensions* (pp. 377–404). Chicago: Aldine.

Lerner, R. M., Orlos, J. B., & Knapp, J. R. (1976). Physical attractiveness, physical effectiveness, and self-concept in late adolescents. *Adolescence, 11*, 313–326.

Lerner, R. M., & Pool, K. B. (1972). Body build stereotypes: A cross-cultural comparison. *Psychological Reports, 31*. 527–532.

Lerner, R. M., & Schroeder, C. (1971a). Kindergarten children's active vocabulary about body build. *Developmental Psychology, 5*, 179.

Lerner, R. M., & Schroeder, C. (1971b). Physique identification, preference, and aversion in kindergarten children. *Developmental Psychology, 5*, 538.

Lerner, R. M., & Spanier, G. B. (1980). *Adolescent development: A life-span perspective*. New York: McGraw-Hill.

Lerner, R. M., Venning, J., & Knapp, J. R. (1975). Age and sex effects on personal space schemata towards body build in late childhood. *Developmental Psychology, 11*, 855–856.

Mead, G. H. (1934). *Mind, self, and society*. Chicago: University of Chicago Press.

Mussen, P. H., & Jones, M. C. (1957). Self-conceptions, motivations, and interpersonal attitudes of late- and early-maturing boys. *Child Development, 28*, 249–256.

Novikoff, A. B. (1945). The concept of integrative levels of biology. *Science, 62*, 209–215.

Padin, M. A., Lerner, R. M., & Spiro, A., III. (1981). The role of physical education interventions in the stability of body attitudes and self-esteem in late adolescents. *Adolescence, 16*, 371–384.

Petersen, A. C. (1983). Pubertal change and cognition. In J. Brooks-Gunn & A. C. Petersen (Eds.), *Girls at puberty* (pp. 179–197). New York: Plenum Press.

Piaget, J. (1950). *The psychology of intelligence*. New York: Harcourt Brace.

Piaget, J. (1970). Piaget's theory. In P. H. Mussen (Ed.), *Carmichael's manual of child psychology* (Vol. 1, pp. 703–732). New York: Wiley.

Reese, H. W., & Overton, W. F. (1970). Models of development and theories of development. In L. R. Goulet & P. B. Baltes (Eds.), *Life-span developmental psychology: Research and theory* (pp. 115–145). New York: Academic Press.

Richardson, S. A. (1971). Handicap, appearance and stigma. *Social Science and Medicine, 5*, 621–628.

Schneirla, T. C. (1957). The concept of development in comparative psychology. In D. B. Harris (Ed.), *The concept of development* (pp. 78–108). Minneapolis: University of Minnesota Press.

Sheldon, W. H. (1940). *The varieties of human physique*. New York: Harper.

Sheldon, W. H. (1942). *The varieties of temperament*. New York: Harper.

Sherrod, L. R., & Brim, O. G., Jr. (1986). Epilogue: Retrospective and prospective views of life-course research in human development. In A. B. Sorensen, F. E. Weinert, & L. R. Sherrod (Eds.), *Human development and the life course: Multidisciplinary perspectives* (pp. 557–580). Hillsdale, NJ: Erlbaum.

Sorel, G. T., & Nowak, C. A. (1981). The role of physical attractiveness as a contributor to individual development. In R. M. Lerner & N.A. Busch-Rossnagel (Eds.), *Individuals as producers of their development: A life-span perspective* (pp. 389–446). New York: Academic Press.

Sorensen, S., Weinert, E., & Sherrod, L. R. (Eds.). (1986). *Human development and the life course: Multidisciplinary perspectives*. Hillsdale, NJ: Erlbaum.

Staffieri, J. R. (1967). A study of social stereotype of body-image in children. *Journal of Personality and Social Psychology, 7*, 101–104.

Staffieri, J. R. (1972). Body build and behavioral expectancies in young females. *Developmental Psychology, 6*, 125–127.

Tanner, J. M. (1962). *Growth at adolescence*. Springfield, IL: Charles C. Thomas.

Tobach, E., & Greenberg, G. (1984). The significance of T. C. Schneirla's contribution to the concept of levels of integration. In G. Greenberg & E. Tobach (Eds.), *Behavioral evolution and integrative levels* (pp. 1–7). Hillsdale, NJ: Erlbaum.

Tobin-Richards, M. H., Boxer, A. M., & Petersen, A. C. (1983). The psychological significance of pubertal change: Sex differences in perceptions of self during early adolescence. In J. Brooks-Gunn & A. C. Petersen (Eds.), *Girls at puberty* (pp. 127–154). New York: Plenum Press.

Tobin-Richards, M. H., Boxer, A. M. McNeill-Karvell, S. A A., & Petersen, A. C. (1984). Puberty and its psychological and social significance. In R. M. Lerner & N. L. Galambos (Eds.), *Experiencing adolescents: A sourcebook for parents, teachers, and teens* (pp. 17–50). New York: Garland.

White, S. H. (1968). The learning-maturation controversy: Hall to Hull. *Merrill-Palmer Quarterly, 14*, 187–196.

PART III

DIVERGENCE AND DYSFUNCTION
OF BODY IMAGES

CHAPTER 6

Objective Bodily Damage: Disfigurement and Dignity

Norman R. Bernstein

> While we are locked in a prison of a body we
> perform duties and burdensome tasks from
> which there is no escape. The soul, you see,
> is of heaven . . .   CICERO

THE DESTRUCTION OF PERSONAL VALUE

Relations with other people are the main measures for judging psychological normality and are a fundamental aspect of ordinary living. People with obvious deformities are disadvantaged in their social relations. A disfigured person is forcibly required to give more attention to his/her body image by his/her surroundings. People stare, and people make job determinations and reject persons with facial scars, or those with severe spinal curvatures, shut and blinded eyes, limps, or paralyzed limbs. The public reacts in terms of how upsetting a disfigured person is to them. People spontaneously and quickly flinch away from disfigurements that scare them. The facially handicapped individual, the blind person feeling his/her way on the street with a cane, and the cerebral palsy victim weaving in a tortured manner are strikingly different in the roles they play in society than those of the fully able person. Their lives differ from the way a man or woman of unremarkable appearance moves along without friction in the social swim. If people are deformed, they may be converted into *things*, and treated in an altered manner. The *contents* of an individual who is visibly marred are devalued, and the person has to struggle to avoid being discredited as an object. The very beautiful are also converted into *objects* by onlookers, but they do not share the negative or frightening tone set by deformity.

SOCIAL PSYCHOLOGY OF BODY IMAGE

In a volume on body image it appears gratuitous to redefine the body-image concept, but it is worth noting that the definition used here comes basically from the writing of Schilder (1935). He states that the

131

image of the human body means the picture of our own body which we form in our mind, that is to say the way in which the body appears to ourselves. There are sensations which are given to us. We see parts of the body-surface. We have tactile, thermal, pain impressions. There are sensations which come from the muscles and their sheaths, . . .sensation coming from the innervations of the muscles . . .and sensations coming from the viscera. Beyond that there is the immediate experience that there is a unity of the body . . .we call it schema of our body or bodily schema . . .the body schema is the tridimensional image everybody has about himself. (p. 527)

Van der Velde (1985) suggests the term *extraneous body image*, and he notes that body images determine individual uniqueness.

The present emphasis will be on the sociology of the body image and the "relations between body images," which Schilder expatiated upon, and which authors such as William James (1890) also discussed, particularly in relation to self-esteem. In this regard, the formulations of Shontz (articulated in Chapter 7 of this volume) about the psychological functions of body experience, the body image as an instrument for action, a stimulus to the self, and a stimulus to others are vital interwoven themes. Fisher's (1986) concept of body prominence also is significant here. However, in the present chapter, the largely clinical formulations will not be fitted neatly into these categories. I will employ the literature on self-concept and the formulations of dynamics in psychiatry and social psychology to describe how a visible disfigurement contributes to a distortion of communications among people.

There is a layered quality to each component of the body image. Lawrence Kolb (1975) says that the term *body image* is too broad. He feels that there are *body percepts*, which include the accumulated experiences of the body, as well as the *body concept*, which includes thoughts, feelings, and memories that evolve as the individual ego views and experiences the body. Each individual develops an idealized image of the body, the *body ideal*, against which he/she measures the percepts and concepts held of his/her body. The ego functions to integrate the disparities among these evaluations, which leads to arousal of either dysphoric or pleasurable affects. Horowitz (1970) sees the body-image constellation as having relevance to the origin of all *self-concepts*, and the differentiation of the self from the world as having relevance to the development of relationships.

McDonald Critchley (1965), the eminent British neurologist, quotes Sapir saying that there is an unwritten code but understood by all when we speak about our bodies. Perhaps the most comprehensive way of looking at this is in terms of Burns's (1979) statement that there is lack of agreement over definition of body image and that the encounter between rival approaches in methodology to the study of psychology and the problems of measuring subjective experiential elements all contribute to difficulties in investigation of the important phenomena of body image and self-concept. Learning about what is and what is not the self, through direct experience and perception of the physical world, is the child's first step in the life journey. Burns sees the body image and body schema as part of the basic identity, which then is a major source of the self-concept. Burns also recognizes that the way people speak of their self-concepts and the feedback received from significant others are very important features of the developing concept. From Burns's perspective, self-concept includes, among its multiple contents, one's physical characteristics, clothing, grooming, and makeup, and health and physical condition.

According to Schonfeld (1966), the whole of social and personality adaptation is affected by body shape. It influences the impression a person makes on others and how he/she views him- /herself. The body image, a biopsycho-social phenomenon, embraces our view of ourselves, not only physically but also physiologically, sociologically, and psychologically. It has also been referred to in the literature as self-awareness, self-concept, the self, body ego, self-identity, ego identity, and body schema. In adolescence, the awareness of the self is particularly intensified (Bernstein 1989) because of the radical physical changes that occur, the increase of introspection, the emphasis assigned to physical traits by the peer group, and the increased tendency to compare oneself with culturally determined standards.

Miller (1978) stated:

> of all the objects in the world, the human body has a peculiar status: it is not only possessed by the person who has it, it also possesses and constitutes him. Our body is quite different from all things we claim as our own. We can lose money, books, and even houses, and still remain recognizably ourselves, but it is hard to give any intelligible sense to the idea of a disembodied person. Although we speak of our bodies as premises in which we live, it has a special form of tenancy: our body is where we can always be contacted. Our body is not, in short, something we have. It is a large part of what we actually are: it is by and through our bodies that we recognize our existence in the world, and it is only by being able to move in and act upon the world that we can distinguish it from ourselves. Without a body, it would be difficult to claim sensations and experiences of our own . . .the body is the medium of experience and the instrument of our action. Through its action we shape and organize our experience and distinguish our perceptions of the outside world from the sensations that arise within the body itself. (p. 6)

Fisher (1986) noted that medical procedures or illnesses that heighten concern about body threat or damage intensify bodily awareness. While his work on body prominence documents the frequency with which research subjects refer to their own body, the disfigured are usually scrupulous in social situations not to mention their disfigurement. Some deformed people feel a need to cope actively with the situation and to control the flood of feelings that may occur when questioned. They have a need to tell people "this happened to me in an accident" or otherwise give a simple explanation of the way they look to forestall probing by strangers. *Body awareness* remains permanently a major issue for the disfigured (Bernstein, 1979). This profoundly shapes the construction of the self-concept. Patients with facial disfigurement are aware of their faces and the feedback their deformities cause. They must constantly work to maintain a sense of self-esteem devoid of reliance upon beauty. They lack a culturally valued ingredient that is difficult to define. They are lodged at the end of a continuum, beginning with beauty, passing through attractive, plain, and ugly. Lakoff and Scherr (1984) explain that all beauty concepts are hemmed in by conflicting images, and these ultimately affect reactions to facially marred men and women. In our society, physical attractiveness is defined in all the media. Our values about beauty are so pervasive they are unconsciously taken for granted. Some of the opposing myths and countermyths we entertain are noted by Lakoff and Scherr:

The myth: Beauty is good for us, allied with innocence and virtue.
Countermyth: Beauty is evil and destructive (e.g., Pandora, the sirens, Delilah, Eve, and Helen of Troy). Because beauty is so powerful and arouses in its observer that most peremptory and inexplicable of impulses, sexual desire, it evokes fear.

The myth: Great beauty brings its possessor misery.
Countermyth: Beauty brings bliss and happiness.

The myth: Beauty goes with stupidity.
Countermyth: Beauty goes with brains.

The myth: Beauty is mentally unsettling.
Countermyth: Beauty is serenity and sanity.

The ambivalence demonstrated by these maxims is part of the complex atmosphere facially impaired people live in.

At the other end of the spectrum, *ugliness* comes from the Old Middle English word *uglike*, meaning fearful, dreadful, unsightly, or vile—reflecting the reactions that the public has toward the disfigured and demonstrating how language is flavored by emotional attitudes. So that when we talk about disfigurement, deformity, and cosmetic damage, we actually use antiseptic words, which carry the older connotations of horror and dread that mere plainness or ordinary ugliness do not evoke.

We should understand that disfigurements in psychologically normal individuals stand in marked contrast to self-mutilation that occurs in response to cultural norms or psychological disturbance. If they are meeting cultural standards, persons are not rejected for the nose piercing, head deforming, and other primitive maneuvers they undertake. (See Fallon's Chapter 4 for a discussion of these practices.) If they are self-inflicted, it appears (Favazza, 1987) that they are doing this in response to intense inner tensions, and achieve relief from their anxiety and desperation by cutting themselves. This disturbed group does not appear to be concerned about their appearance. They cannot be compared to the group we ordinarily consider disfigured, and their treatment must be directed at their inner view of themselves and their tensions, rather than at what society has done in reaction to them.

DEVELOPMENT OF SELF-IMAGE IN THE DISFIGURED

Erikson's Life Stages

Erik Erikson's developmental theory provides a useful format for examining the effects of visible facial disfigurement at different phases of life. Erikson's (1982) overall schema for the major stages in psychosocial development is commonly known and is useful as a basis for examining ways in which children develop and react to their disfigurements. Some issues run through development much like a theme in a piece of music. His schema can be helpful in examining the ways in which a child deals with self-esteem injury and the altered body image resulting from visible disfigurement. This framework will also aid our under-standing of disfigurement during adolesence, adulthood, and old age.

In his first stage, basic *trust* in infancy should lead to "psychosocial strength" or hopefulness in the child. Infants with a visible disfigurement are threatened by an early rearing environment in which this important quality may be impaired. For example, such impairment to a child with a port wine stain may engender a general sense of anxiety, sadness, and dejection.

In a later stage, at school age, conflicts over industry versus inferiority are ideally resolved in a feeling of competence, which many stigmatized children don't develop. One little boy with vitiligo, who had been teased relentlessly about the areas of missing pigment in his skin, being called "map, monster, and creeper," was so dejected that the energy for school work was diminished and he performed poorly and had impaired self-confidence (cf. Hill-Beuf & Porter, 1984; Sensky, 1985).

As Harrison (1985) notes, "a body defect can affect self-esteem directly, by causing negative feedback about appearance, and indirectly, by interfering with the developmental process . . .children will focus on a physical attribute as the organizing factor for feelings of defectiveness" (p. 91). If one compares the trajectory of development of a child who is born with a visible defect such as cleft lip, port wine stain, or cranial deformity, with that of a child who has a less visible defect, it is evident that the world does not impinge so directly. A family worries about a heart murmur, but strangers don't stare and question.

Congenital Deformities, Body Image, and Self-Image

In utero tests during pregnancy can often forewarn patients of the defects in a fetus, but still there are children with Downs' syndrome, babies with cleft palate, hemangiomas, and cranial deformity. The child is shaping a self-concept within the context of surroundings changed by the shock, sorrow, paralysis of the deformity. In other words, there is a muting of the normal baby's environment (cf. Drotar, Baskiewicz, Irwin, Kendl, & Klaus, 1975; Fajardo, 1987). There is also concerned medical involvement, and more worry. The happy and easy smiling, holding, and rocking of the child are tainted by woe, guilt, and anger. The emotional tone is sadder, embittered. Body-image development advances in the first few months of life, the time when the disfigured child learns *where* his/her body parts are in space. He/she sits, stands, and learns size and positional sense, and grasps like a normal child. By age 3, a little boy or girl knows if he/she is cute or pretty and is able to charge into any group of adults and get smiles and cooing encouragement. A child's concept of self is shaped by the standards and values that the child evolves and connects in his/her mental world (Kagan, 1984). The defective child is greeted in a different manner, with more worry and a less relaxed atmosphere. A chronically saddened mother of such a toddler, who does all the right things, cannot substitute for remarks about limping or a cleft palate. The tightness in her chest gets communicated by her taut expression to the child, who is deprived of some of the security and contentment typical of normal child development. Roger-Salyer, Jensen, and Borden (1985) reported that mothers of disfigured newborns held and stimulated their children less than mothers of normal children.

Kindergarten and school entry provide other stresses for the child who then begins to participate in the larger social environment and has to deal with reactions from other children and their parents and from teachers. Whether a mother is supportive, loving, protective, or combative with strangers who stare or remark, the child is imprinted with a feeling that something about him/her is different in a negative way (Goffman, 1963). This experience presents a handicap for developing comfortable self-esteem. Comparisons with others add to the problem. Belfer (1985) notes that "while body image is a stable and complex psychological entity, it is not immutable" (p. 103), and he stresses the benefits to be reaped from early surgical improvement of defects. The work on cleft palate has surgically and psychologically proceeded to include earlier and earlier interventions, producing better results in speech and anatomy improvement as well as providing the earliest change back to normal appearance for the child and thereby the best chance to resume the normal pathway of development (Clifford, 1987). The effects of reconstructive surgeries for such facial deformities receive Pertschuk's detailed attention in Chapter 11 of this volume.

The Case of Phil

He was a 40-year-old doctor who had been born with a cleft lip and palate, but had had incomplete results from surgical repair of this and was always teased in his small southern town, where he was called "Rabbit." For infants with this defect, the smiling response is changed. Mother can't enjoy the baby's expression and doesn't respond as positively. Phil was a very good student but initially faced the common prejudice that people with harelip encounter. They are considered, at first glance, by teachers to be of lower intelligence, hence he became very inhibited about the way he expressed himself verbally in class. As he grew older and his intellectual and professional competence was established more clearly, he found other sources for self-esteem, but only when he could grow a mustache to cover his defect did he feel he had "conquered" it. But the residual social shyness continued to plague him long after he had become an established professional. All his statements in medical groups as well as at cocktail parties were shaped by a very careful and ponderous self-consciousness and care to avoid seeming defective, well after he knew this was not the real issue. Phil's habitual lack of confidence can be viewed in relation to Erikson's observations on the process of building confidence in the young child, as a demonstration of a failure to achieve emotional autonomy with a resultant shame and doubt that influences later performance. This man who did so well in one area still felt damaged in another. Lawn (1989) reports that in some situations a disability serves as a "lightening rod" focusing the "characteristic patterns of response" in shocked onlookers.

Personality theorist George A. Kelly (1953) persuasively argued that individuals who may feel mortified about a particular aspect of their body-image or self-esteem system, may still be arrogant or content and competent within another. In his theory, Kelley defines the "fragmentation corollary": A person may successively employ a variety of construction subsystems that are inferentially incompatible with each other, that is, "miniature systems."

Macgregor et al. (1953) pointed out that, for some individuals, a minor physical defect can be as burdensome and damaging to their self-esteem as a major one. Understanding people whose overall self-system is impaired by a small blemish involves realizing the ancient concept of psychological reality versus objective reality! If individuals believe something is stained and ugly about them, it can cause as much harm to their self-confidence as an objective defect (see Kleck & Strenta, 1980). For the cases included in this chapter the defect is visible and real though not always distinguishable in its effects from those people who view themselves as ugly and deformed but have no anatomical defect.

EARLY AND ABRUPTLY ACQUIRED DISFIGUREMENT

Burn disfigurement accounts for an increasing number of visibly disfigured individuals. The burn patient is usually a physically normal person who has established a good self-system that is abruptly altered by a major accident. The person experiences life-endangering agony in a hospital emergency ward, a busy medical intensive care setting. He/she suffers horrifying agony, isolation, confusion, manipulation, and multiple incomprehensible procedures. Then, in a few weeks, he/she must awaken to a necessary transformation into a very different kind of person, thrust into the sick role, aberrant in appearance, dependent upon others, and unsure of what his/her future means. Certainly no longer able to reply on a pleasant image of his/her body or the certainty of competence of bodily resources. Fingers are stiffened by burns. Scars contract. Eating is more difficult. Exposure to the sun is dangerous. Infections and multiple wound revisions and the pain and work of occupational therapy involve the patient for many months. In the midst of all of this, the burn patient will usually state that the worst of it all is "The way I look!" This transformation from unremarkable appearance to one that is frightful and horrifying is abrupt. But the psychological adaptations that must follow are not as quick. There is a shock phase, a period of depression, gradual inventory of personal resources, and moving forward—to cope and to find people who stand by, people who aren't frightened, and people who are still able to react to the burn disfigured individual in terms of the person within. He has to cast around and try to move to construct a "new self," an altered image that still affords some bearable level of self-esteem, in spite of the way the public reacts.

The burn patient is the prototype of the visibly injured person who must continue to face the rejection and negative pressure of society throughout his/her life. He/she can be readily belittled, humiliated, and devalued for his/her blemishes. The last few decades have shown little improvement in the larger community's toleration of the grossly handicapped or disfigured. The millions and millions of dollare spent in electronic and print media, as well as in the movies, advertising cosmetics and setting beauty standards for society define our standard; they overwhelm the mild and reasonable voices, which tell that these attitudes are superficial. People continue to walk around a blind person trying to cross a street in a big city; they continue to evade a person in a wheelchair. Though the facially disfigured may now have more self-help groups and more determination, they nevertheless remain among the least accepted of the 30 million people in this country who are classified as handicapped and disabled.

The psychology of *differences* still dominates our society, and when the differences are not racial or cultural but are physical handicaps, they bring to the fore everyone's own fears of fragility. Most people are therefore eager to segregate the maimed and unsightly, just as there is resistance to close association among many racial groups. Allport (1954) delineated prejudice "[as] the simple psychological sense of negative over-generalized judgement" (p. 6), which clearly plagues the disfigured.

In school-age children, the peer group shapes the value system of the child regarding skills, intelligence, and social appearance. A limp, scoliosis, or a burn scar can move a child down the pecking order at the time of life when one is so eager to be accepted. The vocabulary of blemishes—"pimple puss," "scar face," "freckles," "rabbit," "bugs bunny," "four eyes"—is all florid and hard to manage. The child with cleft palate and lip may be treated as less intelligent, possibly leading to a sense of inferiority and lack of academic effort (Clifford, 1987). Children with the discoloration of vitiligo may be scapegoated. Let's consider several cases of burn victims and the prototypic importance of visible disfigurement in constructing a self in society and in dealing with the stigma of being handicapped in facial presentation:

The Case of Amy Sue

Amy Sue was burned when her mother spilled hot fat in the kitchen while cooking. The child had startled her. This was a middle-class home where neglect and abuse were not involved. However, Amy was hospitalized at 3 years of age and underwent several surgical procedures, including skin grafting and debridement. Five years after discharge, she returned to the hospital for another minor surgical procedure on her axilla. The family treated her as a "sick" child, whose injuries were mother's cross to bear. Mother felt enormously guilty, always feeling she had done something terrible. This led to inconsistent discipline and excessive indulgence of the child, even when the parents divorced. As Amy Sue grew into adolescence and became concerned about breast development, she was humiliated by having a left nipple that was scarred and abnormally colored. She redoubled her usual efforts to keep her torso and left arm covered to hide her injury. When in college, she sought psychotherapy because, "I have this scar, and because of it I have no confidence in myself." The scar had become a funnel for many of the patient's concerns and a target for blame placing when she didn't study, fought with her mother, or didn't manage well socially. She was, in contrast, feisty and assertive in business situations and school activities. In her frequent sexual relations, she reported that she always kept her scars covered and wore sleeves that shielded from view the minor donor sites on her arms. Overall, the patient funneled most of her insecurities into this bodily focus of dissatisfaction, although she refused to have surgery to remove the deformity of her nipple. Stigmatized people often take on a style of trying to be especially good and friendly to counter public rejection.

The Case of Stacy

This boy was badly scarred on his face at the age of 3, losing his right ear and most of his nasal structure. He also had severe hand burns and much scarring of his cheeks and neck. He had been a victim of a house fire that claimed the life of his sister. Remaining were his mother and father and two other siblings. Stacy was subjected to endless visits to the hospital, multiple skin grafts, and reconstructive surgery to build new nostrils and improve the appearance of his skin and neck. Some attempts were made to reconstruct his ear, but these were abandoned as unsuccessful and more disfiguring. Visitors to his home reported a dark, withdrawn, and dismal atmosphere, with the exception of Stacy's jolly and pleasant demeanor. This was also observed on the hospital ward, where he was uniformly cheerful, always tried to be likeable, and tolerated teasing and rejection in the hospital and in the school situation with remarkable resilience and sweetness of response. Through adolescence and young adulthood, however, he was progressively shunted to the side when it came to social life, and his disabled hands made it hard for him to find employment. The patient was observed in his early 20s living alone, occasionally trying to help out in setting up musical and lighting equipment for a rock band of his peers, but generally spending his time alone in his room, drinking beer and watching television. He was always typically ingratiating in his social interactions. He talked about himself as making a "wonderful adjustment" to his situation, as he tried to hide his misery.

Erikson's schema delineates a struggle in adolescence between identity formation versus role confusion. Disfigured children have to deal with the conflict over maintaining valuable identity versus that of "spoiled identity" (Goffman, 1963). They are often so consumed with this struggle and their own extrusion from the social scene that they cannot work out the issue of loyalty to particular worthwhile individuals in the social group. Rather, the disfigured fall back into a more primitive association with defective individuals who will accept them and confirm their sense of being marred and deficient in their self-worth.

The Case of Bill

This 13-year-old boy suffered a fireworks explosion at a scout camp, which blacked the right side of his face with gunpowder and cost him his right eye. He had 14 operations in the next few years and lost most of the sight of his eye so that only colors could be discerned. Bill went from being a pleasant and attractive, black-haired boy to a socially withdrawn child, who was teased by other boys, socially isolated, academically distracted, and continually sad. He said that he always wondered what other people were thinking of him. He felt that the first impression people had of him was the permanent one. He had had some fights with boys who teased him, but he largely handled his shame over his appearance by wearing dark glasses, indoors and out, even into the swimming pool. At 16, he could be seen at school walking alone, sitting in the farthest corner, and entering and leaving school in isolation. Thus, his identity role was one of ostracism, partly achieved by his behavior and partly by the social pressures to exclude a disfigured individual.

Bull and Rumsey (1988) have delineated the role of facial appearance in liking, dating, and marriage, as well as in persuasion, politics, and employment. In the education system, for example, teachers have lower expectations of children with deviant appearance. As a result, *facially disadvantaged* children are often socially disadvantaged children who must make extra effort to get on in the world. Cooley noted that (1902) "the thing that moves us to self-appraisal, pride or shame is not mere mechanical reflection of ourselves but an imputed sentiment, the imagined effect of this imagination upon another's mind . . .We always imagine and in imagining share the judgments of the others mind" (p. 184). The energy required to prepare oneself for going out in public and to maintain performance in public is much greater for disfigured people than for those with unremarkable faces. This process also alters self-esteem and requires vigilance about appearance in all settings outside of the most familiar ones.

In young adulthood when, according to Erikson's paradigm, intimacy versus isolation are key developmental conflicts, the stigmatized person may bear a load of altered self-sufficiency and self-esteem that make it harder to risk *loving* and feel *loveable*. Isolation is a frequent complaint of the facially marred individual (Macgregor, 1979). Recent theories concerning hostility and aggression have tried to tease out the ways in which anger and its management relate to healthy outcomes (Barefoot et al., 1989). Bitterness, apathy, and cynicism are all emotions of great intensity in the disfigured, and such emotion can, in turn, further affect social relations and self-esteem.

The Case of Carl

A 23-year-old paratrooper and Green Beret was badly scarred on his jaw, neck, and cheeks in an explosion of electrical gear. He also had badly scarred hands. His wife was supportive and attentive, but he derisively said their relationship was like "beauty and the beast," and he apologized for her trials during their occasional sexual relations. Carl felt separated from most of life. His muscular and competent body was gone, along with his self-regard and ability to do a job. He talked endlessly about the soldier's job of killing and spoke of himself as a ruined weapon of destruction. Gallows humor exuded from him.

The Case of Alice

A 30-year-old woman had been injured when a kerosene lamp turned over on a camping trip with her boyfriend. Her face, breasts, neck, and hands were grossly scarred. She had been a perky cheerleader who loved to flirt and greatly enjoyed her femininity and good looks. After the injury, she hid from curious and shocked stares, only occasionally venturing out in public. Once, in a department store, a middle-aged man glanced at her and said, "Oh, I thought Halloween was over." The patient felt shamed and demolished. She stayed in hiding for months; ultimately, she took a job at a radio studio where she saw little of the public. "I am no longer a woman. I am a thing." This was her damaged self-concept, and she could not elude it. Her boyfriend had left her when she came out of the hospital. She had lost her ability to be what Burns (1979) calls "love worthy."

LATER LIFE DISFIGUREMENT

Erikson (1982) writes that in old age the individual achieves some informed and detached concern with life—with minimal emotional involvement. But the elderly still need a link to peers, and must remain attractive enough to not be "scary" to the grandchildren. In his paradigm of the life cycle, the critical theme is *integrity*. While old people talk more about aches and pains and the loss of earlier body-image features, the maintenance of an "acceptable" body image becomes harder as an individual grows older. Aging public figures try to maintain a picture of vigor and authority. One prototype of this is the ancient military leader. Only a few persons who are in the public eye have overcome major physical disfigurement. Gorbachev's port wine stain serves to identify him in photographs but is not itself caricatured. However, we in the West have little knowledge about how it affects Soviet public esteem. Senator Inoye proudly wears his empty sleeve, from his valorous wound in World War II. The enormous struggle for Franklin Roosevelt to maintain a powerful image, while paralyzed by polio, was a success made possible only by the compliance of the press and a less intrusive media relationship with the president. The older Reagan jauntily stepping off his helicopter recapitulates this. However, some older people are troubled by every sunspot, wart, and crease as it appears. Accompanying the literature on health care is the less vivid information about appearance. Among the major appearance-altering diseases in older age are head and neck cancer. When head and neck cancers are diagnosed, the first priority is to save life, but right behind it comes the concern about what a mutilated face will do to one's role in life.

Some of the conventional clinical wisdom about who will handle disfigurement well after cancer surgery may seem logical, but it is anecdotal and sometimes contradictory. For example, it has been said that married women with children will handle mastectomy for cancer much better than single women. This is not necessarily the case, as there are women who make good and poor adjustments in all social and age categories. There is a presumption that people who have had a fuller life can enjoy this memory and have a more mature relation to life's passage that Erikson (1982) sees as the best completion of the life cycle. He reports that "wisdom" is a kind of "informed and detached concern with life itself in the face of death itself, as expressed in age-old adages and yet also potentially present in the simplest references to concrete daily matters" (p. 61).

In terms of body image, this also means being casual about the changes in vigor of appearance. An older man can feel the same in body as a 16-year-old while sitting on a bench, but all of this changes as soon as he makes the effort to get up. Then the problems of stiffness, weakness, and uncertainty of balance come to the fore, along with problems of vision. What makes some older people seem more accepting about their changes is apathy, a devitalized sadness, which is not visible as true depression. Although fond memories of past achievements and pleasures as well as loving grandchildren may all help, the older person can *still* be very concerned about not wanting to look "seedy" or incompetent. Facial blemishes, senile keratoses, and skin cancers and their treatments all provide foci for shame and aggravation in the older person.

The Case of Anton

This 67-year-old salesman had his left eye and cheek removed due to cancer. He was mortified that he was cut down at the time he hoped to begin a fruitful retirement. All his years of confident work were based on presenting a neat and acceptable appearance. He required several years to adjust to the fact that he was going to live after his cancer, and that he would have to learn to live with an appliance that attached to his eyeglass frames, which covered the cavity left by his surgery. His artificial eye took many months to accept and to learn to manage. His adjustment occurred only after he had become forcibly retired from work and placed in a more inactive life role.

The Case of Claudia

A 72-year-old grandmother had mutilating surgery of her right face and neck, leaving her with grossly misshaped features on that side, a neck that was largely cut away, and a missing ear. She was able to cover her ear with hair, her neck with scarves, and she wore glasses to further mask her visible distortion. She was considered a favorite by the hospital staff because she was cheerful and cooperative with her doctors and nurses. However, in her personal life and her self-presentation, her wisdom about life was heavily burdened by her change of appearance. One of the most painful things for her was the sudden awareness that her grandchildren wouldn't kiss her. She had been altered in her appearance into a "thing" that frightened and repelled them. For Claudia, despite help from her grown children and her successful maintenance of an acceptable image in other areas, the disaffection of her grandchildren came to symbolize the pain of her disfigurement.

Freud's Facial Disfigurement

Though many of us are familiar with penetrating and serious posed photos of Freud, careful inspection of them will reveal in the older Freud an extensive asymmetry of his face. Romm (1983) described how, as a result of considerable surgery, Freud had hearing loss on the right side and is said to have had pain and difficulty speaking; his English became muffled, and he is said to have remarked, "My prosthesis does not speak French" (p. 71). His ability to lecture in German was also truncated. "My world is what it was previously, a small island of pain floating on an ocean of indifference" (p. 139). Most of what is written about Freud focuses on his behavior and personality, but his altered appearance was also notable and bothered him.

COPING MECHANISMS OF THE DEFORMED

Goffman (1963) notes that the Greeks used the term *stigma* "to refer to bodily signs designed to expose something unusual and bad about the moral status of the signifier. The signs were cut or burnt into the body and advertised that the bearer was a slave, a criminal or a traitor—a blemished person, ritually polluted, to be avoided, especially in public places . . .'' (p. 1).

In our era the emotional impact of a deformity still hinges on stigma and stigma management. Hiding remains a prominent mode of dealing with the problem. McGregor (1954) has gone further, describing *social death* as a reaction to facial disfigurement, that is, when badly disfigured individuals cut off their relationships with the world and go into a closet existence. The sense of shame of being uncovered, devalued, and diminished in self-esteem must be fought by the visibly damaged. Energy must be used to deal with situations most people handle without much thought. Personal pride is always at risk. While a facially marred individual is cozily talking to a friend, a bystander can gasp and comment, and the disfigured person will be overwhelmed by feelings about his/her defects, sweeping other attitudes aside.

Some young women who have been facially disfigured will become vigorously seductive and promiscuous to repeatedly prove that they are attractive, hoping for love by using sex to prove that they are "love worthy"; a goal they generally fail to achieve. William James (1890) spoke about being a different person in each social situation in which he found himself. Most poignantly, disfigured people may keep trying a different and accepting cordiality in each new social contact. The disfigured person must work to reconstruct his self-presentation and be on guard against stares, evasion, repulsion, and intrusive questions and jokes, which makes the barrier between the self of the disfigured person and others like a high voltage wire. Hay (1754) wrote long ago from the perspective of a socially successful, small hunchback, who met with scorn, revulsion, and contempt. He advised those similarly affected to bear it manfully with Christian forebearance. He advised trying to put onlookers at ease with humor.

The whole concept of fashion and adornment also shifts because of disfigurement. Most people can put on nice clothes and daydream of glorious adventures. Fashion is an effort to gain general acceptance and value (Simmel 1971). But a well-dressed disfigured person will be judged differently (Thomas, 1982). Even in fantasy it is much harder for the scarred, facially palsied, or discolored individual to carry off fashion and show the qualities of inner life when a clear defect distracts onlookers. Fashion attempts to show part of the contents of an individual in a controlled way—the fashionable woman in her "power suit" striding to the bank, the bearded graduate student in jeans and boots at the university, or the young mother in curlers. All are proffering to the world some selected images of themselves that are within the normal range. At another point on the continuum, there is the disfigured trying to *disguise defect* rather than present themselves physically in a special role. They are struggling more intensely to maintain self-esteem and achieve public acceptance, trying to "fade into the background" rather than stand out (deviantly) in the crowd.

The Case of Kathy

Kathy was 18 years of age when she fell water skiing behind the motorboat of a family friend. When she fell, the powerboat operator swung around to pick her up, but tragically the boat's propeller cut off her right arm, slashed her right breast, and severely lacerated the right side of her face, breaking her cheekbone, knocking out several teeth, and leaving her with permanent deformities. She underwent repeated reconstructive procedures, which left her with small but clear improvements, but nothing could bring back the arm or normal facial appearance. It was at first terrifying to her for strangers to glance at her; and after several years of extensive and skilled surgery, it remained unpleasant to her if the public viewed her unexpectedly. The patient experienced a long period of depression. She bravely tolerated the new surgical procedures that were required and worked at trying out each new prosthesis for her arm. Meanwhile, she learned to do almost all of her activities of daily living with her left hand. She got help from her family in washing her hair and setting it, but generally switched to hairdos that were simple and shoes that did not require lacing. She could get into her bra by fastening it and lying it on the floor to squirm into it. Her main social fear was her facial presentation, which caused people to turn away. There was also the humiliation of being unable to perform simple functions in the commercial art courses she tried to pursue.

Additionally, Kathy was caught up in a common struggle with lawyers to obtain a large legal settlement in her suit against the neighbor and the motorboat manufacturer. The nature of the litigation requires that an injured person show that they have indeed experienced an injury, and the visibly disfigured person must show how terrible things are. There is an attempt to place the blame, because of the nature of the adversary process, on the other side, but also to give as graphic and terrible a picture as possible of one's own losses and agonies. This process serves to further imbed one's sense of being a damaged good and exacerbates many of the concerns about being on display—photos to be shown in court, hospital records, testimony by experts, and forced personal testimony.

For Kathy, this was indeed an experience that underscored her sense of loss of worth. She spoke of this repeatedly and with bitterness; at the same time, she hoped the trial's outcome would lead to some wonderful transformation of her problems. She had dreams and fantasies about a wonderful life when all the money ultimately came to her, which included cars, travel, and elegant beaux. However, underneath the dreams was her fantasy that she would get the finest cosmetic surgery, which would make her defects disappear, and that she would buy the finest artificial arm, a true "bionic" appendage. She would be whole and complete once more. She was very explicit about how proud she had been about her beautiful body and her sexual attractiveness. Though she had never felt her face was pretty, it had not always been frightening, and all her teeth had been her own.

Now she was incomplete, unacceptable, depressed, and enraged for long periods. Side by side with the hopes and the medical efforts that dominated her life were her meager social experiences. After some man would politely drive her home, she would wait weeks, immersed in romantic fantasies of his return to become a true boyfriend—a wish that was never fulfilled. After several years, her lawsuit provided her with two million dollars, which she used to fly to Paris (where she was aghast that people still were horrified or shocked by her appearance). There were many other signs that the world did not like her looks and rejected her in spite of her money. Following recurrent depression with suicidal thoughts, she became interested in going back to school. She moved in with a paraplegic young man whom she supported, but who afforded her very little sex. She always worried about how others saw her, reading horror and rejection into their perceptions of her.

CONCLUSION

Myerson (1971) wrote, "Our culture has a well developed value system relating to variations in physique. To change the negative attitudes of the culture towards those who are judged to be disabled may require hundreds of years of systematic labor. In the meantime, we are confronted with the practical problem of helping the handicapped to live with some measure of usefulness and happiness" (p. 16).

Gliedman and Roth (1980) stress the universal concern about how others view us, a preoccupation that endures throughout the life cycle. The visibly handicapped are constantly dealing with an altered relationship between themselves and others, while they must simultaneously try to fit into the *normal* world. Visibly disfigured individuals always face the possibility of being *shamed* or publicly shown to be defective, and as a result feeling devalued. They share a special *vulnerability*, and can be readily viewed as blemished and not quite human.

There is an oppression of the disfigured by society. The fundamental psychological issue is that the facially disfigured individual is suffering not only from an internal change in body image but also from a change in social role. He/she differs from a neurotic or somatoform patient who feels that he/she is ugly when he/she is essentially normal looking. This normal appearing but troubled group comprises the hundreds of thousands who seek cosmetic surgery annually. The facially disfigured group seeks both reconstructive and cosmetic surgery but is *forced* by external as well as internal circumstances to be concerned about appearance. They try to maintain inner normality when they are ugly. The contents of their lives are also revealed by their blemished appearance. The amount of emotional *work* required to be done is part of the great burden born by these individuals.

Our problem then is not to conceive of disfigured individuals in terms of neuroses but rather in terms of an altered social role. They may be quite neurotic but they cannot be dealt with on this basis alone, because so much of the etiology of their problems lies outside of themselves. The problem of changing society's attitudes toward the disfigured is difficult in all countries, from the Hiroshima maidens to the impoverished child whose bad home wiring set the house afire. These people are not readily integrated into society because of their appearance.

REFERENCES

Allport, G. (1954). *The nature of prejudice*. Reading, MA: Addison-Wesley.

Barefoot, J., Dodge, K., Peterson, B., Dahlstrom, G., & Williams, R. B. (1989). The Cook-Medlay Hostility Scale. *Psychosomatic Medicine*, 51, 46–57.

Bernstein, N. R. (1976). *Emotional care of the facially burned and disfigured*. Boston: Little, Brown.

Bernstein, N. R. (1979). Chronic illness and impairment. *Psychiatric Clinics if North America*, 2, 331–346.

Bernstein, N. R. (1989). Psychological problems associated with facial disfigurement. In B. Heller, L. Flobr, & L. Zegous (Eds.), *Psychosocial interventions with physically disabled persons* (pp. 147–161). New Jersey: Rutgers University Press.

Bull, R., & Rumsey, N. (1988). *The social psychology of facial appearance*. New York: Springer.

Burns, R. B. (1979). *The self concept*. London: Longmans.

Cicero (1971). *On old age and on friendship*. Ann Arbor: University of Michigan, Ann Arbor Paperback.

Clifford, E. (1987). *The cleft palate experience*. Springfield, Illinois: Charles C. Thomas.

Cooley, C. H. (1902). *Human nature and the social order*. New York: Scribner's.

Critchley, M. (1965). *The silent language*. London: Butterworth.

Drotar, D., Baskiewicz, A., Irvin, N., Kennell, J., & Klaus, M. (1975). The adaptation of parents to the birth of an infant with a congenital malformation: A hypothetical model. *Pediatrics*, 56, 710–717.

Erikson, E. H. (1982). *The life cycle completed*. New York: W. W. Norton.

Fajardo, B. (1987). Parenting the damaged child: Mourning, regression, and disappointment. *The Psychoanalytic Review*, 74, 19–43.

Favazza, A. R. (1987). *Bodies under siege, self-mutilation in culture and psychiatry*. Baltimore: John Hopkins University Press.

Fisher (1986). *Development and structure of the body image* (Vol. 2). New Jersey: Erlbaum.

Gliedman, J., & Roth, W. (1980). *The unexpected minority: Handicapped children in America* (pp.12). New York: Harcourt Brace Jovanovich.

Goffman, E. (1963). *Stigma, notes on the management of spoiled identity*. New Jersey: Prentice-Hall.

Goffman, E. (1963). *Stigma, notes on the management of spoiled identity*. Englewood Cliffs, NJ: Prentice-Hall.

Harrison, A. (Eds.), (1985). Body image and self-esteem. In J. Mack & M. Abalon (Eds.), *The development and sustenance of self-esteem* (pp. 90–183). New York: International University Press.

Hay, W. (1974). Deformity: An essay. *General Catalogue of Printed Books*, 2314: 10.

Hill-Beuf, A., & Porter, J. D. (1984). Children coping with impaired appearance: Social and Psychological influences. *General Hospital Psychiatry*, 6, 294–301.

Horowitz, M. J. (1970). *Image formation and cognition*. New York: Appleton-Century-Crofts.

James. W. (1890). *Principles of psychology* (Vol. 2). New York: Holt.

Kagan, J. (1984). *The nature of the child*. New York: Basic Books.

Kelly, G. A. (1963). *A theory of personality; The psychology of personal construct*. New York: Norton.

Kleck, R. E., & Strenta, A. C. (1985). Physical deviance and the perception of social outcomes. In J. A. Graham & A. M. Kligman (Eds.), *The psychology of cosmetic treatments* (pp. 161–190). New York: Praeger.

Kolb, L. C. (1959). Disturbance of body image. In S. Arietti (Ed.), *American handbook of psychiatry* (pp. 749–769). New York: Basic Books.

Kolb, L. D. (1975). Disturbances of the body image. In S. Arieti & M. F. Reiser (Eds.), *American handbook of psychiatry* (Vol. 4, 2nd ed., pp. 810–837). New York: Basic Books.

Lakoff, R. T., & Scherr, R. L. (1984). The problem of beauty: Myth and reality. *Face value, the politics of beauty* (pp. 21–43). London: Routledge and Keagan Paul.

Lawn, B. (1989). Experience of a paraplegic psychiatry resident on an inpatient psychiatric unit. *American Journal of Psychiatry, 146*; 771–74.

MacGregor, F. C., Abel, T. M., Bryt, A., & Lauer, E. (1953). *Facial deformities and plastic surgery. A psychosocial study*. Springfield, Illinois.

Macgregor, F. (1979). *After plastic surgery: Adaptation and adjustment*. New York: Praeger Scientific.

Miller, J. (1978). *The body in question*. New York: Vantage Press.

Myerson, L. (1971). Somatopsychology of physical disability. In W. M. Cruickshank (Ed.), *Psychology of exceptional children and youth* (pp. 1–74). Englewood Cliffs, NJ: Prentice-Hall.

Rogers-Salyer, M. A., Jensen, A. G., & Borden, C. (1985). Effects of facial deformities and physical attractiveness on mother–infant bonding. In Daniel Marchac (Ed.), *Craniofacial Surgery, Proceedings of the First International Congress of the International Society of Cranio-Maxillo-Facial Surgery*. New York: Springer-Verlag.

Romm, S. (1983). *The unwelcome intruder, Freud's struggle with cancer*. New York: Praeger.

Schilder, P. (1935). *The image and appearance of the human body*. New York: International Universities Press.

Schonfield, W. A. (1966). Body image disturbance in adolescence. *Archives of General Psychiatry, 15*: 6–21.

Sensky, T. (1985). Family stigma and physical deformity in children. *General Hospital Psychiatry, 7*, 385–386.

Simmel, G. (1971). Fashion. In D. N. Levine (Ed.), *Individuality and social forms* (pp. 294–324). Chicago: University of Chicago Press.

Thomas, D. (1982). *The experience of handicap*. Bungay, Suffolk, England: The Chaucer Press.

Van der Velde, C. (1985, May 5). Body images of one's self and of other: Developmental and clinical significance. *American Journal of Psychiatry, 142*, 527–537.

C H A P T E R 7

Body Image and Physical Disability

Franklin C. Shontz

In order to describe how body image and adjustment to physical disability are related, it is necessary first to examine in depth the various meanings the term *body image* has been given and then to understand the processes by which persons adjust psychologically to physical disability. Neither assignment is simple, but if both can be carried out, there is reason to believe that a description of the relationship between body image and adjustment to disability will emerge along the way.

HISTORICAL CONCEPTIONS OF BODY IMAGE

Body Experience and Injury to the Body

Peculiarities in body experience that occur as a consequence of physical injury or brain damage have been observed for centuries. Ambrose Paré, a 16th-century surgeon, described phantom limbs in patients who had undergone amputations. A report of such phenomena was also published by Weir Mitchell three centuries later in 1871. According to Weinstein and Kahn (1955), cases of denial of personal blindness (now called Anton syndrome) were formally reported by Von Monako in 1885, and a large number of reports of similar cases soon followed. The condition known as anosognosia, described by Babinski in 1914, originally referred to denial to left hemiplegia, but now often refers to a variety of forms of denial of illness.

Seymour Fisher and Sidney Cleveland (1958) credited the French neurologist P. F. Bonnier with the first formal recognition, in 1905, that the body image deserves serious study. Benton (1959) also credits Bonnier with the idea that an organized perceptual model of the body determines how the individual responds to stimuli that are applied to it. Bonnier proposed that this model or *schema* has a topographical organization and imparts a spatial quality to the perception of stimuli on the body. Fisher and Cleveland noted that a few years later, Arnold Pick asserted that each individual constructs an image of the personal body in space and uses that image as a standard for judging current bodily stimulations.

Attempts to Localize Body Perception in the Brain

One way to search for the source of body experience is to examine the types of disturbances in body experience that appear in persons with physical injuries, especially to the brain, and to attempt to relate those types of disturbances to the locations of the injuries. Efforts to localize body experience in this way have not led to much agreement. The minor or non-dominant hemisphere (usually the right) of the brain has been implicated (de Ajuriaguerra, 1965), and some authorities have suggested that body experience is specifically localized in the parietal region of that hemisphere (Critchley, 1965).

Because damage to the brain often produces disturbances in speech and language, it is often difficult to determine whether evidence of a patient's disrupted body experience is to be taken at face value. The actual experience may be undisturbed, but the person may lack the ability to describe it adequately in gestures or words. Gerstmann (1942) believed that he had discovered a particular syndrome, due to central nervous system damage, which consists of inability to recognize one's own fingers, loss of right–left discrimination, and difficulty writing and carrying out arithmetic calculations. Of particular importance was the claim that this syndrome appears in the absence of related disturbances in language (aphasia) and therefore cannot be explained as being a form of language disorder. Gerstmann attributed this syndrome to lesions of the left angular gyrus in its transition to the second occipital convolution. Poeck and Orgass (1971) criticized the idea that disturbances in body schemata occur in such specifically identifiable syndromes or can be precisely localized in the brain. However, cases of Gerstmann's syndrome without aphasia were described in the subsequent scientific literature (Geschwind & Strubb, 1975).

Extensive and intensive studies of the stages of disappearance over time of so-called phantom body parts, which result from amputations and other forms of denervation, led Simmel (1956) to conclude that the sequence of disappearance conforms to the well-known homunculus, which is located in the sensorimotor cortex of the brain (Penfield & Rasmussen, 1950). Simmel also noted that persons who are born without limbs, or who lose limbs early in life, do not experience phantoms, which suggests that body image is at least in part learned. However, as is evident from what has been noted above, phantom limbs are by no means the only type of disturbances of body perception that must be explained. It is not clear whether one hemisphere of the brain is more important in such cases than the other, or to what extent peripheral rather than central neural events contribute to the phenomena.

Despite all these failures to localize body experience physiologically, Fisher (1986) feels it is premature to dismiss the possibility that defects in body perception are caused by localized brain lesions or processes. Fisher also notes, however, that the degree of disturbance in behavior that results from brain damage is partially psychologically determined. Furthermore, he observes that psychological experiences that bring confusion and conflict into body perceptions can also induce behavior anomalies that are analogous to, though less severe than, those that stem from brain damage alone.

Normal Body Experience

The most influential of early attempts to explain normal, as opposed to pathological, body experience in a systematic way was made by the neurologist Henry Head (1920, 1926). Head postulated the operation of neural representations, or *schemata*, that serve as guides in the localization of body stimuli and in steering postural adjustments. According to Head, body schemata are not conscious, although they affect conscious experience. Their influence is automatic, almost mechanical. To explain how they operate, Head used the analogy of the meter in a taxi that automatically converts distance into money without using any intervening processes that could be called conscious.

The following example shows one way in which body schemata work. If someone comes up behind me and touches me on the back, at that instant I know that not only have I been touched but also exactly where I was touched, even though I was probably not thinking about my body at the time. If the touch is on my right side, I am likely to turn my head in that direction automatically, not thinking about what I am doing. A common practical joke is to approach someone from the rear on one side and tap them on the shoulder on the other side. When the victim's head turns toward the tapped side, the perpetrator moves forward on the other side and enjoys the puzzled look on the victim's face.

If a person is to be able to recognize that a touch from an unseen source is on the back, rather than on the top of the head or some other place, it is reasonable to suppose that an overall pattern of neuronal activity (a *schema*, plural *schemata*) within the person was ready to serve as an instantaneously available frame of reference, which localizes the touch accurately. Head maintained that these hypothetical schemata not only organize stimulus location, they also activate postural adjustments. Head used the example of a woman wearing a hat with a tall feather, which, of course, she knows is there but cannot feel directly. She bends down, without consciously realizing that she is doing so, as she goes through a door so that the feather will pass beneath the lintel.

Several decades later, Martin Scheerer (1954) wrote extensively about nonconscious cognitive frames of reference. Scheerer was a psychologist who, in collaboration with the neurologist Kurt Goldstein, had spent years studying persons with central nervous system damage. Using a term from Gestalt psychology, Scheerer called these nonconscious frames of reference "silent organizations" (p. 109), and he acknowledged their functional similarity to Head's concept of schemata. According to Scheerer (1954), the body image is a central structure of cues and traces from diverse sense organs, that are integrated into a plastic model or schema. Being of a holistic turn of mind, Scheerer did not claim that these organizations are purely neurological. Nor did he claim that they are purely mental. Indeed, Scheerer typically argued that the principles of perception were either transcendent to the mind–body distinction or were, in the phrase of Wilhelm Stern (1935), "psychophysically neutral."

Like many Gestalt psychologists, Scheerer was more interested in explaining how silent organizations function in several spheres of psychological experience than in locating them within the human anatomy. He took special interest in the way in which Koffka (1935) related functional schemata to his concept of the ego, the way in which Gibson (1951) used similar ideas in his analysis of visual perception, and the way in which Piaget (1951, 1952) and others used the term schema to refer to essentially similar integrative processes. Scheerer also emphasized that experience of the personal body has special properties that distinguish it from cognition of other objects in the environment. Of particular importance in establishing the body as a perceptual object with special psychological significance are the close, though admittedly imperfect, relationships between the body and the self and the distinctive sense of intimacy, or "mine-ness" that is an integral part of all personal body perception (Shontz, 1960).

Some Other Special Characteristics of Body Experience

Except for Scheerer's ideas about the "mine sphere," which were never fully developed because of Scheerer's death, the theories discussed so far generally emphasize perception of the geometric properties of the personal body. These theories typically take it for granted that the criterion of accuracy, or veridicality, of body experience is the degree to which it corresponds to the actual size and shape of the body as a physical object. Shontz (1969) and Shontz and McNish (1972), however, described a series of experiments that demonstrated that, according to this standard, normal body experience is nonveridical. Among college students, certain body distances (head width and forearm length) were found to be consistently overestimated, while others (hand length, foot length) were underestimated. No obvious explanations, either physiological or environmental, were offered for these findings, but they have been quite dependable, appearing consistently in one experiment after another. Explanations may eventually be derived from ideas that relate personal body perception to values concerning or attitudes toward parts or regions of the body. Perhaps head width is typically overestimated because the head is particularly important to most human beings. However, it is not so obvious why hand length would be underestimated if importance to adaptation were the only determining factor. Whatever the reasons may be, it is obvious that one does not have to search far to find attempts to explain body perception in terms of more inclusive theoretical ideas, such as adaptation, self-concept, and personality.

Paul Schilder (1935) was the first to relate body image to personality in detail. Beginning with Head's ideas about body schemata, Schilder added many concepts drawn from psychoanalytic theory. He developed a theory of body image which tied it closely to individual personality, emphasizing in particular the importance of emotions and of the erogenous zones in its development. In Schilder's theory, the body is more a psychodynamic than a neurological entity, and body experience is viewed mainly as the channel through which libido is expressed upon or exchanged with the environment. Schilder was not an experimentalist, being more concerned with clinical phenomena than with testing specific hypotheses. Some of his ideas did influence later investigators, however, particularly Seymour Fisher, whose work is discussed in Chapter 1 of this volume.

Body and Self

Body perception is usually thought to be so obviously important to personal identity that it is also expected to be closely related to self-perception. Ulric Neisser (1988) recently described a comprehensive theory of selfhood that includes five kinds of self-knowledge. These are called the *ecological self*, the *interpersonal self*, the *extended self*, the *private self*, and the *conceptual self*. The first, the ecological self, seems much like the body schemata discussed above or their associated silent organizations. It is described as being an embodied self, the self as it is perceived in relation to the physical environment.

Neisser is inclined to account for this type of self-knowledge largely in terms of systematic flow patterns in the visual field, or what J. J. Gibson called "visual kinesthesis" (Gibson, 1979, p. 182). Neisser's theory places no special emphasis on what happens in the central nervous system or upon the effects that damage to the central nervous system induces into body experiences. Indeed, it seems in many respects to attribute the ecological self at least as much to environmental events as to innate physiological responses. Nevertheless, Neisser argues that the ecological self is present from earliest infancy, and he acknowledges that, except in "rare pathological cases," such as phantom limbs or distortions of body experience due to brain damage, it is typically highly accurate.

The important point for present purposes is that Neisser's concept of the ecological self seems to be similar to either a silent organization or a set of body schemata. Other aspects of self-knowledge postulated by Neisser also have interesting parallels to ideas that been suggested by others about the various types of body experience. For example, Neisser notes that the body image is part of the conceptual self. Further discussion of other types of self-knowledge is continued when other aspects of body experience are described.

Body Experience as Boundary

Seymour Fisher and Sidney Cleveland (1958) introduced the important idea that the main function of body experience is to provide a personal boundary that more or less effectively separates the self, as an inner psychological entity, from the outer world. Fisher and Cleveland did not assess the "boundary properties" of body experience by comparing them with actual body measurements. Instead, they examined persons' projective responses to inkblots. These responses were coded according to whether the person saw in such ambiguous stimuli things that seem to suggest a firm boundary (Barrier Score) or a boundary that had been violated (Penetration Score). Examples of high Barrier responses are: battleship, turtle, fortress. Examples of high Penetration responses are: person being stabbed, torn fur coat, X-ray picture.

On the basis of considerable empirical evidence, Fisher and Cleveland concluded that the Barrier Score measures a stable characteristic of the body image and that it is linked not only to important personality traits but also to behavior in small groups, responses to stress, physiological activation patterns, body sites of certain physical illness such as cancer, psychopathology, cultural patterns, sex differences, and many other psychologically important characteristics. They felt that the Penetration Score, though useful, is primarily sensitive to more immediate situational conditions.

Fisher (1970) brought his work up to date 12 years later, reporting on new research on Boundary and Penetration Scores and describing a number of new techniques for assessing other relevant aspects of body experience. Fisher noted that the Barrier Score, which had become the indicator of greater research interest, had not been found to correlate with other purported measures of body image, and that most such measures did not correlate with each other. He explained this by arguing that the term body image does not refer to a single variable but to a general class of phenomena that includes many subsystems at different levels of consciousness. For example, inkblot responses tap less conscious response processes than do questionnaire items that ask subjects to make evaluative responses about their bodies, as does Secord and Jourard's Body Cathexis technique (1953).

Other techniques that Fisher developed to define operationally important attributes of body image included the Body Focus Questionnaire (BFQ), the Body Prominence (BP) technique, and the Body Distortion Questionnaire (BDQ). The BFQ asks the person to attend closely to body experience and then to respond to a series of 108 paired comparisons (examples: mouth–neck; heart–shoulder; feet–head) by indicating for each pair the body part more clearly in awareness. Responses are scored to indicate the relative prominence of eight body regions: back, right side, eyes, heart, mouth, stomach, head, and arms. Awareness of a specific body region was expected to be associated with particular personality traits. Although anticipated correspondences did not always emerge, certain associations did appear to be statistically dependable. For example, heart awareness in men is apparently associated with high religiosity and low aesthetic or artistic interest. Also, among men, heterosexual difficulties seem to be associated with a focus on the right side of the body as opposed to the left. In general, women's scores were found to be less stable over time than men's.

The BP technique requires the person to list "twenty things that you are aware of or conscious of right now." The person is told to use several words in each description. All responses that make direct or indirect reference to the body are scored. Among men, prominence of the body seems to be associated with concern over oral stimuli, whereas among women it is associated with personal strength and self-steering.

The BDQ contains 82 items, each describing a form of distorted body experience. Scores are obtained for several types of distortions: feeling larger, feeling smaller, weakened boundary, blocked body openings, unusual feelings in the skin, feeling dirty, depersonalization. The BDQ was expected to reveal distortions of body perception in psychopathological states. Surprisingly, though, high levels of admission of distortion in body experience were not unique to schizophrenic samples of subjects. The averages for these groups were about the same as those for neurotics and were not much higher than for those of normals. In his later work, Fisher (1986) did not place much emphasis upon findings from this instrument.

When summarizing his overall conclusions from the extraordinarily comprehensive research base that he has amassed over at least 30 years, Fisher characterized the High Barrier individual as being person centered—self-driven, ambitious, and optimistic. They are not anxious about their bodies: "Even with a highly defective body, they continue to operate relatively satisfactorily at a psychological level" (1986, p. 526). Low Barrier persons are, of course, just the opposite.

With respect to Body Focus and Body Prominence, Fisher continued to find consistency in how much attention people pay to particular parts of their bodies, men being more consistent than women overall. His later thinking continued to emphasize the importance of body landmarks in personality. However, it placed less emphasis on the attempt to find more or less universal one-to-one correspondences between specific personality characteristics and specific landmark emphases. Later research also continued to show that high-body prominence is associated with guilt in males, and with sharpened boundedness in females, but Fisher was by no means certain how to explain this.

In general, Fisher has not been favorable toward attempts to develop unifying theories about body image. He feels that body experience is so complex, operates at so many levels, and is influenced by so many different kinds of variables that it is at best premature and at worst impossible to attempt to explain the findings with a single theory.

Psychologizing the Body Image

Clearly, as Fisher himself has articulated in Chapter 1 of this volume, his extensive research program follows Paul Schilder's lead by concentrating more heavily on body image as a psychological entity than as a neurological structure. Not that Fisher's research program has ignored the physical body, for many studies were carried out in which body experience or body perception was deliberately altered in order to examine the psychological effects of these manipulations. For example, Fisher summarized studies in which body perception was directly altered by the use of aniseikonic lenses. These lenses affect perception by causing retinal images to differ from normal. They may cause the image in one eye to differ in size and shape from the image in the other. They often produce a tilting of the visual field and can alter mirror images in a variety of ways. Fisher also cited research that assessed the effects of injections of epinephrine on measures of responses to inkblot tests and rating scales, such as the BFQ. What was most impressive about these studies was that they did not yield expected correspondences between experimental manipulations and performances on psychological tests, the results of which tended to remain stable despite changes in perceptual experience. Fisher concluded that responsiveness to such manipulation is determined less by the manipulation itself than by the level of anxiety that happens to be aroused in the perceiver. Gender is also an important factor. The importance of both variables is evident in the finding that sexually anxious women showed the highest resistance to acknowledging lens-induced changes in the pelvic region of their bodies (Fisher, 1986).

As is evident from the above, Fisher's explanations of the results of the research he summarized have tended to stress the emotional influences of body experience on cognition. For example, Fisher argues that parents who foster feelings of inadequacy and dependency in their children will induce feelings of body vulnerability and limited body differentiation (1986). Furthermore, Fisher maintains that the learned ascription of personal values to different sectors of the body induces differential levels of physiological activation within these sectors. This, in turn, may influence the development or course of physical symptoms in illness. In short, for Fisher, the specific locations or physical properties or conditions of body parts are not nearly as important as are the cognitive–affective, which is to say "attitudinal," significance that is assigned to those parts and to the body as a whole. These develop in the individual as a result of his/her total life time of experiences and learning.

Summarizing their first series of investigations, Fisher and Cleveland (1958) recognized that research had led them to regard the body image less as a geometric representation of the body in space than as a projection screen for emotional learning and experience. Fisher and Cleveland acknowledged that they had almost taken the body out of the body image. Thirty years later, a commentator observed that by then Fisher seemed to have taken the image out of it as well (Shontz, 1987).

A COMPREHENSIVE THEORY

Functions and Levels of Body Experience

Although body experience is admittedly extremely complex, at least one attempt has been made to summarize its most important features in a comprehensive theory (Shontz, 1974, 1975). This was accomplished by identifying seven *functions* that body experience performs and four *levels* at which one or more of these functions are carried out.

Functions

Being essential to all perception, learning, and memory, the body serves as a *sensory register and processor of sensory information*. Because it provides the tools with which behavior is carried out, the body serves as an *instrument for action*. As a biologically self-regulating mechanism, the body is the ultimate *source of needs, drives, and reflexes*. Body experience is also personal; as Scheerer would have said, it is uniquely "mine." Therefore, body experience constitutes a *private world*, which is typically shared with others only under conditions of closest intimacy. Self-generated and integrated body experiences guide the use of the personal body in its above-mentioned function as an adaptive instrument for action. Eye–hand coordination would not be possible without self-guidance. I know that I am touching myself because I feel both the afferent stimulation and the efferent response—except when part of me is anesthetized and feels strangely like an extended object that is no longer mine. Therefore, the body is also an essential *stimulus to the self*. Externally, body appearance is an extremely important *social stimulus*. It identifies age, gender, ethnicity, attractiveness, and sometimes occupation or social role. Among persons with physical disabilities, appearance can be a stigma that closes off opportunities that are open to others without hesitation (Wright, 1983). Finally, the body is an *expressive instrument*, the medium through which individuality is communicated. People use body language constantly, whether deliberately or unconsciously. They communicate, or attempt to conceal, their inner psychological states and emotions by gesture, posture, and facial movements.

Obviously, the seven functions are not discrete. To list them is not to describe different classes of behavior but to suggest manifold possibilities. A hungry person, who dresses stylishly, picks up a companion and drives to a well-appointed restaurant for an evening of dinner and dancing, is probably engaging in all seven functions at several points throughout the behavioral sequence.

Levels

As indicated above, body image is, to use another of Wilhelm Stern's (1935) phrases, a *unitas multiplex*. It is unified, yet it is made up of identifiably different components. One way to describe these is to examine their functions, as was done in the preceding section. Another way is to see them as being organized into several levels, depending upon how closely dependent each level is upon immediate sensory input. Four such levels have been identified and may be discussed under the headings: *body schemata, body, body self, body fantasy*, and *body concept*. The term *body image* is not used here but is reserved for use only when discussing body experience as a whole.

Body Schemata

The most fundamental level of body experience involves perception of the body as an object in space. Perception at this level of experience provides information about the topographic location of stimuli on the body surface, and about the arrangement and spatial orientation of body parts. It also communicates a basic distinction between that which is pleasurable and that which causes pain. Although schemata are to some extent affected by learning, they remain remarkably stable over both time and changes in the person's psychological state.

Body Self

At this level, experiences are differentiated into those that happen to "me" and those that do not. These experiences may be considered elaborations of the topographic and structural aspects of the body schemata. Most of the research on Body Barrier and Penetration scores was carried out at this level. Also involved at this level is the learning of ego-centric directionality. Many concepts that are crucial to successful adaptation are body-centered. Among these are the ideas of up and down, far and near, in front of and behind, this and that, and, even, now and then. These distinctions represent elaborations of the postural aspects of body schemata. Finally, as an extension of the pleasure–pain experiences that occur in the body schemata, the body self incorporates evaluative judgments about body experiences. These experiences then become not merely pleasurable or painful, but good or bad, desirable or undesirable, moral or immoral.

The distinction between body schemata and body self is apparent in the findings of research by Mayer and Eisenberg (1988), who studied mental representations of the body in four medical groups. The groups consisted of persons in a cardiac rehabilitation program, persons with spinal cord injuries, persons in an alcoholism rehabilitation program, and persons in a domiciliary unit of a VA Hospital. All participants were asked to sort 33 cards, each containing the name of a body part, into as many categories as they wished (preferably not more than ten). The participants were then asked to rate each of the body parts according to how good or bad they felt about it.

The initial sorting procedure yielded three clearly defined dimensions according to which body parts had been classified by the participants: Head–Body, Arm–Leg, and Inside–Outside. The same dimensions appeared in data from all groups. Mayer and Eisenberg related this classificatory scheme to the Penfield and Rasmussen sensory and motor homunculi (1950). They commented that this way of representing the body mentally "appears to be so fundamental that paradoxically, severe physical incapacitation yields only modest changes in it" (p. 170). Ratings of body parts as good or bad, however, were quite sensitive to medical conditions. The *arm* was rated as "bad" by people with spinal cord injuries; the *heart* was rated as "bad" by people with cardiac conditions.

Although Mayer and Eisenberg referred to the results of their classification procedure as relating to body concept, their findings clearly describe phenomena at the level of the body schemata, as that term is used here. The investigators related their findings regarding ratings of the goodness or badness of body parts to what they called "body esteem," but those findings clearly belong at the level of the body self.

Body Fantasy

Dreams and spontaneous images about the body may be quite elaborate, and often contain irrational content that is none the less symbolically meaningful. According to the earliest versions of Freudian theory, elongated objects symbolize the male sexual organ, while encapsulating objects and cavities symbolically represent female genitals. In everyday life, someone may characterize their personal body, or someone else's body or body-language as being like a machine, or an animal, perhaps a swan, or in a less complimentary way, a pig or a donkey. Such symbolic or metaphorical images are the stuff of dreams, and they provide a wealth of material for artists and cartoonists. The connectedness that exists at the higher levels of body experience is shown by the fact that Fisher and Cleveland could successfully use fantasy-like responses to inkblots as sources of data for assessing the boundary properties of the body self.

Body Concept

This term covers knowledge about the body that has been acquired through education rather than direct experience. It is expressible in terms of verbal labels, anatomical drawings, photographs or descriptions of body parts and functions. Accuracy of the body concept is typically used to promote health and well being, although a high level of conceptual knowledge is ordinarily not necessary for basic survival.

Integration

Body experience is usually an integrated totality. Separate levels and functions are distinguishable, but they constantly work together as do the parts of any structured system, such as a university, a hospital, or a community. Similarly, body experience works together with the still more inclusive Self, or personality as a whole. None can exist alone, and each may be examined from the perspective of the others. When body image is disturbed, the Self is disturbed. When the Self is disturbed, the body image suffers to some extent as well. Although higher-order programming functions may serve to coordinate the four levels, it is not necessary to postulate a superordinate psychological entity, such as an overarching Ego, that integrates body, body image, and personality. They are all parts of a whole that functions as do all integrated systems, and they must continue to do so if the person is to survive and individuate.

All that being said, it is nonetheless possible to speculate that a single dimension underlies both the levels and the functions of body experience that have been described. The relevant dimension was mentioned in the earlier discussion of the levels of body experience. It begins at one extreme with levels and functions that are completely dependent upon body processes, and it extends to levels and functions that are completely or nearly completely independent from direct body processes at the other extreme.

With respect to the levels of body experience, the lower or anchor point of the dimension is made up of the body schemata, which are closely tied to neurological processes. At the upper end of the dimension is the body concept, which is essentially cognitive, consisting as it does of material that could be learned entirely by exposure to information from outside sources: textbooks, lectures, diagrams, dissection, etc. Because the body self is based on direct learning about personal experiences from the body, it is closer to the body schemata than to the body concept. Body fantasy lies between the body self and cognitive processes, because body fantasy uses thought or imagery to give form to body experiences that originate at lower levels of the continuum and filter upward through the body self.

The seven functions served by body experience may be related to the four levels by arranging the functions along the same hypothetical dimension. The result appears in Table 7.1. In this table, the function of the body as a sensory register and processor of sensory information has been placed next to the body schemata because this function is highly dependent upon direct body experience. Only slightly less dependent on direct experience is the function of the body as a source of biological needs, drives, instincts, and reflexes.

Body experience begins to enter the realm of selfhood when the body is used as an instrument for purposive action and when it serves as a stimulus to the self that aids in self-control and evaluation. In Table 7.1, expressive functions have been placed at the high end of the range of the body self. That is because expressive activities are closely related to the body's function as a stimulus to others; most of what is done expressively is for the purpose of influencing others' impressions. Furthermore, when operating as a social stimulus, body experience frequently involves fantasy activities, as can be readily observed in any

TABLE 7.1. HYPOTHETICAL RELATIONS BETWEEN LEVELS AND FUNCTIONS OF BODY EXPERIENCE

Levels	Functions
Body concept	Body is known cognitively as an abstract entity
	Body experience consitutes a private world
Body fantasy	Body serves as stimulus to others
	Body serves as expressive instrument
Body self	Body serves as stimulus to self
	Body is used as an instrument for purposive action
	Body serves as source of biological needs, drives, reflexes, instincts
Body schemata	Body serves as a sensory register and information processor

television commercial for clothing, jewelry, or cosmetics. Fantasy also has a private aspect, for it is in fantasy that the person lives out his/her dreams of athletic prowess and sexual success.

Strictly speaking, the body as a cognitive entity is not necessarily a form or function of body experience at all. For example, one's knowledge of the operation of the body's immune system is not based on personal experience but on abstract learning. This should not be taken to imply that cognitive processes do not influence or are not influenced by lower level experiences. Why would one become interested in learning about the immune system if one had never had the experience of being ill or had no hope that knowledge of that system's functioning would reduce the likelihood of having that experience in the future? In general, however, we are inclined to believe that conceptual knowledge is best acquired and used when it is kept as free as possible from the influence of lower, less rational, process.

Conceptual schemes, such as the one described here, are useful ways of organizing and communicating ideas, but they can not do full justice to the phenomena they conceptualize. Few philosophers, and virtually no psychologists or physicians, seem to have understood that any attempt to discuss body "experience" as a mental (i.e., cognitive or imaginal) entity must be incomplete. Such attempts ignore the essential point that human experience cannot be definitively separated from the lived body and the lived world, as these are given directly in existence. Only the philosopher Maurice Merleau-Ponty, whose work is rarely mentioned by body-image researchers, fully recognized that consciousness and body, body and world, are not merely interrelated, they are virtually inseparable under ordinary conditions of human life (Barral, 1965). The thinking of this philosopher is too subtle and complex to be summarized briefly, but it is appropriate to recommend that anyone who seriously considers working on the topic of body image have some acquaintance with Merleau-Ponty's ideas.

Effects of Physical Disability on Body Image

Bearing in mind the actual inseparability of body-image functions and levels, it is still possible to anticipate certain more or less direct correspondences between physical illness or injury and body image. The following list, adapted from Gerstmann (1958) and Kolb (1959), classifies conditions that are likely to induce long-term disorders in body experience:

1. Damage to the brain.
2. Damage to other parts of the nervous system, without loss of body parts (e.g., paraplegia).
3. Acute dismemberment.
4. Toxic or metabolic disturbance.
5. Psychosomatic conditions, or body states with high levels of involvement of personality factors (e.g., obesity, disfigurement).
6. Faulty personality development (e.g., serious personality disorder, especially such as might lead to conditions such as bulimia or anorexia).

Any of these conditions is likely to induce effects of more than one kind in any given person, although in individual cases effects of one particular sort may be more noticeable than others. For example, amputation not only alters direct body sensations, and therefore affects body schemata through such phenomena as phantom limbs; it also changes the operation of the body as an instrument for action, as a stimulus to the self and as a social stimulus. If it should re-activate psychopathological processes that began in early childhood, it may also induce an emotional disorder such as denial or inappropriately prolonged depression. Therefore, to understand how a given physical condition affects the body image of a particular person, it is necessary to fully describe the range and extent of its effects on each of the *functions* and at each of the *levels* discussed above. A schedule for organizing such descriptions is suggested in Shontz (1974).

ADJUSTMENT TO PHYSICAL DISABILITY

Outsiders' Perspectives

The personal implications of the problems posed by a physical disability may be viewed in any of several different ways, or from several different standpoints. As in the preceding sections, a researcher or clinician may focus on the *effects of* a physical condition on certain aspects of the patient or client. This view conceives of the client as a passive victim of illness or disability. It is a useful vantage point for a professional who is acting as a diagnostician in assessing the impact of a specific condition on a relatively narrow band of personal functions.

From another standpoint, the researcher or clinician may be most concerned with the behavior exhibited by the person as the person attempts to manage the problems in living that a disability precipitates. From this stand-point, the client is seen as one who is not entirely passive but who *reacts to* the effects of his/her disability (Shontz, 1980). It serves the professional by guiding rehabilitation efforts in such a way as to ensure that the affected individual responds to diagnosed problems in ways that the professional has been taught are best suited to the well-being of the client, the agency, and society.

Taking either of the above vantage points leads the observer to perceive the process of adaptation to disability primarily with an *outsider's* perspective (Dembo, 1964/1970, 1969; Shontz, 1982). Both standpoints are useful, but they are also limited because they tend not to acknowledge, or not to take as seriously as they should, the way the situation may look to the person who has the disability. As an outsider, the service provider recognizes only those problems and therapies that are officially sanctioned by society's official gate-keepers: physicians, judges, social workers, etc.

Insiders' Persepectives

An insider is a person who is actually suffering a misfortune such as a physical disability. Although insiders are expected to, and often do, adopt the outsiders' perspective, it is not uncommon for the way an insider perceives the treatment situation to differ considerably from the way outsiders, including both profes-sionals and nonprofessionals, see it. For instance, the insider is less likely than the researcher to be interested in making a contribution to scientific knowledge by participating in a risky experiment in order to solve a purely theoretical problem. An insider may not respond to a formal diagnosis but may be willing to admit that a *problem* exists only when personal suffering, or the anticipation of it, is intense and cannot be relieved by the insider's own efforts.

Other differences between outsiders' and insiders' perspectives have been identified (Shontz, 1982). The insider is likely to want relief only from what he or she is personally willing to acknowledge as being a source of unresolvable misfortune. The outsider is likely to regard the insider's judgments about such matters as being insufficiently reliable or as too subjective or ill-informed to serve as a basis upon which to make important treatment plans or decisions. A person who is suffering is likely to want immediate relief, whereas the professional thinks in terms of the entire course of patient care, from admission to discharge. In addition, whereas the researcher or clinician is primarily interested in the *facts* about a disability, the person with the disability is more likely to be interested in its *implications* for the future conduct of his/her life. The physiatrist wants to be sure that the patient is performing as well as possible, given the direct effects of the client's disabling physical condition. The client may only want to know how soon, or whether, he/she will be able to go back to work, eat a regular diet, or have sex.

A Personological Approach

A fully personological approach to understanding physical disability or illness (Shontz, 1984) would take all of the above perspectives into account. To be more specific, it would recognize that the concept of the body image can be studied only if one adopts the outsider's perspective. Nothing about body-image theory or research on body experience can be taken to suggest, even remotely, that the body image is a readily recognizable, concrete entity in anyone's immediate psychological awareness. A phantom limb is real enough to the person who feels it, but its source, whether physical or mental, lies outside of consciousness to the insider. What phantom limbs or any other forms of body experience "are," how they develop, where they reside, and what forms they assume are questions for the scientist and medical or rehabilitation professionals. Rarely does the scientific study of such matters concern clients themselves.

Indeed, the limitations that are automatically imposed when an investigator chooses to employ conventional research methodology virtually precludes studying whole persons. These limitations are such as to discourage investigators from being open to the complex set of events that are constantly occurring to and within a person. For example, conventional experimental methods restrict investigators to testing specific sets of hypotheses about relationships among narrowly operationally defined variables. Rigorous control is required over all possible sources of "error," and if control cannot be imposed physically it is necessary that possible sources of error, such as individual differences on unwanted variables, be measured and "adjusted out" of the data by statistical means. Such practices are intended to eliminate not highlight the peculiarities of individuals.

The study of the dimensions of body perception by Mayer and Eisenberg, cited in an earlier section of this chapter, shows how a research can contribute to general theoretical knowledge without telling a counselor or clinician anything that will be of value in treating individuals. Although the results of this study make an important point about how body experience in general is probably organized, a rehabilitation professional is not likely to gain very much by knowing how a particularly difficult client dimensionalizes his/her body schemata. Perhaps certain special conditions can be imagined in which such knowledge *might* be useful if it led to the employment of a specific treatment regimen that would change a client's entire life by helping that client redimensionalize his/her body experience. However, Mayer and Eisenberg's research report does not recommend this, nor is there any reason why it should. Their study concerned only the abstract, general properties of body experience. In fact, the investigators used highly sophisticated quantitative techniques of multidimensional scaling in order to be as certain as possible that the peculiarities of any individual's responses did not inordinately affect the conclusions that were drawn from the data on the groups as wholes.

Scientists and professionals, especially those who work in service delivery settings and are directly responsible for individual patient care, should learn to regard the body image as being only one component, albeit a complex and multifaceted one, of the total life situation of the person. Furthermore, it is a component that is discussable only when one assumes an outsider's standpoint.

To the extent that it becomes necessary (and it may not always be) to examine this component in detail, the researcher or professional help-giver should ask three basic questions:

1. What effects are this condition having on the various functions and levels of the person's body experience?
2. How is this person reacting to those effects?
3. What is the personal meaning of body experience to the client, in the context of his/her total life situation?

Generally speaking, conventional research and clinical practices devote a great deal of time and effort to the first two of these questions and spend relatively little on the third. However, some personological research, examining individuals intensively, has appeared in the rehabilitation literature. For example, Heinemann and Shontz (1984) examined in systematic fashion insiders' views of the roles that spinal cord injury play in their lives. These investigators selected for study two persons with quadriplegia who displayed contrasting rehabilitation outcomes. In order to obtain normative information about the cognitive abilities and general life styles of these persons, both were first administered standard tests of intelligence and personality. The life history of each person was then examined, with each person choosing several critical life episodes to serve as reference points for further study. Spontaneous and guided imagery were employed to induce re-experiencing of these episodes, and several morphogenic measures (Allport, 1962) were administered after each re-experiencing to assess reactions to the episodes. The measures included a set of Q-sort items, which had been devised to represent hypothesized stages of reaction to crises; investigator-provided as well as individually-generated role repertory constructs, which were used by the person to rate his/her own characteristics; and dimensional measures that produced ratings of depression and adjustment to disability.

The findings of this research highlight the importance of previously established coping styles as well as the role of environmental events in adjustment. Stages of adaptation were found to occur cyclically in one person (Deirdre), although they did not occur in the theoretically expected order, and they were usually triggered by external events. The other person (Craig) denied ever having experienced depression or having had any noticeable changes in his emotional state. Although both persons were making satisfactory behavioral adjustments at the time of the study, Craig had previously attempted suicide, an act which he regarded not as a response to depression but as a way to regain control over his life. The study seemed to show that some form of felt or expressed mourning, with or without the subjective experience of depression, is necessary if personal growth is to take place following the occurrence of profound life crisis.

Six Principles

By way of summarization, six principles relating disability and psychological adjustment have been formulated (Shontz, 1977). These apply to body image as well as to the adjustment process as a whole:

1. Psychological reactions to the onset or imposition of physical disability are not uniformly disturbing or distressing and do not necessarily result in maladjustment. By the same token, psychological reactions to the removal of physical disabilities are not uniformly or necessarily pleasant and do not necessarily lead to improved adjustment. Even though direct body experience is affected by the onset of most disabilities, the impact of the effects are not always negative. For example, Beecher (1956) found that hospitalized combat soldiers who were wounded on the Anzio beachhead in World War II suffered less than civilians who were in civilian hospitals for surgery. For civilians, the physical disorder that brought them in for care often constituted a threat to an otherwise satisfactory way of living. For soldiers, however, an honorably acquired wound is a way out of an extremely threatening situation. Anxiety arises in persons who recover from disabilities when they are forced to face problems that never arose before or that could be successfully avoided during the period of disablement.

2. Favorable or unfavorable psychological reactions to disabilities are not related in a simple way to the physical properties of the disabilities. As noted in preceding sections, physical impairment usually affects body image at more than one level and influences more than one type of body-image function. Further-more, the work of Fisher and others has shown that reactions to changes in body experience are probably more a function of how much anxiety is generated by the experience than by the location, severity, or type of experience itself.

3. The shorter and less complex the causal linkage is between the body structure affected by a disability and the adaptive behavior in question, the more predictable the latter is from the former. With regard to body image, it is perhaps obvious that the occurrence of phantom-limb experiences is more readily predictable from the knowledge that a person's arm has been amputated than is the occurrence of a maladaptive reaction to the body as stimulus to others (a function that is further removed from the direct source of stimulation). It is easier to anticipate that any person with paraplegia will have trouble walking than to predict that every such person will become bitter and angry about the condition.

4. The less direct the linkage between the body structure affected and the behavior in question, the more appropriate it is to describe the influence of disability as facilitative, rather than as causal or coercive. It is probably safe to say that a condition such as anosognosia is "caused" by damage to the central nervous system. It is less obvious that a divorce that follows the third exacerbation of multiple sclerosis in one member of a married couple was caused

by the medical condition alone. Body-image effects may be caused by physical states, but the ways in which people react to those states and the meanings those states acquire are not caused either by the states themselves or the influence they have upon the body image as such.

5. Environmental factors are at least as important in determining psychological reactions to disabilities as are the internal states of the persons who have the disabilities. A simple example: How well integrated the body-image disturbances of a person with quadriplegia may be does not matter if architectural barriers prevent the person from getting into public buildings or using public transportation. A person with cerebral palsy who has athetoid movements may feel comfortable with his/her physical state, but the prejudices of others that are aroused by the person's social stimulus value may prevent that person from engaging in a full or satisfying life and may induce serious states that others will perceive as maladjustment.

6. The final, and most important, principle is that, of all the factors that affect the total life situation of a person with a disability, the disability itself is only one, and often its influence is relatively minor. People are notoriously adaptive. They have shown themselves to be capable of living with all sorts of difficulties, pains, and discomforts, if they feel there is a good reason for doing so. If life has meaning and purpose, then a disorder of body image may fade into insignificance. On the other hand, a life that has no meaning, purpose, or overriding goal is easily disrupted. When a physical disability or the body-image problems that result from it become the main focus of concern in a person's life, that life becomes narrowed and restricted. Psychologically, to overcome a disability means to stop thinking about it all the time and to get on with the business of living as best one can. Indeed, it has been said that a person with a chronic illness or disability has satisfactorily come to terms with a personal medical condition to the extent that the problem of contending with it ceases to be the dominant element in that person's total psychological structure or life space (Shontz, 1982).

This brings about a paradox for professionals whose job it is to help others adjust to physically disabling conditions. The process of treatment and rehabilitation requires concentration upon the illness or disability-related difficulties that arise, in order that they can be overcome. This means that patients, who may already be under severe emotional stress from their physical conditions, are often forced to concentrate upon their body-image problems, to spend a good deal of time and effort examining their own deficiencies and difficulties, even if they find the task to be less than worthwhile. Perhaps it also means placing more emphasis or a different kind of emphasis upon the body and its functions than the patient has done before in his/her life. The job often cannot be done without requiring the person to abandon, if only temporarily, many of the most important aspects of his/her life that have nothing whatever to do with the medical conditions being treated. Fortunately, for the most part, people with chronic illnesses and disabilities possess sufficient integrative resources and capacity for delay of gratification to absorb the stress of rehabilitative care and to benefit from it, provided that they can see themselves making progress and that they have sufficient hope in the future to justify the effort it requires.

REFERENCES

Allport, G. W. (1962). The general and the unique in psychological science. *Journal of Personality, 30*, 405–421.

Barral, M R. (1965). *Merleau-Ponty: The role of the body-subject in interpersonal relations.* Pittsburgh, PA: Duquesne University Press.

Beecher, H. K. (1956). Relationship of significance of wound to pain experienced. *Journal of the American Medical Association, 161*, 1609–1613.

Benton, A. L. (1959). *Right–left discrimination and finger localization: Development and pathology.* New York: Harper & Row.

Critchley, M. (1965). Disorders of corporeal awareness in parietal disease. In S. Wapner & H. Werner (Eds.), *The body percept* (pp. 82–106). New York: Random House.

de Ajuriaguerra, J. (1965). Discussion. In S. Wapner & H. Werner (Eds.)., *The body percept* (pp. 82–106). New York: Random House.

Dembo, T. (1969). Rehabilitation psychology and its immediate future: A problem of utilization of psychological knowledge. *Rehabilitation Psychology (Formerly Psychological Aspects of Disability)*, 16, 63–72.

Dembo, T. 1964/1970). Sensitivity of one person to another. In R. L. Noland (Ed.), *Counseling parents of the metally retarded: A sourcebook* (pp. 71–82). Springfield, IL: Charles C. Thomas.

Fisher, S. (1970). *Body experience in fantasy and behavior.* New York: Appleton-Century-Crofts.

Fisher, S. (1986). *Development and structure of the body image* (Vols. 1 & 2). Hillsdale, NJ: Erlbaum.

Fisher, S., & Cleveland, E. E. (1958). *Body image and personality.* Princeton, NJ: Van Nostrand.

Gerstmann, J. (1942). Problem of imperception of disease and of impaired body territories with organic lesions. Relation to body schema and its disorders. *Archives of Neurology and Psychiatry, 48*, 890–913.

Gertsmann, J. (1958). Psychological and phenomenological aspects of disorders of the body image. *Journal of Nervous and Mental Disease, 126*, 499–512.

Geschwind, N., & Strub, R. (1975). Gerstmann syndrome without aphasia: A reply to Poeck and Orgass. *Cortex, 11*, 296–298.

Gibson, J. J. (1951). Theories of perception. In W. Dennis (Ed.), *Current trends in psychological theory* (pp. 85–110). Pittsburgh, PA: University of Pittsburgh Press.

Gibson, J. J. (1979). *The ecological approach to visual perception.* Boston: Houghton Mifflin.

Head, H. (1920). *Studies in neurology* (Vol. 2). London: Oxford University Press.

Head, H. (1926). *Aphasia and kindred disorders of speech.* London: Cambridge University Press.

Heinemann, A. W., & Shontz, F. C. (1984). Adjustment folowing disability: Representative case studies. *Rehabilitation Counseling Bulletin, 28*, 3–14.

Koffka, K. (1935). *Principles of Gestalt psychology.* New York: Harcourt, Brace.

Kolb, L. C. (1959). Disturbances of the body image. In S. Arieti (Ed.), *American Handbook of Psychiatry* (Vol. 1, pp. 749–769). New York: Basic Books.

Mayer, J. D., & Eisenberg, M. G. (1988). Mental representation of the body: Stability and change in response to illness and disability. *Rehabilitation Psychology, 33*, 155–171.

Neisser, U. (1988). Five kinds of self-knowledge. *Philosophical psychology*. *1*, 35–59.

Penfield, W., & Rasmussen, T. (1950). *The cerebral cortex of man*. New York: Macmillan.

Piaget, J. (1951). *Play, dreams and imitation in childhood* (C. Gattegno & F. M Hodgson, Trans.). New York: Norton.

Piaget, J. (1952). *The origins of intelligence in children*. New York: International Universities Press.

Poeck, K., & Orgass, B. (1966). Gerstmann's syndrome and aphasia. *Cortex*, *2*, 421–437.

Poeck, K., & Orgass, B. (1971). The concept of the body schema: A critical review and some experimental results. *Cortex*, *7*, 254–277.

Scheerer, M. (1954). Cognitive theory. In G. Lindzey (Ed.), *Handbook of social psychology* (pp. 91–142). Reading, MA: Addison-Wesley.

Schilder, P. (1935). *The image and appearance of the human body*. London: Kegan, Paul, Trench, Trubner & Co.

Secord, P. F., & Jourard, S. L. (1953). The appraisal of body cathexis: Body cathexis and the self. *Journal of Consulting Psychology*, *17*, 343–347.

Shontz, F. C. (1960). Cognitive processes, cognitive theories and rehabilitation. In L. H. Lofquist (Ed.), *Psychological research and rehabilitation* (pp. 13–51). Washington DC: American Psychological Association.

Shontz, F. C. (1969). *Perceptual and cognitive aspects of body experience*. New York: Academic Press.

Shontz, F. C. (1974). Body image and its disorders. *International Journal of Psychiatry in Medicine*, *5*, 461–471.

Shontz, F. C. (1975). *The psychological aspects of physical illness and disability*. New York: Macmillan.

Shontz, F. C. (1977). Six principles relating disability and psychological adjustment. *Rehabilitation Psychology*, *24*, 207–210.

Shontz, F. C. (1980). Theories about the adjustment to having a disability. In. W. M. Cruickshank (Ed.), *Psychology of exceptional children and youth* (4th ed., pp. 3–44). Englewood Cliffs, NJ: Prentice-Hall.

Shontz, F. C. (1982). Adaptation to chronic illness and disability. In. T. Millon, C. Green, & R. B. Meagher (Eds.), *Handbook of clinical health psychology* (pp. 153–172). New York: Plenum Press.

Shontz, F. C. (1984). A personologic approach for health psychology research. *American Behavioral Scientist*. 28, 510–524.

Shontz, F. C. (1987, November 12–14). Seymour Fisher's contribution to research on body image. In *The Body and Literature*. An interdisciplinary conference at SUNY-Buffalo, Buffalo, New York.

Shontz, F. C. & McNish, R. D. (1972). The human body as stimulus object: Estimates of distances between body landmarks. *Journal of Experimental Psychology*, *95*, 20–24.

Simmel, M. L. (1956). On phantom limbs. *Archives of Neurology and Psychiatry*, *75*, 637–647.

Stern, W. (1935). *General psychology from the personalistic standpoint* (H. D. Spoerl, Trans.). New York: Macmillan.

Weinstein, E. A., & Kahn, R. L. (1955). *Denial of illness*. Springfield, IL: Charles C. Thomas.

Wright, B. A. (1983). *Physical disability —a psychosocial approach* (2nd ed.). New York: Harper & Row.

CHAPTER 8

Psychopathology of Body Experience: Expanded Perspectives

Thomas Pruzinsky

The vast majority of contemporary research on body-image psychopathology focuses on the eating disorders (Rosen, Chapter 9, this volume; Thompson, 1990). This research provides important information regarding the roles of body image in the etiology, maintenance, relapse, and treatment of anorexia and bulimia nervosa. On the other hand, the domination of eating-disorders research risks inhibiting the development of a comprehensive understanding and treatment of the vast range of body-image psychopathologies (Cash, 1988). Many other forms of pathology are expressed primarily through bodily feelings, attitudes, or symptoms (Bix & Snaith, 1988; Cumming, 1988; Kolb, 1975; Lacey & Birtchnell, 1986; Nightingale, 1982; Shontz, 1974; Sims, 1988; Vaeth, 1986), and some have not been adequately elucidated from a body-image perspective—for example, hypochondria, body dysmorphic disorder, somatic delusions, transsexualism, and self-mutilation. Existing research on these disorders is scattered across the general medicine, psychiatric, dermatological, and plastic surgery journals. The perspectives on body image offered by these disciplines allows us to expand our thinking and knowledge about body-image psychopathology.

Much of the scholarly literature reviewed in this volume focuses on appearance-related variables. However, individuals focus on many aspects of body experience other than appearance, including feelings regarding strength, size, degree of masculinity and femininity, experience of body boundaries, overall level of body security, and feelings about emotional arousal (see Fisher, 1986, 1989). Thus, this chapter focuses not only on physical appearance but also on subjective body experiences including perceptions, beliefs, and emotions vis-a-vis bodily functions (Lipowski, 1977). Body-image dysfunctions associated with eating disorders are examined in great detail by Rosen in Chapter 9 of this volume.

BODY-EXPERIENCE PSYCHOPATHOLOGIES

There are two major categories of body-experience psychopathology. In the first group the body-image problem is a central defining feature of the disorder—as in hypochondria, body dysmorphic disorder, somatic delusions, gender identity disorders, koro, and self-mutilation. The second group consists of psychological disorders *associated* with but *not* primarily focused on body image, including depression, sexual dysfunction, and schizophrenia.

Hypochondria

Hypochondria is a classic psychopathology of body experience and is one of the Somatoform Disorders listed in the revised third edition of the Diagnostic and Statistical Manual of Mental Disorders (American Psychiatric Association [APA], 1987). Many reviews of the etiology and treatment of hypochondria already exist (e.g., Barsky & Klerman, 1983; Kellner, 1986; Kenyon, 1965). The central defining characteristic of hypochondria is the patient's fear that they have a serious illness, despite the fact that there is no objective medical evidence that such a disease exists. The patient's fear of illness and the subsequent preoccupation with this fear is ". . . based on the person's interpretation of physical signs or symptoms as physical illness" (APA, 1987, p. 261).

Hypochondriacal patients often experience impaired functioning as a result of their beliefs about their medical condition and are usually unshakable in their beliefs. There is a clear relationship between hypochondria and the sense of self.

> the primary theme of hypochondriacal communication is, "There is something wrong with me," it is proposed that the symptom serves a symbolic representation of low self-esteem. The mechanism of symptom formation is a simple displacement of the feeling that there is something wrong with the self from the psyche to the soma. The transformation of the amorphous feeling into a somatic disease enables the patient to define and communicate his problem in a concrete form. (McCranie, 1979, p. 12)

Despite clarification of the diagnostic criteria for hypochondria (e.g., in DSM-III-R), there is still much confusion regarding the specific meaning of hypochondriacal symptoms. Part of this confusion is because a hypochondriacal focus on bodily symptoms can take many forms, including a somatic hallucination, a somatic delusion, a somatic delusion secondary to another form of psychopathology, an overvalued idea, an obsessional rumination, or an anxious preoccupation (Sims, 1988). Another source of confusion is the wide range of extant conceptual and etiological perspectives. For example, hypochondria is regarded as a form of masked depression, an anxiety disorder, as well as a body-image disturbance (see Kellner, 1986, pp. 9-10). Additionally, hypochondria has been viewed in terms of psychodynamic processes, perceptual or cognitive abnormalities, or learned social behavior (Barsky & Klerman, 1983). In light of this confusion, Barsky and Klerman (1983) suggest replacing the term *hypochondria* with the alternative term *amplifying somatic style*.

> Individuals with an amplifying somatic style scrupulously monitor their normal body sensations and functions; they scrutinize trivial and transitory symptoms that others might note but dismiss as insignificant; they react to these perceptions with apprehension and alarm; they readily attribute them to physical disease. (Barsky & Klerman, 1983, p. 280)

Thus, for the hypochondriacal individual, the body is in the foreground of life experiences, whereas the rest of the world is background. For most individuals the reverse is true, except in times of illness, bodily threat, or bodily change. This "hypochondriacal somatic style" leads to chronic anxiety and misperceptions of bodily experience.

Body Dysmorphic Disorder

Another DSM-III-R Somatoform Disorder is Body Dysmorphic Disorder (APA, 1987). Historically, Body Dysmorphic Disorder (BDD) has been referred to as "beauty hypochondria" (Ladee, 1966) and more commonly as "dysmorphophobia" (Andreasen & Bardach, 1977; Birtchnell, 1988; Braddock, 1982; Connolly & Gipson, 1978; Crisp, 1981; Hardy & Cotterill, 1982; Hay, 1970, 1983; Thomas, 1984). BDD is a "preoccupation with some imagined defect in a normal-appearing person" (APA, 1987, p. 255), which is not a somatic delusion nor due to an eating disorder or Gender Identity Disorder (APA, 1987). DSM-III-R (1987) also states that if the person does have some "slight physical anomaly" (p. 256) but reacts to it in a manner grossly out of proportion to the actual deformity than he/she would also be classified as having BDD. BDD is attributed to a body-image disturbance (Hardy, 1984; Thomas, 1984). The focus of the individual's concern can be on any body part, though it is most commonly on the face (APA, 1987).

These patients often repeatedly seek medical consultations and are frequently treated by plastic surgeons and dermatologists (Thomas, 1984). Contemporary descriptions of dysmorphophobia are largely based on reports of plastic surgery patients who seek treatment for "minimal deformities" (Connolly & Gipson, 1978; Edgerton, Jacobson, & Meyer, 1960; Hay, 1970). Dysmorphophobic patients often evidence obsessional, depressive, schizoid, and narcissistic traits (Cotterill, 1981; Hardy & Cotterill, 1982; Stekel, 1950; Thomas, 1984). The degree of social, occupational, and psychological impairment varies from individual to individual but can be severe (Birtchnell, 1988; Thomas, 1984). In the past, dysmorphophobic symptoms were considered to be prognostically ominous (Bychowski, 1943; Hay, 1970; Stekel, 1950).

Despite increasing clinical attention being paid to dysmorphophobia, many questions remain regarding the classification of these symptoms (Birthchnell, 1988; Thomas, 1984). First, there is no evidence of a phobia in dysmorphophobia; there is no fear of other individuals with a physical deformity. There is no fear of an existing deformity or a fear of becoming deformed in the future. Thus, "dysmorphophobia" is a misnomer (APA, 1987; Thomas, 1984), and the more accurate term to describe these problems is BDD. The term *phobia* in dysmorphophobia has been employed because these individuals often report apprehensiveness regarding the reaction that their perceived appearance will evoke from others. This concern often leads to social avoidance and inhibition. Furthermore, "it is not yet determined whether dysmorphophobia is one presentation of an underlying disease, or exists in its own right as a separate disease entity" (Lacey & Birtchnell, 1986, p. 628, citing Andreasen & Bardach, 1977). However, there is agreement that *dysmorphophobia* should not be used to describe body-image disturbances associated with organic diseases (Birtchnell, 1988; Hay, 1970; Thomas, 1984). Additionally, dysmorphic symptoms in the presence of psychotic symptomology or severe mood disorders are considered "secondary" dysmorphophobia (Thomas, 1984).

Some confusion is evident regarding the definition of dysmorphophobia because its symptoms "may range from obsessional preoccupation to a frank delusion, whilst the accompanying self-consciousness may similarly range to delusions of reference" (Lacey & Birtchnell, 1986, p. 627). DSM-III-R diagnostic criteria clarify that the critical differential diagnosis with respect to Delusional Disorder, Somatic Type, hinges upon the intensity of the patient's belief in the defectiveness of their appearance. The nondelusional patient "can acknowledge the possibility that he or she may be exaggerating the extent of the defect or that there may be no defect at all" (APA, 1987, p. 256). In delusional disorder, this ability to disengage or distance one's self from the perception of the deformity is not present.

Despite this attempted distinction between delusional and nondelusional dysmorphic beliefs, it remains "unclear . . . whether or not the belief is a delusion, or whether they are merely variants of the same disorder" (APA, 1987, p. 256). However, it does appear that BDD experiences are characteristic of an overvalued idea (Andreasen, 1977; Birtchnell, 1988; de Leon, Bott, & Simpson, 1989; Sims, 1988; Thomas, 1984), which is "a solitary, abnormal belief that is neither delusional nor obsessional in nature, but which is preoccupying to the extent of dominating the suffer's life" (McKenna, 1984, p. 579).

> The phenomenology of the overvalued idea seems to combine the unlikely elements of non-delusional conviction, non-obsessional preoccupation and non-phobic fear. At the heart of all the disorders is an abnormally intense

conviction that has been repeatedly observed not to be delusional. . . . The preoccupation that inevitably accompanies the beliefs shows none of the features of obsessional preoccupation; the idea is seen as natural rather than intrusive, is acquiesced to without resistance, and is not regarded as senseless or even futile. (McKenna, 1984, p. 583)

Summary

Given that BDD is new to the official diagnostic nomenclature, it will take time to evaluate its usefulness (de Leon et al., 1989; Munro, 1987). An important step will be the refinement of the definition of the "degree of physical deformity present" (Birtchnell, 1988). In other words, what is a "minimal deformity?" The plastic surgery literature clearly documents that there is no necessary relationship between the degree of physical deformity and the degree of psychological distress experienced by the patient (Edgerton & Langman, 1982; Pruzinsky, 1988). This is a critical maxim for the psychologically astute plastic surgeon. Very large physical deformities may cause little psychological distress, and small deformities often cause great psychological distress. Just because a patient's physical deformity is objectively "minimal" does not necessarily rule out the possibility of a positive impact from surgery (Edgerton & Langman, 1982). Additionally, the patient's degree of distress regarding the physical deformity must be considered in his or her unique cultural context (Birtchnell, 1988; Macgregor, 1981, 1989). For example, in some cultures, even small facial scars on women have profound social and psychological implications (Birtchnell, 1988; Macgregor, 1981, 1989).

The experience of BDD can be usefully interpreted in terms of a "somatic style." As Barksy and Klerman (1983) point out, just as there is an "amplifying somatic style" evident in hypochondria, "[t]here are surely other somatic styles . . . [which] include ways of dealing with physical appearance and physical attractiveness; attitudes toward physical fitness, strength, and activity; perceptions of aging and other non-pathological deviations such as baldness, short stature, infertility, myopia, and colorblindness . . . " (p. 281). Thus, in BDD, as in hypochondria, the individual pays a great deal of attention to bodily processes (i.e., appearance factors in BDD and arousal factors in hypochondria). In hypochondria, this attentional focus leads to increased accuracy in the perception of some aspects of bodily arousal, but with concomitant overreaction to this arousal as well as oversensitivity to any type of arousal fluctuation (Fisher, 1986). A similar process occurs in BDD, where the attentional focus leads the individual to be more discerning of their physical appearance, but also more distressed about and likely to misinterpret or exaggerate their perceptions. Fisher (1986) states that "although a good deal of the research dealing with the impact of being exposed to one's mirror image has shown that it stirs guilt and self-disapproval, evidence has also emerged that it increases the accuracy of perception of other events" (Fisher, 1986, p. 288). Thus, the person who spends an inordinate amount of time looking at their reflection in the mirror can become very discerning regarding the details of their physical appearance and experience a range of negative emotions (e.g., shame) (Fisher, 1986).

In the two forms of Somatoform disorders described in this chapter (Hypochondriasis and BDD), two different "somatic styles" are evident. The hypochondriacal somatic style focuses on bodily sensations and the BDD somatic style focuses on bodily appearance.

Somatic Delusions

Somatic delusions are classified in DSM-III-R under the rubric of Delusional (Paranoid) Disorder, which is described as "the presence of a persistent, nonbizzare delusion that is not due to any other mental disorder, such as Schizophrenia, Schizophreniform Disorder, or a Mood Disorder" (APA, 1987, p. 199). There are five common variants of Delusional (Paranoid) Disorders described in DSM-III-R (i.e., erotomanic, grandiose, jealous, persecutory, and somatic). The somatic type is a "disorder in which the predominant theme of the delusion(s) is that the person has some physical defect, disorder or disease" (APA, 1987, p. 203).

Development of this DSM-III-R category was partially based on Munro's description of monosymptomatic hypochondriacal psychosis (MHP) (Munro, 1978, 1980, 1983, 1988; Munro & Chmara, 1982; Munro & Pollock, 1981). MHP "is characterized by a single hypochondriacal, delusional system, distinct from the remainder of the personality" (Munro & Chmara, 1982, p. 374). MHP "appears to be a form of paranoia and is distinct from the neurotic dysmorphophobias, and from hypochondriasis arising from other neurotic or personality disorders" (Munro, 1978, p. 497).

There are three common presentations of MHP: delusions of dysmorphosis (i.e., belief that one's body or parts are ugly or misshapen), delusions of body odor (e.g., halitosis), and delusions of infestation (e.g., with insects, worms) (Munro, 1988; Munro & Chmara, 1982; Munro & Pollock, 1981). These three types of MHP are similar in terms of descriptive features, predisposing factors, associated symptomology, and treatment outcome (Munro & Chmara, 1982). Delusions of infestation appear to be the most commonly reported somatic delusions (see Bishop, 1980, 1983, as well as Wykoff, 1987, for reviews of delusions of infestation).

The onset of MHP can be abrupt or insidious and is sometimes associated with a particular stressor (Frances & Munro, 1989). The predisposing psychological characteristics of these individuals include personality disorders, as well as obsessional and schizoid traits (Frances & Munro, 1989). The condition dominates the individual's life as the person searches for medical "cures" for the problems.

These patients experience profound disturbance of their lives as a result of their illness. Its chronicity, the tension it generates, the endless quest for unavailing treatments, and the conflicting and inappropriate advice they are given, cause enormous concern and anguish to them and their families. The more distressed and delusional they become, the more frantically they seek the wrong kind of help and the more antagonistic they become towards psychiatric help. The literature suggests that some may commit suicide. (Munro, 1988, p. 38)

As stated earlier, the main distinction between dysmorphic delusions and BDD is the intensity of the belief held by the patient. However, while "most experienced clinicians can describe delusional beliefs and can distinguish between ideas that are delusional and those that are not, it is very difficult to obtain consensus on a specific definition of delusions (Oltmanns & Maher, 1988, p. ix). The "difference between body-dysmorphic disorder and delusional disorder, somatic type, depends on whether the thoughts of the defect in appearance represent an overvalued idea (with uncertainty) as in dysmorphophobia . . . or reach delusional intensity (with certainty) as in monosymptomatic hypochon-driacal psychosis" (Hollander, Liebowitz, Winchel, Klumker, & Klein, 1989, p. 768), though some clinicians do not believe that such a distinction can be made (de Leon et al., 1989)

The psychological condition of most MHP patients does not appear to deteriorate over time (Frances & Munro, 1989), and there are effective treatments available. The most frequently cited treatment for delusional disorder is with the drug Pimozide (Frances & Munro, 1989; Munro, 1988; Munro & Chmara, 1982), which

is a powerful neuroleptic, closely related to haloperidol . . . The patient's usual course with treatment, even in chronic cases, is of substantial symptom-atic recovery within two weeks and continued improvement over a period of several months . . . Some patients eventually come off all medication, but many require prolonged maintenance therapy . . . The success rate in treat-ment compliant patients is 60 to 80 percent, with complete or substantial return to normal existence. (Frances & Munro, 1989, p. 1114)

Despite this effective treatment, patients often remain susceptible to heightened sensitivity regarding their previously delusional concern as well to recurrence of the full-blown delusional disorder during periods of increased stress.

Gender Identity Disorders

Gender identity is a basic component of our sense of self and body image (Fisher, 1986, 1989; Fleming et al., 1982). "Gender identity is the sense of knowing to which sex one belongs, that is, the awareness that 'I am a male' or 'I am a female.' Gender identity is the private experience of gender role, and gender role is the public expression of gender identity" (APA, 1987, p. 71). Gender identity problems exist when an individual is concerned about discrepancies between biological sex, gender identity, and gender role. Under the rubric of gender identity disorders are patients with various degrees of gender identity disturbance. The most extreme form of gender identity disturbance is transsexualism, in which "the person not only is uncomfortable with the assigned sex but has the sense of belonging to the opposite sex" (APA, 1987, p. 71). Transsexuals are so disturbed by the discrepancy between their physical characteristics and their psychological gender that they seek surgical correction. Transsexuals are born with normal male or female anatomy, but they firmly believe that they were born "in the wrong body"—clearly a body-image problem.

> The concept of body image has particular relevance to the phenomenon of transsexualism . . . The transsexual is unable to form a satisfactory body image because of the dissonance between his (or her) anatomic sex and gender identity (psychological sex). The reality of the transsexual's body does not conform to the preferred and desired body image. The result is a disturbance of a complete and consistent self-concept. (Pauly & Lindgren, 1976–1977, p. 134).

Despite the obvious relevance, little has been written regarding the relationship between body image and transsexualism (Fisher, 1989). Much of the extant empirical work utilizes projective methodologies of body-image assessment (Fisher, 1989; Freytag, 1977).

Transsexuals represent a fascinating group of patients to study in terms of body-image transformation. Although much speculation exists regarding the etiological factors of transsexualism (Hoenig, 1985), among professionals experienced in treating transsexualism there is agreement regarding the current treatment of choice (Pauly & Edgerton, 1986). The goal of the treatment process is the reduction of discrepancies between the patient's biological sex and their subjective self-perception. This is accomplished by facilitating the patient's progressive body-image transformation, which initially requires "cross-dressing" in the desired gender and taking on the social role of the gender of choice. In addition to cross-dressing in all social situations and living completely in the desired gender, these patients undergo hormone treatment to facilitate the masculinization or feminization process.

Only after patients have successfully traversed these initial treatment stages (cross-living and hormone treatment) can they be candidates for surgical modifications. Surgical intervention often begins with reduction of the breasts of biological females and breast augmentation in biological males. Patients experience psychological satisfaction from these surgeries, yet many still desire reconstructive genital surgery.

Lindgren and Pauly (1975), using the Lindgren–Pauly Body Image Scale, found that as patients progress through treatment, from the initial use of hormones followed by surgery, there is a progressive increase in body-image satisfaction. Clinically, patients report some positive change in body image when they begin cross-dressing. As they undertake hormone treatment, biological males reduce beard growth, experience testicular atrophy, and may experience moderate breast development. Biological females may experience beard growth, voice deepening, and cessation of menstruation. As these changes occur patients report greater body-image satisfaction (Langman, Pruzinsky, Edgerton, & Nachbar, 1987). Thus, properly treated transsexuals experience a progressive transformation of their bodies to match their self-perceptions. However, different patients have different goals. Most patients do not experience relief from their sense of body-image discrepancy until undergoing genital surgery. Other patients do not psychologically require genital surgery; that is, some experience sufficient psychological relief from cross-dressing and hormonal interventions alone. Still other patients psychologically require hormonal treatment, genital surgeries, and multiple facial surgeries to feminize or masculinize appearance. In one patient I assessed, after all of the standard medical interventions had been successfully completed, surgical reduction of the ankle and shin bones was relentlessly pursued by a biological male (who underwent surgery to become female). The patient's goal was to achieve a "feminine" contour of the leg. This patient was not satisfied until this change occurred.

It is important to note that these patients do not experience genital surgery (or *any* medical intervention) as facilitating "gender reassignment." Rather, for the "true" transsexual the medical–surgical interventions are experienced as "gender confirmation"—that is, having the physical body "confirm" what has "always" been internally experienced.

Koro

A fascinating form of body-experience psychopathology is koro, an apparently rare syndrome (Ang & Weller, 1984; Fishbain, Barsky & Goldberg, 1989; Mellor, 1988; Rubin, 1982; Yap, 1965) composed of the belief that the penis is retracting into the abdomen, leading to the experience of intense anxiety and panic and the use of mechanical devises to prevent the retraction of the penis into the abdomen. "The strength of the delusory belief determines the degree of fear and panic, which in turn determines the vigor with which the remedies are attempted, leading to various degrees of physical damage to the genitals" (Rubin, 1982, p. 155).

There is a strong cultural influence regarding the experience of koro (Yap, 1965). Most victims are Chinese males (Rubin, 1982). There are very few reports of cases of koro in Western cultures. The cultural impact most likely occurs because:

> of the long tradition in Chinese culture of attaching great importance to the preservation of sexual function. . . . Thus, guilt over excessive masturbation, unsatisfactory intercourse with one's wife, promiscuity . . . frequently have been psychological precipitants of an acute koro attack. . . . Thus . . .

hearsay information about koro, along with preexisting sexual fears and subjective sensations in the genitalia . . . leads to a vicious circle of the delusion of genital shrinkage, attendant panic, and enhanced fears of a delusory nature, with even greater panic and crude attempts to prevent the disappearance of the penis. (Rubin, 1982, pp. 156–157)

Koro is described here to emphasize the critical interaction among cultural–social, perceptual (i.e., proprioceptive), and intrapsychic–situational factors in the etiology of psychopathology of body experience.

[T]he visual angle subtended by one's own penis on casual self-inspection is less than that of the view of another man's genitals, which may be the basis of a general regard of one's own genital apparatus as smaller than another's. Under normal circumstances this remains but a fleeting impression, being counteracted by one's adequacy of sexual performance and competence in other areas of life. However, in men with predisposing sexual conflicts or with . . . culturally determined beliefs, an otherwise innocuous phenomenon such as the normal retraction of the penis after a bath or on a particularly cold day may serve to trigger the koro fear of the penis completely shrinking into the abdomen . . . (Rubin, 1982, p. 171)

Self-Mutilation

Self-mutilation is a symptom occurring in a range of psychiatric disorders (Walsh & Rosen, 1988). Because of their physical injuries, many self-mutilating patients are treated in the general hospital setting (DeMuth, Strain, & Lomabardo-Maher, 1983; Drinker, Knorr, & Edgerton, 1972; Goldwyn, Cahill, & Grunebaum, 1967; Phelps, Buchler, & Boswick, 1977).

Walsh and Rosen (1988) describe a study (Walsh, 1987) that found that "body alienation" was the single-most important predictor of self-mutilation in adolescents. Body alienation refers to the individuals' experience of "their bodies as somehow separate from their real selves—as contaminated, alien and grotesque" (Walsh & Rosen, 1988, p. 74). Walsh (1987) found that body alienation was related to childhood experiences of physical illness and/or hospitalization, physical or sexual abuse, family violence and substance abuse, and parental loss (through death, divorce, or foster home placement) (Walsh, 1987). Body alienation resulted in a range of body-related problems, including eating disorders, a disregard for physical appearance, sexual identity problems, distortions in the thoughts and feelings about body size and shape, as well as higher incidence of physical illnesses (Walsh, 1987).

It is clear that self-mutilation was only one way in which these adolescents expressed their body alienation. For most, there was a pervasive pattern of disrespect, discomfort and debasement of their physical selves. Self-mutilation was simply the most dramatic form of expression of body dissatisfaction. (Rosen & Walsh, 1988, p. 70)

Self-mutilation is directly related to the belief that one deserves to be mutilated. "The belief that self-injury is deserved derives from a broader condemnation of self. Self-mutilators report that they loathe and hate themselves" (Walsh & Rosen, 1988, pp. 156–157).

> Especially common are derogatory thoughts about their bodies. . . . These mutilators have thoughts such as . . . : "I hate my body. I'm so ugly. I'm so disgusting. I can't stand looking at myself in the mirror." These negative thoughts about body image are critical since they establish the person's own body as repulsive and as a likely target for abuse. When guilt or other emotions become intolerable, the mutilator has psychologically established his or her body as target for self-sacrifice. (p. 157)

In treating adolescents who are self-mutilators, Walsh and Rosen (1985, 1988) utilize a multimodal approach emphasizing body alienation. This approach attempts to facilitate the patient's more adaptive and integrated bodily experience, including cognitive changes of the self-statements and beliefs regarding body and self, as well as direct approaches to body care (e.g., personal grooming, makeup, and the selection of clothes). This treatment regimen has shown initial promise in the reduction of self-mutilative behavior.

Another important component of the treatment of self-mutilation is the development of social skills. The scarring that results from the self-mutilation further exacerbates these patients' feelings of unacceptability and repulsiveness to others, leading to a decrease in social interaction (Walsh & Rosen, 1988). In my own clinical work, I have evaluated patients seeking plastic surgery for removal of the physical stigmata of self-mutilation, including the replantation of amputated body parts. These patients are usually hesitant to discuss the cause of their scars and experience a great deal of shame. However, they are willing to discuss their motivations for surgery as part of their preoperative evaluation. In properly selected patients, these surgical interventions greatly benefit the patient and facilitate positive body-image change.

Other Dysfunctional Body Experiences

There are a number of other psychiatric disorders that can be considered within the realm of body experience psychopathology. For example, conversion disorders "may be viewed as a particular distortion of body image, and much attention has been given by psychoanalysts to the symbolic values which may be ascribed to certain body parts and how these may become the vehicle for the expression of psychopathology" (Lacey & Birtchnell, 1986, p. 628). Although depersonalization is a very common psychological experience, which is considered by many to be a body-image problem (Fisher, 1986; Mellor, 1988; Schilder, 1935), little research exists relating body-image variables and depersonalization (Fisher, 1986). There are also the more rare autoscopic phenomenon "in which a person visualizes a veritable hallucinatory image of his double"

(Grotstein, 1982, p. 77), which Schilder (1935) described as the external projection of body image (Grotstein, 1982). A range of body-image related problems are variants of self-mutilation, including Munchausen syndrome (Nadelson, 1986) and surgical addiction (Menninger, 1939; Wright, 1985). In this regard, it is interesting to note the relatively high incidence of self-mutilation in patients with eating disorders (Garner, Garfinkel, & O'Shaughnessy, 1982). Moreover, "Crisp (1977) reports that some anorexic patients, especially the young, undergo laparotomy or appendectomy to correct an uneasy sense that there is something wrong within the body" (Yates, Shisslak, Allender, & Wolman, 1988, p. 557).

PSYCHOPATHOLOGIES WITH A POSSIBLE BODY-IMAGE COMPONENT

There are other psychiatric problems that are proposed to have an important, though not a defining body-image component. Such syndromes include depression, sexual dysfunctions, and schizophrenia.

Depression

The proposition that there is a relationship between depression and body-image disturbances has drawn from many theoretical perspectives, including the cognitive (Noles, Cash, & Winstead, 1985) and the psychodynamic (Peto, 1972). The relationship between depression and body-image disturbance can range from the appearance-related concerns of patients with general self-esteem problems (e.g., Teri, 1982) to patients who are so depressed that their body-image disturbances are manifested in terms of "hypochondriacal preoccupations, which may reach the intensity of delusions concerning disease and decay" (Lacey & Birtchnell, 1986, p. 628). Significant empirical documentation exists regarding the relationship between depression and body-image problems (Fisher, 1986; Marsella, Shizuru, Brennan, & Kameoka, 1981; Noles et al., 1985; Taylor & Cooper, 1986; Teri, 1982; Thompson, 1990; Thompson & Psaltis, 1988). It is clear from the available research that depressed individuals view their appearance more negatively than nondepressed individuals, despite the lack of objectively evaluated differences in appearance (Noles et al., 1985). Furthermore, there is a relationship between depression and requests for cosmetic surgery (Cash & Horton, 1983, 1990; Harris, 1982; Schlebusch, 1989).

Currently, no empirical investigation has addressed the question of causation. Does the experience of depression lead to increased negative perception of appearance or does the negative evaluation of appearance lead to the depressive symptoms? Regardless of causal direction, enough research and clinical evidence exists to warrant the routine evaluation of body-image experiences in depressed patients in order to assess the salience and role of this dimension vis-à-vis the patient's depression.

Sexual Dysfunction

Clear relationships exist among bodily experience, body image, and sexual functioning (Fisher, 1989). For example, the experience of sex guilt, the impact of parental attitudes toward bodily processes and sexuality, and the manner in which one integrates the powerful emotional experiences of sexual arousal are critical to body-image development (Fisher, 1989).

Furthermore, among physically traumatized persons, body-image variables influence sexual experience. For example, it is not difficult to imagine that cancer affecting the sexual organs (Derogatis, 1986; Pruzinsky, 1990; Vaeth, 1986), burns resulting in disfigurement (Tudahl, Blades, & Munster, 1987), or spinal cord injury (Wilmuth, 1987) could negatively affect sexual functioning.

However, the effect of body-image variables on sexual functioning is not limited to the dramatic and obvious impact of physical disability and disease (Fisher, 1989; Freedman, 1989). While there is little empirical research on the relationship between body-image attitudes and sexual functioning, it is easy to imagine that if individuals are uncomfortable with their bodily appearance then it would be difficult to enjoy sexual contact or be comfortable, with sexual expression (Freedman, 1989; Hangen & Cash, 1990).

Citing empirical research documenting a positive relationship between the quality and quantity of sexual experience and degree of body satisfaction (MacCorquodale & DeLamater, 1979), Cash (1985) states that "An aversion to one's own body parts or appearance. . . . or the belief that the partner is repulsed by some aspect of one's body may heighten sexual anxiety and avoidance" (p. 203). In DSM-III-R (American Psychiatric Association, 1987), these problems are potentially classifiable under the rubric of "Sexual Disorders Not Otherwise Specified," which include "marked feelings of inadequacy concerning body habitus, size and shape of sex organs, sexual performance, or other traits related to self-imposed standards of masculinity or femininity" (p. 296). Of course, body-image concerns attenuate desire, promote aversion and avoidance, or engender sexual anxiety and spectatoring that inhibit arousal or orgasm (Hangen & Cash, 1990). If so, such difficulties may represent dysfunctions of sexual desire, arousal, or orgasm.

In summary, there is clear rationale for assessing the sexually dysfunctional individual's body experience and body image. Body-image problems can potentially interfere with any phase of the sexual response cycle. Failure to address these issues in sex therapy could decrease treatment efficacy.

Schizophrenia

Much theoretical speculation and clinical observation has focused on the role of body-image disturbance in schizophrenia (e.g., Blatt & Wild, 1976; Lacey &

Birthchnell, 1986; Schilder, 1935). Observations regarding schizophrenic body-image disturbances were often made by psychodynamic theorists (e.g., Rose, 1966; Woodbury, 1966), though many clinicians have commented on this issue.

> Leading psychopathologists . . . have described schizophrenic's deviant perceptions, feelings and beliefs concerning their bodies. Every experienced clinician has encountered schizophrenics who report delusions of rotting organs or changed sex, or perceptions of alterations in the size and shape of their bodies, or feelings of unreality of the body, of the merging of the body with external objects, and of the body not being one's own. These experiences have come to be described as disturbances of body image. (Chapman, Chapman, & Raulin, 1978, p. 399)

Despite the widespread description of body-image deviations in schizophrenia, Fisher (1986), after a thorough review of the literature "unequivocally" concludes:

> there is no solid evidence that adult schizophrenics experience their bodies in any unique fashion or that they suffer from some extraordinary "body image deficit." Why empirical studies fail to verify the flamboyant body image dramas that abound in the many clinical vignettes about schizophrenics remains a mystery. (Fisher, 1986, p. 299)

SUMMARY AND CONCLUSIONS

This chapter has reviewed a range of psychopathologies focusing on bodily experience. Mental health professionals have experience treating some of these disorders (e.g., hypochondria, self-mutilation, depression, and sexual dysfunction), though there has not been adequate attention paid to their body-image components. Patients with body dysmorphic disorder, somatic delusions, and transsexualism, however, are not in the usual bailiwick of most mental health professionals. These individuals seek out dentists (Marbach, 1978), dermatologists (Cotterill, 1981; Gould & Gragg, 1976; 1983; Van Moffaert, 1974, 1982, 1986), internists, and primary care physicians (Barsky & Klerman, 1983), as well as plastic surgeons (Pruzinsky, 1988; Pruzinsky & Persing, in press). Given the ego-syntonic nature of their body-image complaints, these patients are very resistant to psychological treatment. Therefore, mental health professionals have had contact with only a small proportion of the total patient population (Barsky & Klerman, 1983). This lack of experience has resulted in a paucity of research regarding the body-image components of these disorders. However, learning more about these disorders can teach us a great deal about body image.

Some of the disorders described in this chapter are rare (e.g., koro). However, many of the disorders are quite common (e.g., hypochondriasis). Additionally, some of these symptoms are common to many other forms of psychopathology (e.g., self-mutilation). Furthermore, patients with BDD and somatic delusions are more common than previously thought (APA, 1987; Frances & Munro, 1989; Munro, 1988).

Individuals with these disorders experience much psychological suffering. Even brief contact with individuals with hypochondria, body dysmorphic disorder, somatic delusions, or transsexualism reveals the profound impact of these disorders on the individual's quality of life (Edgerton et al., 1990; Pruzinsky & Persing, in press). For many of these patients, life is put "on hold" until a "cure" is found for their problems. These patients go from physician to physician, often traveling many miles at great monetary expense and disruption to their lives.

In view of such suffering, we must learn more about these patients in order to develop effective interventions for them. Effective treatments already exist for some of these disorders. For example, for patients with somatic delusions, Pimozide holds hope for approximately 80% of treatment compliant patients (Frances & Munro, 1989). Currently, however, our treatment goals are limited to relieving the symptomatic distress and disability resulting from these disorders. That is, it appears that for patients with overvalued ideas and somatic delusions, the realistic therapeutic goal is symptom reduction, not symptom eradication. Munro (1988) has noted that most of the MHP patients retain their delusional beliefs despite drastic symptom reduction—a finding consistent with what we know about delusions (Oltmanns & Maher, 1988), about individuals with eating disorders, and about the more seriously disturbed patients treated by plastic surgeons. These patients are able to find some relief, but retain residual sensitivity regarding their bodily experience (Frances & Munro, 1989).

In order to capitalize on what these patients have to teach us about body image and to maximize our treatment effectiveness, we (as mental health professionals) need to *go to the patients* by establishing collaborative relationships with the health professionals most likely to see these patients. Models for these inter-professional relationships already exist in plastic surgery (Pruzinsky, 1988, 1990; Pruzinsky, Edgerton, & Barth, in press), oral surgery, (Buffone, 1989), and dermatology (Gould & Gragg, 1983; Van Moffaert, 1974, 1982, 1986). These health professionals often will welcome our contributions. Our continuing education of these professionals allows for more frequent and precise identification of patients who can benefit from psychological treatment.

For the mental health professional willing to venture from the familiar territory of the mental health clinic, these collaborations hold the promise of a great education about body-image psychopathology and body experience in general. These unique treatment contexts (e.g., the dermatologist's office) provide opportunities for in vivo study of body-experience psychopathological processes not available elsewhere.

In conclusion, it is clear that despite the compilation of known body-image psychopathologies, no current synthesis of these currently exists (Fisher, 1986; Sims, 1988). Such a synthesis must take into account contemporary knowledge regarding the neurological and psychophysiological aspects of body image, along with the sociocultural, psychodynamic, and phenomenological characteristics of these disorders (Schilder, 1935). I agree with Sims (1988) that "unification of the concepts used to describe body image disorders is not possible" (Sims, 1988, p. 51)—at least given our present understanding of these variables.

The best we can presently do is to ensure that our description of body-image problems is as comprehensive as possible. Too narrow a focus just on eating disorders and just on physical appearance in defining the study of body image psychopathology is limiting. Our knowledge will be vastly increased by taking a more expanded perspective on the relationship between body experience and psychopathology.

REFERENCES

American Psychiatric Association (1987). *Diagnostic and statistical manual of mental disorders*. (3rd ed., rev.). Washington, DC: Author.

Andreasen, N. C., & Bardach, J. (1977). Dysmorphophobia: Symptom or disease? *American Journal of Psychiatry, 134*, 673–676.

Ang, P. C., & Weller, M. P. (1984). Koro and psychosis. *British Journal of Psychiatry, 145*, 335.

Barsky, A. J., & Klerman, G. L. (1983). Overview: Hypochondriasis, bodily complaints, and somatic styles. *American Journal of Psychiatry, 140*, 273–283.

Birtchnell, S. A. (1988). Dysmorphophobia: A centenary discussion. *British Journal of Psychiatry, 153*, (Whole Supplement Number 2), 41–43.

Bishop, E. R. (1980). Monosymptomatic hypochondriasis. *Psychosomatics, 21*, 731–741.

Bishop, E. R. (1983). Monosymptomatic hypochondriacal syndromes in dermatology. *Journal of the American Academy of Dermatology, 9*, 152–158.

Bix, K. J. B., & Snaith, R. P. (Eds.). (1988). The psychopathology of body image: Proceedings of the Second Leeds Psychopathology Symposium. *British Journal of Psychiatry, 153* (Whole Supplement Number 2), 1–55.

Blatt, S. J., & Wild, C. M. (1976). *Schizophrenia: A developmental approach*. New York: Academic Press.

Braddock, L. (1982). Dysmorphophobia in adolescence: A case report. *British Journal of Psychiatry, 140*, 199–210.

Buffone, G. W. (1989). Consultation with oral surgeons: New roles for medical psychotherapists. *Medical Psychotherapy: An International Journal, 2*, 33–48.

Bychowski, G. (1943). Disorders of the body image in the clinical pictures of the psychoses. *Journal of Nervous and Mental Disorders, 97*, 310–334.

Cash, T. F. (1985). Physical appearance and mental health. In J. A. Graham & A. M. Kligman (Eds.), *The psychology of cosmetic treatments* (pp. 196–216). New York: Praeger.

Cash, T. F. (November, 1988). *Body image and beyond*. Paper presented at the annual meeting of the Association for the Advancement of Behavior Therapy, New York.

Cash, T. F., & Horton, C. E. (1983). Aesthetic surgery: Effects of rhinoplasty on social perception of patients by others. *Plastic and Reconstructive Surgery, 72*, 543–548.

Cash, T. F., & Horton, C. E. (1990). A longitudinal study of the psychological effects of aesthetic surgery. Unpublished research, Old Dominion University, Norfork, VA.

Chapman, L. J., Chapman, J. P., & Raulin, M. L. (1978). Body-image aberration in schizophrenia. *Journal of Abnormal Psychology, 87*, 399–407.

Connolly, F. H., & Gipson, M. (1978). Dysmorphophobia—A long-term study. *British Journal of Psychiatry, 132*, 568–570.

Cotterill, J. A. (1981). Dermatological non-disease: A common and potentially fatal disturbance of cutaneous body image. *British Journal of Dermatology, 104*, 611–619.

Cumming, W. J. K. (1988). The neurobiology of body schema. *British Journal of Psychiatry, 153* (Whole Supplement Number 2), 7–11.

Crisp, A. H. (1977). The differential diagnosis of anorexia. *Proceedings of the Royal Society of Medicine, 70*, 686–690.

Crisp, A. H. (1981). Dysmorphophobia and the search for cosmetic surgery. *British Medical Journal, 282*, 1098–1099.

de Leon, J., Bott, A., & Simpson, G. M. (1989). Dysmorphophobia: Body dysmorphic disorder or delusional disorder, somatic subtype? *Comprehensive Psychiatry, 30*, 457–472.

DeMuth, G. W., Strain, J. J., & Lomabardo-Maher, A. (1983). Self-amputation and restitution. *General Hospital Psychiatry, 5*, 25–30.

Derogatis, L. R. (1986). The unique impact of breast and gynecologic cancers on body image and sexual identity in women: A reassessment. In J. M. Vaeth (Ed), *Body image, self-esteem, and sexuality in cancer patients* (2nd ed., rev., pp. 1–14). Basel: Karger.

Drinker, H., Knorr, N. J., & Edgerton, M. T. (1972). Factitious wounds: A psychiatric and surgical dilemma. *Plastic and Reconstructive Surgery, 50*, 458–461.

Edgerton, M. T. (1975). The plastic surgeon's obligation to the emotionally disturbed patient. *Plastic and Reconstructive Surgery, 55*, 81–83.

Edgerton, M. T., Jacobson, W. E., & Meyer, E. (1961). Surgical–psychiatric study of patients seeking plastic (cosmetic) surgery: Ninety-eight patients with minimal deformity. *British Journal of Plastic Surgery, 13*, 136–145.

Edgerton, M. T., & Langman, M. W. (1982). Psychiatric considerations. In E. H. Courtiss (Ed.), *Male aesthetic surgery* (pp. 17–38). St Louis: C. V. Mosby.

Edgerton, M. T., Langman, M. W., & Pruzinsky, T. (1990). Patients seeking symmetrical recontouring for perceived deformities in the width of the face and skull. *Aesthetic Plastic Surgery, 14*, 59–73.

Fishbain, D. A., Barksy, S., & Goldberg, M. (1989). "Koro" (genital retraction syndrome): Psychotherapeutic interventions. *American Journal of Psychotherapy, XLIII*, 87–91.

Fisher, S. (1986). *Development and structure of the body image* (Vols. 1 & 2). Hillsdale, NJ: Erlbaum.

Fisher, S. (1989). *Sexual images of the self: The psychology of erotic sensations and illusions.* Hillsdale, NJ: Erlbaum.

Fleming, M., MacGowan, B. R., Robinson, L., Spitz, J., & Salt, P. (1982). The body image of the post-operative female to male transsexual. *Journal of Consulting and Clinical Psychology, 50*, 461–462.

Frances, A., & Munro. A. (1989). Treating a woman who believes she has bugs under her skin. *Hospital and Community Psychiatry, 40*, 1113–1114.

Freedman, R. (1989). *Bodylove: A practical guide for women.* New York: Harper & Row.

Freytag, F. F. (1977). *The body image in gender orientation disturbance.* New York: Vantage.

Garner, D. D., Garfinkel, P., & O'Shaughnessy, M. (1982). Clinical and psychometric comparison between bulimia in anorexia nervosa and bulimia in normal weight women. In *Fourth Ross Conference on Medical Research* (pp. 6–13). Colombus, Ohio: Ross Laboratories.

Goldwyn, R. M., Cahill, J. L., & Grunebaum, H. U. (1967). Self-inflicted injury to the wrist. *Plastic and Reconstructive Surgery, 39*, 583–589.

Gould, W. M., & Gragg, T. M. (1976). Delusions of parasitosis. *Archives of Dermatology, 112*, 1745–1748.

Gould, W. M., & Gragg, T. M. (1983). A dermatology–psychiatry liaison clinic. *Journal of the American Academy of Dermatology, 9*, 73–77.

Grotstein, J. S. (1982). Autoscopic phenomena. In C. T. H. Friedmann & R. A. Fauget (Eds.), *Extraordinary disorders of human behavior* (pp. 65–77). New York: Plenum Press.

Hangen, J., & Cash, T. F. (1990). *The relationships of body-image attitudes to sexual experiences and sexual dysfunctions.* Unpublished research, Old Dominion University, Norfold, VA.

Hardy, G. E. (1982). Body image disturbance in dysmorphophobia. *British Journal of Psychiatry, 141,* 181–185.

Hardy, G. E., & Cotterill, J. A. (1982). A study of depression and obsessionality in dysmorphic and psoriatic patients. *British Journal of Psychiatry, 140,* 19–22.

Hay, G. G. (1970). Dysmorphophobia. *British Journal of Psychiatry, 116,* 399–406.

Hoenig, J. (1985). Etiology of transsexualism. In B. W. Steiner (Ed.), *Gender dysphoria: Development, research and management* (pp. 33–73). New York: Plenum Press.

Hollander, E., Liebowitz, M. R., Winchel, R., Klumker, A., & Klein, D. F. (1989). Treatment of body-dysmorphic disorder with serotonin reputake blockers. *American Journal of Psychiatry, 146,* 768–770.

Kellner, R. (1986). *Somatization and hypochondriasis.* New York: Praeger.

Kenyon, F. E. (1965). Hypochondriasis: A survey of some historical, clinical and social aspects. *British Journal of Medical Psychology, 38,* 117–133.

Knorr, N. J., & Edgerton, M. T. (1967). The insatiable cosmetic surgery patient. *Plastic and Reconstructive Surgery, 40,* 554–558.

Kolb, L. C. (1975). Disturbances of the body image. In M. F. Reiser (Eds.), *American Handbook of Psychiatry,* (Vol. 4, 2nd ed., pp. 810–837). New York: Basic Books.

Lacey, J. H., & Birtchnell, S. A. (1986). Body image and its disturbances. *Journal of Psychosomatic Research, 30,* 623–631.

Ladee, G. A. (1966). *Hypochondriacal syndromes.* New York: Elsevier.

Langman, M. W., Pruzinsky, T., Edgerton, M. T., & Nachbar, J. (June, 1987). Specific satisfying results in post-operative patients. Presented at the Tenth International Symposium on Gender Dysphoria, Amsterdam, The Netherlands.

Lindgren, T., & Pauly, I. A body image scale for evaluating transsexuals. *Archives of Sexual Behavior, 4,* 639–656.

Lipowski, Z. J. (1977). The importance of body experience for psychiatry. *Comprehensive Psychiatry, 18,* 473–479.

MacCorquodale, P., & DeLamater, J. (1979). Self-image and premarital sexuality. *Journal of Marriage and the Family, 41,* 327–339.

Macgregor, F. C. (1981). The place of the patient in society. *Aesthetic Plastic Surgery, 5,* 85–93.

Macgregor, F. C. (1989). Social, psychological and cultural dimensions of cosmetic and reconstructive plastic surgery. *Aesthetic Plastic Surgery, 13,* 1–8.

Marbach, J. J. (1978). Phantom bite syndrome. *American Journal of Psychiatry, 135,* 476–479.

Marsella, A. J., Shizuru, L., Brennan, J., & Kameoka, V. (1981). Depression and body image satisfaction. *Journal of Cross-Cultural Psychology, 12,* 360–371.

McCranie, E. J. (1979). Hypochondriacal neurosis. *Psychosomatics, 20,* 11–15.

McKenna, P. J. (1984). Disorders with overvalued ideas. *British Journal of Psychiatry, 145,* 579–585.

Mellor, C. S. (1988). Depersonalization and self-perception. *British Journal of Psychiatry, 153* (Whole Supplement Number 2), 15–19.

Menninger, K. A. (1939). Polysurgery and polysurgery addiction. *Psychoanalytic Quarterly, 3,* 173–198.

Morrison, J. (1989). Childhood sexual histories of women with somatization disorder. *American Journal of Psychiatry, 146,* 239–241.

Munro, A. (1978). Monosymptomatic hypochondriacal psychoses. *Canadian Psychiatric Association Journal, 23,* 497–500.

Munro, A. (1980). Monosymptomatic hypochondriacal psychoses (MHP): New aspects of an old syndrome. *Journal of Psychiatric Treatment and Evaluation, 2,* 79–86.

Munro, A. (1983). Treatment of monosymptomatic hypochondriacal psychosis with imipramine. *Canadian Journal of Psychiatry, 28*, 236–237.

Munro, A. (1987). Paranoid (Delusional) disorders: DSM-III-R and beyond. *Comprehensive Psychiatry, 28*, 35–39.

Munro, A. (1988). Monosymptomatic hypochondriacal psychosis. *British Journal of Psychiatry, 153*, (Whole Supplement Number 2), 37–40.

Munro, A., & Chmara, J. (1982). Monosymptomatic hypochondriacal psychosis: A diagnostic checklist based on 50 cases of the disorder. *Canadian Journal of Psychiatry, 77*, 374–376.

Munro, A., & Pollock, B. (1981). Monosymptomatic psychoses which progress to schizophrenia. *Journal of Clinical Psychiatry, 42*, 474–476.

Nadelson, T. (1986). The false patient: Chronic factitious disease, munchausen syndrome, and malingering. In J. L. Houpt & H. K. H. Brodie (Eds.), *Consultation-liaison psychiatry and behavioral medicine* (Vol. 3, pp. 195–205). New York: Basic Books.

Nightingale, S. (1982). Somatophrenia: A case report. *Cortex, 18*, 463–476.

Noles, S. W., Cash, T. F., & Winstead, B. A. (1985). Body image, physical attractiveness, and depression. *Journal of Consulting and Clinical Psychology, 53*, 88–94.

Oltmanns, T. F., & Maher, B. A. (Eds.) (1988). *Delusional beliefs.* New York: Wiley.

Pauly, I. B., & Edgerton, M. T. (1986). The gender-identity movement: A growing surgical–psychiatric liaison. *Archives of Sexual Behavior, 15*, 315–329.

Pauly, I. B., & Lindgren, T. W. (1976–1977). Body image and gender identity. *Journal of Homosexuality, 2*, 133–142.

Peto, A. (1972). Body image and depression. *International Journal of Psychoanalysis, 53*, 259–263.

Phelps, D. B., Buchler, U., & Boswick, J. A. (1977). The diagnosis of factitious ulcer of the hand: A case report. *The Journal of Hand Surgery, 2*, 105–108.

Pruzinsky, T. (1988). Collaboration of plastic surgeon and medical psychotherapist: Elective cosmetic surgery. *Medical Psychotherapy: An International Journal, 1*, 1–13.

Pruzinsky, T. (1990). Book review: *Body Image, self-esteem, and sexuality in cancer patients (2nd ed.), J. M. Vaeth (Ed), Basel, Switzerland: Karger, 1986. Canadian Journal of Psychiatry; 35*, 193–194.

Pruzinsky, T., & Cash, T. F. (in press). Medical interventions for the enhancement of physical appearance. In T. P. Gullotta (Ed.), *Advances in adolescent development.* Beverly Hills, CA: Sage.

Pruzinsky, T., Edgerton, M. T., & Barth, J. T. (in press). Medical psychotherapy and plastic surgery: Collaboration, specialization and cost-effectiveness. In K. Anchor (Ed.), *The Handbook of Medical Psychotherapy.* Toronto: Hans Huber Publishers.

Pruzinsky, T., & Persing, J. (in press). Psychological perspectives on applications of reconstructive surgery techniques. In D. K. Ousterhout (Ed.), *Aesthetic applications of craniofacial techniques.* Boston: Little, Brown.

Riding, J., & Munro, A. (1975). Pimozide in the treatment of monosymptomatic hypochondriacal psychosis. *Acta Psychiatrica Scandinavia, 52*, 23–30.

Rose, G. (1966). Body ego and reality. *International Journal of Psychoanalysis, 47*, 502–509.

Rubin, R. T. (1982). Koro (Shook Yang): A culture-bound psychogenic syndrome. In & C. T. H. Friedmann & R. A. Fauget (Eds.), *Extraordinary disorders of human behavior* (pp. 155–172). New York: Plenum Press.

Schlebusch, L. (1989). Negative bodily experience and prevalance of depression in patients who request augmentation mammaplasty. *South African Medical Journal, 75*, 323–326.

Schilder, P. (1935). *The image and appearance of the human body: Studies in the constructive energies of the psyche.* New York: International Universities Press.

Shontz, F. C. (1974). Body image and its disorders. *International Journal of Psychiatry in Medicine, 5*, 461–472.

Sims, A. C. P. (1988). Towards the unification of body image disorders. *British Journal of Psychiatry, 153* (Whole Supplement Number 2), 51–56.

Stekel, W. (1950). *Compulsion and doubt* (Vol. 2). London: Peter Nevill.

Teri, L. (1982). Depression in adolescence: It's relationship to assertion and various aspects of self-image. *Journal of Clinical Child Psychology, 11,* 101–106.

Taylor, M. J., & Cooper, P. J. (1986). Body size overestimation and depressed mood. *British Journal of Clinical Psychology, 25,* 153–154.

Thomas, C. S. (1984). Dysmorphophobia: A question of definition. *British Journal of Psychiatry, 144,* 513–516.

Thompson, J. K. (1990). *Body image disturbance: Assessment and treatment.* New York: Pergamon Press.

Thompson, J. K., & Psaltis, K. (1988). Multiple aspects and correlates of body figure ratings: A replication and extension of Fallon and Rozin (1985). *International Journal of Eating Disorders, 7,* 813–818.

Tudahl, L. A., Blades, B. C., & Munster, A. M. (1987). Sexual satisfaction in burn patients. *Journal of Burn Care and Rehabilitation, 8,* 292–293.

Vaeth, J. M. (Ed.) (1986). *Body image, self-esteem, and sexuality in cancer patients* (2nd ed.). Basel, Switzerland: Karger.

Van Moffaert, M. (1974). The importance of permanent psychiatric consulting in a dermatologic clinic. *Archives of Belgium Dermat, 30,* 215–220.

Van Moffaert, M. (1982). Psychosomatics for the practicing dermatologist. *Dermatolgica, 165,* 73–78.

Van Moffaert, M. (1986). Training future dermatologists in psychodermatology. *General Hospital Psychiatry, 8,* 115–118.

Walsh, B. W. (1987). *Adolescent self-mutilation: An empirical study.* Unpublished doctoral dissertation, Boston College Graduate School of Social Work.

Walsh, B. W., & Rosen, P. M. (1985). Self-mutilation and contagion: An empirical test. *American Journal of Psychiatry, 141,* 119–120.

Walsh, B. W., & Rosen, P. M. (1988). *Self-mutilation: Theory, research and treatment.* New York: Guilford Press

Wilmuth, M. E. (1987). Sexuality after spinal cord injury: A critical review. *Clinical Psychology Review, 7,* 389–412.

Woodbury, M. (1966). Altered body-ego experiences: A contribution to the study of regression, perception and early development. *Journal of the American Psychoanalytic Association, 14,* 273–304.

Wright, M. R. (1986). Surgical addiction: A complication of modern surgery? *Archives of Otolaryngology Head and Neck Surgery, 112,* 870–872.

Wykoff, R. F. (1987). Delusions of parasitosis: A review. *Review of Infectious Diseases, 9,* 433–437.

Yap, P. M. (1965). Koro—A culture bound depersonalization syndrome. *British Journal of Psychiatry, 111,* 43–50.

Yates, A., Shisslak, C. M., Allender, J. R., & Wolman, W. (1988). Plastic surgery and the bulimic patient. *International Journal of Eating Disorders 7,* 557–560.

CHAPTER 9

Body-Image Disturbances in Eating Disorders

James C. Rosen

The term *eating disorder* generally refers to psychological disorders involving gross abnormalities in eating. However, body-image disturbance is essentially what distinguishes them from other psychological conditions that occasionally involve eating abnormalities and weight loss. The purpose of this chapter is to present the different manifestations of body-image disturbance in eating disorders and to examine the empirical literature dealing with the causes of these disturbances in eating disorder patients, the importance of body image to the maintenance of the other symptoms of eating disorders, and the treatment of body image in eating disorder patients. Besides clinical eating disorders, which fall at the endpoint of a continuum of disordered eating and negative body image, there are milder but distressing forms of the disorders which fall at intermediate points along the continuum and are widespread among women (Polivy & Herman, 1987). Nonetheless, this review is limited mainly to clinical populations of anorexia nervosa and bulimia nervosa subjects. Obesity is excluded from the domain of eating disorders in this review due to the lack of compelling evidence that obesity results from or is characterized by abnormal eating behavior. Cash discusses obesity and body image in Chapter 3 of this volume.

DEFINITION OF EATING DISORDERS

Bulimia nervosa (Russell, 1979) refers to a severe eating disorder in which individuals, almost always women, habitually vomit or more rarely abuse laxatives after binge eating or after eating even minimal amounts of "forbidden" foods that they consider dangerously fattening. Vomiting is self-induced and typically occurs daily. As many as 10 episodes per day have been reported in the treatment literature, but the mean frequency per week typically reported is between 7 and 15. According to Russell's definition, bulimia nervosa is also accompanied by a morbid fear of becoming fat. The prevalence of bulimia nervosa is about 2–4% (Johnson & Conners, 1987).

The diagnostic criteria for bulimia nervosa according to DSM-III-R (APA, 1987) include "recurrent episodes of binge eating" (p. 68) (averaging at least two binge episodes per week for three months), an experience of a "lack of control over eating behavior" (p. 68) during the binges, the regular occurrence of purgative behavior (by self-induced vomiting, use of laxatives or diuretics, strict eating restraint, or vigorous physical exercise) to avoid weight gain, and the "persistent overconcern with body shape and weight" (p. 69).

This definition sets no boundaries for weight, though clinical, descriptive studies of women with bulimia nervosa reported that the overwhelming majority are within the normal weight range. Moreover, all the major clinical treatment trials for bulimia nervosa have been conducted exclusively with subjects who are normal weight. Nonetheless, according to current diagnostic criteria, the term may also be applied to women who are obese or below normal weight. Thus, an anorexia nervosa patient, for example, may also meet the criteria for bulimia nervosa.

A major problem with these criteria is that they fail to distinguish between those individuals who purge after eating and those who do not purge. These groups seem to be very different from each other. For example, normal-weight, purging, bulimics were much more disturbed than nonpurging bulimics on measures of eating behavior, psychological adjustment, body image, depression, and eating attitudes (Willmuth, Leitenberg, Rosen, & Cado, 1988). In any case, the body-image and treatment studies of bulimia nervosa that could be located for this review involved almost exclusively patients who self-induce vomiting after eating. In fact, there are probably very few normal-weight women[1] who meet the other criteria for bulimia nervosa but who do not vomit. Or if they do exist, they seldom seek treatment (Willmuth et al., 1988). Bulimia without purging, on the other hand, is more common in obese individuals.

According to the DSM-III-R, the criteria for anorexia nervosa are met by: a "refusal to maintain body weight over a minimal normal weight for age and height" (p. 67) (i.e., weight 15% below the appropriate standard), an intense anxiety about "gaining weight or becoming fat, even though underweight" (p. 67), and a disturbance of body experience (e.g., "feeling fat" or believing a body area is "too fat," even when emaciated). Among females, amenorrhea is an additional criterion (for "at least three consecutive menstrual cycles when otherwise expected to occur") (p. 67).

In most cases of anorexia nervosa, weight loss is achieved through fasting or reduction in food intake, but as much as 50% of samples in clinical, descriptive

---

[1]The feminine noun and pronoun will be used throughout with reference to individuals with eating disorders because the overwhelming majority of patients with eating disorders are women.

studies use vomiting and purging as a form of weight reduction (Fairburn & Garner, 1986). According to the current diagnostic criteria, bulimia nervosa would also be present in these cases. The prevalence of anorexia nervosa has ranged from reports of 1 in 100 young women to 1 in 250 (Garfinkel & Garner, 1982).

Most bulimic women maintain normal weight because they are able to eat some food without vomiting, whereas anorexic women are emaciated because they engage in starvation. Anorexia nervosa tends to occur in young adolescents who are still living at home. The patient's obvious physical ill health and irrational state are frightening to parents and can provoke attention that inadvertently complicates the disorder. Social attention plays a less important role in bulimia nervosa because the disorder is inconspicuous, and it tends to be secretive. It is more common in older adolescents and young adults no longer living at home. Although anorexia nervosa is much more likely to lead to serious physical ill health and even to death, both disorders are associated with widespread psychopathology and eventually interfere with normal functioning in relationships, work, and school.

BODY-IMAGE DISTURBANCES IN EATING DISORDERS

Although there is remarkable agreement that eating disorders involve a disturbance of body image, there is considerable variation in the specific disturbance believed to be most characteristic of these disorders. The most appropriate resolution to disparate definitions of body-image disturbance in eating disorders is that it is a multidimensional phenomenon that involves perceptual, attitudinal, and behavioral features (Cash & Brown, 1987; Garfinkel & Garner, 1982; Rosen, Saltzberg, & Srebnik, 1989; Thompson, 1990; Williamson, 1990).

Disturbances in Perception

Bruch (1962) was the first to postulate that body-image disturbance was a pathological feature of anorexia nervosa, which she referred to as: "the absence of concern about emaciation, even when advanced, and the vigor and stubbornness with which the often gruesome appearance is defended as normal and right" (p. 189). This gap between the reality of the patient's appearance and her self-perception is captured by a quote from an anorexic that was reported by Garner and Garfinkel (1981–82): "I look in a full length mirror at least four or five times daily and I really cannot see myself as too thin. Sometimes after several days of strict dieting, I feel that my shape is tolerable, but most of the time, odd as it may seem, I look in the mirror and believe that I am too fat" (p. 265). At this time, the patient weighed 33 kg at 168 cm tall. Eventually she gave up weighing herself because the numbers on the scale did not agree with her visual image.

In essence, patients with eating disorders tend to perceive themselves as unrealistically big or fat and as being grossly out of proportion or protruding at certain body regions, such as having excessively wide hips or a stomach that sticks out too far. The distortion of normal size is often evident by the unrealistic standards that the patient attempts to achieve. For example, she must be able to put a ruler on both hips without it touching her abdomen, or the inner surface of her thighs must not touch when standing. Eating disorder patients exhibit a mistrust or disbelief in more conventional standards for comparing their weight to normal, such as tables of weight norms. No matter what feedback the patient may receive about her size, she relies on her own perceptions and feelings of being too big.

Bruch also postulated that distorted perceptions of body size in anorexia nervosa were related to a more general perceptual disturbance of interoceptive awareness, such that eating disorder patients were inaccurate or unable to identify a variety of internal sensations such as emotions and hunger and satiety. Presumably the perception of any other somatic activity (e.g., pain, postural changes, movement) could be distorted by individuals with eating disorders. This hypothesis that a global abnormality of perception underlies both body-image disturbance and eating abnormalities in these patients is appealing by virtue of its simplicity. However, supportive data currently are very limited.

Garner and associates developed a self-report measure of interoceptive awareness that was contained in the Eating Disorders Inventory (EDI) (Garner, Olmsted, & Polivy, 1983). On the Interoceptive Awareness scale, the subject is asked to report how well she can identify emotions or how confused she is by them. In support of Bruch's hypothesis, individuals with eating disorders reported a much higher level of confusion about these internal sensations compared with normals. Moreover, reports of disturbed interoceptive awareness were associated with higher scores on the EDI Body Dissatisfaction scale in both normal and anorexia nervosa samples (Garner & Olmsted, 1984), suggesting that the two facets of perceptual disturbance go together. However, it should be noted that this Interoceptive Awareness scale taps into complaints of emotional confusion but not the perception of visceral sensations. Also, it is questionable whether subjects can accurately appraise and report the type of disturbance in perception that was originally proposed by Bruch.

Another line of research revealing data consistent with Bruch's hypothesis deals with the study of eating behavior in anorexia nervosa patients. There have been several reports that satiety in anorexics is less responsive to experimental manipulations of food consumption than normals, who are more responsive to the energy value of food (Garfinkel & Garner, 1982). Further, anorexics who overestimated their body size were less likely to show an aversion to high concentrations of sucrose compared to anorexics who had little size distortion (Garfinkel, 1981), suggesting that body-image disturbance and abnormal eating may both be tied to an underlying disturbance in perceptual processes. However, another interpretation of these findings is that the satiety abnormality in anorexics is not a perceptual abnormality, but a behavioral consequence of the anorexic's strict dieting. A vast literature on laboratory studies of restrained eaters has shown that they will overeat or "counterregulate" when their restraint is broken, unlike nonrestrained eaters who have a regulatory style of eating and eat less food after having consumed a preload (Herman & Polivy, 1980).

Despite widespread clinical agreement that patients with eating disorders are remarkable for their belief in being abnormally big or fat, the measurement of these perceptions often have been eluded in standardized size-perception tests, casting some doubt on the validity of perceptual distortion as a fundamental feature of eating disorders. One controversy stems from reports of inconsistent intercorrelations between the size distortion of different body parts (Cash & Brown, 1987). Some would argue that if eating disorder patients possess a perceptual abnormality, it should be manifested consistently in body image. Or should it? Because different body parts are likely to be more or less salient, depending on the individual, it should not be surprising that size distortion is inconsistent when measured piecemeal. Eating disorder patients, in fact, can be quite idiosyncratic in their body preoccupation. Negative feelings and distortion may be traced to one perceived defect in appearance, for example, thick thighs. Thus, a low internal consistency on measures of size distortion does not necessarily invalidate the concept.

A second and more important controversy stems from the finding (e.g., Cash & Brown, 1987) that noneating-disorder control subjects often overestimate their size as much as do women with anorexia nervosa. This has led some investigators to argue that size distortion is ephemeral and not unique to this population, thus perceptual body-image disturbance should not be a criterion for eating disorders (Hsu, 1982). There are several reasons to reject this view. In two recent and excellent reviews on size perception, the tally of studies that did find greater overestimation of body size in eating disorder patients than controls is greater than the number of studies with negative findings (Cash & Brown, 1987; Cooper & Taylor, 1987), especially in the case of bulimia nervosa. Second, size distortion can be remarkably stable, even after the patient has been partially rehabilitated (Garfinkel, 1981). Third, it is not surprising that "normal" women also overestimate their size, given the ubiquitous concern with weight in the current culture. There is a vast number of women with subclinical eating disorder syndromes. Fourth, body-size distortion is only one symptom of body-image disturbance in eating disorder patients, and because it is a multidimensional problem, the absence of one type of disturbance is not sufficient evidence to rule out the entire concept.

In a frequently cited study by Crisp and Kalucy (1974), anorexia nervosa patients decreased their overestimation upon a second testing when told by the experimenter, "We both know you are thin. Being able to acknowledge this . . . is not going to be used . . . in evidence against you. Taking all this into account, I would like you to drop your guard for a moment and tell me again how wide you really judge yourself" (p. 352). Some investigators have interpreted this finding to mean that size overestimation is not perceptual error at all but simply an attempt by the patient to impress the examiner with her belief she is not sick or in need of treatment (Hsu, 1982). However, the concept of size distortion is not invalid simply because it can be influenced by situational factors. As a matter of fact, subjects in the Crisp and Kalucy study still grossly overestimated their size by 45% after being instructed to give more accurate estimates. The lower estimate was just as likely to be a compliant response to experimenter demand as a more accurate reflection of their perception. If size distortion was simply used by the patient to impress the clinician, then one should witness a change in size estimation after rapport has been established. To the contrary, size distortion persists after this early stage of treatment, when the patient has become committed to receiving treatment (Garfinkel, Moldofsky, & Garner, 1979).

Disturbances in Attitudes

Body dissatisfaction often can be traced to particular body areas such as the width of the hips or thighs, the protrusion of the abdomen, or the dimpled flesh on the back of the legs. Dissatisfaction is expressed in terms of dislike for the body part, thoughts that the part appears ugly or disgusting, and beliefs that the part is too fat or lacking muscle tone. As Thompson and colleagues delineated in Chapter 2 of this volume, this type of body-image attitude is assessed by self-report inventories such as the EDI Body Dissatisfaction Scale (Garner et al., 1983), the Body Esteem Scale (Franzoi & Shields, 1984), and the Multidimensional Body–Self Relations Questionnaire (Cash, Winstead, & Janda, 1986). More specific to eating disorders are reports of painful social self-consciousness about appearance, for example, "When I hear people whisper as I walk by, I think they've probably been commenting on my weight" (Thompson, Berg, & Shatford, 1987).

Cooper and Fairburn (1987) argue that the more clinically remarkable beliefs pertain to the eating disorder patient's investment of self-worth in her appearance. For example, women with eating disorders feel that other people evaluate them mainly on their appearance and that other personal attributes do not mean as much. Being thin is the only important aspect of their self-image; if they are not exceedingly thin, it proves they are weak, lazy, unlovable, and incompetent. Other typical thoughts are: "I gained two pounds this year, so people will think I'm gross." "Because I'm big, people don't like me." "People look at me when I walk across campus—they think I'm gross." "Because I'm big, I'm not feminine." "If I was thinner, I would be more successful." "I am a bad person (weak, selfish, greedy, irresponsible, inadequate, stupid, dull, etc.), but if I lose weight I will be different." "My legs have fat dimples in them (or some other minor imperfection), therefore, men don't like my body."

Cooper and Fairburn believe that responses to questions about "feeling fat" or "being afraid of gaining weight" are not representative of the morbid and overvalued concern about appearance that is typical of individuals with eating disorders. Their interview, the Eating Disorders Examination (1987), contains the Shape Concern and Weight Concern scales, which were designed to probe for these rigid beliefs. The Body Image Automatic Thoughts Questionnaire also was designed to tap into distorted thoughts about being a good or bad and desirable or undesirable person on account of physical appearance (Brown, Johnson, Bergeron, Keeton, & Cash, 1988; Cash, Lewis, & Keeton, 1987). Relative to weight-matched controls, not only do binge–purging adolescents have more negative affect and distorted beliefs about their weight and appearance but they are also more cognitively and behaviorally invested in their appearance (Brown, Cash, & Lewis, 1989). Indeed, it appears that eating disorder subjects cannot be distinguished from other weight preoccupied women on ratings of body dissatisfaction alone (Garner, Olmsted, & Garfinkel, 1983; Wilson & Smith, 1989). However, they are distinguished by the importance they place on weight and shape for self-worth (Wilson & Smith, 1989).

Disturbances in Behavior

Negative body image also can be accompanied by a lifestyle that revolves around the individual's physical self-consciousness. This can include tendencies to avoid situations that provoke concern about physical appearance such as avoiding social outings where the person believes her body will be scrutinized, wearing baggy clothes instead of more revealing and tight fitting clothes, avoiding physical intimacy, and eating less. Other habits such as frequent weighing or inspection in the mirror are also typical. Patients with eating disorders who distort or devalue their appearance learn to reduce anxiety about their appearanceby avoiding certain triggering situations. This type of extensive behavioral avoidance itself can augment social and psychological impairment.

Although there has been extensive clinical observation that certain practices involving dressing, grooming, social outings, etc., stem from or co-occur with negative body image, little attention has been given to this behavioral component in descriptions of body-image disturbance. Recently, a scale that taps into this feature was shown to successfully discriminate women with bulimia nervosa and was sensitive to change following treatment for negative body image (Rosen, Srebnik, Saltzberg, & Wendt, 1989).

DEVELOPMENT OF NEGATIVE BODY IMAGE

Body-image disturbances in women with eating disorders have been attributed to cultural standards for beauty, learning within the family, disturbances in development of self-identity and effectiveness, disturbances in psychosexual development, and deficits in self-esteem.

Cultural Influences

Certainly a background factor for the development of body-image concerns in women with eating disorders is the prevailing ideal of thinness as a marker of beauty in women. Were it not for this, there would be no epidemic of eating disorders. Several other chapters in this volume have pointed to the importance of culture and gender in body-image development. In a classic paper by Garner and his associates (Garner, Garfinkel, Schwartz, & Thompson, 1980), it was shown that exemplars of female beauty (e.g., models and beauty contestants) have become thinner over the last couple of decades—to the point that the ideal physique is below the actuarial norm. This change has been accompanied by an apparent increase in the prevalence of eating disorders and more reports of subclinical eating and body-image disturbances among women. In non-Western cultures where plumpness is valued, or at least not devalued (e.g., where it is associated with wealth, sexuality, fertility, womanhood, etc.) eating disorders are rare (Nasser, 1988). Also, Third World immigrants to industrialized countries have a higher rate of eating disorders than people of the same nationality who remain in their own country (Nasser, 1988). The correlation between weight standards for beauty and the prevalence of eating disorders suggests culture plays a very important etiological role. However, it should be noted that epidemiological studies of eating disorders across time and cultures have been inconsistent and nonstandard. Thus, the true relation between these two variables is unknown.

Within the United States, there appears to be a racial difference in body-size preference. Specifically, compared to white girls, fewer black girls reported that they were overweight or were trying to lose weight and more reported that they were trying to gain weight (Gray, Ford, & Kelly, 1987; Rosen & Gross, 1987). These findings were not attributable to socioeconomic class differences. Perhaps these racial differences in body image explain the lower reported rate of bulimia nervosa in black women (Gray et al., 1987; Gross & Rosen, 1988).

In addition to the messages about beauty that women receive from society as a whole, there is evidence to suggest that women with eating disorders and body-image disturbance may have had personal experiences of social rejection in connection with their appearance. According to a popular woman's magazine survey of 33,000 people, those with negative body image were more likely to report having had mothers who were critical of their appearance (Wooley & Kearney-Cooke, 1986). Another large-scale survey of body-image attitudes (Cash, Winstead, & Janda, 1986; see also Cash, Chapter 3, this volume) similarly found a link between reported childhood teasing about appearance and negative body-image affect and eating disturbance in adolescence (Brown et al.,

1989). And negative body self-esteem and size overestimation in teenage girls were associated with a higher frequency of being teased about weight or size by other people (Fabian & Thompson, 1989). An unusually high proportion of bulimic women had been overweight prior to the onset of their disorder (Fairburn & Cooper, 1982; Garfinkel, 1981; Striegel-Moore, Silberstein, & Rodin, 1986), which would suggest that these individuals were actually subjected to more than a normal degree of negative feedback about their appearance.

In sum, women who live in cultures that view thinness as an important feature of beauty are more at risk for negative body image and eating disorders. This may be especially true for women who are somewhat overweight or are subjected to negative feedback about their appearance. These social factors by themselves cannot explain the development of body-image disturbance in eating disorders as most women are exposed to the cultural pressure to be thin, yet only a small minority develop eating disorders. The cultural attitude toward body weight may provide the background for the disorder, but this must be combined with other predisposing psychosocial factors for true pathology to develop.

Self-Identity and Effectiveness

According to Bruch (1973), young girls with eating disorders come from families with domineering, intrusive, overprotective parents who make it difficult for the developing adolescent to become autonomous of parental control and to formulate her own sense of identity. Palazzoli (1974) added that the child's struggle with autonomy is even more difficult during puberty because her body begins to approximate her mother's body at a time that she is seeking differentiation from an overcontrolling parent. As a result, the rapid physical development causes the child to feel less, rather than more, in command of her own life. According to Bruch, pursuit of thinness is an adaptive effort for the adolescent to take charge of herself in the midst of this conflict. While other things are out of control, weight may be the one issue that remains within self-control. Losing weight may enhance perceptions of self-effectiveness, which helps the adolescent to separate from parents and to reduce the threat of other developmental stressors (Cattanach & Rodin, 1988; Striegel-Moore et al., 1986). Another interpretation is that the emaciation of anorexia nervosa is a regressive defense mechanism that allows the child to preserve the pubertal look, to avoid growing up, and to remain in childhood (Crisp, 1980). In any case, the body becomes the focus of attention in the afflicted adolescent as an outward manifestation of a rapid change in self-image.

Although widely held by psychodynamically oriented clinicians who work with eating disorder patients, there has been little empirical investigation of these explanations. Developmental studies of body image have shown that girls perceive their body size more accurately with age (Garner & Garfinkel, 1981–82). Thus, the inaccurate perception by girls with eating disorders would be consistent with the general notion of a developmental delay. Body dissatisfaction is significantly correlated with feelings of ineffectiveness and perfectionism but not with maturity fears (Garner & Olmsted, 1984). Apparently, more study is needed concerning the importance of deviations in social development as risk factors for body-image disturbance and eating disorders.

Sexuality, Sexual Abuse, and Sex-Role Orientation

The drive toward emaciation in young anorexia nervosa patients, at a time when they otherwise would be developing physically, clearly raises the possibility of an underlying fear of emerging sexuality. Indeed, it has been proposed that anorexics have little more than the usual concern about fatness, but somehow eating and weight become linked with sexual development, which is the true object of fear (Crisp, 1980). Food may be viewed as aversive to the anorexic because it represents the building blocks to breasts and hips. Self-starvation is the patient's attempt to forestall the outward signs of her sexuality.

Women with bulimia nervosa generally are older than anorexics and are normal weight. Thus, they are past the stage of physical sexual development and apparently are not engaged in an effort to deny their sexuality. Nonetheless, they too express strong feelings of disgust toward their bodies and feel that their bodies are out of control. Attitudes toward sexuality among bulimics often seem to be laced with guilt. Many clinicians seem to believe that the sexual connotation of disturbed body image in bulimia nervosa stems from a history of physical or sexual trauma. Thus, for both types of eating disorders, sexual fears, sexual immaturity, or sexual trauma possibly are important etiological factors.

In a study of antecedents to bulimia nervosa, 72% of bulimics recalled stressful triggers suggestive of a sexual conflict (Lacey, Coker, & Birtchnell, 1986). In contrast to this impressionistic and uncontrolled study, more objective comparisons of eating disorder patients with normal or psychiatric controls have not found unusual patterns of sexual attitudes, behavior, or experiences (see Scott, 1987, for review). Comparisons of anorexics with normals showed no significant differences in sexual fears, desire to menstruate or to have children, fear of pregnancy, frequency of masturbation, or the number of subjects who had a boyfriend and were sexually active. Compared to normals or psychiatric controls, bulimic women were not significantly different in sexual activity, sex guilt, or sex knowledge (Haimes & Katz, 1988; Johnson & Conners, 1987; Mizes, 1988). The only difference between groups was that bulimics were somewhat older at the time of their first sexual intercourse (Haimes & Katz, 1988).

There are several case reports of sexual abuse history in eating disorder patients; however, there appears to be only two controlled studies. Finn, Hartman, Leon, and Lawson (1986) compared samples of sexually abused and nonabused women. All subjects were receiving group therapy for psychological disorder. Although the rate of eating disorder symptoms was fairly high for all the women, there were no differences between the groups with respect to past or present eating disorder. Similarly, in a survey of college females, Smolak, Levine, and Sullins (1990) found no differences between abused and nonabused groups on the subscales of the EDI.

With respect to sex-role orientation, it has been proposed that the emaciation in anorexia nervosa is an attempt by the person to deny her femininity, whereas bulimic women supposedly have an excessive desire to attain some ideal version of femininity. But according to the research literature, there is no consistent evidence that eating disorder groups are less or more feminine in traditional sex-role orientation (e.g., being passive, dependent, or concerned with social approval). However, they do appear to endorse fewer masculine traits, which might reflect their lower self-esteem or sense of autonomy (Scott, 1987; Striegel-Moore, Silberstein, & Rodin, 1986).

In conclusion, ideas about the importance of sexuality for the development of body-image disturbance in eating disorders are wide ranging. However, the empirical literature indicates that no matter how important sexual concerns might be to eating disorder patients, these issues are not unique to them as compared to other groups.

Self-Esteem

Body-satisfaction or physical self-esteem is closely associated with more global feelings of self-esteem (Cash et al., 1986; Rosen & Ross, 1968; Secord & Jourard, 1953). Women with eating disorders have extremely low self-esteem, feelings of being a bad person, and dread of rejection or abandonment (Garfinkel & Garner, 1982; Johnson & Conners, 1987). Given the importance placed on appearance in our weight-conscious society, it is not difficult to see how a young woman (with or without an eating disorder) might take the view that her self-worth is dependent on having a perfect body and that if only she were able to lose some weight, or look more perfect on the outside, then no one would know just how bad a person she is on the inside. Although all women are exposed to cultural messages extolling thinness, there may be a synergistic relationship between this pressure and the drive from within to compensate for perceptions of personal deficits.

In women with established eating disorders, body-size perception and satisfaction are more disturbed among those who have the most negative self-esteem (Cooper & Taylor, 1987; Dunn & Ondercin, 1981; Garfinkel, 1981; Garner & Garfinkel, 1981–82; Strober, 1981; Wingate & Christie, 1978). In a few laboratory studies, eating disorder subjects were exposed to cues designed to provoke negative moods and self-evaluation. Although the experimental stimuli were purposely unrelated to body image, subsequent to the induction of negative self-evaluation, the subjects reported more body dissatisfaction and greater size overestimation compared to their reports under neutral stimulus conditions or to normal subjects (Freeman, Thomas, Solyom, & Miles, 1983;

Lindholm & Wilson, 1987; Taylor & Cooper, 1989). These laboratory findings indicate that negative self-evaluation can trigger more negative body images in eating disorder patients and that physical appearance may become a focus of attention in these women when their self-worth sinks.

BODY-IMAGE DISTURBANCE IN THE DEVELOPMENT AND MAINTENANCE OF EATING DISORDERS

The essential features of eating disorders are not completely independent but are linked together and mutually sustaining. The best example is that extreme weight control by dieting or vomiting contributes to the development of binge eating in bulimia nervosa (Polivy & Herman, 1985; Rosen & Leitenberg, 1988). Does body-image disturbance also play a role in the development of the other characteristics of eating disorders? Fairburn and Garner (1986, 1988) have asserted that is does—that the extreme eating abnormalities and weight control in these disorders are secondary to overconcern with weight and shape. This seems perfectly sensible. Except for those individuals needing to lose weight purely for matters of physical health, why would a young woman begin dieting unless she first was displeased with her appearance? Why would she suffer the consequences of fasting or purging unless she was desperate to lose weight?

Among young women in general, body dissatisfaction is associated with various problematic eating attitudes and habit including a perceived lack of control over food, dietary restraint, and binge eating (Kiemle, Slade, & Dewey, 1987; Striegel-Moore, McAvay, & Rodin, 1986; Wiedel & Dodd, 1983; Wolf & Crowther, 1983; Zakin, 1989). Moreover, body dissatisfaction was a better predictor of bulimic eating attitudes and behaviors in teenage girls than self-esteem, depression, and social anxiety combined, which contributed very little unique variance after body dissatisfaction (Gross & Rosen, 1988). Similarly, Brown et al. (1989) found that body-image parameters continued to differentiate binge-purgers from controls even after psychosocial adjustment was statistically controlled. Among women with bulimia nervosa, the severity of eating and dieting symptoms were correlated with body dissatisfaction (Post & Crowther, 1987; Ruderman & Grace, 1988).

In a prospective study, the EDI was administered to ballet students who were evaluated 2 years later for eating disorders. Among the eight scales, only Body Dissatisfaction and Drive for Thinness significantly predicted individuals with eating disorder symptoms (Garner, Garfinkel, Rockert, & Olmsted, 1987). However, baseline levels of eating disorder symptoms were not controlled and the unique predictive contribution of body image could not be determined. Another relevant study used measures of body dissatisfaction, perceived attractiveness, perfectionism, ineffectiveness, stress, competitiveness, and body weight as independent variables to predict increased binge eating, dieting, and purging among female college students from the beginning to the end of their freshman year (Striegel-Moore, Silberstein, Frensch, & Rodin, 1989). The best predictors were change scores in the pathologic direction, from time 1 to time 2, on measures of body dissatisfaction and perceived attractiveness. Changes in weight and the other psychological variables added little to the prediction of eating pathology and dieting beyond the measures of body image. In sum, there is consistent evidence that negative body image predicts severity of eating and dieting pathology and does so to a greater extent than other psychological variables, although no truly adequate prospective study has been conducted.

PROGNOSTIC SIGNIFICANCE OF BODY-IMAGE DISTURBANCE

The majority of anorexic and bulimic patients appear to improve with psychological treatment, particularly treatments that use cognitive–behavioral techniques (Bemis, 1987; Brownell & Foreyt, 1986; Fairburn, 1988; Gwirtsman, Kaye, Weintraub, & Jimerson, 1984; Mitchell, 1988; Rosen, 1987). However, even the most successful published accounts of treatment outcome at follow-up indicate a significant minority of treatment failures (i.e., anorexics still well below their appropriate weight and bulimics who dropped out of therapy prematurely or continued to binge and vomit regularly). Given the complexity of these disorders, the fact that most individuals are helped is encouraging, but the results are still far from optimal. Thus, it would be extremely useful to identify the risk factors for treatment failure.

In the earliest publications on body image in eating disorders, Bruch (1962) said that normalization of body image was a precondition for recovery. She also noted that anorexic patients may gain weight for many reasons while hospitalized and may seem to progress well in psychotherapy; however, the improvement is apt to be only temporary unless it is accompanied by a correction of distorted body image. What evidence is there to support body image as a prognostic variable in the treatment of eating disorders?

Body-size distortion was measured in several prognostic studies of treatment response in anorexia nervosa (Button, 1986; Casper, Halmi, Goldberg, Eckert, & Davis, 1979; Garfinkel, Moldofsky, & Garner, 1977; Leon, Lucas, Colligan, Ferdinande, & Kamp, 1985). In all these studies, more extreme overestimation of body size at the beginning of inpatient treatment predicted less weight gain by the subjects at discharge. Among those who had completed treatment and successfully restored their weight, weight-loss relapse was predicted by the severity of size overestimation at pretreatment, during treatment, and at discharge (Button, 1986; Button, Fransella, & Slade, 1977; Slade & Russell, 1973). Vandereychken and colleagues (Vandereychken, Probst, & Meermann, 1988) also reported that anorexics who were pleased with their emaciated appearance as shown to them on a videotape at pre- and posttreatment were less likely to gain weight during treatment and were more likely to relapse after discharge.

Compared to other variables, body image appears to be among the most important prognostic factors. In two large samples of anorexia nervosa patients, baseline distorted body image was among a couple of significant predictors of weight gain during hospitalization and weight maintenance at follow-up (Button, 1986; Strober, Bowen, & Preble, 1985). A large set of psychological, familial, and other measures of illness severity did not add anything beyond body image to the prediction of weight restoration. On balance, body image has emerged as a significant prognostic factor in the treatment of anorexia nervosa. However, the evidence is not entirely consistent. In one study, size overestimators did not gain less weight than size underestimators (Touyz, Beumont, & Collins, 1988). In another, negative body-image attitudes at baseline were not associated with weight gain (Strober, Goldenberg, Green, & Saxon, 1979).

Less information on prognostic factors in the treatment of bulimia nervosa is available, but a few published studies indicate that body image is an important predictor of treatment outcome. One problem in outpatient treatment of bulimia nervosa is that a significant number (as high as 35%) of patients drop out of therapy (Rosen, 1987). Wilson has noted (Rossiter & Wilson, 1985; Wilson, Rossiter, Kleinfield, & Lindholm, 1986) that dropping out is often precipitated by fears of weight gain, especially when the patient is instructed to eat forbidden foods without vomiting. At the end of treatment, bulimics who improved the most on measures of body dissatisfaction had also made the greatest reductions in binge-eating and vomiting (Conners, Johnson, & Stuckey, 1984). Of patients who were free from binge eating and vomiting at the end of therapy, body dissatisfaction at the end of treatment was one of two best predictors of relapse 6 months later (Freeman, Beach, Davis, & Solyom, 1985).

TREATMENT OF BODY-IMAGE DISTURBANCES

Treatment of body image in eating disorders could be arranged in accord with the different body-image components outlined earlier, that is, perceptual, cognitive, and behavioral disturbances. With respect to perceptual disturbances, Garner and Garfinkel (1981–82) offered this analogy to their patients for treatment of distorted body–size perception: "When I try to estimate my own dimensions, I am like a color blind person trying to coordinate her wardrobe. I will have to rely on objective data or someone I can trust to determine my actual size" (p. 279). This can be accomplished in several ways. One method has subjects repeatedly estimate their body size until they are able to do so accurately. Two studies of women without eating disorders have demonstrated that it is possible to decrease size overestimation with such training (Goldsmith & Thompson, 1989; Rosen et al., 1989). In a related study, women with anorexia nervosa and bulimia were able to reduce their size overestimation after being directed in an exercise to study their shape objectively in a mirror (Norris, 1984). Another technique frequently recommended is to provide the patient with normative information on her weight compared to other women of similar age and height (Andersen, 1987; Rosen et al., 1989). Even if this information shows the patient that she is normal or below normal weight, it is common for the patient to protest that normal is still too big, that she still feels fat compared to her peers. It might be possible to combat these negative social comparisons further by having the patient collect height and weight data on the friends with whom she is comparing herself (Rosen et al., 1989). The purpose of these exercises is for the patient to discover that she is not as large as she believed, that in most cases she is average or below-average weight, and that she is about the same size or even smaller than peers whom she believed look ideal.

The disturbed body-image attitudes of eating disorder patients are amenable to cognitive–behavioral strategies (Agras, 1987; Anderson, 1987; Fairburn, 1988; Garner & Bemis, 1982; Rosen et al., 1989) that essentially are adapted from the treatment of cognitive distortions in depressed or anxious patients (Beck & Emery, 1985). The patient should be directed to self-monitor thoughts about perceived defects in her appearance and, more importantly, thoughts about the perceived significance of her appearance for her self-worth or relationships. Thoughts of being weak willed and inadequate or being unattractive or disgusting to other people are appropriate targets for modification. The therapist should allow the patient to take the active role in examining the evidence that she has to support or to refute these beliefs. After the patient has generated arguments to counter her maladaptive beliefs, positive and more accurate substitute thoughts should be formulated to be rehearsed in their place. Although the maladaptive beliefs will not be dispelled entirely at first, the immediate objective is to bring her to the point of reasonable uncertainty about them, so that she can begin to recognize truth in the alternative beliefs. It also has been recommended that the patient be helped to investigate whether traumatic events such as rape or physical abuse initially provoked these thoughts (Andersen, 1987).

Women with eating disorders tend to avoid situations that they feel will call attention to their shape or weight, such as wearing tight-fitting clothes or allowing boyfriends to see or touch certain parts of their body. Besides causing even more disruption of normal social functioning, this can prevent the patient from discovering that some of the predicted consequences of not hiding her body actually will not come to pass. Thus, exposure to these avoided situations not only can reduce behavioral dysfunction, but can help to extinguish some of the patient's negative beliefs about her appearance (Fairburn, 1988; Leitenberg & Rosen, 1988; Rosen et al., 1989). For example, a patient might predict that if she was to wear tight jeans to school instead of a baggy skirt people would remark that she has fat thighs and consequently she would panic. For homework between therapy sessions, the patient could be asked to practice facing this feared situation and to compare the actual and expected outcomes. Typically, the patient will discover that anxiety in the situation was more tolerable than she had predicted, that the dreaded consequences did not occur, and that by "coming out of hiding" she actually had received positive feedback from other people.

EFFECTS ON BODY IMAGE OF TREATING EATING DISORDERS

In this section, I will review what we know about the effects of existing eating disorder treatment programs on body-image disturbance. All published treatment outcome studies of anorexia nervosa and bulimia that have been cited previously in more detailed reviews (Bemis, 1987; Brownell & Foreyt, 1986; Fairburn, 1988; Garner, 1987; Gwirtsman, Kaye, Weintraub, & Jimerson, 1984; Halmi, 1985; Mitchell, 1988; Rosen, 1987) were examined for the extent to which body image was targeted in treatment or assessment. A few recent studies were also examined that have emerged since these reviews. Both psychological and pharmacological treatment programs were considered. Among the more than 75 studies, the overwhelming majority fell into one of two categories: (1) treatment trials that neither directly treated nor measured body-image disturbance, or (2) treatment programs that did not measure changes in body image after treatment, even though body image was targeted for intervention. Only those few studies that actually reported specific data on body-image changes will be cited and discussed.

The first question of treatment outcome is: Does pharmacologic therapy lead to improvements in body image? Most of the studies reviewed involved a controlled comparison of an active drug with placebo or no-drug control conditions. The medication was always delivered in a minimal or no-therapy context, devoid of any specific education or therapy for body-image disturbance. Unfortunately, none of the over 20 published studies for either anorexia nervosa or bulimia measured body image. Recently, some unpublished data emerged on the effect of medication on body image (Mitchell, Pyle, Eckert, Hatsukami, Pomeroy, & Zimmerman, 1989). In this study, bulimia nervosa patients were randomly assigned to anti-depressant medication, placebo medication control, group psychotherapy, or group psychotherapy plus anti-depressant medication. Subjects in the drug-alone condition remained unimproved in body image at the end of treatment, whereas subjects in psychotherapy and psychotherapy plus medication did show reductions in body dissatisfaction. Psychotherapy and combined treatment conditions did not differ in body-image improvements, indicating that the medication did not add anything to psychotherapy for body-image disturbance.

The next question is: Does psychotherapy, behavior therapy, or behavior modification lead to improved body image in anorexia nervosa and bulimia? Among over 40 psychological treatment-outcome studies, about one-third of the treatment programs involved some attempt to modify body image directly.

However, the effects of these attempts are unknown. Information about changes in body image among anorexics is limited to a few contradictory treatment reports. In three reports, anorexics decreased the severity of their size overestimation after they had regained weight in the hospital (Beaumont, 1989; Button, 1986; Crisp & Kalucy, 1974; Slade & Russell, 1973), whereas in three others they did not (Button, Fransella, & Slade, 1977; Garfinkel, 1981). Also, all these studies were uncontrolled, thus any changes that did occur may have been influenced by repeated assessment and experimenter demand as opposed to the active ingredients of treatment. Still, it would be inappropriate to be overly discouraged by these mixed results. These treatment programs were not specifically geared to modify body image. There may have been improvements on other dimensions of body image that were not measured. Finally, although size distortion did not decrease in some subject samples, nor did it worsen, which is impressive given that subjects had gained significant amounts of weight.

The bulk of data on body image after treatment has only recently emerged in the bulimia nervosa treatment trials. It is generally believed that one way eating disorder patients can be helped is to persuade them that they have "bought into" a cultural fashion for physical appearance in women, that body weight is less modifiable than they think, that they are capable of rising against this social pressure, and so on. In short, armed with facts about the sociocultural origins of their body image, the patient may be able to change her body-image attitudes. Such an educational approach has been tried in two studies of bulimia nervosa patients, but both failed to produce significant reductions in body dissatisfaction (Berry & Abramowitz, 1989; Conners et al., 1984). As was demonstrated in a study of non-eating-disordered women, education must be accompanied by actively involving the patient in therapeutic exercises in order for her to change body-image attitudes and behaviors (Rosen et al., 1989). Wooley and Kearney-Cooke (1986) described a group therapy for women with bulimia nervosa that was educationally oriented, utilizing consciousness-raising plus experiential exercises and social-resistance training. This program resulted in significant decreases in body dissatisfaction, but the study was uncontrolled. The only controlled investigation of a treatment for bulimia nervosa that involved a strong educational component concerning body image coupled with experiential exercises was by Wolchik, Weiss, and Katzman (1986). At the end of therapy, treatment subjects reported significantly less body dissatisfaction, but they were no more improved than the no-treatment control subjects.

Several studies used cognitive–behavior therapy for body image with bulimia nervosa patients. In addition to education, these treatment programs were mainly concerned with helping the patient to challenge and replace irrational, self-defeating thoughts with more realistic self-perceptions and to practice facing situations that normally would trigger body dissatisfaction. Wilson and colleagues (1986) reported significant reductions in body dissatisfaction at posttreatment and follow-up. The only two controlled studies of cognitive–behavior therapy versus minimal or no-treatment reported that treated bulimics were significantly more satisfied with their appearance (Ordman & Kirschenbaum, 1985) and more accurate in size estimation (Leitenberg, Rosen, Gross, Nudelman, & Vara, 1988). Birtchell, Lacey, and Harte (1985) also reported that size distortion decreased in their treated bulimics in an uncontrolled study of psychotherapy. Most recently, the preliminary report on a controlled study of cognitive–behavior therapy (Fairburn, 1988) showed that it was equally effective as interpersonal psychotherapy for improving over-concern with weight and shape, whereas a purely behavior therapy that was focused only on controlling eating behavior was relatively ineffective for body image. Thus, control over eating and vomiting alone is not sufficient to alter body image. Also the core cognitions of eating disorder patients may not need to be addressed, as the interpersonal psychotherapy that dealt with more global self-evaluation also was effective in reducing body dissatisfaction. The reader is referred to Chapters 12 and 13 of this volume for Krueger's discussion of psychodynamic perspectives on body-image treatment and Freedman's further discussion of cognitive–behavioral procedures.

CONCLUSION

Body-image disturbance in eating disorders is a multidimensional problem that includes perceptual, attitudinal, and behavioral features. Not all persons with eating disorders, however, suffer from each of these different types of body-image disturbance, and strong correlations among them should not be expected.

Several explanations for the development of negative body image in women with eating disorders have been reviewed. Without discounting their impor-tance, it is essential to note that these ideas have been tested mainly in studies with cross-sectional, correlational designs. The problem with this approach is that the chronology of body-image disturbance and other psychosocial variables is not clear, making it is difficult to draw meaningful distinctions between premorbid characteristics from those which might arise as a consequence of the body-image disorder.

Women who engage in bulimic episodes of overeating and purging usually experience a great sense of self-disgust. Feelings of inadequacy or worthlessness could easily result from failed weight change attempts in young women who believe weight control is only a matter of will power. Life stresses and low self-esteem are likely to be increased in individuals who are ashamed of their appearance. Furthermore, biological investigators of anorexia nervosa have argued persuasively that impaired concentration, mood disturbance, obsessions, and other mental processes relevant to body image are directly attributable to the effects of starvation (Kaplan & Woodside, 1987). Even though they are not emaciated, the same may be true in bulimia nervosa, possibly because they are biologically starved compared to a naturally determined premorbid weight (Kaplan & Woodside, 1987). Only prospective studies can be used to determine the true role of psychosocial variables in the etiology of body-image disturbance, but this approach in body-image research has been neglected.

Concerning the idea that eating and dieting pathology are secondary to body image, the data indicate that body image is, indeed, the best predictor of these other symptoms. However, to date, there is no completely adequate prospective study to examine whether negative body image truly is a precursor to the onset of a full-blown eating disorder. The possibility remains that body-image disturbances in many eating disorder patients are promoted by their dieting attempts, preoccupation with eating, etc. Therefore, the same caveat concerning the need for longitudinal studies is applicable to this question as well.

Based simply on a tally of studies with positive results, it could be concluded that severe body-image disturbance is predictive of treatment failure. However, this conclusion can only be tentative because there just are not enough large case series that included body image as a predictor variable. Also, in order to learn whether body image is truly an important risk factor for poor outcome, more multivariate research designs are needed to examine its predictive power in relation to other risk factors. Finally, in most prognostic studies body image has been defined in terms of body-size distortion. But recently, there has been a tremendous advance in delineating other clinical features of body-image disturbance (e.g., Brown et al., 1988; Cash et al., 1986; Cooper & Fairburn, 1987; Rosen, Srebnik, et al., 1989) that also should be incorporated into future studies of prognosis.

Given the critical importance of body image to eating disorders and the vast literature on this subject, it is ironic and alarming that there is still no definite answer to questions of treatment effectiveness for body-image disturbance. With respect to anorexia nervosa, the primary, and often only, outcome variable in treatment trials has been weight gain. Although most anorexia nervosa patients do gain weight in the hospital, weight gain itself certainly is not a guarantee of improved body image. Anorexic patients gain weight for many reasons other than coming to terms with their distorted body image, including being allowed access to hospital privileges and eventually to gain release from the hospital. Despite the reversal of their starvation, patients who are treated simply with contingency management for weight gain may have their body-image disturbance reinstated or intensified after hospitalization (e.g., Bruch, 1974, 1978). Similarly, with respect to bulimia nervosa, it has been argued that too much attention has been focused on achieving total abstinence from binge-eating and vomiting without regard to other important clinical features of the disorder (Bemis, 1985). Anorexia nervosa and bulimia nervosa are multidimensional problems, so body weight and frequencies of binge-eating and vomiting cannot give a complete picture of clinical severity. People with the same level of improvement on these variables are likely to vary on other measures of psychopathology. Thus, improvement in body image needs to be measured directly, not merely inferred.

REFERENCES

American Psychiatric Association. (1987). *Diagnostic and statistical manual of mental disorders* (3rd ed., rev.). Washington, D.C.: Author.

Agras, W. W. (1987). *Eating disorders: Management of obesity, bulimia, and anorexia nervosa.* New York: Pergamon Press.

Andersen, A. E. (1985). *Practical comprehensive treatment of anorexia nervosa and bulimia.* Baltimore: Johns Hopkins University Press.

Andersen, A. E. (1987). Contrast and comparison of behavioral, cognitive–behavioral, and comprehensive treatment methods for anorexia nervosa and bulimia nervosa. *Behavior Modification, 11,* 522–543.

Beaumont, P. J. V. (1989). Trying to make sense of body-image data. *The BASH Magazine, 8,* 160–167

Beck, A T., & Emery, G. (1985), *Anxiety disorders and phobias: A cognitive perspective.* New York: Basic Books.

Bemis, K. M. (1985). "Abstinence" and "nonabstinence" models for the treatment of bulimia. *International Journal of Eating Disorders, 4,* 407–437.

Bemis, K. M. (1987). The present status of operant conditioning for the treatment of anorexia nervosa. *Behavior Modification, 11,* 432–463.

Berry, D. M. & Abramowitz, S. I. (1989). Educative/support groups and subliminal psychodynamic activation for bulimic college women. *International Journal of Eating Disorders, 8,* 75–85.

Birtchell, S. A., Lacey, J. H. & Harte, A. (1985). Body image distortion in bulimia nervosa. *British Journal of Psychiatry, 147,* 408–412.

Brown, T. A., Cash, T. F., & Lewis, R. J. (1989). Body-image disturbances in adolescent female binge-purgers: A brief report of the results of a national survey in the U.S.A. *Journal of Child Psychology and Psychiatry, 30,* 605–613.

Brown, T. A., Johnson, W. G., Bergeron, K. C., Keeton, W. P., & Cash, T. F. (1988, November). *Assessment of body-related cognitions in bulimia: The Body Image Automatic Thoughts Questionnaire.* Paper presented at the meeting of the Association for the Advancement of Behavior Therapy, New York.

Brownell, K. D., & Foreyt, J. P. (Eds.). (1986). *Handbook of eating disorders: Physiology, psychology, and treatment of obesity, anorexia, and bulimia.* New York: Basic Books.

Bruch, H. (1962). Perceptual and conceptual disturbances in anorexia nervosa. *Psychosomatic Medicine, 24,* 187–194.

Bruch, H. (1973). *Eating disorders: Obesity, anorexia nervosa, and the person within.* New York: Basic Books.

Bruch, H. (1974). Perils of behavior modification in treatment of anorexia nervosa. *Journal of the American Medical Association, 230,* 1419–1422.

Bruch, H. (1978). Dangers of behavior modification in treatment of anorexia nervosa. In J. P. Brady & H. K. H. Brodie (Eds.), *Controversy in psychiatry* (pp. 645–654). Philadelphia: W. B. Saunders.

Button, E. (1986). Body size perception and response to in-patient treatment in anorexia nervosa. *International Journal of Eating Disorders, 5,* 617–629.

Button, E. J., Fransella, F., & Slade, P. D. (1977). A reappraisal of body perception disturbance in anorexia nervosa. *Psychological Medicine, 7,* 235–243.

Cash, T. F., & Brown, T. A. (1987). Body image in anorexia nervosa and bulimia nervosa: A review of the literature. *Behavior Modification, 11,* 487–521.

Cash, T. F., Lewis, R. J., & Keeton, P. (1987, March). *Development and validation of the Body-Image Automatic Thoughts Questionnaire: A measure of body-related cognitions.* Paper presented at the meeting of the Southeastern Psychological Association, Atlanta.

Cash, T. F., Winstead, B. A., & Janda, L. H., (1986, April). Body image survey report: The great American shape-up. *Psychology Today, 20*, 30–37.

Casper, R. C., Halmi, K., Goldberg, S. C., Eckert, E. D., & Davis, J. M. (1979). Disturbances in body image estimation as related to other characteristics and outcome in anorexia nervosa. *British Journal of Psychiatry, 134*, 60–66.

Cattanach, L., & Rodin, J. (1988). Psychosocial components of the stress process in bulimia. *International Journal of Eating Disorders, 7*, 75–88.

Conners, M., Johnson, C. L., & Stuckey, M. K. (1984). Treatment of bulimia with brief psychoeducational group therapy. *American Journal of Psychiatry, 141*, 1512–1516.

Cooper, Z., & Fairburn, C. G. (1987). The Eating Disorder Examination: A semi-structured interview for the assessment of the specific psychopathology of eating disorders. *International Journal of Eating Disorders, 6*, 1–8.

Cooper P. J., & Taylor, M.Æ. (1987). Body image disturbance in bulimia nervosa. *British Journal of Psychiatry, (Suppl. 2)*, 34–38.

Crisp, A. H. (1980). *Anorexia nervosa: Let me be*. London: Academic Press.

Crisp, A. H., & Kalucy, R. S. (1974). Aspects of the perceptual disorder in anorexia nervosa. *Journal of Medical Psychology, 47*, 349–361.

Dunn, P., & Ondercin, P. (1981). Personality variables related to compulsive eating in college women. *Journal of Clinical Psychology, 37*, 43–49.

Fabian, L. J. & Thompson, J. K. (1989). Body image and eating disturbance in young females. *International Journal of Eating Disorders, 8*, 63–74.

Fairburn, C. G. (1988). *Cognitive treatment of bulimia nervosa*. Unpublished treatment manual, Department of Psychiatry, University of Oxford, Oxford, England.

Fairburn, C. G., (1988). The current status of the psychological treatments for bulimia nervosa. *Journal of Psychosomatic Research, 32*, 635–645.

Fairburn, C. G., & Cooper, P. J. (1982). Self-induced vomiting and bulimia nervosa: An undetected problem. *British Medical Journal, 284*, 1153–1155.

Fariburn, C. G., & Garner, D. M. (1986). The diagnosis of bulimia nervosa. *International Journal of Eating Disorders, 5*, 403–419.

Fairburn, C. G., & Garner, D. M. (1988). Diagnostic criteria for anorexia nervosa and bulimia nervosa: The importance of attitudes to shape and weight. In D. M. Garner & P. E. Garfinkel (Eds.), *Diagnostic issues in anorexia nervosa and bulimia nervosa*. New York: Brunner/Mazel.

Finn, S., Hartman, M., Leon, G. R., & Lawson, L. (1986). Eating disorders and sexual abuse: Lack of confirmation for a clinical hypothesis. *International Journal of Eating Disorders, 5*, 1051–1060.

Franzoi, S. L., & Shields, S. A. (1984). The Body Esteem Scale: Multidimensional structure and sex differences in a college population. *Journal of Personality Assessment, 48*, 173–178.

Freeman, R. J., Beach, B., Davis, R., & Solyom, L. (1985). The prediction of relapse in bulimia nervosa. *Journal of Psychiatric Research, 19*, 349–353.

Freeman, R. J., Thomas, C. D., Solyom, L., & Miles, J. E. (1983). Body image disturbances in anorexia nervosa: A reexamination and a new technique. In P. L. Darby, P. E. Garfinkel, D. M. Garner, & D V. Coscona (Eds.), *Anorexia nervosa: Recent developments in research* (pp. 117–127). New York: Alan R. Liss.

Garfinkel, P. E. (1981). Some recent observations on the pathogenesis of anorexia nervosa. *Canadian Journal of Psychiatry, 26*, 218–223.

Garfinkel, P. E., & Garner, D. M. (1982). *Anorexia nervosa: A multidimensional perspective*. New York: Brunner/Mazel.

Garfinkel, P. E., Moldofsky, H., & Garner, D. M. (1977). The outcome of anorexia nervosa: Significance of clinical features, body image, and behaviour modification. In R. Vigersky (Ed.), *Anorexia nervosa* (pp. 315–330). New York: Raven Press.

Garfinkel, P. E., Moldofsky, H., & Garner, D. M. (1979). The stability of perceptual disturbance in anorexia nervosa. *Psychological Medicine, 9,* 703–708.

Garner,D. M. (1987). Psychotherapy outcome research with bulimia nervosa. *Psychotherapy and Psychosomatics, 48,* 129–140.

Garner, D. M., & Bemis, K. M. (1982). A cognitive–behavioral approach to anorexia nervosa. *Cognitive Therapy and Research, 6,* 123–150.

Garner, D. M., & Garfinkel, P. E. (1981–82). Body image in anorexia nervosa: Measurement, theory, and clinical implications. *International Journal of Psychiatry in Medicine, 11,* 263–284.

Garner, D. M., Garfinkel, P. E., Rockert, W., & Olmsted, M. P. (1987). A prospective study of eating disturbances in the ballet. *Psychotherapy and Psychosomatics, 48,* 170–175.

Garner, D. M., Garfinkel, P. E., Schwartz, D., & Thompson, M. (1980). Cultural expectations of thinness in women. *Psychological Reports, 47,* 483–491.

Garner, D. M., & Olmsted, M. P. (1984). *Eating Disorder Inventory.* Odessa, Florida Psychological Assessment Resources.

Garner, D. M., Olmsted, M. P., & Garfinkel, P. E. (1983). Does anorexia nervosa occur on a continuum? *International Journal of Eating Disorders, 2,* 11–20.

Garner, D. M., Olmsted, M. P., & Polivy, J. (1983). Development and validation of a multidimensional Eating Disorder Inventory for anorexia nervosa and bulimia. *International Journal of Eating Disorders, 2,* 15–34.

Goldsmith, D., & Thompson, J. K. (1989). The effect of mirror confrontation and size estimation feedback on perceptual inaccuracy in normal females who overestimate body size. *International Journal of Eating Disorders, 8,* 437–444.

Gray, J. J., Ford, K., & Kelly, L. M. (1987). The prevalence of bulimia in a black college population. *International Journal of Eating Disorders, 6,* 733–740.

Gross, J., & Rosen, J. C. (1988). Bulimia in adolescents: Prevalence and psychosocial correlates. *International Journal of Eating Disorders, 7,* 51–61.

Gwirtsman, H., Kaye, W., Weintraub, M., & Jimerson, D.C. (1984). Pharmacologic treatment of eating disorders. *Psychiatric Clinics of North America, 7,* 863–878.

Haimes, A. L., & Katz, J. K. (1988). Sexual and social maturity versus social conformity in restricting anorectic, bulimic, and borderline women. *International Journal of Eating Disorders, 7,* 331–341.

Halmi, K. A. (1985). Behavioral management for anorexia nervosa. In D. M. Garner & P. E. Garfinkel (Eds.), *A handbook of psychotherapy for anorexia nervosa and bulimia* (pp. 147–159). New York: Guilford Press.

Hsu, L. K. G. (1982). Is there a disturbance in body image in anorexia nervosa? *Journal of Nervous and Mental Disease, 82,* 305–306.

Johnson, C., & Conners, M. E. (1987). *The etiology and treatment of bulimia nervosa: A biopsychosocial perspective.* New York: Basic Books.

Kaplan, A. S., & Woodside, D. B. (1987). Biological aspects of anorexia nervosa and bulimia nervosa. *Journal of Consulting and Clinical Psychology, 55,* 645–653.

Kiemle, G., Slade, P. D., & Dewey, M. E. (1987). Factors associated with abnormal eating attitudes and behaviors: Screening individuals at risk of developing an eating disorder. *International Journal of Eating Disorders, 6,* 713–724.

Lacey, J. H., Coker, S., & Birtchnell, S. A. (1986). Bulimia: Factors associated with its etiology and maintenance. *International Journal of Eating Disorders, 5,* 475–487.

Leitenberg, H., & Rosen, J. C. (1988). Cognitive–behavioral treatment of bulimia nervosa. in M. Hersen, R. M. Eisler, & P. M. Miller (Eds.), *Progress in Behavoir Modification, Vol. 23* (pp. 11–35). Beverly Hills, CA: Sage.

Leitenberg, H., Rosen, J. C., Gross, J., Nudelman, S., & Vara, L. (1988). Exposure plus response prevention treatment of bulimia nervosa. *Journal of Consulting and Clinical*

Psychology, 56, 535–541.

Leon, G. R., Lucas, A. R., Colligan, R. C., Ferdinande, R. J., & Kamp, J. (1985). Sexual, body-image, and personality attitudes in anorexia nervosa. *Journal of Abnormal Child Psychology, 13*, 245–258.

Lindholm, L., & Wilson, G. T. (1987). *Body image assessment in patients with bulimia nervosa and normal controls.* Unpublished manuscript, Rutgers University, New Brunswick, New Jersey.

Mitchell, J. E., Pyle, R. .L., Eckert, E. .D., Hatsukami, D., Pomeroy, C., & Zimmerman, R. (1989). *A comparison study of anti-depressants and structured intensive group psychotherapy in the treatment of bulimia nervosa.* Unpublished manuscript, Department of Psychiatry, University of Minnesota, Minneapolis.

Mitchell, P. B. (1988). The pharmacologic management of of bulimia nervosa: A critical review. *International Journal of Eating Disorders, 7*, 29–42.

Mizes, J. S. (1988). Personality characteristics of bulimic and non-eating-disordered female controls: A cognitive–behavioral perspective. *International Journal of Eating Disorders, 7*, 541–550.

Nasser, M. (1988). Culture and weight consciousness. *Journal of Psychosomatic Research, 32*, 573–577.

Norris, D. L. (1984). The effects of mirror confrontation on self-estimation in anorexia nervosa, bulimia and two control groups. *Psychological Medicine, 14*, 835–842.

Ordman, A. M., & Kirschenbaum, D. S. (1985). Cognitive–behavioral therapy for bulimia: An initial outcome study. *Journal of Consulting and Clinical Psychology, 53*, 305–313.

Palazzoli, M. S. (1974). *Self-starvation.* London: Chaucer.

Polivy, J., & Herman, C. P. (1985). Dieting and binge eating. *American Psychologist, 40*, 193–201.

Polivy, J., & Herman, C. P. (1987). Diagnosis and treatment of normal eating. *Journal of Consulting and Clinical Psychology, 55*, 635–644.

Post, G., & Crowther, J. H. (1987). Restricter–purger differences in bulimic adolescent females. *International Journal of Eating Disorders, 6*, 757–761.

Rosen, G. M., & Ross, A. O. (1968). Relationship of body image to self-concept. *Journal of Consulting and Clinical Psychology, 32*, 100.

Rosen, J. C. (1987). A review of behavioral treatments for bulimia nervosa. *Behavior Modification, 11*, 464–486.

Rosen, J. C., & Gross, J. (1987). Prevalence of weight reducing and weight gaining in adolescent girls and boys. *Health Psychology, 6*, 131–147.

Rosen, J. C., & Leitenberg, H. (1988). Eating behavior in bulimia nervosa. In B. T. Walsh (Ed.), *Eating behavior in eating disorders* (pp. 161–174). Washington, DC: Author.

Rosen, J. C., Saltzberg, E., & Srebnik, D. (1989). Cognitive behavior therapy for negative body image. *Behavior Therapy, 20*, 393–404.

Rosen, J. C., Srebnik, D., Saltzberg, E., & Wendt, S. (1989). Development of a Body Image Questionnaire. Manuscript submitted for publication, Department of Psychology, University of Vermont, Burlington, Vermont.

Rossiter, E., & Wilson, G. T. (1985). Cognitive restructuring and response prevention in the treatment of bulimia nervosa. *Behavior Research and Therapy, 23*, 349–360.

Ruderman, A. J., & Grace, P. S. (1988). Bulimics and restrained eaters: A personality comparison. *Addictive Behaviors, 13*, 359–367.

Russell, G. F. M. (1979). Bulimia nervosa: An ominous variant of anorexia nervosa. *Psychological Medicine, 9*, 429–448.

Scott, D. W. (1987). The involvement of psychosexual factors in the causation of eating disorders: Time for a reappraisal. *International Journal of Eating Disorders, 6*, 199–213.

Secord, P., & Jourard, S. (1953). The appraisal of body-cathexis: Body cathexis and the self. *Journal of Consulting Psychology, 17*, 343–347.

Slade, P. D., & Russell, G. F. M. (1973). Awareness of body dimensions in anorexia nervosa: Cross-sectional and longitudinal studies. *Psychological Medicine, 3,* 188–199.

Smolak, L., Levine, M. P., & Sullins, E. (1990). Are child sexual experiences related to a college sample? *International Journal of Eating Disorders, 9,* 167–178.

Striegel-Moore, R. H., McAvay, G., & Rodin, J. (1986). Psychological and behavioral correlates of feeling fat in women. *International Journal of Eating Disorders, 5* 935–947.

Striegel-Moore, R. H., Silberstein, L. R., Frensch, P., & Rodin, J. (1989). A prospective study of disordered eating among college students. *International Journal of Eating Disorders, 8,* 499–509.

Striegel-Moore, R. H., Silberstein, L. R., & Rodin, J. (1986). Toward an understanding of risk factors for bulimia. *American Psychologist, 41,* 246–263.

Strober, M. (1981). The relation of personality characteristics to body image disturbances in juvenile anorexia nervosa: A multivariate analysis. *Psychosomatic Medicine, 43,* 323–330.

Strober, M., Bowen, E., & Preble, J. (1985). Predictors of weight change in juvenile anorexia nervosa. *International Journal of Eating Disorders, 4,* 605–608.

Strober, M., Goldenberg, I., Green, J., & Saxon, J. (1979). Body image disturbance in anorexia nervosa during the acute and recuperative phase. *Psychological Medicine, 9,* 695–701.

Taylor, M. J., & Cooper, P. J. (1989). *Body size perception and depressed mood: A mood induction study.* Unpublished manuscript, Department of Experimental Psychology, University of Cambridge, Cambridge, England.

Thompson, D. A., Berg, K. M., & Shatford, L. A.(1987). The heterogeneity of bulimic symptomatology: Cognitive and behavioral dimensions. *International Journal of Eating Disorders, 6,* 215–234.

Thompson, J. K. (1990). *Body image disturbance: Assessment and treatment.* New York: Pergamon Press.

Touyz, S., Beumont, P., & Collins, J. (1988). Does over- or underestimation of body shape influence response to treatment in patients with anorexia nervosa? *International Journal of Eating Disorders, 7,* 687–691.

Vandereycken, W., Probst, M., & Meermann, R. (1988). An experimental video-confrontation procedure as a therapeutic technique and a research tool in the treatment of eating disorders. In K. M. Pirke, W. Vandereycken, & D. Ploog (Eds.), *The psychobiology of bulimia nervosa* (pp. 172–178). Heidelberg: Springer-Verlag.

Wiedel, T. C., & Dodd, J. M. (1983). The relationship between dietary restraint, personality measures and weight in college students. *Journal of Obesity and Weight Regulation, 2,* 88–96.

Williamson, D.A. (1990). *Assessment of eating disorders: Obesity, anorexia, and bulimia nervosa.* New York: Perganan Press.

Willmuth, M. E., Leitenberg, H., Rosen, J. C., & Cado, S. (1988). A comparison of purging and nonpurging normal weight bulimics. *International Journal of Eating Disorders, 7,* 825–836.

Wilson, G. T., Rossiter, E., Kleinfield, E. I., & Lindholm, L. (1986). Cognitive–behavioral treatment of bulimia nervosa: A controlled evaluation. *Behaviour Research and Therapy, 24,* 277–288.

Wilson, G. T., & Smith, D. (1989). Assessment of bulimia nervosa: An evaluation of the Eating Disorders Examination. *International Journal of Eating Disorders, 8,* 173–179.

Wingate, B. A., & Christie, M. J. (1978). Ego strength and body image in anorexia nervosa. *Journal of Psychosomatic Research, 22,* 201–204.

Wolchik, S. A., Weiss, L., & Katzman, M. K. (1986). An empirically validated, short term psycho-educational group treatment program for bulimia. *International Journal of Eating Disorders, 5,* 21–34.

Wolf, E. M., & Crowther, J. H. (1983). Personality and eating habit variables as predictors of severity of binge eating and weight. *Addictive Behaviors, 8*, 335–344.

Wooley, S. C., & Kearney-Cooke, A. (1986). Intensive treatment of bulimia and body-image disturbance. In K. D. Brownell & J. P.Foreyt (Eds.), *Handbook of eating disorders: Physiology, Psychology, and treatment of obesity, anorexia, and bulimia* (pp. 476–502). New York: Basic Books.

Zakin, D. F. (1989). Eating disturbance, emotional separation, and body image. *International Journal of Eating Disorders, 8*, 411–416.

BODY-IMAGE CHANGE THROUGH BODILY CHANGE

C H A P T E R 10

Body-Image Change in Cosmetic Plastic Surgery

Thomas Pruzinsky
Milton T. Edgerton

Although aesthetic or cosmetic surgery is undertaken to improve the patient's appearance, the purpose of aesthetic surgery is to facilitate positive psychological changes—a goal articulated by the earliest developers of plastic surgery (e.g., Joseph, 1931; translated in Milstein, 1984) and contemporary surgeons (e.g., Edgerton, 1975; Goldwyn, 1981). In fact, the *only* rationale for performing aesthetic plastic surgery is to improve the patient's psychological well-being (Edgerton & Langman, 1982). To conduct safe and successful surgery, the plastic surgeon must evaluate the potential patient's subjective body image and the emotional and interpersonal contexts of this body-image experience (Edgerton & Langman, 1982; Pruzinsky, 1988). Thus, the plastic surgeon is continually involved in learning about body-image development, deviance, and change.

There have been dramatic increases in the numbers of patients seeking cosmetic plastic surgery in the United States over the past decade (American Society for Plastic and Reconstructive Surgery [ASPRS], 1989). In 1988, over 680,000 aesthetic procedures were performed in the United States by board-certified plastic and reconstructive surgeons. Additional thousands of cosmetic surgery procedures are performed each year by other types of surgeons (e.g., otolaryngologists, dermatologists). The most common surgical procedures are liposuction, breast augmentation, blepharoplasty (eyelid surgery), rhinoplasty (nose surgery), and rhytidectomy (face-lift) (ASPRS, 1989).

This chapter explores the nature of body image and the change in body image brought about by cosmetic plastic surgery. What are the motivations for cosmetic plastic surgery, and how are these motivations related to the patient's body image? What changes in body image result from cosmetic plastic surgery?

How do these changes in body-image result in behavioral and self-image change? These questions are both clinically and theoretically significant. If we better understand body-image processes, we can facilitate achievement of the psychosocial goals of surgery. Furthermore, the "laboratories" of the cosmetic surgeon (i.e., their consultation and operating rooms) provide a unique opportunity to study body-image development, deviance, and change.

The psychological meaning and impact of surgery is highly dependent upon the patient's developmental stage. Plastic surgeons assess and treat patients across the life span—including the young boy who wants his "ears pinned back," the adolescent female who does not want to live with her "father's big nose" on her own face, the attractive female in her early 20s who has "always" been self-conscious about her "small breasts," and the 65-year-old, energetic female executive who feels that the wrinkles on her skin "make me look different from the way I feel inside." Thus, the plastic surgeon has the opportunity to learn about and to alter the psychosocial experiences of patients at various developmental points across the life span.

In addition to treating patients who experience moderate levels of self-consciousness and anxiety regarding their appearance, plastic surgeons also witness the emotional struggles of individuals who have placed an exaggerated importance on their physical attractiveness (see Pruzinsky, Chapter 8, this volume). Such individuals often feel ugly and deformed beyond what others would expect on judging their objective appearance. The plastic surgeon also sees patients who have undergone multiple cosmetic surgeries and who are unlikely ever to be satisfied with their physical appearance (Knorr, Edgerton, & Hoopes, 1967). While all individuals who seek cosmetic surgery do so largely for psychological reasons (Edgerton & Langman, 1973), the "insatiable" cosmetic surgery patients are more psychologically disturbed and need to be managed with special care (Edgerton, Langman, & Pruzinsky, 1990). Such patients have much to teach us about body-image psychopathology. The plastic surgeon is also in a unique position to study body-image changes resulting from surgery. The surgeon observes the patient's reactions to surgery in the immediate postoperative visits, and in the long-term follow-up period. However, little has been written regarding the process and outcome of long-term psychological changes. This chapter explicates the processes by which these body-image changes take place.

A MODEL OF BODY-IMAGE CHANGE

We propose a model of body-image change in cosmetic plastic surgery; a model based on changes in perceptual, cognitive, affective, and behavioral aspects of body image. We first describe the positive impact of cosmetic surgery. Later, we describe the less common negative impacts of cosmetic surgery.

Perceptual Changes

The first step in the process of body-image change is the patient's perception of change in appearance, as well as sensory (e.g., tactile) changes resulting from surgery. Patients undergo cosmetic plastic surgery to change their appearance. The surgical changes in appearance that routinely occur from cosmetic surgery are significant. For example, Figure 10.1 shows the effects of a modest reduction rhinoplasty procedure. In Figure 10.2 we see the pre- and post-operative photographs of a woman in her late 50s who underwent both a face-lifting procedure as well as rhinoplasty. In Figure 10.3 we see the effects of an augmentation mammaplasty procedure for a woman in her mid-20s. Perception of appearance involves the evaluation of the aesthetic effect of surgery. How does it look? Is the nose shorter, longer, straighter? How does the nose look in relation to the rest of the face? Does the nose appear to be more in proportion to the rest of the face? Does the nose appear to be more masculine or more feminine? Does the physical change remove or enhance the individual's ethnicity? Does the change serve to make the patient appear more dominant or perhaps more submissive? Are there noticeable scars? Any of these factors can be important in the patient's perception of the surgical outcome.

Perceptual changes also include sensory modifications (e.g., tactile sensations), which are especially important when considering their role in developing and maintaining body image (Mahler & McDevitt, 1982; Pruzinsky, Chapter 14, this volume). Many sensory changes occur in cosmetic plastic surgery. For example, patients undergoing breast augmentation or reduction often experience reduced sensation in the skin of the nipples and areolae. There may also be

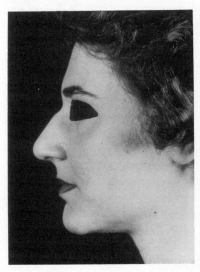 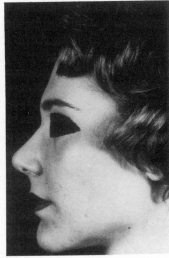

FIGURE 10.1

FIGURE 10.2

change in the breast's weight, firmness, or relative position (Goin, Goin, & Gianini, 1977). Breast reduction patients report a number of body-image changes. These patients are especially interesting because they are almost always satisfied with the surgery and are among the least psychologically complicated cosmetic surgery patients. Their body-image changes include the frequent loss of nipple sensation, occasional grief and mourning responses to this loss, and other experiences similar to phantom-limb phenomenon (Gifford, 1976; Goin & Goin, 1981). A lifetime of having to work around very large breasts may suddenly be removed. There can be marked reduction in breast sensitivity, which can affect sexual experience and functioning. Face-lift surgery also brings about sensory changes that can lead to transient body-image disturbances.

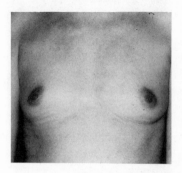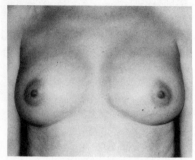

FIGURE 10.3

Most patients experience transient hypesthesia of the skin of the face and the neck. The boundaries between the self and the non-self become blurred. . . . It is disconcerting to try and sleep on a pillow which cannot be felt, or which is felt less distinctly than is usual. This rather odd experience may cause uneasiness, anxiety and sleeplessness. Rarely do such patients understand what it is that is keeping them awake. (Goin & Goin, 1986, p. 94)

Sensory changes occur in virtually all types of cosmetic plastic surgery. In blepharoplasty (eyelid surgery), a patient may experience an increase in range of vision and other changes associated with the sensitive muscles and skin around the eyes. In rhinoplasty, the nose may feel different and there may be permanent change in respiratory sensations. Postoperative reductions in skin sensation in the operated body area also routinely occur with liposuction (Courtiss & Donelan, 1988).

In the facilitation of body-image change, there is nothing more psychologically fundamental than the physical sensation that something feels "different" than before, in addition to seeing that something has changed. Thus, the perceptual changes in appearance and sensation are the foundation for the cognitive, emotional, and behavioral changes that result from cosmetic surgery. However, "[i]t is important to understand that it takes many patients a significant period of time after a body change for the picture in their mind's eye to assimilate the actual, physical change" (Goin & Goin, 1986, p. 1131). Patients need to understand that it takes time to adjust to these changes so that they will not be disturbed by the sometimes strange sensations that are a normal accompaniment of surgery. Also quite important is the realization that in cosmetic surgery there are often "tradeoffs." That is, scars or permanent changes in sensation are traded for improvements in appearance (Goin & Goin, 1981). The body-image implications of the scars, lost sensitivity, and so forth must be considered by both patient and surgeon in the total configuration of postsurgical body-image changes.

Cognitive Changes

Perceptual changes provide the foundation for important cognitive changes— that is, changes in the way that the patient thinks about his/her appearance and body experience.

Patients undergoing cosmetic surgery are strongly motivated to reduce self-consciousness (Harris, 1982; 1983; Pruzinsky & Cash, in press). Self-consciousness is the experience of self-focused attention, associated with negative cognitions and emotions regarding one's self or the evaluation of the self by others (Buss, 1980, 1985). These patients experience an anxious preoccupation with their physical appearance (Harris, 1982, 1983). This self-consciousness is perpetuated by the individual's self-criticism and constant comparison of their appearance with the appearance of others, a process that can diminish self-perceived attractiveness (e.g., Cash, Cash, & Butters, 1983) as well as reduce self-esteem and foster anxiety or depression. The amount of time and emotional energy that can be taken up by negative self-focused attention is phenomenal, with some self-conscious individuals (i.e., "worriers") reporting negative self-focused attention up to 90% of the day (Borkovec, Robinson, Pruzinsky, & Depree, 1983). This cognitive experience greatly disrupts the individual's positive perception of the self and augments perceiving the negative social evaluations of others (Borkovec, Metzger, & Pruzinsky, 1986).

The most important psychological impact of cosmetic surgery is the reduction in self-consciousness. If patients perceive the surgical change positively, they can be more positive in their self-statements and in their self-images, as well in their beliefs about themselves. For example, when patients see their postsurgical reflection in the mirror, they no longer say to themselves "What an ugly nose." Rather, they more likely say, "My nose sure looks better than it did before!" They may come to believe "I'm not so bad looking after all," and may develop a different mental picture of their appearance. Clinically, it is consistently reported that surgery reduces the amount of time that patients spend thinking about their appearance, comparing their appearance with others, and thinking about what others are thinking of their appearance. This can lead to greater amounts of time and emotional energy being focused on other areas of their life.

Emotional Changes

Cosmetic surgery patients often experience poor self-esteem, general feelings of inferiority, and mild to moderate depression (e.g., Beale, Lisper, & Palm, 1980; Goin & Goin, 1981, 1987; Harris, 1982; Robin, Copas, Jack, Kaeser, & Thomas, 1989; Schlebusch, 1989; Schlebusch & Levin, 1983). Central to their motivation for surgery is the elimination of these adverse experiences.

The vast majority of patients undergoing cosmetic surgery are satisfied with the surgical outcome (Wengle, 1986a). They report feeling more positive about their surgically changed appearance, and would undergo the procedures again if given the choice (Wengle, 1986a). Cash and Horton's (1990) longitudinal, psychological study of cosmetic surgery revealed an 86% rate of satisfaction with the physical results of surgery a month afterwards. This rate is similar to that observed in other studies (see Cash & Horton, 1983, for a summary). In a national body-image survey (Cash, Winstead, & Janda, 1986), among those who had cosmetic surgery, 95% of the females and 78% of the males would be willing to have additional cosmetic surgery (Cash & Pruzinsky, 1990).

Patients also feel positive about the fact that they had the initiative to seek out the surgical change. Most patients report that they thought about undertaking the surgery for many months and often for years before seeing the plastic surgeon (ASPRS, 1989; Pruzinsky, 1988). Cash and Horton (1990) found that nearly two-thirds of their cosmetic surgery subjects had a longstanding desire for cosmetic surgery. After surgery most patients report pleasure in having "finally" accomplished a goal that they had set for themselves to increase their self-esteem and self-efficacy.

Empirical evaluations document a positive emotional impact of cosmetic surgery (Goin & Goin, 1981, 1986; Pruzinsky, 1988; Wengle, 1986a). The most frequently documented emotional reactions are increased self-esteem and reductions in depression and anxiety associated with self-consciousness (Goin & Goin, 1981, 1986). For example, women undergoing reduction mammaplasty (Hollyman, Lacey, Whitfield, & Wilson, 1986) reported an overall improvement in body image and increased self-esteem, perception of sexual attractiveness, and feelings of femininity. Wright and Wright (1975) conducted a 18–24-month follow-up of rhinoplasty patients that included the Minnesota Multiphasic Personality Inventory (MMPI) and clinical interviews. The researchers observed improvements in self-concept, reduction in feelings of agitation and depression, "fewer aggressive impulses," and changes from a somewhat neurotic style to a more normal level of psychological adjustment, including more socially self-assured interpersonal relationships. Cash and Horton (1990) examined a variety of psychological change variables at 1 month and 1 year after cosmetic surgery. The picture is not one of major personality change. However, two key psychological conditions changed significantly from presurgery to postsurgery and 1-year follow-up: Patients did indeed report sustained improvements in their body-image satisfaction. Also, depression (assessed by the Beck Depression Inventory) was at a significantly lower level 1 month and 1 year after cosmetic surgery than was experienced before receiving surgery.

Behavioral Changes

Plastic surgery has been posited to have potential impact on a range of behaviors (Edgerton, Webb, Slaughter, & Meyer, 1964). Clinically, although patients often report resultant behavior changes, little empirical research has been conducted to validate the self-reported behavioral changes. Nevertheless, when an individual experiences positive perceptual, cognitive, and emotional changes after surgery, then behavioral changes logically could follow.

An important behavioral change brought about by successful cosmetic surgery is a reduction in the use of "camouflage techniques" (Harris, 1982). That is, patients do not need to engage in behavior aimed at concealing the body part that they are self-consciousness about. Patients no longer have to be constantly monitoring to prevent someone from viewing them from a "negative" vantage point (i.e., one that exposes their unattractive preoperative nasal profile, malocclusion, or breast size). This impact can be substantial in that it allows the individual the freedom to be more spontaneous in his/her behavior and social interactions. Patients may also take a new approach toward their grooming and self-care. They may have renewed motivation to take on a weight-loss or exercise program and make adjustments in their grooming. They may experiment with new makeup or hair styles, which further enhance appearance and can also add to the positive emotional effects the patient is experiencing. Self-conscious individuals often employ clothing styles that hide certain physical features (Harris, 1982). After surgery, patients may experiment with changes in clothing style. For example, Hetter (1979) reported that 60% of his breast augmentation patients began wearing more revealing clothing after surgery.

Individuals who feel better about their appearance may even begin to adopt new forms of movement and nonverbal behavior. Such a change can have considerable psychosocial importance, given the movement and nonverbal aspects of body image (e.g., Pruzinsky, Chapter 14, this volume), and the role of nonverbal behavior in interpersonal communication. Two persons, who are identical in appearance but who move or gesture differently from one another, are readily perceived to have different personality characteristics (Kleinke, 1975). Body movement and body language change are very powerful modes of communication, often providing unconscious (tacit) information to the self as well as to others.

The positive changes in appearance, cognitive and emotional evaluations of appearance, and behavioral changes can directly impact social relationships. Self-conscious individuals can become socially avoidant and socially withdrawn, as well as avoidant of photograph taking and situations requiring bodily exposure (Harris, 1982). They are shy or socially anxious/phobic and have difficulty in all types of social interactions, including public and intimate social interactions. They are hypersensitive to any sign of social rejection (Harris, 1982). Furthermore, this fear of rejection and preoccupation with their physical appearance make it very difficult for the individual to put his/her attention toward maintaining normal social interactions. They are so distracted and preoccupied with their own self-consciousness that they cannot adequately allocate attention to the person they are interacting with. Eventually, this pattern can result in actual (as opposed to perceived) social rejection, which further negatively impacts the self-conscious individual (Harris, 1982).

With positive changes in appearance and associated cognitive and emotional changes, it logically follows that patients would become more outgoing or at least less socially inhibited, thus allowing for a reversal of this downward spiral. For example, nearly half (47%) of a sample of breast augmentation patients reported being "more outgoing" (Hetter, 1979). More than half (53%) reported positive impacts on their sexual experiences. Other people's reactions toward the patient are a direct result of the patient's behavioral changes. If an individual has more confidence, is more pleasant and optimistic, as well as more outgoing (in addition to being objectively better looking), the social response to that individual is likely to be more positive.

Marcus aptly summarizes the process by which the relatively simple intervention of surgery can engender a "domino effect" or a series of mutually interactive changes:

it would appear that a surgical operation has long-term positive effects and by releasing previously repressed and inaccessible energies allows the patient to develop a significantly different life-style. This sequence of events is analogous to Leichter's "ripple effect," namely the long-term generalised therapeutic advantage of removing a single persistent symptom which obstructs any genuine emotional growth (Spiegel and Linn, 1969). With removal of the symptom in question (the hated nose) the stage is set for the learning of new skills, a sense of mastery and increased self-esteem. This in turn may lead to a significant improvement in the life style and the personality of the . . . patient. (Marcus, 1984, p. 317)

FACTORS INFLUENCING THE CHANGE PROCESS

The sequence of events leading to the favorable impact of cosmetic surgery described above is dependent upon the patient's positive perception of the surgical outcome. A negative perception of the surgical result precludes its cognitive, emotional, and behavioral benefits. A discussion of factors influencing the patient's evaluation of the surgical outcome teaches important lessons regarding body image. These factors include the patient's expectations regarding surgery, the nature and degree of surgical change undertaken, the patient's gender and age, the response of others to the surgical change, and the influence of time.

Perception of Surgical Change

Patients interpret the visual and sensory changes resulting from surgery according to their own subjective standards. Patients may believe that their nose was made too small or interpret the "pulling" sensation of the face-lifting as their face looking "stretched." The patient's perception of the change does not necessarily correspond with objective reality (Albino & Tedesco, 1988; Edgerton & Langman, 1982). However, it is not the reality of the patient's appearance that is primary; rather, the patient's perception of reality is most important in determining the psychological outcome. The emphasis here is on the *subjectivity* of body-image experience.

Expectations

In their longitudinal study of cosmetic surgery, Cash and Horton (1990) found the following reasons for seeking surgery were endorsed by the majority of the study's patients: (1) to have considerable improvement in my looks (87%); (2) to improve my feelings about myself (80%); (3) to receive more compliments about my appearance (67%); (4) to decrease my self-consciousness (64%); (5) to look younger (64%); and (6) to feel younger (54%). Cash and Horton's (1990) results indicated that 76% of the participating patients reported that their physical expectations had been mostly or completely fulfilled by surgery; only 4% responded with "did not look at all as I wanted."

Individuals have a current conception of their body as well as expectations regarding their future body image. These current and future body images correspond to components of actual (present) and ideal (future) "selves" (Markus & Nurius, 1986). The patient is motivated to reduce the discrepancies between their actual and ideal physical appearance by undergoing surgery (Burk, Zelen, & Terino, 1985). Patients have a picture in their mind of what they will look like postsurgically. They have expectations regarding changes in attractiveness, the feminization or masculinization of their appearance, or alteration of the symbolism (e.g., ethnicity) (Macgregor, 1989) of some physiognomic characteristic. The patient's perception of the surgical change is dramatically influenced by such expectations. If surgery was technically successful but does not match the patients conception of their appearance, the patient will react negatively.

Patients ideally should (and *usually* do) have a clear idea of the type and degree of surgical change they are expecting. Pre-operatively, the surgeon must also have a *very* clear understanding of these expectations and explain to the patient the degree to which these changes can or cannot be achieved. The cosmetic surgery literature constantly reiterates the importance of clarifying a patient's preoperative expectations regarding surgical change (e.g., Edgerton & Langman, 1982; Goin & Goin, 1981; Gorney, 1982; Lavell & Lewis, 1984; Pruzinsky, 1988; Wengle, 1986b; Wright, 1984).

Nature of Surgical Change

Cosmetic plastic surgery procedures can roughly be categorized as type-changing versus restorative surgeries (Goin & Goin, 1986). Much of cosmetic plastic surgery is restorative; that is, the surgery restores the person to their previous physical characteristics (e.g., face-lift, blepharoplasty). Type-changing operations create an appearance that the person has not previously had, for example, changing the basic shape of the nose. As a general rule, the psychological impact of type-changing operations is more profound than for restorative procedures.

> It is quite unusual for a restorative operation, such as a face-lift, to cause serious body image disturbances. Following a standard face-lift operation patients do not look "different." Their basic appearance is unchanged but they look younger and generally feel "refreshed.". . . Thus, the average face-lift patient has little or no need to adjust psychologically to a sudden alteration in the size and shape of a body part with the attendant possibility of body image distortions. (Goin & Goin, 1986, p. 94)

When patients undergo restorative procedures, assimilation of appearance change is much less likely to be psychologically challenging or disruptive. The "restored image" exists in the memory stores of the patient's experience. The possible body-image disturbances resulting from type-changing surgeries are most frequently associated with rhinoplasty, though other procedures (e.g., breast augmentation, blepharoplasty) have brought about these effects (Goin & Goin, 1986). In rhinoplasty, the psychological impact of the surgery has been hypothesized to relate to the symbolic significance of the nose (e.g., Book, 1971; Saul, 1948) and the role of the nose in determining facial identity (i.e., what makes a face recognizable as a particular face). Facial identity is heavily determined by nasal appearance, and personal identity is often thought to be psychologically "wrapped up" in the nose. Furthermore, very dramatic changes in nasal structure are routinely obtained with modest and acceptable risk of surgical complications.

The interactions between type-changing surgery and patient expectations regarding that surgical change are very important. A dramatic change in appearance that was close to that expected by the patient and that also matches the patient's ideal body image is likely to have a positive psychological impact. However, a dramatic physical change that is not expected and that is discrepant from the patient's idealized image carries a greater probability of problems of adjustment to the surgical change. The interaction between expectations, actual surgical change, the particular body part operated on, the patient's personality, and perceptions of change all influence the impact of surgery.

Degree of Surgical Change

When "more" is done (i.e., the change is more extensive), there is a greater likelihood that a restorative procedure would actually produce physical changes that seem "type-changing" to the patient. Thus, surgical procedures that recapture a former image can also precipitate psychological difficulties. The degree of surgical change undertaken can determine the patient's perception of the appearance change. For example, an extensive face-lift procedure may involve a change in the slant of the eyelid fissures or a minor change in the shape of the smile along with the expected substantial removal of tissue laxity. Such a patient may experience negative psychological reactions to this particular "image recapture," such as the feeling that "too much was done."

The line between the type-changing and restorative procedures can often be blurred. For example, face-lifts may involve sub-malar implants which not only alter skin laxity but also change the basic facial contour and movements. Furthermore, the ability of plastic surgeons to produce massive bony-structure changes in addition to soft-tissue changes is increasing with the rapidly developing application of craniofacial (reconstructive) surgical techniques for *aesthetic* purposes (Edgerton, 1987; Edgerton, Langman, & Pruzinsky, 1987; Edgerton, Langman, & Pruzinsky, 1990; Nahas, 1987; Ousterhout, 1987; Ousterhout, 1989; Whitaker, 1982). These procedures allow for changes in facial shape well beyond the removal of fat (as in liposuction) or the tightening of skin and muscle (as in face-lifting procedures). Do these changes, which involve "deeper" anatomical levels, produce more profound psychological changes? Are there greater psychological risks with undertaking these more complex procedures? Data regarding these questions have yet to be collected and represent one of many challenges for students of body-image change in plastic surgery.

Some surgeons maintain, especially for some emotionally fragile patients, that surgical changes be staged so that the patient has the opportunity to assimilate smaller sequential changes as opposed to one massive change.

Social Evaluation of Surgical Change

Social evaluations are critical in determining the patient's ultimate adjustment to surgical changes. Social evaluation of the surgical change comes from the surgeon, or other health-care personnel (e.g., nurses), and individuals in the patient's social world. The surgeon's evaluation of the patient's surgical result can greatly influence the patient's perception of the result. Hearing the surgeon say that the surgical outcome is "one of the best I have ever seen" versus "not what I had hoped," can influence the patient's perception of the surgical outcome. At times, patients will perceive some negative aspect of the surgical outcome that is genuinely not perceived by the surgeon. There are also instances when the surgeon sees flaws in the surgery that are not perceived by the patient.

Once again, the patient's perception of the surgical outcome is paramount. However, this perception can be influenced by significant others in the patient's life. A husband's comment that his face-lifted wife now looks more relaxed and rested, or looks like she did 20 years ago, can be a very positive experience for the patient. Empirical studies have documented that the patient's appearance can often be judged to be improved postoperatively (Cash & Horton, 1983; Kalick, 1979). Thus, the patient may not only look better to themselves and to the surgeon but also, in many instances, objective perceivers can discern and appreciate positive changes in the patient's appearance. Some patients have the dilemma of wanting others to see them as more attractive without those individuals knowing that plastic surgery produced the change (Cash & Horton, 1983). Unfortunately, there are also instances where individuals close to the patient, in an effort to show support for the pre-operative condition, point out negative features of the patient's postsurgical appearance. This only initiates the patient's insecurity and any negative perception of the surgery. As research indicates, dissatisfied patients often attribute their dissatisfaction to others having reacted negatively (Reich, 1975).

Age

An interesting and consistent observation in the literature is that younger patients psychologically adapt to type-changing surgical procedures more easily than do older patients (Belfer, Harisson, Pillemer, & Murray, 1982; Goin & Goin, 1981, 1986; Goldwyn, 1981). For example, older patients undergoing rhinoplasty often have a longer and more difficult course of postoperative psychological adjustment and have more frequent psychological problems (especially feeling a loss of identity following surgery). The most common explanation for this consistent clinical observation is the common-sense notion that older patients have a much stronger and longer-term bond between their perception of their physical appearance and their sense of personal identity. Younger patients have not had as long to develop the bond between their appearance and identity. That is, early in life, the body image is more malleable.

Gender

One's gender may be a salient determinant of one's psychological response to plastic surgery. Males request cosmetic surgery less often than females. In 1988, males accounted for 16% of cosmetic surgery (ASPRS, 1989). Moreover, males are more likely to be anxious and psychologically disturbed pre-operatively and are more likely to experience postoperative psychological disturbances than females receiving the same aesthetic operations (Edgerton & Langman, 1982; Wright, 1987).

> Whether it is because the man comes in with a greater level of disturbance or because of a basic difference in response, the adult male patient (not the adolescent) more frequently experiences a stormy period of adjustment postoperatively. He may be preoccupied with small irregularities and impatient for the resolution of postoperative artifacts. Many male patients describe going through an extreme "identity crisis." In fact, most male secondary rhinoplasty (which represent a higher percentage of secondary cases) request a reconstruction that closely resembles their original nose. (Sheen & Sheen, 1987, p. 653)

Fisher (1986) reports that on the basis of the extant body-image literature, it appears that females, while being more critical of their appearance and less satisfied with their bodies, are much more psychologically comfortable with body changes. Males, on the other hand, are more satisfied with their appearance but appear to be more threatened by body changes (Fisher, 1986).

When patients are dissatisfied with surgery one focus of dissatisfaction is sometimes on the lack of congruence between the surgical change and gender-related aspects of the patient's appearance. That is, for the most part (but not always), male patients want to appear more masculine and female patients more feminine. For example, female desires for nasal changes or breast augmentation procedures are very often to move the patient toward the feminine ideal. Thus, in terms of the actual and the ideal body images that cosmetic plastic surgery patients hold, one of the primary characteristics is to maximize one's sense of femininity or masculinity.

Stages of Change

Time heals, it is said, and the passage of time can dramatically change the patient's perception of appearance and experience of sensations associated with the surgery. Patients soon forget what their appearance was like before the surgery (Goin & Goin, 1986). This may be due to deliberate repression of memories of one's previous appearance, to the assimilation of the new appearance into one's body image, or to a combination of these and other factors. In any case, the inherent malleability of the body image allows most patients to assimilate the new identity.

The positive postoperative changes in perception, cognition, emotion, and behavior outlined above do not occur immediately after the removal of the surgical bandages. The psychosocial changes, including body-image change, are gradual (Goin & Goin, 1986). Patients report a postsurgical increase in the amount of attention they pay to the physical feature of concern, an increase that may continue for weeks or even months after surgery is completed. Thus, there is an initial exacerbation in the emotion, time, and attention given to one's appearance and to the physical feature of concern. Postoperatively, many patients experience anxiety about the temporary scarring or discoloration from surgery, an experience that dissipates with continued healing (Cash & Horton, 1990). Over time, as one becomes adapted to the new appearance and sensations, the amount of attention given to the body part diminishes.

Interestingly, we have clinically observed that those individuals who undergo the most marked emotional reactions in the initial postoperative period (as long as those reactions are not psychologically devastating) may experience the *most positive* psychological outcomes in long-term follow-up. Why this is so is difficult to say. This clinical phenomenon, which is not empirically documented, may be related to the theories of psychological change that propose that any type of psychotherapeutic change must initially be preceded by a period of emotional disruption before reorganization and lasting benefit can take place (Mahoney, Chapter 15, this volume). That is, important psychological change does not always come about as a smooth transition from one steady state to another. Rather, for important psychological change to occur, there must often be a period of emotional disruption (i.e., disorder). Those individuals who are able to experience and tolerate this moderate, nondebilitating level of emotional disruption are among those more likely to experience a major and permanent and positive therapeutic benefit.

POSTSURGICAL NEGATIVE PSYCHOLOGICAL CHANGES

Despite the prevalent reports of patients being very satisfied with cosmetic surgery, there is evidence in the literature concerning negative psychological reactions (e.g., Goin & Goin, 1986). For the most part, as implied above, these negative psychological reactions are transient. However, any account of body-image change in cosmetic surgery must consider these negative emotional changes. There are three types of negative emotional change that plastic surgery patients experience: the experience of no emotional change (i.e., no relief), dissatisfaction with the surgical outcome, and overwhelming negative emotional reactions.

No Emotional Change

Patients undergoing cosmetic plastic surgery not only expect to look better, they expect to feel better about their appearance and themselves. However, some patients still feel somewhat depressed and dissatisfied with their lives and their appearance, despite their perception of a technically satisfactory surgical result. This reaction has not been evaluated in the literature, and it is difficult to determine how often such reactions occur. This result may be analogous to the phenomenon among overweight individuals who have experienced significant weight loss yet still feel as though they are a "fat person" (Stunkard & Burt, 1967; Stunkard & Mendelson, 1967). Cash and his colleagues (Cash, Counts, & Huffine, in press) have documented the psychological impact of "vestigial" effects of being overweight. They have empirically documented that the "adverse body experience [of formerly overweight individuals] may not be shed with weight loss." Thus, some cosmetic surgical patients may acknowledge a positive change in appearance but not be able to integrate this change into their self-concepts. They still perceive and conceive of themselves as unattractive.

Some individuals will experience a constant refocusing of their self-conscious bodily concerns on other body parts, which could be conceptualized as a form of symptom substitution (Gordon & Zax, 1981). Body parts are the inkblots onto which some people project their discontent. This may account, in part, for the recent increase in the numbers of patients requesting cosmetic plastic surgery who have previously undergone cosmetic surgery procedures on other parts of their bodies.

There are also those patients, referred to in the literature as "insatiable" patients (Groenman & Sauer, 1983; Knorr, Edgerton, & Hoopes, 1967), who appear to be more psychologically disturbed than those patients who simply experience no change or who refocus their self-consciousness on another body part. Insatiable patients repeatedly request cosmetic surgery, often requesting multiple operations on the same body part. These patients often have borderline personality organizations (Groenman & Sauer, 1983), characterized by a general instability in psychological identity that likely includes body-image diffuseness. Such diffuseness and/or volatility makes it very difficult for the patient to experience a "match" between the desired body-image change and the change brought about by surgery. These patients experience such confusion regarding their identity and their body image that to attempt to match the surgical results to their desires is tantamount to "hitting a moving target."

Patient Dissatisfaction with Surgical Outcome

Patient dissatisfaction with the results of technically satisfactory surgery may be the result of one or several factors (Macgregor, 1981). Patient-related causes for dissatisfaction include patient psychopathology (e.g., borderline personality organizations). Patients may also unrealistically expect too great an impact of surgery on their lives and are disappointed when these do not occur. Surgery alone will not augment external outcomes (e.g., surgery does not necessarily lead to positive changes in one's social life). Surgery is mostly a catalyst for changing one's relationship with one's self.

Dissatisfaction can occur if the surgeon has not explained the nature of the surgery in terms that the patient can understand. Patient dissatisfaction is ultimately the physician's responsibility. The surgeon must establish clear communication and maintain positive rapport with the patient in order to learn about the patient's current and anticipated body images. This is a difficult and challenging task that surgeons are seldom trained to carry out. A knowledgeable psychologist or psychiatrist can be invaluable in the therapeutic team of individuals treating plastic surgery patients (Pruzinsky, 1988; Pruzinsky, Edgerton, & Barth, 1990).

Serious Psychological Problems

The most common serious psychological problems associated with cosmetic surgery include postoperative psychosis (Schweitzer & Hirschfeld, 1984) or loss of identity (Knorr, 1972). Thankfully, these are rare. Only a small number of cases of postoperative psychosis are reported in the literature (Schweitzer & Hirschfeld, 1984). This is an important point. Early psychoanalytic observations regarding cosmetic surgery indicated that surgical removal of the patient's "symptom" (or "crutch") or excessive concern about some part of the body frequently would result in the patient's psychological decompensation (Meerloo, 1956). However, clinical experience has consistently proven such dire predictions to be false.

One of the most disturbing changes associated with cosmetic surgery is the "loss of identity." Loss of identity has been reported with type-changing and restorative surgical procedures (Goin & Goin, 1986). Loss of identity refers to the patient's expressing depersonalization ("I don't feel like myself") coupled with generalized anxiety (Knorr, 1972). In most cases, the loss of identity is transient, rarely lasting more than a few months. However, there is a small group of patients for whom there is a continued sense of identity loss. These patients may be hesitant to talk about, or have difficulty articulating their concerns. In the more extreme cases of identity loss, we have found it imperative to surgically return the patients as closely as possible to their previous appearance, even though such surgery will leave them aesthetically less attractive in the eyes of others! In our experience, these patients consistently report a marked reduction in negative psychological symptoms after surgery returns them even partially to their previous appearance.

SUMMARY AND CONCLUSIONS

The setting of cosmetic plastic surgery provides a unique opportunity to learn much more about body-image development, deviance, and change. In studying body images, we need to draw from as many sources and perspectives as possible.

A clear understanding of the nature of body image is critical to evaluating cosmetic surgery patients. Change in body image following cosmetic surgery results is an interaction among perceptual, cognitive, emotional, and behavioral processes. Perception of appearance and sensation are critical to facilitating the cognitive, emotional, and behavioral changes, which can often be quite profound.

Many factors influence the patient's perception of the surgical outcome and determine the nature and degree of psychological and body-image change. These factors include the patient's subjective perception of the surgical outcome, his/her expectations regarding the outcome, the nature and degree of surgical change, the patient's gender and age, plus the social evaluation of the surgical change and the passage of time. Each of these factors teaches us an important lesson regarding the nature of body image. They point to many avenues for empirical research and clinical exploration.

Negative psychological reactions to plastic surgery also occur, including the lack of desired psychological relief, patient dissatisfaction, and sometimes even more serious psychological reactions of psychosis and identity loss. Proper screening, evaluation, and clear doctor–patient communication regarding expected surgical changes are critical for the prevention of postoperative psychological problems. However, even the clearest communication cannot screen out all the potentially fragile patients. A more detailed examination of patients who represent "failures" in terms of the ultimate goals of cosmetic surgery deserve special attention and would be a sign of the maturity of the discipline. We should exam all psychologic failures with the hopes of learning from them (e.g., Foa & Emmelkamp, 1983). The exploration of the influence and mechanism of action of cosmetic plastic surgery on body image is still in a very early stage of development.

REFERENCES

Albino, J. E., & Tedesco, L. A. (1988). The role of perception in treatment of impaired facial appearance. In T. R. Alley (Ed.), *Social and applied aspects of perceiving faces* (pp. 217–237). Hillsdale, NJ: Erlbaum.

American Society for Plastic and Reconstructive Surgery (1989). *Estimated number of cosmetic surgery procedures performed by ASPRS members* (Report of surgical procedures conducted by Board Certified Plastic and Reconstructive Surgeons). Chicago, IL: Director of Communications Executive Office.

Beale, S., Lisper, H. O., & Palm, B. (1980). A psychological study of patients seeking augmentation mammaplasty. *British Journal of Psychiatry, 136*, 133–138.

Belfer, M. L., Harisson, A. M., Pillemer, F. C., & Murray, J. E. (1982). Appearance and the influence of reconstructive surgery on body image. *Clinics in Plastic Surgery, 9*, 307–315.

Book, H. E. (1971). Sexual implications of the nose. *Comprehensive Psychiatry, 12*, 450–455.

Borkovec, T. D., Metzger, R. L., & Pruzinsky, T. (1986). Anxiety, worry and the self. In L. Hartman & K. R. Blankstein (Eds.), *Perception of self in emotional disorders and psychotherapy* (pp. 219–260). New York: Plenum Press.

Borkovec, T. D., Robinson, E., Pruzinsky, T., & Depree, J. A. (1983). Preliminary exploration of worry: Some characteristics and processes. *Behavior Research and Therapy, 21*, 9–16.

Burk, J., Zelen, S. L., & Terino, E. O. (1985). More than skin deep: A self-consistency approach to the psychology of cosmetic surgery. *Plastic and Reconstructive Surgery, 76*, 270–280.

Buss, A. H. (1980). *Self-consciousness and social anxiety.* San Francisco: Freeman.

Buss, A. H. (1985). Self-consciousness and appearance. In J. A. Graham & A. M. Kligman (Eds.), *The psychology of cosmetic treatments* (pp. 125–132). New York: Praeger Scientific.

Cash, T. F., Cash, D. W., & Butters, J. W. (1983). "Mirror, mirror on the wall . . . ?" Contrast effects and self-evaluations of physical attractiveness. *Personality and Social Psychology Bulletin, 9*, 351–358.

Cash, T. F., Counts, B., & Huffine, C. E. (in press). Current and vestigial effects of overweight among women: Fear of fat, attitudinal body image, and eating behaviors. *Journal of Psychopathology and Behavioral Assessment.*

Cash, T. F., & Horton, C. E. (1983). Aesthetic surgery: Effects of rhinoplasty on social perception of patients by others. *Plastic and Reconstructive Surgery, 72*, 543–548.

Cash, T. F., & Horton, C. E. (1990). *A longitudinal study of the psychological effects of aesthetic surgery.* Unpublished research.

Cash, T. F., & Pruzinsky, T. (1990). *Who wants cosmetic surgery? Survey results.* Unpublished manuscript.

Cash, T. F., Winstead, B., & Janda, L. H. (1986). The great American shape-up: Body image survey report. *Psychology Today, 126*, 305–316.

Courtiss, E. H., & Donelan, M. B. (1988). Skin sensation after suction lipectomy: A prospective study of 50 consecutive patients. *Plastic and Reconstructive Surgery, 81*, 550–553.

Edgerton, M. T. (1975). The plastic surgeon's obligation to the emotionally disturbed patient. *Plastic and Reconstructive Surgery, 55*, 81–83.

Edgerton, M. T. (1987). Discussion of D. K. Ousterhout's Feminization of the forehead: Contour change to improve facial aesthetics. *Plastic and Reconstructive Surgery, 99*, 712–713.

Edgerton, M. T., & Knorr, N. J. (1971). Motivational patterns of patients seeking cosmetic (esthetic) surgery. *Plastic and Reconstructive Surgery, 48*, 551–557.

Edgerton, M. T., & Langman, M. W. (1982). Psychiatric considerations. In . E. H. Courtiss (Ed.), *Male aesthetic surgery* (pp. 17–38). St. Louis: C. V. Mosby.

Edgerton, M. T., Langman, M. W., & Pruzinsky, T. (1987, October). *Patients seeking symmetrical recontouring for perceived deformities in the width of the face and skull.* Paper presented at the Annual Meeting of the International Society of Aesthetic Surgery, New York City.

Edgerton, M. T., Langman, M. W., & Pruzinsky, T. (1990). Patients seeking symmetrical recontouring for perceived deformities in the width of the face and skull. *Aesthetic Plastic Surgery, 14*, 59–73.

Edgerton, M. T., Webb, W. L., Slaughter, R., & Meyer, E. (1964). Surgical results and psychosocial changes following rhytidectomy. *Plastic and Reconstructive Surgery, 33*, 503–521.

Fisher, S. (1986). *Development and structure of the body image*. Hillsdale, NJ: Erlbaum.

Foa, E. B., & Emmelkamp, P. M. G. (Eds.). (1983). *Failures in behavior therapy*. New York: Wiley.

Gifford, S. (1976). Emotional attitudes toward cosmetic breast surgery: Loss and restitution of the "ideal self." In R. M. Goldwyn (Ed.), *Plastic and Reconstructive Surgery of the Breast* (pp. 103–107). Boston: Little, Brown.

Goin, J. M., & Goin, M. K. (1981). *Changing the body: Psychological effects of plastic surgery*. Baltimore: Williams & Wilkens.

Goin, M. K. (1982) Psychological reactions to surgery of the breast. *Clinics in Plastic Surgery, 9*, 347–354.

Goin, M. K., & Goin, J. M. (1986). Psychological effects of aesthetic facial surgery. *Advances in Psychosomatic Medicine, 15*, 84–107.

Goin, M. K., Goin, J. M., & Gianini, M. H. (1977). The psychic consequences of a reduction mammaplasty. *Plastic and Reconstructive Surgery, 59*, 530–534.

Goldwyn, R. M. (1981). *The patient and the plastic surgeon*. Boston: Little, Brown.

Gordon, K. S., & Zax, M. (1981). Once more into the breach dear friends. . . A reconsideration of the literature on symptom substitution. *Clinical Psychology Review, 1*, 33–47.

Gorney, M. (1982). Patient selection: An ounce of prevention. In E. H. Courtiss (Ed.), *Male aesthetic surgery* (pp. 11–16). St Louis: C. V. Mosby.

Groenman, N. H., & Sauer, H. C. (1983). Personality characteristics of the cosmetic surgical insatiable patient. *Psychotherapy and Psychosomatics, 40*, 241–245.

Harris, D. L. (1982). The symptomatology of abnormal appearance—An anecdotal survey. *British Journal of Plastic Surgery, 35*, 312–323.

Harris, D. L. (1983). Self-consciousness of disproportionate breast size: A primary psychological reaction to abnormal appearance. *British Journal of Plastic Surgery, 36*, 191–195.

Hetter, G. P. (1979). Satisfactions and dissatisfactions of patients with augmentation mammaplasty. *Plastic and Reconstructive Surgery, 64*, 151–155.

Hollyman, J. A., Lacey, J. H., Whitfield, P. J., & Wilson, J. S. P. (1986). Surgery for the psyche: A longitudinal study of women undergoing reduction mammoplasty. *British Journal of Plastic Surgery, 39*, 222–224.

Joseph, J. (1931). (S. Milstein, Trans., 1984). Motivation for reduction rhinoplasty and the practical significance of the operation in life. *Plastic and Reconstructive Surgery, 73*, 692–693.

Kalick, S. M. (1979). Aesthetic surgery: How it affects the way patients are perceived by others. *Annals of Plastic Surgery, 2*, 128–133.

Kleinke, C. L. (1975). *First impressions*. Englewood Cliffs, NJ: Prentice-Hall.

Knorr, N. J., Edgerton, M. T., & Hoopes, J. E. (1967). The "insatiable" cosmetic surgery patient. *Plastic and Reconstructive Surgery, 400*, 285–288.

Knorr, N. J., (1972). Feminine loss of identity in rhinoplasty. *Archives of Otolaryngology, 96*, 11–15.

Lavell, S., & Lewis, C. M. (1984). SAFE: A practical guide to psychological factors in selecting patients for facial cosmetic surgery. *Annals of Plastic Surgery, 12*, 256–259.

Macgregor, F. C. (1981). Patient dissatisfaction with results of a technically satisfactory surgery. *Aesthetic Plastic Surgery, 5*, 27–32.

Macgregor, F. C. (1989). Social, psychological, and cultural dimensions of cosmetic and reconstructive plastic surgery. *Aesthetic Plastic Surgery, 13*, 1–8.

Mahler, M. S., & McDevitt, J. B. (1982). Thoughts on the emergence of self, with particular emphasis on the body self. *Journal of the American Psychoanalytic Association, 32*, 827–848.

Marcus, P. (1984). Psychological aspects of cosmetic rhinoplasty. *British Journal of Plastic Surgery, 37*, 313–318.

Markus, H., & Nurius, P. S. (1986). Possible selves. *American Psychologist, 41*, 954–969.

Meerloo, J. A. M. (1956). The fate of one's face. *Psychiatric Quarterly, 3*, 31–43.

Nahas, L. F. (1987). Workshop on aesthetic surgery of the facial skeleton. *Plastic and Reconstructive Surgery, 79*, 1008.

Ousterhout, D. K. (1987). Feminization of the forehead: Contour changes to improve female aesthetics. *Plastic and Reconstructive Surgery, 99*, 701–711.

Ousterhout, D. K. (1989). Feminization of the skull. In J. L. Marsh (Ed.), *Current therapy in plastic and reconstructive surgery* (pp. 483–491). Philadelphia: Decker.

Pruzinsky, T. (1988). Collaboration of plastic surgeon and medical psychotherapist: Elective cosmetic surgery. *Medical Psychotherapy: An International Journal, 1*, 1–13.

Pruzinsky, T., & Cash, T. F. (in press). Medical interventions for the enhancement of physical appearance. In T. P. Gullotta (Ed.), *Advances in adolescent development*. Beverly Hills, CA: Sage.

Pruzinsky, T., Edgerton, M. T., & Barth, J. T. (in press). Medical psychotherapy and plastic surgery: Collaboration, specialization and cost-effectiveness. In K. Anchor (Ed.), *The Handbook of Medical Psychotherapy*. Toronto: Hans Huber Publishers.

Reich, J. (1975). Factors influencing patient satisfaction with results of aesthetic plastic surgery. *Plastic and Reconstructive Surgery, 55*, 5–13.

Robin, A. A., Copas, J. B., Jack, A. B., Kaeser, A. C., & Thomas, P. J. (1988). Reshaping the psyche: The concurrent improvement in appearance and mental state after rhinoplasty. *British Journal of Psychiatry, 152*, 539–543.

Saul, L. J. (1948). Feminine significance of the nose. *Psychoanalytic Quarterly, 17*, 51–57.

Schlebusch, L. (1989). Negative bodily experience and prevalence of depression in patients who request augmentation mammoplasty. *South African Medical Journal, 75*, 323–326.

Schlebusch, L., & Levin, A. (1983). A psychological profile of women selected for augmentation mammoplasty. *South African Medical Journal, 64*, 481–483.

Schweitzer, I., & Hirschfeld, J. J. (1984). Postrhytidectomy psychosis: A rare complication. *Plastic and Reconstructive Surgery, 74*, 419–422.

Sheen, J. H., & Sheen, A. P. (1987). *Aesthetic rhinoplasty* (2nd ed.). St Louis: C. V. Mosby.

Spiegel, H., & Linn, L. (1969). The "ripple effect" following adjunct hypnosis in analytic psychotherapy. *American Journal of Psychiatry, 126*, 53–58.

Stunkard, A. J., & Burt, V. (1967). Obesity and body image: II. Age at onset of disturbances of body image. *American Journal of Psychiatry, 123*, 1443–1447.

Stunkard, A. J., & Mendelson, M. (1967). Obesity and body image: I. Characteristics of disturbances in the body image of some obese persons. *American Journal of Psychiatry, 123*, 1296–1300.

Wengle, H. P. (1986a). The psychology of cosmetic surgery: A critical overview of the literature 1960–1982—Part 1. *Annals of Plastic Surgery, 16*, 435–443.

Wengle, H. P. (1986b). The psychology of cosmetic surgery: Old problems in patient selection seen in a new way—Part 2. *Annals of Plastic Surgery, 16*, 487–493.

Whitaker, L. (1982). Skeletal foundations of aesthetic cranial and facial surgery. In E. H. Courtiss (Ed.), *Male aesthetic surgery* (pp. 145–160). St. Louis: C. V. Mosby.

Wright, M. R. (1987). The male aesthetic patient. *Archives of Otolaryngology and Head and Neck Surgery, 113*, 724–727.

Wright, M. R., & Wright, W. K. (1975). A psychological study of patients undergoing cosmetic surgery. *Archives of Otolaryngology, 101*, 145–151.

CHAPTER 11

Reconstructive Surgery: Objective Change of Objective Deformity

Michael J. Pertschuk

Until the 1950s, plastic surgery was primarily surgery of soft tissues (e.g., skin, cartilage, and muscle). Unfortunately, many cases of facial trauma and congenital facial deformities involve hard tissue (i.e., bone). Beginning in the 1950s, Paul Tessier, a French plastic surgeon, initiated studies on the surgical alteration of the facial skeleton. He demonstrated that segments of facial bone could be surgically relocated to correct deformities. Because bone growth usually continued after such surgical intervention, the procedures could be implemented with children. The bony orbits could be cut free and moved closer together to correct a condition of extremely widely spaced eyes known as *hypertelorism*. The maxilla could be brought forward and the mandible moved to at least partially correct the multiple facial malformations in congenital conditions such as *Apert* or *Crouzon syndrome*.

Tessier's work was truly revolutionary. In the late 1960s and early 1970s, he attracted the interest of the "best and the brightest" of younger plastic surgeons who went to Paris to learn this new field of craniofacial surgery. By the mid-1970s, craniofacial surgery was established as a plastic surgery subspecialty around the world.

A curious aspect in the development of craniofacial surgery was that these complex procedures, with significant morbidity and mortality risks, were used to treat largely nonlife-threatening conditions. Children do not die from Crouzon syndrome or Hemifacial microsomia, two diagnoses associated with severe facial deformities. They could die, however, from the attempts at surgical correction. This was especially true during the early years of craniofacial surgery. How could such risks be justified?

That was the question presented to this author approximately 13 years ago when given the project of conducting psychosocial studies of children with craniofacial anomalies. The assumption was that the risks *were* justified. Tessier (1971) described children with craniofacial birth defects being hidden away by their families and treated like "monsters." Other surgeons (Edgerton, Jane, Berry, & Marshall, 1975) held similar beliefs concerning grave emotional consequences of facial deformity. This led to the recommendation that the sooner the surgery could be performed, the better. These were, however, only impressions based on limited clinical experience, not the result of systematic inquiry.

Years before, Macgregor et al. (1955) studied a series of patients with a range of facial deformities from minor to severe. She observed that while many were functional in their lives, they suffered marked emotional impairments. More severe deformities were associated with serious psychosocial difficulties, although not invariably. Aside from this and scattered anecdotal reports (Easson, 1966; Hogeman & Willman, 1974), little psychosocial data were available about patients with craniofacial malformations.

There was more information about one group with corrected facial deformities, those with cleft lip and/or palate. Surgery for these conditions had been available since the latter part of the last century (Waite & Kersten, 1980). While major surgical improvement is possible, correction of a cleft lip invariably leaves a noticeable scar. Correction of a cleft palate does not totally solve the associated problem of hypernasal speech. Initial surgery for these conditions is undertaken during the first year of life; additional procedures are performed well into childhood and adolescence.

Prior to the late 1970s, the research literature on these patients indicated that they were generally doing well psychologically (see below). To an extent, these data could be considered as supporting surgical intervention on psychosocial grounds. If cleft patients were leading relatively normal lives with their surgical corrections, presumably patients with correction of more severe deformities could do likewise.

The documentation of the psychosocial impact of facial deformities and their correction would seem a simple enough task: evaluate the psychological and emotional status of patients before and after surgery to assess the effects of facial deformity. The task has proven anything but simple because a wide range of variables influence the psychosocial effects of deformity. Deformities arise in different ways. Facial deformities can be congenital, resulting from genetic or toxic factors—cleft lip and cleft palate are examples. Deformities can be progressive, beginning at birth or later and worsening over time. An example is *neurofibromatosis*, which can be associated with facial tumors that develop and enlarge during the course of years. Deformities can be acute traumas from physical insults, such as an orbital fracture secondary to an auto accident. Deformities can be iatrogenic, such as the surgical removal of a cancer that also necessitates the removal of a large segment of facial soft and hard tissues. It is probable that these different etiologies, with different onsets and circumstances, have potentially very distinct influences on the individual.

There are a range of factors associated with facial deformity that influence psychosocial adjustment. Certain congenital forms of craniofacial deformity (e.g., Apert syndrome) coexist with brain abnormalities associated with mental retardation (Cohen & Kreiborg, 1989). Craniofacial injuries can traumatize the central nervous system, reducing the individual's ability to cope with the stress of injury and limiting the potential for recovery. Life-threatening illnesses like cancer that require ablative surgery have psychological and physical implications for the individual apart from deformity.

The age of the individual is also important. The social consequences of a cleft lip at age 3 are different from the consequences of the same deformity at age 13 and at age 43. Gender is also significant. A scar may have quite different social meanings on a man's face than on a woman's. Age at the time of corrective surgery is a third pertinent factor. A deformity that is largely eliminated in early childhood can have a different impact on the individual than a deformity that can be removed only in mid-adolescence.

The social and psychological resources of the individual provide contexts that mitigate or magnify the psychosocial impact of facial deformity. Consider the potential adjustment of two similar appearing children with cleft lip and palate. One scores in the superior range on the Wechsler Intelligence Scale for Children and comes from an intact, supportive family with financial security. The other scores in the dull–normal range of intellectual ability and comes from a single parent family, headed by a clinically depressed mother with limited income. Implicit here is the proposition that there are critical developmental and sociocultural factors that will affect the internalization of the deformity vis-à-vis body image and self-concept.

To fully understand the meaning of facial deformity and its correction, it would be essential to recognize and control a staggering array of variables. It would require an extensive and systematic program of research along with a lot of funding. This is not how research in this area has progressed. Instead, as is typical with clinical research, investigations have been undertaken as need, opportunity, and funding have allowed. Far from a systematic "whole-cloth" knowledge, what has evolved is a "patchwork" of information about different patient groups with, at best, limited consideration of the variables that might influence adjustment apart from abnormal facial appearance. The balance of this chapter focuses on elements of this patchwork to better understand the rationale and results of correcting facial deformity.

CLEFT LIP AND PALATE

Cleft lip and palate are by far the most common of congenital facial deformities. Because of the relatively large patient population and the need for a variety of services, multispecialty clinics developed relatively early. The first was established in the late 1930s by a Pennsylvania orthodontist, Dr. Herbert Cooper (Millard, 1980). The bringing together of surgeons, dentists, and (later) speech therapists and social workers promoted the consideration of the whole patient, rather than just the deformity.

Over the past 30–35 years, literature has accumulated on the psychosocial adjustment of these patients. There has been a trend, which has been repeated in the study of craniofacial patients, to move from global negative impressions of adjustment, to impressions of relative normality, to more detailed assessments revealing specific areas of vulnerability. Articles dating from the 1950s were often suggestive of wide-ranging difficulties for these patients. The children were seen as passive and anxious (Tisza, Silverstone, Rosenblum, & Hanlon, 1958) and possibly at risk for long-term emotional problems and anxiety (Kahn, 1956; Kinnis, 1954).

These dire predictions were not borne out by direct measurement. Watson (1964) compared scores on the Rogers Personal Adjustment Inventory of boys with cleft lip and palate, boys with physical handicaps other than facial deformity, and normal boys. He was unable to find between-group differences and was led to question whether cleft lip and palate was associated with any personality disturbance, at least in boys. Using multiple measures of cognitive style, body image, and self-concept, Brantley and Clifford (1978) could detect few significant differences between adolescents with clefts and normal adolescents. Their measures of body image included attitudinal as well as perceptual indices and they found no between-group differences on either. Curiously, the adolescents with clefts scored *higher* than normals on self-concept measures. The authors could not explain that particular finding.

Follow-up surveys conducted in the 1970s also supported the contention that individuals with clefts achieved relatively normal psychosocial adjustment. McWilliams and Paradise (1973) surveyed 115 adult cleft palate patients and their families who previously attended the University of Pittsburgh clinic. The cleft palate patients were not significantly different from their noncleft, nearest-age siblings in educational or occupational attainment; however, only 40% of the cleft patients were or had been married, compared to 72% of the normal siblings. Peter and Chinsky followed up a group of 195 cleft patients from a Lancaster, Pennsylvania clinic. They found a lower rate of marriage and later marriage in the cleft group as compared to normal siblings and normal controls (Peter & Chinsky, 1974a). The educational attainments of the cleft group were similar to those of the normal sibling and normal control groups (Peter & Chinsky, 1974b). Occupational status and employment stability did not vary between groups, although cleft patients did earn significantly less than the other two groups (Peter, Chinsky, & Fisher, 1975a). Cleft patients were found to stay closer to home, have fewer close friendships, and report more social anxiety than normal controls (Peter, Chinsky, & Fisher, 1975b).

The accumulated data clearly did not support the gloom and doom predictions of early investigators. This led some to emphasize the positive and view these patients as functioning in a largely normal manner. Clifford (1983), one of the pioneers in psychosocial research in this area, posed the question in an editorial appearing in the *Cleft Palate Journal*, "Why are they so normal?" He suggested that the answer lay partly in the treatment and partly in the possible lack of significance of the deformity to the individual and family.

If the cup is not empty, others have suggested it is not entirely full. Richman and Eliason (1982) reviewed the extant psychosocial research on cleft lip and palate and identified specific areas of vulnerability. They concluded that significantly depressed Verbal Intelligent Quotient (IQ) and language disability could be associated with clefts. School achievement for these children tended to be below expectations based on intellectual ability. Teachers and parents tended to maintain lower academic expectations for children with clefts. Behavioral inhibition was a problem for this group along with heightened concern and dissatisfaction with appearance, especially for girls. Research since this review has generally confirmed the presence of identifiable difficulties at least within subsets of the cleft palate population.

Richman (1983), using the Minnesota Multiphasic Personality Inventory (MMPI) along with ratings of appearance and speech concerns, found that, overall, "cleft" adolescents did not exhibit more personality or adjustment problems than controls. He was able to identify a subgroup of slightly more than half the cleft subjects with one or more MMPI scale scores significantly elevated. The Social Introversion scale was the most frequent scale elevation. Further, cleft adolescents with a greater degree of facial concern had significantly higher scores on the Social Introversion scale than cleft adolescents with only slight facial concern. In a later study, Richman, Holmes, and Eliason (1985) investigated the relationship between accuracy in physical self-perception and personality adjustment. They found that cleft adolescents who perceived their appearance accurately (i.e., their appearance rating scores were similar to scores given them by independent raters) scored normally on a measure of conduct and personality problems. Cleft adolescents who overestimated their appearance (i.e., their appearance rating scores were higher than scores given them by independent raters) scored in a range indicating social inhibition.

Kapp-Simon (1986) investigated self-concept in a younger group of cleft patients between the ages of 5 and 9 years. She used the Primary Self-Concept Inventory and found that relative to a control group, the children reported lower global self-concept. They tended to perceive themselves as less socially adept and more frequently sad and angry than their peers. Within-group differences based on cleft type (e.g., cleft palate only, cleft lip and palate) were not observed. It was also apparent that many in the cleft group did not have unusually low self-concept. Broder and Strauss (1989), utilizing the same self-concept measure in a group of 7-year-old cleft patients, had somewhat similar results. The children with clefts, as a group, had lower self-concept scores than did normal controls. Unlike Kapp-Simon, these authors found that the cleft lip and palate group had the lowest self-concept scores.

There is clearly heterogeneity within the cleft population in morphology, etiology, and associated anomalies. The deformity can range from entirely invisible (cleft palate only) to conspicuous (cleft lip and palate). With cleft lip only, speech is normal; with cleft palate, there are hypernasality and articulation problems. Some clefts are associated with hearing deficits. In recent years there has been growing interest in identifying patterns of genetic abnormalities associated with these disorders. It is becoming apparent that clefting can be one manifestation of a syndrome of abnormalities caused by specific genetic abera-tions. *Stickler syndrome* is one such genetic abnormality. An autosomal dominant disorder, it may underly a significant number of cases with cleft palate only (McDonald, personal communication, June, 1989; Temple, 1989).

The data suggest that these variations affect psychosocial outcome. For whatever reason, patients with only cleft palate seem to have more difficulties. Richman, Eliason, and Lindgren (1988) observed that this subgroup had the highest incidence of reading problems. Peter et al. (1975b) found males in this subgroup to be the least socially integrated of all the cleft patients. The presence of other congenital anomalies is also predictive of greater psychosocial difficul-ties. This was evident from the Richman and Eliason (1982) review of the literature in which they found more frequent reports of problems in intellectual functioning for this subgroup. Tobiasen, Levy, Carpenter, and Hiebert (1987) reported that irrespective of cleft type, children with associated congenital malformations had more serious school and conduct problems.

While there are specific areas of vulnerability, most clearly in socialization and self-concept, it is apparent that Clifford was not entirely wrong about these patients' normality. Overall, the children, adolescents, and adults who were studied appear to lead lives that do not differ markedly from the lives of noncleft individuals. There may be a number of reasons for this. Surgical techniques of the last 30 years considerably reduce deformities, typically to small areas around the lip and nose. Although conspicuous enough to engender teasing, the deformities are not so extreme as to cause involuntary revulsion or physical withdrawal. Since the conditions are relatively common, the deformities are correctly recognized by many lay individuals as representing residuals of a cleft. The public may be less prone to misconstrue the deformity as signifying either mental retardation or other psychological deviance. Because clefts are usually treated in clinics, patients and families have exposure and access to others with similar difficulties. Accordingly, the potential for social isolation is reduced.

Clefts are also congenital, which means the individual and family have time to deal with the deformity. The major part of the surgery is done early in life, during infancy and early childhood, so that the child only has to integrate the corrected deformity into a sense of self (including body image). The residual deformity, whatever else it may be, is not foreign to the individual.

Returning to the primary question of how deformity influences psychosocial adjustment, it should be apparent from the above discussion that the relationship is by no means clear for cleft patients. One of the more psychosocially problematic subgroups, the cleft palate only, exhibits no visible deformity, although sufferers do have speech problems. To this writer's knowledge, no study with these persons has involved the direct correlation of appearance, measures of self-perceived appearance, attitudes toward appearance, and psychosocial adjustment. Only Richman et al. (1985) and very few others have considered even subsets of these variables. What little information there is suggests that individuals who have negative body-image attitudes seem prone to social difficulties. This was true in Richman's (1983) study where adolescent cleft patients highly concerned with appearance had elevations on the MMPI Social Introversion scale. However, individuals who underrate the extent of their deformity, through perceptual error or denial, are also more vulnerable to social problems. Adolescents, with inflated appearance self-ratings scored high on behavioral inhibition in the study of Richman et al. (1985). Taken together these limited findings suggest a conclusion verging on a cliche: Psychosocial adjustment will be maximized when the individual is able to realistically perceive his/her appearance and accept what is perceived. While this homily is quite possibly true, more specific correlational studies between appearance, perceived appearance, and adjustment are needed.

As an aside to this, it might be debated what actually constitutes "realistic perception" of deformity. Is the "true" perception that of independent raters judging only from photographs? Is it the impression gained from spending time with the individual, allowing other facets of self-presentation to influence perception? Arguably, the former is "purer," but it is the latter that may be more relevant in real-life settings.

CRANIOFACIAL MALFORMATIONS

Favorable psychosocial adjustment with corrected clefts was used to justify early efforts in craniofacial surgery. Still, there are clearly major differences between the cleft and craniofacial groups. Most of the aforementioned mitigating factors do not apply to craniofacial patients. Although some craniofacial deformities can be eliminated through surgery, most are just reduced, leaving many patients with significant residual deformity. Moreover, the conditions are diverse and rare. The lay public does not recognize these deformities as specific syndromes and may incorrectly associate some of them with other abnormalities like mental retardation. Because the deformities are novel to the observing public and in some cases are very marked, there may be a greater tendency to stare at and withdraw from these patients. The rarity of the conditions also means that there are fewer opportunities for patients and their families to interact with others who have the same condition, possibly compounding social isolation.

Before considering the psychosocial research, it might be helpful to briefly describe some of the syndromes. *Plagiocephaly* is a distortion of the skull caused by premature closure of one or more of the cranial sutures. *Isolated craniosynostosis*, the premature closure of only one suture, is readily treatable by reopening the suture and is one of the few craniofacial conditions in which entirely normal appearance can be achieved. Cruzon syndrome, also called *craniodysostosis*, is shown in Figure 11.1. The syndrome is characterized by shallow orbits with protruding eyes (exophthalmus). The midface is poorly developed and has a pushed-in appearance. The condition can be associated with increased intracranial pressure, although mental retardation has not been reported with any frequency. A postoperative outcome is also shown in Figure 11.1. *Teacher–Collins syndrome* is identifiable by the absence of cheek bones, incomplete orbits, hypoplastic jaw, and retruded chin (before and after surgery shown in Figure 11.2). *Hemifacial microsomia* is a condition of facial asymmetry caused by poor growth of one side of the mandible. As seen in Figure 11.3, the cheek bone on the affected side is hypoplastic and the muscles of mastication on that side are underdeveloped. Figure 11.3 also shows a surgical correction of this condition. The extent of deformity within each diagnostic group varies. It is not uncommon in a clinic to see a mother, with only traces of a craniofacial syndrome, bringing her child in with a severe form of the same anomaly.

The heterogeneity of the craniofacial population goes well beyond that of the cleft group. Compounding the difficulty for research is the limited number of patients within each diagnostic category. This has meant that researchers have either had to combine diagnoses within specific age groups, or include widely disparate ages within the same diagnosis. Early research tended to lump diagnoses; most recently there has been some effort to separate them.

The surgeons initially painted a very bleak picture of the craniofacial child's psychosocial prospects. The first order of business in psychosocial research was to establish how the patients were faring prior to surgery. Lefebre and Barclay

FIGURE 11.1. Cruzon syndrome before and after craniofacial surgery.

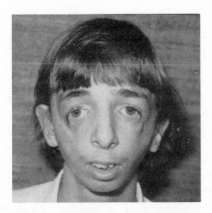
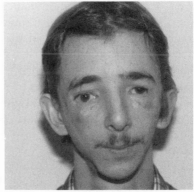

FIGURE 11.2.   Treacher–Collins syndrome before and after craniofacial surgery.

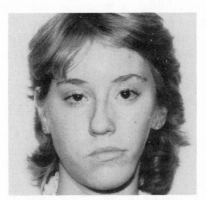
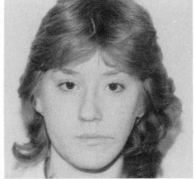

FIGURE 11.3.   Hemifacial microsomia before and after craniofacial surgery.

(1982) evaluated a diverse group of craniofacial patients at the University of Toronto clinic and found that most of the preadolescents in their sample scored in the average or above-average range on a measure of self-concept. The patients were leading relatively normal lives, attending school, and participating in the usual childhood activities.

At the University of Pennsylvania, Pertschuk and Whitaker (1985) evaluated 43 children between the ages of 6 and 13 years prior to craniofacial surgery. They also evaluated a group of control subjects matched on the basis of sex, age, intelligence, and economic background. The measures included the Piers–Harris Self-Concept Scale, State–Trait Anxiety Scale for Children, Junior Eysenck Personality Inventory, the Childhood Experience Questionnaire (a measure of negative social experiences), Missouri Behavior Checklist, and the Pupil Behavior Rating Scale. Almost across the board, scores for the craniofacial subjects indicated more difficulties. Relative to the controls, the craniofacial children demonstrated higher state anxiety, more introversion, poorer self-concept, more frequent negative social experiences, more hyperactive behavior at home, and poorer behavior in the classroom. The differences between the craniofacial and control subjects were pervasive, but not profound. The children in the craniofacial group, like their counterparts in the Canadian study, were attending school and appeared to be functioning adequately in their home and school environments. None had required the intervention of a mental health professional. Had a matched control group not been included, the limitations might have gone undetected.

If psychosocial deficits are evident prior to surgery, does corrective surgery reduce them along with the deformity? Pertschuk and Whitaker (1988) followed up 34 of the original patient sample, 12–18 months after surgery. Differences between the craniofacial and control subjects were diminished. Only the reported frequency of negative social encounters differentiated the groups with craniofacial patients reporting more negative interactions. Relative to their presurgical scores, the craniofacial subjects exhibited a decrease in trait anxiety and a trend toward decreases in inhibited and hyperactive behavior. It was noted that with age, extraversion increased and negative social encounters decreased for the normal controls. No such relationship was found for the craniofacial subjects.

It appeared that postoperatively some of the abnormal personality traits and behaviors changed in a direction toward normality, whether because of surgery or simply time. The social gulf between these children and their normal peers had not narrowed and perhaps had even widened. Recently, Pillemer and Cook (1989) reported more significant psychosocial deficits in a group of postoperative craniofacial patients ages 6 through 16 years. Subjects demonstrated problems in the areas of inhibition, depression, dependency, and socialization. Interpretation of their findings is at least partially limited by lack of a control group.

If craniofacial malformations are associated with psychosocial deficits that can be only partially alleviated with surgery in middle to late childhood, might earlier surgery result in a better psychosocial outcome? Pertschuk, Trisdorfer, and Whitaker (1989) followed up a group of 20 children who had undergone craniofacial surgery prior to age 4 years. At the time of evaluation the children were between the ages of 6 and 13 years. Utilizing a test battery similar to that used in their earlier studies, they found no differences in scores between the craniofacial and a matched control group. Unfortunately, this favorable outcome could not be attributed just to surgical timing. The early operated craniofacial patients had generally less severe malformations. Almost half had isolated craniosynostosis with excellent cosmetic outcomes. Most of the subjects in the later operated group had more involved syndromic malformations with definite residual deformity. When the early operated group was divided on the basis of presence or absence of residual deformity, it was found that the subjects with residual deformity had more abnormalities in their test score profiles. When early surgical correction of a craniofacial malformation left little or no deformity, psychosocial adjustment was excellent. Early surgery with residual deformity was still associated with adjustment difficulties. Whether these difficulties were less than those with later surgery could not be determined from the study.

Lost in the combined data was the extreme variability in adjustment of the study children as observed informally at the craniofacial clinic in Philadelphia. Some of the most deformed children were excelling at school and doing well socially, seemingly on the basis of intelligence and charm. Others, who may have had less severe malformations, were having major difficulties in school and appeared relatively discouraged.

To assess whether another factor, namely learning disabilities, might be influencing school adjustment, a survey of patients attending this craniofacial clinic was conducted (Trisdorfer, Pertschuk, & Whitaker, 1989). Sixty children without mental retardation were seen with their families. Twenty-six, or 43%, had evidence of learning disability based on information derived from the children's school or parents. The possibility that facial deformity might have contributed to learning disabilities through psychosocial mechanisms cannot be ruled out entirely. It should be noted, however, that learning disabilities are thought to arise from subtle neurological deficits rather than from intrapsychic or interpersonal stresses. Problems such as elevated intracranial pressure known to be associated with some of these disorders, may be a more likely etiologic factor. This pilot study underscores the importance of considering other variables influencing psychosocial adjustment rather than assuming that all functional difficulties in this population necessarily derive from emotional or social reactions to facial deformity.

Given the social and psychological importance of appearance documented elsewhere in this volume, why are these often markedly deformed patients not doing worse? The psychosocial deficits demonstrated thus far have not been profound and may not even be entirely attributable to appearance. It is not that the appearance of these patients goes unnoticed. Whether they are viewed as physically handicapped or just extremely unattractive, all the patients experience teasing and staring.

Most of the research with craniofacial patients has focused on children. The negative impact of the deformities may be reduced by the restricted environments typical for children in our society. Until the end of latency or early adolescence, children usually attend relatively small schools where they are known. They tend to interact with limited neighborhood or club groups outside of school. Enforced intimacy may maximize the opportunity for peers to get past initial negative reactions to the child's malformation. Were this the case, then greater problems could be anticipated with adolescence and adult life as the individual's social world expands and enforced contacts become more limited.

The Pertschuk and Whitaker (1988) data suggest that social deficits seen in this group may persist or possibly increase as adolescence approaches. Their results may portend problems similar to those seen in the cleft palate population. In previously cited surveys (Peter et al., 1975a, 1975b), the most significant long-term difficulties for the cleft patients were in marriage and friendship patterns.

Perhaps individuals with craniofacial malformations cope as best they can by controlling what they can control, namely their own actions and attitudes. They do not have control over the reactions of others and therefore are most vulnerable in social settings. It is not that patients with congenital facial deformities are immune or exempt from the consequences of negative appearance. Rather, some areas of functioning are more affected than others. While characterologic traits such as self-concept are influenced, the greatest impact of deformed appearance may be on social interaction, which becomes more obvious with age.

CRANIOFACIAL TRAUMA

There are approximately 20 centers in North America treating congenital craniofacial anomalies. There are between 100 and 200 cleft-palate centers in North America, depending on the definition of a "center." But there are literally thousands of hospitals treating facial trauma, and oddly, the least psychosocial data are available about this patient group. To this author's knowledge, there have been no published systematic surveys or follow-up studies on craniofacial trauma. Lacking this, there is only personal experience to report.

In contrast to the infrequent use of mental health services by cleft palate or craniofacial patients, the Philadelphia experience with the trauma group has been that between 10% to 20% require some intervention. The most common presenting problems are debilitating anxiety or depression. Symptoms can be divided into those relating to the accident itself and those caused by concerns with altered appearance. In the former category are problems such as driving phobias after an auto accident or chronic posttraumatic stress syndrome with nightmares and flashbacks relating to the circumstances of the accident.

In the appearance-related category are preoccupation with appearance, social withdrawal, and depression. Working with these patients permits the observation of a pattern of reactions. Initially there is relief just to have survived the trauma. This is followed by an early realization of the extent of injury. The patient may defend against incipient panic by placing tremendous faith in the skill of the plastic surgeon. Days or weeks later, depression or panic may break through as the patient recognizes that there are limits as to what can be surgically accomplished, and that the process will be long and arduous.

If the patient maintains composure despite internal panic, the surgeon may never know that there is a problem unless direct inquiry is made. Psychological consultation is requested most often when the patient's composure does, in fact, break down. Possible dysfunctional patterns of behavior include postponing all social contacts pending restoration of pretrauma appearance, withdrawal from loved ones, refusal to leave the house, and "doctor shopping." Clinical depression with anhedonia, suicidal thoughts, and psychomotor retardation can occur. Retreat into substance abuse is another possibility, which is facilitated by the routine medical prescription of large quantities of analgesics and tranquilizers. Two recurrent themes are "Why me?" and "Why can't I look the way I used to?"

Part of the reason for the extreme emotional reactions that occur is the monumental stress these patients undergo. With congenital anomalies, there is time to incorporate the malformation into a sense of self. The individual may not like what is reflected in the mirror, but recognizes the image as his/her own, for better or worse. Further, there is a lifetime to prepare for the problems of being identifiably different. The trauma patient has had a lifetime of looking one way, and now must cope with looking both different and worse. At least temporarily, the trauma patient must deal with the novel experience of being stared at by strangers, and having to explain altered appearance in social situations should he/she venture into any. While dealing with this, the individual is also caught up in the often uncomfortable role of being a patient in a complex medical system. Work and family must be disrupted periodically over the course of years for successive surgical procedures.

Some of the emotional reactions have to do with the nature of this particular patient group. A number of craniofacial trauma victims are inherently more psychologically vulnerable. Accidents do not randomly distribute across the population. There is some self-selection. Alcohol and substance abusers are more prone to accidents for obvious reasons. Depressed individuals are also at greater risk as some "accidents" are veiled suicide attempts. Other psychological conditions like anxiety and eating disorders can increase the probability of accidents through impaired concentration. The stresses involved with surgery and rehabilitation strain the coping abilities of even the most well adjusted. Such stresses can certainly exceed the capacities of those who are already compromised.

Therapeutic intervention can involve a variety of strategies depending on the specific symptoms. Depression can be treated pharmacologically and/or psychotherapeutically. Social withdrawal and isolation can be managed through behavioral contracting, sometimes with the enlistment of family members' active involvement. Ventilation and support can go a long way as many patients have previously remained silent about their concerns, fearing that other caregivers would take offense and withdraw. A cognitive–behavioral approach can be used to help patients adjust their expectations to the cosmetically achievable and avoid unnecessary postponements of normal responsibilities. Finally, in the realm of external realities, a consultation with a skilled cosmetologist can help the patient hide what the surgeon cannot now, or ever, make normal.

CONCLUSIONS

Multiple factors determine psychosocial functioning. Because one very conspicuous element is aberrant, namely facial appearance, it does not follow that every problem demonstrated necessarily derives from that aberration. Nor does it follow that amelioration or elimination of the abnormality will invariably lead to resolution of whatever problems may be present.

The naive view has been that facial deformity must cause major psychosocial trauma, if not ruin existence altogether. The realization that people often cope with what they have to, that life goes on regardless of deformity, can lead to the other extreme of assuming that everything is normal. Psychosocial research has progressed to the point of defining the middle ground. Specific psychosocial problems associated with facial deformity are there to be found, even if they do not all stem directly from abnormal appearance.

The importance of exploring this middle ground is to better predict patterns of difficulties associated with specific deformities in order that treatment interventions can be made more effective. For example, recognizing that some children with craniofacial malformations have learning problems is one step. Identifying which diagnoses are associated with which neuropsychological deficits is another. Developing intervention strategies with these particular children to forestall educational failure is a third. Delineating the areas of vulnerability, discovering their origins, and developing intervention strategies will continue to be the major thrust of psychosocial research in this area.

Just as it is incorrect to assume that all problems for the patient with facial deformity are caused by appearance, it is unrealistic to assume that none derive from that source. To a major extent, the psychological consequences of abnormal appearance are mediated by social response. If social response could be altered, some of the consequences might be reduced. Educating the public about facial deformity might never entirely eliminate negative social responses but could diminish them appreciably.

In a limited way, educating the public about facial deformity has been the mission of some patients and families. Recently, researchers also have begun to take on this challenge (Tobiasen, Collins, Heitland, & Wood, 1988). There is a whole area of social science devoted to measuring and producing attitude change. To date, very little from this science has been brought to bear on the social perceptions of facial deformity. What information would need to be promulgated? How is this best done and with which target populations? Bull and Rumsey (1988) suggest that media needs to deemphasize physical attractiveness in advertising and programming, and concomitantly needs to place greater emphasis on the competence of the facially disadvantaged. As seat belts and air bags are preventive measures for facial trauma, public education may be the means to prevent some of the psychosocial trauma of facial deformity. This should be another important area for future psychosocial research.

REFERENCES

Brantley, H. T., & Clifford, E. (1978). Cognitive, self-concept and body image measures of normal, cleft palate and obese adolescents. *Cleft Palate Journal, 16,* 177–182.

Broder, H., & Strauss, R. P. (1989). Self-concept of early primary school age children with visible or invisible defects. *Cleft Palate Journal, 26,* 114–117.

Bull, R., & Rumsey, N. (1988). *The Social psychology of facial appearance* (pp. 232–237). New York: Springer-Verlag.

Clifford, E. (1983). Why are they so normal? *Cleft Palate Journal, 20,* 83–84.

Cohen, M. M., Jr., & Kreiborg, S. (in press). The central nervous system in the Apert's syndrome. *American Journal of Medical Genetics.*

Easson, W. M. (1966). Psychopathological environmental reaction to congenital defect. *Journal of Nervous and Mental Diseases, 142,* 453–457.

Edgerton, M. T., Jane, J. A., Berry, F., & Marshall, K. A. (1975). New surgical concepts resulting from cranio–orbito–facial surgery. *Annals of Surgery, 182,* 228–264.

Hogeman, K. E., & Willman, K. (1974). On LeFort III osteotomy for Crouzon's disease in children. *Scandinavian Journal of Plastic Surgery, 8,* 169–173.

Kahn, J. P. (1956). Operations for hare lip and cleft palate: The emotional complications in children. *California Medicine, 84,* 334–338.

Kapp-Simon, K. (1986). Self-concept of primary-school-age children with cleft lip, cleft palate, or both. *Cleft Palate Journal, 23,* 24–27.

Kinnis, G. C. (1954). Emotional adjustment of mother to child with a cleft palate. *Medical Social Work, 3,* 67–71.

Lefbvre, A., & Barclay, S. (1982). Psychosocial impact of craniofacial deformities before and after reconstructive surgery. *Canadian Journal of Psychiatry, 27,* 579–582.

Macgregor, F. C., Abel, T. M., Byrt, A., Lauer, E., & Weissman, S. (1955). *Facial deformities and plastic surgery: A psychosocial study.* Springfield, IL: Charles C. Thomas.

McWilliams, B. J., & Paradise, L. P. (1973). Educational, occupational and marital status of cleft palate adults. *Cleft Palate Journal, 10,* 223–229.

Millard, R. D. (1980). *Cleft craft—The evolution of its surgery. Volume III. Alveolar and palatal deformities.* (pp. 1018–1019). Boston: Little, Brown.

Pertschuk, M. J., & Whitaker, L. A. (1985). Psychosocial adjustment and craniofacial malformations in childhood. *Plastic and Reconstructive Surgery, 75,* 177–182.

Pertschuk, M. J., & Whitaker, L. A. (1988). Psychosocial outcome of craniofacial surgery in children. *Plastic and Reconstructive Surgery, 82,* 741–744.

Pertschuk, M. J., Trisdorfer, A., & Whitaker, L. A. (1989). *Long-term follow-up of craniofacial surgery in early childhood.* Paper presented at the American Cleft Palate Association Meetings, San Francisco.

Peter, J. P., & Chinsky, R. R. (1974a). Sociological aspects of cleft palate adults: I. Marriage. *Cleft Palate Journal, 11,* 295–309.

Peter, J. P., & Chinsky, R. R. (1974b). Sociological aspects of cleft palate adults: II. Education. *Cleft Palate Journal, 11,* 443–449.

Peter, J. P., Chinsky, R. R., & Fisher, M. J. (1975a). Sociological aspects of cleft palate adults: III. Vocational and economic aspects. *Cleft Palate Journal, 12,* 193–199.

Peter, J. P., & Chinsky, R. R., & Fisher, M. J. (1975b). Sociological aspects of cleft palate adults: IV. Social integration. *Cleft Palate Journal, 12,* 304–310.

Pillemer, F. G., & Cook, K. V. (1989). The psychosocial adjustment of pediatric craniofacial patients after surgery. *Cleft Palate Journal, 26,* 201–207.

Richman, L. C. (1983). Self-reported social, speech, and facial concerns with personality adjustment of adolescents with cleft lip and palate. *Cleft Palate Journal, 20,* 108–112.

Richman, L. C., & Eliason M. (1982). Psychological characteristics of children with cleft lip and palate: Intellectual, achievement, behavioral and personality variables. *Cleft Palate Journal, 19*, 249–257.

Richman, L. C., Eliason, M. J., & Lindgren, S. D. (1988). Reading disability in children with clefts. *Cleft Palate Journal, 25*, 21–25.

Richman, L. C., Holmes, C. S., & Eliason, M. J. (1985). Adolescents with cleft lip and palate: Self-perceptions of appearance and behavior related to personality adjustment. *Cleft Palate Journal, 22*, 93–96.

Temple, I. K. (1989). Stickler's syndrome. *Journal of Medical Genetics, 26*, 119–126.

Tessier, P. (1971). The definitive plastic surgical treatment of the severe facial deformities of craniofacial dysostosis, Cruzon's and Apert's diseases. *Plastic and Reconstructive Surgery, 48*, 419–442.

Tisza, V., Silverstone, B., Rosenblum, O., & Hanlon, N. (1958). Psychiatric observations of children with cleft palates. *American Journal of Orthopsychiatry, 28*, 416–423.

Tobiasen, J. M., Levy, J., Carpenter, M. A., & Hiebert, J. M. (1987). Type of facial cleft, associated congenital malformations, and parents' ratings of school and conduct problems. *Cleft Palate Journal, 24*, 209–215.

Tobiasen, J. M., Collins, D., Heitland, K, & Wood, A. (1988, April 26–29). *Growing up with . . . cleft lip and palate.* Paper presented at the American Cleft Palate Association Meetings, Williamsburg, Virginia.

Trisdorfer, A., Pertschuk, M. J., & Whitaker, L. A. (1989, June 14–16). *Learning disabilities associated with craniofacial malformations.* Paper presented at the Second International Congress, International Society of Cranio–Maxillo–Facial Surgery, Florence, Italy.

Waite D. E., & Kersten, R. B. (1980). Residual alveolar and palatal clefts. In W. H. Bell, W. R. Proffit, & R. P. White (Eds.), *Surgical correction of dentofacial deformities.* Philadelphia: W. B. Saunders.

Watson, C. G. (1964). Personality adjustment in boys with cleft lips and palates. *Cleft Palate Journal, 1*, 130–133.

BODY-IMAGE CHANGE THROUGH PSYCHOLOGICAL CHANGE

C H A P T E R 12

Developmental and Psychodynamic Perspectives on Body-Image Change

David W. Krueger

THE ROLE OF BODY IMAGE IN THE DEVELOPMENT OF THE SELF

The body and its evolving mental representations are the foundation of a sense of self. Freud (1923/1961) recognized the ego as first and foremost a body ego. The body ego, or body self, refers to a combination of the psychic experience of body sensation, body functioning, and body image (Krueger, 1989a; Lichtenberg, 1985). The consensus of most developmentalists is that body-self formation includes the full range of kinesthetic experiences on the body's surface and in its interior, as well as the body's functions (Faber, 1985; Lichtenberg, 1978). *Body image*, in this developmental and psychodynamic context, is operationally defined as the mental representations of the body self. It is important to note that these representations are not limited to visual "images" (i.e., pictures in one's head of one's body) but comprise the schema of all sensory input, internally and externally derived—lived experiences processed and represented within a maturing psychic apparatus.

The development of an intact body image and physical boundaries, and the subsequent evolution of ego boundaries fall along a continuum. This parallel developmental line of body self and psychological self moves from states of primary narcissistic fusion or merger to stages of separation–individuation—from body-boundary consistency to ego-boundary coherence. Seymour Fisher in Chapter 1 of this volume and elsewhere (Fisher, 1986) has described an extensive research program concerning dimensions of the psychodynamic concept of body boundaries.

Stages of Development of the Body Self

From infancy onward, normal development is characterized by a progressively more complete, integrated *body schema*. Self-awareness incorporates the awareness of one's own body as well as the perception of another's responses to it (Spitz, 1957). The development of a body self can be conceptualized as occurring in a three-stage process.

1. *Early Psychic Experience of the Body.* Specific and time-appropriate stimuli are crucial for psychic recognition and registration of physical experiences. The infant's body, affects, and movements are initially experienced through the mirroring selfobject (the mother). At the earliest stage of development, these experiences coalesce and are not differentiated from the mother.

2. *Early Awareness of a Body Image with an Integration of Inner and Outer Experience.* In this stage, there is definition of body-surface boundaries and distinction of the body's internal state from the external world. This stage of development, beginning at a few months and extending into the toddler phase, is characterized, in normal development, by a sense of reality based on an integrated body self emerging from newly discovered body boundaries and the perception of differentiated body states. The representation of body self evolves as an increasingly definite articulation of boundary and content. Body experiences start to become coherent in the first months of an infant's life as awareness of the internal and surface aspects of the body increases. Critical to this process is the development of the infant's imaging capacity. Neurobiologists (e.g., Horowitz, 1983) speak of the psychological and anatomical substrates of images, including image formation.

An infant's imaging capacity begins at Piaget's (1945) sensorimotor stage IV (8–13 months), at which time the image and its properties seem to exist independently of the object or person perceived. As the capacity to make images and internal representations develops, people or objects can exist apart from the infant's sensory perception of them. This imaging capacity is initially primitive and is limited to identification of symbols of transitional objects, for example, a thumb to suck rather than a breast, or a blanket to rub rather than the mother's skin.

With the achievement of imaging capacity, the infant comprehends the distinctiveness of body and object and develops an awareness of space beyond the body. From these faculties emerges the sense that the infant creates his/her own image and thereby his/her own action. The infant distinguishes between his/her own body and the body "out there"—his/her image. The toddler thus seems to recognize that the mirror imparts information about his/her own body and his/her own actions in a definite and objectifiable manner, and the movement of that image is created directly by his/her own actions (Modaressi & Kinney, 1977).

The individual develops a full imaging capacity at about 18 months, corresponding with Piaget's description of *object permanence*. By this time the toddler can extend his/her conceptual capacity beyond himself/herself to include the body of others, for example, drinking from his/her cup and offering a drink from the cup to a parent or doll (Nicholich, 1977). Through the period of 13–18 months an object must be reexamined and verified (i.e., *recognition memory*). After about 18 months of age, the toddler is able to evoke an image of the absent object and pursue it without any immediate perceptual cues (i.e., *evocative memory*) (Fraiberg, 1969).

3. Definition and Cohesion of the Body Self as a Foundation of Self-Awareness. A new level of organized self-awareness begins at about 15 months. This is confirmed by observational studies of the infant discovering himself/herself in the mirror at 15–18 months (Emde, 1983) and by the acquisition of the semantic "no." The capacity for and function of the child's ability to say "no" is defined by Spitz (1957) as evidence of the emerging distinctness of the "I" and "Non-I." Autonomy and self-awareness are emerging. "No" encapsulates developmental statements that: "I am not an extension of you and your body or your desire; this is where you end and I begin—my body is mine and mine alone."

Mahler (Mahler & Furer, 1968) and Piaget (1945) agree (from different theoretical vantage points) that a cognitive sense of separate existence and of body self can normally exist by age 18 months. In normal development, the experiences and images of the inner body and the body surface become organized and integrated into an experiential and conceptual whole. They are felt as a coherent unit of body self, which becomes integrated and uncritically accepted as a higher-order self-experience. Consolidation of a stable, integrated, cohesive mental representation of one's body is a key developmental task during this period. This entails delineation of what is inside and what is outside, with clear, distinct boundaries. Internal body-self awareness and intact internal/external boundaries communicate a distinctiveness from others which promotes individual mastery and the experience of effectiveness.

Cohesion and Integration of Body Images

The body-self experience, body images, and self images cohere to form the sense of self. This synthesis of body and psychological selves provides a unity and continuity over time, space, and state (Bauman, 1981). There is a developmental sequence to the formation of the body self. First, the body self is the *function* of another (a caretaker). Next, it is immediate, felt *experience*: the emerging experience of unsatisfied need (e.g., hunger). Next, the body self is *form*, objectively distinct patterns of behavior, as well as the subjective and systematic experience of reality. Finally, it is *concept*, a relatively enduring internal frame of reference, comprised of bodily and emotional images, concepts, and experiences. The quality of relative stability over time comprises the aspect of identity.

The process of *symbolization* is a step in the abstraction and internalization process toward self constancy and cohesiveness, toward self and object differentiation (Krueger, 1988). This process facilitates self-awareness (subjectivity), the connection of meaning to experience and then to understanding (objectivity). The pathological opposite is an equation of experience with action (Ogden, 1985), when urge and action are fused without intermediating evaluation. Contemplation and judgment reside in this potential space between urge and action. Without it, one is reflexly active, or "impulsive."

The experience of subjectivity introduces the experience of objectivity. In these simultaneous processes, there is distinction between symbol and symbolized, thought and the object of thought, experience and the naming of it, feeling and action, thought and action (Hegel, 1807/1977). It is the beginning of a delay between impulse and action. One component of this developmental maturation is the consolidation of an accurate internal representation of one's body, including its seamless integration with psychological self to form a sense of self.

What is first and most clearly observed is also what was first experienced: the body and bodily sensations. This leads to the more developmentally advanced experience of self, then to most abstract conceptualizations and representations of the self, including body image and self image. However, this unity of body and self (body and mind) may suffer developmental interruption or arrest at any point, creating a deficit ("nonintegration" as opposed to "split") in the progression and integration of body self and psychological self (Krueger, 1989a).

Just as the first subjective awareness is of the body, the first symbol is also of the body—a part of the oneness of mother and infant and a bridge to something external, such as food, a blanket, a thumb. The imaging capacity of the infant matures and symbols are used more flexibly and reliably, undergoing refinement into various internalizations, including the formation of a body image.

Developmental research (Spitz, 1965) and clinical observation (Blatt, 1974) emphasize the significance of developing boundaries between inner and outer experience as well as between self and others. It is necessary for these basic boundary distinctions to be established before the mental representations of self and other can undergo more complex differentiation, articulation, coherence, and integration in the developmental process.

What becomes internalized is not the object or its functions but one's *experience* of and with the object. One uses this experience to form images and fantasies of internal objects (Grotstein, 1983). Images are concrete and easily accessible ways to code, store, and retrieve information. The transformation of information into an image is a standard mnemonic device. Visual images are probably the first means of thinking or processing information. There appears to be a hierarchy of intellectual mechanisms ranging from images, to words, to organizing patterns, to superordinate abstractions and inferences that regulate the entire experience of the self. Some people characteristically use visual images more than others. Grinder and Sandler (1976) characterized the three commonly employed representational models as auditory, visual, and kinesthetic.

The body self seems to consist of a group of images that are dynamically and preconsciously centered on body experiences. A body image is a conceptual composite from all sensory modalities; the individual's sense of cohesion is also a conceptualization because the entire body cannot be simultaneously visualized nor can all images/sensations be simultaneously retrieved from a memory. Body image has been assumed to be something that one either has or does not have, as if it is fixed and either accurate or distorted (Bauman, 1981; VanderVelde, 1985). In addition to the mental representations, later developmental influences include the reactions of others to one's appearance. Usually preconscious and uncritically internalized, they are not as static as the term "image" might imply. One's body and body-self representation are developmental processes undergoing gradual maturational change with a cohesive core, analogous to the psychological self.

Body self and its derivative representation, body image, are fluid processes interconnected to the psychological self and its derivative representation, self-image. They are mutually complementary. The accurate empathic mirroring of the entire depth and range of the infant and child's responses establishes the basis for the subjective experience of the body and self. The imaging capacity is crucial to establishment of the objective experience of the body self (Lichtenberg, 1985) and the associated distinctness between self and object. The emerging capacities to subjectively and objectively experience one's body and one's self—as object and as origin of contemplation—parallel the increasing ability to use symbols. This developmental attainment of experiencing the self as a whole includes being an initiator and a director of intentional actions.

PATHOLOGICAL SEQUENCES IN BODY SELF AND BODY IMAGE

The disruption of the normal developmental integration of body self and psychological self can result in abrupt, symptomatic, and prominent changes of self state (such as empty depleted depression, affect regulation problems) and body-image distortions. Research on deficiency states in infancy has demonstrated that failure to develop a normal psychic representation of the body may result from insufficient intensity of stimulation as well as from cognitive and emotional overstimulation (Dowling, 1977; Shevrin & Toussieng, 1965; Wolff, 1960).

When a body image has been insufficiently formed to sustain the stresses of developmental maturation, one's functioning and body image both regress in response to emotional events. Both self-image and body image will display rapid oscillations in narcissistically vulnerable individuals. When such individuals are in regressed states such as narcissistic rage or depression, their body images oscillate precipitously. Comparisons of body images drawn at different times within a day show remarkable parallels to emotional states; that is, at a time of particular emotional turmoil, body image becomes distorted, vague, or regressed (Krueger, 1989a). In the course of successful therapy, patient and therapist will see a process of maturation, cohesiveness, distinctness, and consistency of body image that parallels developmental maturation (Krueger & Schofield, 1987)— that is, the resumption of previously arrested emotional development parallels resumption of development of body self and image as well.

Substantial research reviewed by Cash (1981, 1985), as well as by Hatfield and Sprecher (1986), has demonstrated that an individual's objective physical attractiveness influences both one's psychosocial experiences and development. Yet, an individual's self-perception of physical appearance may not correspond meaningfully with objective perceptions (Cash, 1985; Noles, Cash, & Winstead, 1985).

The subjective versus objective experiences and representations of the body self and image have the same disparity as the true self and false self described by Winnicott (1965). For individuals with developmental disruptions of body self and psychological self (e.g., narcissistic disorders), distortions exist within the self-image and body image, as well as a vertical split between the two, that is, nonintegration. They do not use objective data—such as being quite attractive or being normal weight—to alter internal representations of body image (such as being ugly or fat). They compulsively pursue physical attractiveness and social affirmation and acceptance to supply vital narcissistic needs, to counter an inner emptiness, and to insure against expected abandonment. Beauty, social, and aesthetic standards are pursued due to the lack of internal standards and the absence of an internal point of reference.

Types of Developmental Arrest Involving Body Self and Body Image

The context of the patient population that I will describe now should be kept in mind as I discuss developmental theory and clinical implications. The population, from which the implications emerged, is to be clearly distinguished from nonpatient (e.g., college student) populations. "Negative body image" in a college student population, for example, has quite different meanings than for eating disorder inpatients. For nonpatient populations, the applicability of cognitive and behavioral approaches (as in Butters & Cash, 1987; Freedman, Chapter 13, this volume) seems quite a different matter than for patients who are suffering from substantial developmental arrest, including nonformed or distorted body image, or for whom body image is a focal point of other significant pathology (Krueger, 1989b). The present patient population consisted of late adolescents and young adults with a substantial degree of developmental arrest: diagnostically, primarily narcissistic with some borderline personality disorders. The manifestations of this pathology include depressions, eating disorders, and impulsive behaviors.

My conclusions are based largely on psychoanalytic and psychotherapeutic work with patients suffering disorders of the self. Some observations were provided by a multispecialty inpatient treatment team who have worked with 425 hospitalized patients. Developmental data and reconstructions from this group of adolescents and young adults emerge from dynamically oriented individual therapy, serial projective drawings of body image and other psychological testing, family therapy, neurosensory integration, and dance-movement therapy. In the inpatient setting, specific techniques and studies focusing on body-self development include developmental sequences within dance-movement therapy, videotape analysis and feedback, body-image tracing, clay sculpting of body image, neurosensory evaluation/integration, family-history evaluations, and biofeedback techniques developed to address body image and simulation of preverbal mirroring.

I would like to propose a specific link between certain developmental disruptions and resulting psychopathology. Early developmental arrests in the process of establishing a stable, integrated, cohesive body image seem to result from one or several maladaptive interactions (Krueger, 1989a, 1989b). These early pathological sequences fall roughly into three groups. Although not mutually exclusive, the types of interaction can be described as (1) overintrusiveness and overstimulation, (2) empathic unavailability, and (3) inconsistency or selectivity of response.

1. Overintrusiveness and overstimulation. Overly intrusive parents attempt to remain merged with their children from infancy onward, impeding the processes of separation, individuation, and growth toward autonomy. When extreme enough to produce developmental arrest, this controlling and enmeshed parental behavior, with predominant demands for conformity (Bosormenyi-Nagy & Spark, 1973), result in the body self and image experienced as indistinct and blurred, or alternatively, as small, prepubescent, asexual, and undifferentiated (Krueger, 1989a). They experience their bodies as separate from themselves and easily invaded, and they carefully guard their body integrity. They may attempt to establish their body- and self-distinctness in rudimentary ways—by exercising to feel physical sensation, refusing to eat, having aversion to touch, compulsive weight-lifting to establish a firm body outline, or engaging in various sexual behaviors (e.g., exhibitionism) that elicit social recognition and response (Krueger, 1989b).

When an individual experiences physical and emotional intrusiveness and overstimulation, primitive protective measures may be mobilized that result in a higher threshold to stimuli, including a tuning-out or withdrawal (Demos, 1985). This tuning-out may subsequently interfere with psychic representation at a higher level, affecting integration of physical and psychic representation. The consequent pathology in later life requires a more intense or extreme experience to produce psychic representation of feeling. Sequelae include such distortions of tactile stimulation as limpness when held, an intense fear of or wish for being touched, a desire/avoidance for physical intimacy, sensations of numbness or somatic inattentiveness, or misperceived body image (Donatti, Thibodeaux, Krueger, & Strupp, 1989).

The transsexual male is an extreme clinical example of overstimulation. His body and psyche were so intermingled with that of his mother that he can make no somatic or psychic distinction between the two (Krueger, 1983). This intermingling and continued fusion of the body of both mother and son is illustrated by a transsexual male who recalled that, at approximately age 4 years, he looked at his arms as they were moving and asked, "Are these my arms, or are these Mother's?" The mother had carried him and physically intermingled with him to the extent that he had no independent psychic representation of his body or self. When he tried to picture his own body, the image evoked was that of his mother.

Intrusiveness upon the privacy of personal and inner space may result from actual invasion of the child's body space, including sexual assault, forced feedings (Dowling, 1977) or evacuations, operations, illnesses, and unrelenting body contact. Intrusiveness also results from penetration of the child's emotional world by manipulation of feelings or thoughts, devaluation of attempts at mastery, or demands that negate or deny the child's own perceptions. Overstimulation can occur in both physical as well as psychic trauma, resulting in the inability to integrate or control bodily sensations. During these overwhelming states, there may be a regression to (or if early enough, nondevelopment beyond) preoccupation with the body self and archaic imagery (Peto, 1959).

If development of a complete and distinct body self is arrested, a later compensatory attempt to supply this experience may involve intense sensory stimulation to provide perceptions of the body, such as compulsive exercise, induction of physical pain (e.g., wrist-cutting), intense physical stimulation, or extreme physical risk-taking. At time of emotional stress, there may be regression to the body self as an attempt to regulate affect and reduce tension. Stimulation and reintegration of the basic body self is the most primitive adaptive attempt at psychic reorganization.

A 16-year-old girl tried desperately to control her overwhelming compulsion to exercise. She reported, "I tried and tried not to give in and exercise, but the anxiety was overwhelming. I felt that if I didn't exercise, I would lose it— that I would just fade into everyone else and my body would just become a blob mixed in with everyone else around me. Then I'd be like everyone else—not special." Through compulsive exercise she regressively attempted to vividly reestablish her body-self experience and boundaries—to feel real and distinct.

She later showed me a letter written to her by her parents. Her mother wrote, "We need to give you our love and receive yours in return. We are all hurting so much. You are and always will be a part of our bodies." In a family therapy session, the mother told the therapist, "When she left home, it was like losing a part of me—like my arm or part of my body."

2. *Empathic Unavailability and Nonresponse.* The parent may be unable to resonate accurately and consistently with the child's internal experiences, or to the subtleties of the child's emotional and physical experiences, movements, and affects. If so, then the infant's experience does not become a point of reference for evolving self-development. Body boundaries of these individuals may not have been consistently defined by caress, touch, or secure holding. The affective interchange between infant and mother may not have supported and sustained the body experience. When these basic experiences are not accurate or consistent, the infant does not develop a reliable body boundary, sensory awareness,

or body image. Later, this individual experiences body self as incomplete and body image as distorted. The projective drawings of body images of these individuals are distorted, without shape, with blurred boundaries, and are excessively large (Krueger, 1989b). These findings are most notable in individuals diagnostically bulimic, borderline, or chronic depressive characters. Their body images often fluctuate with their mood and self-image, oscillating several times a day to a body image larger than actuality.

Many behaviors regarded as impulsive, addictive, or unrelenting are designed to evoke or establish boundaries. Stimulation of skin affirms and delineates a body boundary: wearing large, loose clothes to feel the rubbing sensation, wrist cutting, compulsive sexuality. Stimulation of internal body awareness includes binge-eating, vomiting, and using laxatives or diuretics.

Later in development, temporary losses of body control, such as soiling, crying, or even tripping and falling, can create insults to the body self and may intolerably strain the sense of self-cohesion and body reality. These experiences are often expressed as a desire to escape from one's body or shed one's skin (Lichtenberg, 1978).

At times of intense affect, an individual's focus of attention shifts from mastery to basic aspects of body-self intactness and preoccupations with body sensations, body schema, and body language.

In response to feeling abandoned, 15-year-old Cindy repeatedly rubbed the skin on her arms with a pencil eraser until she bled. When she could not evoke or provoke responses from her parents, she felt as if she did not exist. She had no body image to evoke. Lacking an internal image, she created an external sensation in order to reassure herself that she was real. She tried to establish real sensations through pain (and, unconsciously, establish the boundaries of her skin), validated by blood and confirmed later by scarring. She was further reassured when she found that she could not erase herself. She was indelible, permanent. The pain, as well as her primitive sense of existence, relieved her anxiety. The reality of her most basic self—her body—buttressed her feelings of realness. Body boundaries were restored, outlined by pain and accentuated by scars. This action, to her, was calming, as it affirmed her own existence and experience of her self via body sensation.

3. Inconsistency or Selectivity of Response. Parental response to selective stimuli from the infant creates a selective reality for the infant. For example, the mother may ignore affective and kinesthetic stimuli and respond only to physical needs or physical pain. This response pattern teaches the infant to perceive and organize experiences around pain and illness in order to obtain attention and affection. Effectiveness is via the body self; affect regulation never gets desomatisized. The affirmation of body self and psychological self through pain and discomfort entrenches itself in personality and characteristic modes of expression.

Ashley, now 19 and a very attractive television model and college student, described a ritual of several years duration. Whenever she felt overwhelmingly anxious and fragmented, she would get into very hot bath water and scrub herself so hard with a brush that her skin would be raw and bleeding. She indicated that this actually did not cause pain, but was relieving and reassuring to do. It outlined and defined her when she felt disorganized and could not picture how she looked. Her "scrubbings" began at pubescence, when she felt "dirty" and needed to "scrub away the dirtiness." She later recognized that illnesses and accidents were the only way to effectively engage the concern and attention of her highly self-absorbed and largely absent mother. Earlier physical and sexual abuse had skewed the experience of her body and of pain, heightening an already-elevated pain threshold because of empathic neglect of sensorimotor development.

Psychopathology with Intact Body Self and Body Image

There is a developmental continuum of psychopathology here. I have just characterized three facets at a very early level. These patients are not really denying body awareness and feelings, because they have never distinguished affects and bodily sensations or integrated mind and body enough to split and deny them. At times ofemotional insult, the organizing function is a directed focus on the first and most basic organizer of ego experience and structure: the body self.

Higher-order psychopathology involves regressive retreats to more intact body self-representations and regulation that occur at a time of threatened self-representation. In more developmentally advanced psychopathology, there is an integrated body schema with more highly organized and dynamically significant loss fantasies, such as bodily damage (e.g., castration anxiety) or immobilization. Unconscious fantasies of losing vital body parts or functions occur in conjunction with emotionally charged social interactions and Oedipal issues. In those individuals with less psychopathology (e.g., psychoneurosis), the fantasies of loss occur without severe threat to a sense of self-cohesion. Body-self cohesion, representation, and image are basically intact and accurate and play an important role in these instances, but these symptoms occur at the level of fantasy.

Body-image content and distortions may represent fragments of a dissociated memory. Behavioral, affective, and sensory fragments of repressed or dissociated memories may emerge in body-image alterations. For example, some obese individuals describe their obesity as a way to distance themselves from a thin, fragile, helpless, and vulnerable child state or experience. The obesity also may decrease possibilities of dating and being confronted by adult sexuality. Incest victims may pursue thinness to retreat to a prepubertal body to avoid feared rape, impregnation, and traumatic memories. We have also seen that body-image incongruities may represent dissociated or alternative personalities in patients with multiple personality disorder.

THERAPEUTIC IMPLICATIONS

Mind–Body Integration

Therapeutic interventions for the improvement of distorted and dysfunctional body-image perceptions must occur in the context of understanding the disordered self which is perceiving. That is, in individuals with developmental arrest of the psychological self, concurrent arrest of body self and body-image development is also found. The therapeutic focus must include both body self (and image) and psychological self, and it also must address integration of the two.

These individuals are guided by the responses of others, by external points of reference, so they may not even know or have developed their true selves. A gifted young woman, doing poorly in college, indicated: "Sometimes I feel really empty. When I feel unfocused and confused, I have no image of myself. I get really scared. It's like looking in the mirror and seeing no image, and I ask myself, 'Do I exist? Where am I? Who am I?' " These patients typically are limited in their ability to describe themselves and their feelings in a meaningful way. They constrict emotional expression and tend to describe endless details of symptoms as substitutes for feelings and internal experiences; they inhibit fantasy and thus limit their capacity to symbolize and play. Though often quite successful, such patients describe a vague sense of incompleteness or emptiness, a feeling that something is missing. Often they express some specific external focus of conflict or disruption, ranging in presentation from a separation crisis to an eating disorder.

Individuals with more significant developmental arrests usually have an incomplete, noncohesive body self and image. These early deficits in differentiation affect the body self, with later difficulties of the desomatization of the body self to its representational position in the psychological self. Lacking a consistent, internally regulated image of a body self or psychological self, they rely on external feedback and referents, such as other people or mirrors. Narcissistic individuals have little experience of themselves as the same persons over an extended period of time (Geist, 1985). Patients with profound early developmental arrests involving the sense of self do not form a cohesive body image and often exhibit significant defects of sensory integration (Donatti et al., 1989).

Therapy for patients with early developmental arrests must address the nascent sense of self that emerges from mirroring experiences with the primary parent in the first weeks of life and extends in changing form throughout development. Deficits in early mirroring experiences with this parent either creates an inner fragmentation that does not allow the development of a cohesive sense of self (Shane & Shane, 1985) or prevents the development of a psychological and body self separate from the parent. With these early developmental disruptions, it is as if the individual has been looking in a distorted "fun-house" mirror and only recognizes in adolescence (or beyond) what an image in an accurate mirror can be.

Such deficits in self-regulation mean that these vulnerable individuals must rely on external sources to supplement deficient internal regulation. Through their reliance on others for affirmation, enhancement, function, and esteem, they attempt to internalize these sources symbolically by acquisition or admiration of material goods and money, or of substances such as food, alcohol, or drugs. Still, the desire for a more permanent solution exists. The wish to engage meaningfully with the therapist as with other people, is experienced as unsafe and possibly threatening because of the patient's assumption that such a relationship would be as unreliable as past relationships have been. The desire to be effective and to impose predictability is a major factor that may have to be addressed early in the therapeutic encounter.

Patients may be quite invested in their symptomatology since symptoms are immediate and powerful in affect regulation and tension reduction. For example, a bulimic binge is instantly effective in creating calmness and the illusion of nurturance. It is difficult and anxiety-provoking for a patient to consider relinquishing the power that symptoms confer. Such symptoms often cannot be abandoned as a prerequisite to therapy, but they may diminish in intensity and utility over time in therapy. Consistent therapeutic attention must focus on the use of the symptoms: the motivation, enactment, and experience of the symptomatic act itself, and its change throughout the course of therapy.

Body-image distortion and malformation are a necessary component of the treatment focus and contribute significantly to clinical outcome (Krueger, 1989b). The degree of body-image disturbances is predictive of relapse for a patients with significant narcissistic pathology (Garner & Garfinkel, 1981).

Empathic Listening

The therapist must place himself/herself inside the entire experience of the patient, understanding and resonating with the patient's subjective reality. Empathy does not mean being kind, sympathetic, consoling, gratifying, or commiserating. Empathy describes a listening position, a particular way of listening from inside another individual's experience that permits appreciation from that person's own frame of reference. "Listening from the inside" includes an awareness of the patient's internal and perceived external systems and of the representational model (whether auditory, visual, or kinesthetic) that individual uses to describe his/her body, psyche, and world.

Patients whose basic pathology lies in the formation and synthesis of body self and psychological self have helped us understand the nature of empathy through their particular sensitivity to it. It is by empathic failures in the developmental past that their pathology has been created—the sense that their feelings, internal experience's, and perceptions have not been listened to. The therapist's insistence on his/her own separateness will engender these individuals to feel, as they have in the past, that they are not being listened to or validated.

Developmentally arrested patients may see a therapist as a part or of function of themselves (i.e., self–object transference); hence, the therapist becomes increasingly important as part of the structure of the patient's self-experience. The therapist becomes the personification of the patient's own listening and experiencing process and becomes a developmental organizer in the growth of the patient. Through dynamic understanding of this entire process, the patient develops self-empathy and self-structure (Kohut, 1977; Krueger, 1989a).

"Listening" for Nonverbal Material

In the beginning, developmentally, there are no words. Words are not necessary for the original self, the body self, or early communication. Before language exists, we communicate facially, posturally, gesturally, affectively, and vocally. Initial communication takes place at a nonverbal, affective level; verbal language is a relatively late acquisition ontogenetically and phylogenetically. Even in the adult, nonverbal communication accompanies every word. Nonverbal information emerges steadily from the patient in therapy. Posture, gesture, body rumblings, voice changes and quality, as well as silence, are all means of expression available to the apparently immobile patient.

Attention to a patient's behavior is not new; however, the understanding and decoding of nonverbal behavior has traditionally been in structural terms, that is, as manifestations of sexual or aggressive drive-derivatives or in other object-related terms. Transference material has been understood, until recently, in the model of object-differentiated transferences. What has been omitted in our conceptualizations of this behavior is its preverbal origin. The simplest explanation deserves consideration first: that nonverbal behavior is communication with a significant nonverbal implication. Just as we now consider selfobject transferences to arise from this developmental time frame, we must also be alert to the affective and autonomic communication from a patient (Krueger, 1989a).

Nonverbal behaviors are rich in meaning and history and are indicators of motivation, fantasy, and dynamics. Gesture and movement predate speech and reveal basic and powerful affect.

Gestures and movements may be scrutinized for the following characteristics:

1. Symbolic content.
2. Unity of movement, affect, and words.
3. Position of the body and interrelationships of the body (position of hands, arms, feet, and legs in relation to the rest of the body).
4. Coordination of verbal and nonverbal movement in regard to timing, intensity, and change over time.

5. Symbolic reenactments: movements that recreate an object or selfobject relationship.
6. Associations of the patient to movements and gestures.
7. Kinesthetic patterning and meanings in terms of the transference.

Therapy as a Developmental Experience

Psychotherapy may be conceived as a corrective developmental experience with the therapist as developmental organizer (Krueger, 1989a). The therapeutic setting contains symbolic equivalents of the mother–child relationship, consistency, reliability, empathic attunement, specific and defined boundaries, focus on the patient, acceptance of what is otherwise alienating, and a holding environment. These factors are of even greater importance in the treatment of patients with early developmental issues and arrests than for patients with more consistent internal structure (i.e., neurotic patients). The body self as well as psychological self must be integrated in the developmental march of therapy.

The function of the therapist is to accurately recognize and assist in articulating affective states and to help the patient develop an internal point of reference. Affect evolves from somatic experience, to differentiation of types of affect, to verbalization about them. Verbalization not only provides mastery by articulating feelings but also, more importantly, it facilitates the accurate perception of body self and image, perception of the psychological self, and integration of the two. The blending of affective and cognitive, bodily and psychic self, consolidate a sense of self.

Additional Therapeutic Modalities

Especially for patients with more significant developmental arrest, the creative and expressive art therapies offer more direct access to the unconscious and symbolic processes as well as to more basic experiences of the body self. The methodologies of expressive therapies allow direct experience of body self and basic affect without guilt by bypassing later developmental structures, such as superego, to directly access experience (Fink, 1985; Krueger, 1989b). In inpatient or day treatment settings, these therapies can provide nonverbal, expressive, and experiential integration of mind and body through movement-dance techniques, psychodrama, art therapy, biofeedback, and sensory integration.

These modalities can be utilized in psychodynamically oriented, developmentally informed sequences and can be cohesively integrated with a treatment team. The results can be quite powerful, partly because of these therapies' intrinsic relationship with primary process and preverbal and nonverbal developmental issues.

Additional techniques address development of body self and psychological self for patients with significant arrest through videotape feedback, body-image tracing, sequential clay sculpting of body image, mask and marionette making, and projective collages and drawings of body image. Each of these therapeutic techniques can result in heightened self-experience, an effective communication of affect and internal reality, and an objective depiction of the patient's experience in a form that can be validated by both patient and therapist.

The emergence of material rooted in the preverbal period is easily obstructed. It is undifferentiated and unstructured since it existed when there were no mind–body or self–object differentiations. The preverbal period encompasses basically the first 3 years of life. Although some verbalization begins in the second year of life, the major expressive behaviors are motoric, mimetic, and gestural. As verbal and cognitive capacities increase, the experience shifts, and the capacity for verbal and encoding mastery heightens. Still, by age 2 to 3, a child does not yet have language or concepts to match the complexities of fantasies, thoughts, and affects.

These expressive treatment modalities can be combined with verbal therapy to promote a cohesive and complete developmental sequence. Integrated therapy begun at a basic level of awareness of body self allows resumption of the growth process in a more profound and rapid manner. Additionally, the patient's desperate sense of helplessness and ineffectiveness is immediately addressed by techniques that deal with primitive and preverbal issues and integrate them with higher–level verbal and symbolic functions and experiences to provide cohesive development of a sense of self.

A basic aspect of therapeutic approach for an individual coming from a severely growth-inhibiting environment and having distortions in the perception of emotional and somatic experiences and communications may be to focus initially on the accurate reading and labeling of signals, both somatic and affective. A therapeutic task can be to focus on those particular internal signals that patients may be neglecting, deleting, or distorting. Some of these signals or experiences may be quite threatening, such as the experience of emptiness or of internal disorganization. As this close attunement of both therapist and patient concerns the patient's internal experiences, the patient may fear reexperiencing the disappointment and emptiness of earliest empathic failures.

The therapist must respond contingently to the productions of the patient. A basic sense of causality thereby becomes established. It is the empathic emersion, resonance, and response with the internal experience of the patient in therapy that provides a new framework of experience. The experience of effectiveness and process of empathic attunement can then become internalized by the patient as self-empathy. Ultimately, the individual can internalize the entire process for self-regulation from the newly developed internal center of initiative, affects, esteem, and initiative. In this manner, the healthy development of body self and image as well as psychological self can resume.

REFERENCES

Bauman, S. (1981). Physical aspects of the self. *Psychiatric Clinics of North America, 4,* 455–469.

Blatt, S. (1974). Levels of object representation in analytic and intrajective depression. *Psychiatric Study of the Child, 29,* 107–157.

Bsormenyi-Nagy, I., & Spark, G. (1973). *Invisible loyalties* . New York: Harper & Row.

Butters, J., & Cash, T. (1987). Cognitive–behavioral treatment of women's body-image dissatisfaction. *Journal of Consulting and Clinical Psychology, 55,* 889–897.

Cash, T. F. (1981). Physical attractiveness: An annotated bibliography of theory and research in the behavioral sciences. *JSAS Catalog of Selected Documents in Psychology, 2* (Ms. 2370).

Cash, T. F. (1985). Physical appearance and mental health. In J. A. Graham & A. Kligman (Eds.), *The Psychology of cosmetic treatments* (pp. 196–216). New York: Praeger.

Demos, V. (1985). Affect and the development of the self: A new frontier. Paper presented at the Self Psychology Conference, New York, New York.

Donatti, D., Thibodeaux, C., Krueger, D., & Strupp, K. (1989). *Sensory integrations of body image distortion in eating disorder patients.* Unpublished paper.

Dowling, S. (1977). Seven infants with esophageal atresia; a developmental study. *Psychoanalytic Study of the Child, 32,* 215–256.

Emde, R. (1983). The prerepresentational self. *Psychoanalytic Study of the Child, 38,* 165–192.

Faber, M. (1985). *Objectivity and human perception.* Alberta, Canada: University of Alberta Press.

Fink, P. (1985). In looking ahead, planning together: The creative arts in therapies. Symposium published by Hahnemann University, Philadelphia, Pennsylvania.

Fisher, S. (1986). *Development and structure of the body image.* Hillsdale, NJ: Erlbaum.

Fraiberg, S. (1969). Libidinal object constancy and mental representation. *Psychoanalytic Study of the Child, 24,* 9–47.

Freud, S. (1961). The Ego and the Id. In J. Stratchey (Ed. and Trans.), *The standard edition,* (vol. 19, pp. 12–60). London: Hogarth Press. Original work published 1923 of the complete psychological works of Sigmund Freud

Garner, D., & Garfinkel, P. (1981). Body image in anorexia nervosa: Measurement, theory and clinical implications. *International Journal of Psychiatric Medicine, 11,* 263–284.

Geist, R. (1985). Therapeutic dilemmas in the treatment of anorexia nervosa: a self-psychological perspective. In S. Emmett (Ed.), *Theory and treatment of anorexia nervosa and bulimia.* New York: Brunner/Mazel.

Grinder, J., & Sandler, R. (1976). *The structure of magic: II.* Palo Alto, CA: Science and Behavior Books.

Grotstein, J. (1983). Perspectives on self psychology. In A. Goldberg A. (Ed.), *The future of psychoanalysis.* New York: International Universities Press.

Hegel, G. (1977). *Phenomenology of spirit* (A. V. Miller, Trans). London: Oxford University Press. (Original work published 1807)

Horowitz, M. (1983). *Image formation and psychotherapy.* New York: Jason Aronson.

Kohut, H. (1977). *The restoration of the self.* New York: International Universities Press.

Krueger, D. (1983). Diagnosis and management of gender dysphoria. In Fann, W., Karacan, I., Pokorny, A., & Williams, R., (Eds.), *Phenomenology and treatment of psychosexual disorders.* New York: SP Medical and Scientific.

Krueger, D., & Schofield, E. (1987). An integration of verbal and nonverbal therapies in eating disorders patients. *Journal of Arts in Psychotherapy, 13,* 323–331.

Krueger, D. (1988). Body self, psychological self, and bulimia: Developmental and clinical consideration. In H. Schwartz, (Ed.), *Bulimia: Psychoanalytic treatment and theory.* New York: International Universities Press.

Krueger, D. (1989a). *Body self and psychological self: Developmental and clinical integration in disorders of the self.* New York: Brunner/Mazel.

Krueger, D. (1989b). The "parent loss" of empathic failures and the model symbolic restitution of eating disorders. In D. Dietrich, & P. Shabab (Eds.), *The problems of loss and mourning: New psychoanalytic perspectives.* New York: International Universities Press.

Lichtenberg, J. (1978). The testing of reality from the standpoint of the body self. *Journal of*

American Psychoanalytic Association, 26, 357–385.

Lichtenberg, J. (1985). *Psychoanalysis and infant research.* Hillsdale, NJ: The Analytic Press.

Mahler, M., & Furer, M. (1968). *On human symbiosis and the vicissitudes of individuation.* New York: International Universities Press.

Modaressi, T., & Kinney, T. (1977). Children's response to their true and distorted mirror images. *Child Psychiatry and Human Development, 8,* 94–101.

Nicolich, L. (1977). Beyond sensorimotor intelligence: Assessment of symbolic maturity through analysis of pretend play. Merrill-Palmer Quarterly, 28, 89–99.

Noles, S. W., Cash, T. F., & Winstead, B. A (1985). Body image, physical attractiveness, and depression. *Journal of Consulting Clinical Psychology, 53,* 88–94.

Ogedn, T. (1985). On potential space. *International Journal of Psycho-Analysis, 66,* 129–142.

Peto, A. (1959). Body image and archaic thinking. *International Journal of Psychoanalysis, 40,* 223–231.

Piaget, J. (1945). *Play, dreams and imitation in childhood.* New York: Norton.

Shane, M., & Shane, E. (1985). *Self change and development in the analysis of an adolescent patient: The use of a combined model.* Paper presented at the American Psychoanalytic Association Meeting, Denver.

Shevrin, H., & Toussieng, P. (1965). Vicissitudes of the need for tactile stimulation in instinctual development. *Psychoanalytic Study of the Child, 20,* 310–339.

Spitz, R. (1957). *No and yes.* New York: International Universities Press.

Spitz, R. (1965). *The first year of life.* New York: International Universities Press.

VanderVelde, C. (1985). Body images of one's self and of others: Developmental and clinical significance. *Journal of American Psychiatric Association, 142,* 527–537.

Winnicott, D. (1965). *Maturational processes and the facilitating environment.* New York: International Universities Press.

Wolff, P. (1960). *The developmental psychologies of Jean Piaget and psychoanalysis (Psychological issues. Monograph 5)* New York: International Universities Press.

C H A P T E R 13

Cognitive–Behavioral Persepctives on Body-Image Change

Rita Freedman

As a psychological phenomenon, we experience our bodies through a collection of multidimensional cognitive constructs. These mental images are not static, but develop as part of the dynamic process by which we continuously try to organize and understand our experiences. Though somewhat stable, body images do vary around a modal point, depending on internal, external, and contextual factors. They are also filtered through social reality, through the expectations and judgments we think others form of us (Cash, 1988; Keeton, Cash, & Brown, 1989; Lacey & Birtchnell, 1986; McCrea, Summerfield, & Rosen, 1982; van der Velde, 1985).

A cognitive–behavioral model for understanding body images includes perceptual and affective components as well as attitudinal ones, for whatever is seen or felt is inevitably thought about (Garner & Garfinkel, 1981). *Body-image percept* refers to the cognitive interpretation of such external sensations as observing one's reflection, or of such internal sensations as feeling hungry. *Body-image affect* includes the emotional responses generated by conscious thoughts about the body. *Body-image attitude* refers to the ideas and rules that organize our view of the physical self. These beliefs solidify over time, forming part of the "permanent core of the personality," which is resistant to change (van der Velde, 1985).

Behavior both reflects and affects body image by influencing cognitions. When you run a race, for example, you may think "I'm strong and healthy," a thought that in turn alters body-image percept and affect. The circular interaction among behaviors, cognitions, and emotions is explained by the rational–emotive model of Albert Ellis (Ellis, 1962): First, A, an activating event (stepping on the scale), leads to B, a bridging thought and self-statement ("I'm too heavy"), which triggers C, a conditioned emotional response (anxiety, disgust). The behavior generates new cognitions which then induce new feelings and behavior (dieting). Behavioral disturbances may thus be both a cause and an effect of faulty thinking.

DYSFUNCTIONAL PROCESSES

From a cognitive perspective, body-image distortion and dysphoria result from irrational thoughts, unrealistic expectations, and faulty explanations. The idea that the meaning of an event determines our emotional responses to it, forms the core of the cognitive model of emotional disorders. It is not so much the body but the view that we take of it that creates problems. Dysphoria can occur without distortion and distortion may be present without dysphoria. The direction and magnitude of the misinterpretation determine its emotional impact. Seeing oneself as more attractive than is objectively true can enhance satisfaction and thereby serves as "an adaptive self-deception in the service of one's emotional well being" (Noles, Cash, & Winstead, 1985).

Body images serve as cognitive organizations. In the development of obsessive thoughts and compulsive behavior patterns, the body often becomes a target for various problems and the object of intense judgment. Growing evidence suggests that the cumulative adverse effects of body-image dysphoria are associated with anxiety, sexual difficulties, social introversion, depression, and low levels of self-esteem (Archer & Cash, 1985; Cash, 1985; Cash, Cash, & Butters, 1983; Cash, Winstead, & Janda, 1986; Lerner, Orlos, & Knapp, 1976).

Dysfunctional cognitions clearly play a crucial role in the development and maintenance of eating disorders (Brown, Cash, & Lewis, 1989; Cash & Brown, 1987; Fairburn, Cooper, & Cooper, 1986). Negative thoughts about appearance is one of the most reliable body-image variables in discriminating bingers from normal eaters (Cash, Lewis, & Keeton, 1987; Dykens & Gerrard, 1986; Katzman & Wolchik, 1984). As Rosen indicated in Chapter 9 of this volume, unaltered body-image disturbances are good predictors of relapse of an eating disorder after treatment (Freeman, Beach, Davis, & Solyom, 1985). Such patients see their behavior as following logically from the premise that thinness is admirable and essential. Since this belief drives the disorder, therapeutic interventions invariably must confront disturbances in information processing that support this basic premise (Garner & Bemis, 1982). Bruch (1973) considered the correction of body-image distortion a precondition to recovery for anorectics.

Body-image constructs relate to personality types and to the cognitive styles associated with them. For instance, depressive personality types chronically interpret events in terms of deficiencies and get trapped by habitual self-defeating thoughts (e.g., "I'll never be thin enough"). Depressed people are less satisfied with their bodies (Archer & Cash, 1983; Noles et al., 1985), and "distortion of body image" is listed among the cognitive symptoms of depression (Beck, 1973). Anxious personality types who chronically overestimate risks become hypervigilant (e.g., "Everyone is staring at me"). They may defensively avoid mirrors or social events where feedback about appearance is likely, and their avoidant behavior in turn isolates them from experiences that could modify their fears. Habitual overmonitoring or avoidant undermonitoring of body processes leads to maladaptive feelings of self-consciousness and to maladaptive behavior such as compulsive weighing. Hyperactive cognitive sets seem to operate independently of outside stimuli, governed mainly by internal drives to avoid anxiety (Beck, 1970). People who overestimate risks suffer unnecessary anxiety and may lead constricted lives.

An unique closeness exists between one's body and one's identity. The somatic self is a central part of self-concept. High positive correlations are found between body image and self-image (Dworkin & Kerr, 1987), between body cathexis and self-cathexis (Secord & Jourard, 1953), and between body satisfaction and self-esteem (Berscheid & Walster 1974; Cash et al., 1986; Franzoi & Shields, 1984; Striegel-Moore, Silberstein, & Rodin, 1986). Although objective physical attractiveness is only modestly related to personality traits, subjective physical attractiveness (body image) is strongly related to them (Cash, 1985; Cash & Smith, 1982). People who view their bodies unfavorably tend to suffer from a variety of problems, regardless of how attractive they may actually be. The interdependence of body image and self-esteem means that distortion of one will affect the other, although the direction of effect may be hard to determine. Lack of self-esteem can stem from an underlying body loathing, while body loathing may be a product of low self-esteem (Freedman, 1989; Mintz & Betz, 1986; Thompson & Thompson, 1986).

We each operate with a system of rules or "shoulds" that shape our experiences of ourselves and our environments. When these rules are too rigid, too personalized, or are used too arbitrarily, they act as burdensome imperatives or constraints. Examples of dysfunctional rules that filter out positive information and cause negative automatic thoughts include: "I should always look my very best so everyone will like me." "My value as a person depends on how thin I am."

The therapeutic process opens the cognitive system to new information by challenging such underlying rules, making them less rigid and showing that "shoulds" can be shed without dire consequences. Beck's well-known taxonomy of cognitive errors (Beck, 1976) is useful in explaining misperceptions of body related experiences. Several examples from his more extensive list of common cognitive errors include:

1. *Personalization*—Misinterpreting events in terms of self-reference. ("They're talking about hair transplants because they notice my hair is thinning.")

2. *Polarized thinking*—Misinterpreting events in extremes such as good/bad. ("With skin like this I'll always look ugly.")
3. *Arbitrary inference*—Jumping to conclusions when evidence is lacking. ("I lost the promotion because I'm so fat.")

These types of cognitive errors generate automatic thoughts which in turn cause body-image problems. Irrational thoughts are not consciously initiated but arise spontaneously, almost reflexively, and serve as self-administered cognitive reinforcements or punishments. Because they seem so plausible, they are resistant to invalidation through experience and therefore tend to recur (Beck, 1976).

TECHNIQUES OF COGNITIVE BEHAVIOR THERAPY

Cognitive behavior therapy (CBT) attempts to detect automatic thoughts and correct the underlying belief structures that are dysfunctional. (For a basic review of principals of CBT, see Beck, 1976; Ellis & Greiger, 1977; Hollon & Beck, 1979; Kaplan, 1986; Meichenbaum, 1977; and Wilson & Franks, 1982.) Clients are taught to become more aware of their faulty cognitions and are taught techniques to make these thoughts more rational, more self-enhancing, and less self-defeating. CBT is an especially suitable therapeutic approach to body-image change precisely because body-image problems are more closely connected with thoughts about the body than with the objective reality of the body itself. Moreover, cognitive–behavioral techniques have proven effective with a variety of conditions known to be associated with body-image disturbance such as depression, anxiety, and eating disorders (Freeman et al., 1985; Garner & Bemis, 1982; Kazdin & Wilson, 1978; Kendall and Hollon, 1979; Miller & Berman, 1983). Since body images reside in the eye of the beholder, the therapeutic goal is to teach the mind's eye to see the body more adaptively.

Beck (1976) has delineated three distinct components of CBT: (1) The Behavioral Approach systematically introduces new forms of behavior such as wearing makeup or practicing assertion skills. By rehearsing new responses and confronting feared situations in small steps, avoidant behavior is gradually overcome. (2) The Experiential Approach provides new "corrective emotional experiences" that are powerful enough to challenge current beliefs, such as relaxation, guided imagery, physical activity, or group interactions. (3) The Intellectual Approach focuses on body-image cognitions — what, where, when, and how often they occur. Cognitive restructuring is then used to identify misconceptions, test their validity, and explore alternative thoughts. The basic steps in cognitive restructuring include (Beck, 1976):

1. Monitoring thoughts about the body, clarifying them, and determining the events that trigger them.

2. Demonstrating the connection between dysfunctional thoughts, behaviors, and emotions.
3. Examining the origins and validity of certain beliefs and gathering evidence to support or refute them.
4. Exploring the advantages and disadvantages of holding on to a belief.
5. Developing more adaptive interpretations and actively rehearsing them.
6. Modifying underlying rules that lead to dysfunctional thoughts.

The example presented in Table 13.1 illustrates how Beck's triple column technique for correcting dysfunctional thoughts can be adapted to body-image treatment. Clients first track their automatic thoughts and list them in Column 1. These thoughts are analyzed in terms of the cognitive errors being made (i.e., polarized thinking, personalizing, etc.), which are then recorded in Column 2. Rational counterarguments that refute the automatic thoughts are placed in Column 3. Counterarguments should be reality-based, persuasive, self-defensive, and adaptive. After the columns are worked through on paper, clients rehearse the counterarguments aloud and practice catching automatic thoughts as soon as they occur and challenging them with ready responses (Butters & Cash, 1987; Freedman, 1988; Hollon & Beck, 1979).

Standard cognitive and behavioral techniques are easily adapted to treating negative body image as shown in these brief examples (Beck & Emery, 1979; Kendall & Korgeski, 1979). Table 13.2 depicts the application of specific cognitive interventions, and Table 13.3 presents the application of behavior techniques. These kinds of behavioral changes elicit cognitions relevant to body image and provide practice in responding to previously avoided emotions and experiences.

Implementation of CBT is facilitated by a warm therapeutic relationship that includes a genuine respect for the client's intelligence and lifestyle. It is a

TABLE 13.1. APPLICATION OF TRIPLE COLUMN TECHNIQUE

Automatic thought	Cognitive error	Rational counterargument
"I look hideous. This haircut is a disaster."	Exaggerating	"It's not great, but it's not hideous. Looking scalped isn't really earthshaking."
"I always make such a mess of everything."	Personalizing	"I wanted a new look. Just because it didn't turn out as I expected this time doesn't mean I mess up all the time."
"I'm ashamed to go out. Everyone will laugh."	Emotional reasoning	"I'm entitled to make a mistake. Some people may laugh, others will sympathize. Most won't care."
"I can't go. I'll die if anyone sees me."	Jumping to conclusions; exaggeration	"I can go or not go. Either way I won't die. At home I'll be safe and lonely. If I go, I'll have more risk but more to gain."

TABLE 13.2. COGNITIVE INTERVENTIONS

Technique	Procedure
Operationalizing beliefs	Articulating precisely what is expected or feared, such as ridicule if a full meal is eaten in public.
Testing prospective hypothesis	Devising mini experiments that demonstrate whether the prediction is correct. (Ordering dessert in front of a critical parent to see what actually happens.)
Decatastrophizing	Using "what if" questions to articulate feared outcomes, then formulating coping tactics to deal with them.
Reframing cognitions	Restating negatives in either neutral or positive terms. "My thighs are disgusting" becomes "My thighs are the heaviest part of me."
Evaluating basic assumptions	Questioning the evidence and examining the consequences of a certain belief such as "bald heads are unsightly."
Systematic desensitization	Overcoming the fear of wearing a bathing suit by combining relaxation with a hierarchy of images.
Reattribution	Altering interpretations about causality. "My weight may be due as much to my genes as to anything else."

TABLE 13.3. BEHAVIORAL INTERVENTIONS

Technique	Procedure
Response initiation	Developing new grooming practice or joining an exercise class.
Assertion training and behavioral rehearsal	Practicing assertive responses to social criticism about weight. ("My weight is my own concern, not yours.")
Diversion techniques	Delaying a bulimic attack by changing into tight clothes.
Graded task assignment	Overcoming avoidance of one's nude reflection by gradual brief exposure in dim light.
Scheduling pleasant events	Taking time out on a regular basis for the sensuous reward of a massage, a long bath, a manicure.

collaborative partnership aimed at problem solving, where the client takes active responsibility for change. Therapy becomes a process of exploring new hypotheses. The therapist takes a supportive rather than a confrontational role, slowly challenging and encouraging clients to test the consequences of their attitudes and to consider what would happen if they altered them. Although certain beliefs may be distorted, they should never be overtly deprecated or torn down too fast but rather should be tested gently. An honest, nonmanipulative therapeutic alliance allows the client to overcome deficits in self-esteem and in personal trust. As a role model, therapists may use self-disclosure or self-presentation to illustrate body-image conflicts. As a source of information, they provide facts about the client's body, other people's bodies, norms of behavior, and scores on assessment instruments. Therapists also convey a basic understanding of how events, beliefs, and emotions interact to cause problems (Beck, 1976; Fairburn, Cooper, & Cooper, 1986).

Resistance is overcome by setting modest goals, breaking problems into small parts, working on them one by one, and concentrating on progress rather than on set-backs. A good starting point may be some tangible act (e.g., not weighing in for several days), which can serve as a catalyst for further change. Homework assignments are mutually devised and clients develop their own therapeutic style as they test what works for them. The self-management techniques that are rehearsed will be useful later on as life circumstances change.

RESEARCH REVIEW

Although body-image disturbances are widespread and clinically significant, the development and empirical testing of treatment interventions for them has been minimal. Few studies meet the basic methodological criteria of random assignment of subjects, inclusion of a control group, and posttreatment follow-up (Butters, 1985). Perhaps the paucity of work reflects a continued reluctance to admit the impact of body-image variables on psychological disorders. Thorough systematic outcome research requires that cognitive, affective, and behavioral approaches are all included in the assessment as well as in the treatment plan. This section reviews the major studies of therapeutic interventions that include a cognitive–behavioral component.

Butters and Cash (1987) tested the effectiveness of CBT with normal-weight, college women who showed substantial body-image dissatisfaction on the Body–Self Relations Questionnaire (Cash et al., 1986). Doctoral students conducted six individually structured, 1-hour counseling sessions. A diverse treatment protocol included cognitive restructuring, relaxation, systematic desensitization, guided desensitization in front of a mirror, physical mastery assignments, and stress inoculation techniques to prevent relapse.

Assessment of perceptual, affective, and attitudinal aspects of body image was conducted pretest and again at 2 and 7 weeks after treatment. Results were impressive. Relative to pretreatment levels and compared to untreated controls, the treatment group reported less preoccupation and greater satisfaction with physical appearance, enhanced social self-esteem, improved sexual interest, more positive evaluations of physical fitness, and more accurate assessment of body size and attractiveness. Favorable outcomes remained unchanged 7 weeks after treatment. Butters and Cash (1987) subsequently treated the control group by CBT and generally replicated its efficacy for improving dysfunctional body images. While all these subjects initially had low body-image scores (as well as poor self-esteem), they were drawn from a "normal population," and the authors caution that results may not generalize to clinical populations.

Dworkin and Kerr (1987) tested several treatment interventions with college women who identified themselves as overweight or unattractive, but fell within 20% of recommended weight ranges. The Body Cathexis and Self-Cathexis Scales (Secord & Jourard, 1953) were employed for pretest and posttreatment assessment. Subjects with moderately to highly negative body-image scores were randomly assigned to one of three interventions or to a waiting-list control group.

The first intervention, called "cognitive therapy," focused on reducing negative self-statements, challenging faulty beliefs and developing more rational ones. The second, termed "cognitive–behavior therapy," extended the cognitive approach by assigning daily practice in self-reinforcement for positive thoughts and guided fantasy to envision oneself as an attractive person. The third, "reflective therapy," was more psychodynamic, focusing on developmental issues and exploring current feelings about the body. In all interventions, a female graduate student conducted three 30-minute individual counseling sessions.

Cognitive therapy proved the most effective in improving body-image scores but was no more effective than the other two treatments in improving self-concept scores. Results suggest that even very short term CBT can be helpful in increasing body acceptance and self-esteem, even in severe cases of body-image dissatisfaction. Whether these results apply only to self-referred clients and whether improvement would persist over time is not clear from this study. Because of the high correlation found between body-image and self-esteem, the authors suggest that many people who exhibit low self-esteem might benefit from brief body-image therapy.

Addressing some of the limitations in the previous research, Rosen, Saltzberg, and Srebnik (1989) tested the stability of treatment effects, while adding a behavioral dimension so that the design included perceptual, cognitive, and behavioral components during assessment as well as during treatment. Subjects were normal-weight college women free of eating disorders, who had negative body-image scores on the Body Shape Questionnaire (Cooper, Taylor, Cooper, & Fairburn, 1987).

Six treatment sessions of 2 hours each were led by college seniors or graduate students in small group settings. The cognitive–behavioral intervention involved retraining in size and weight perception, modifying distorted negative thoughts about appearance, rehearsing positive self-statements, and practicing exposure to stressful situations. In contrast, a nondirective intervention provided support and information but no structured exercises for correcting perceptions or dysfunctional thoughts. Results at posttreatment and at a 2-month follow-up were described as "quite striking." As a result of CBT, there was a decrease in body-size overestimation, a reduction of behavioral avoidance, and a decrease in body dissatisfaction from pathological to normal ranges. CBT proved more effective than nondirective therapy on all three dimensions (i.e., body-image perception, cognition, and behavior). The nondirective intervention failed to produce clinically significant changes in body-image attributes. As Rosen et al. (1989) concluded: "Thus, it seems that education and support alone are not sufficient to improve negative body image and the benefits of cognitive–behavior therapy were not a function of the nonspecific effects of therapeutic attention" (p. 402).

Two other important studies combine experiential elements of CBT with psychodynamic and feminist approaches. Hutchinson (1982; see also Sankowsky, 1981) worked with psychologically healthy women ages 24–40 years in eight weekly group meetings. The Body Cathexis and Self-Cathexis Scales were used as pre- and posttreatment measures along with personal interviews. Treatment focused on the use of visualization and guided imagery in conjunction with a journal process that helped translate visual experiences into words. Controlled imaging was chosen as an appropriate tool for accessing and altering the subjective experience of the body because body image is, in part, an image that patients have the potential to control. As a clinical tool, guided imagery promotes development and rehearsal of new mental patterns while conveying a sense of the power of the imagination to reshape reality. (See Hutchinson, 1985, for a detailed account of imagery exercises.) Although systematic desensitization is a basic tool of CBT (combining imagery with relaxation to reduce anxiety), it was also employed here as a form of experiential therapy to uncover "repressed material."

Hutchinson reported a dramatic positive improvement in body and self-image on both quantitative and qualitative measures. Group imagery exercises were highly effective in accessing and reworking emotional material related to gender and body-image development. Hutchinson unexpectedly discovered, while working with these normal-weight women, that most of them were preoccupied with weight and food. She concluded that for females today, body-image struggles are inseparable from eating issues.

In contrast to the previous experimental studies involving "nonclinical" populations, Wooley and Kearney-Cooke (1986) and Kearney-Cooke (1989) report on an intensive treatment program for women with a long history of bulimia. During the 1-month program, they received 6–8 hours per day of individual and group therapy. Treatment goals were to correct body-image distortion, to establish realistic weight goals, to explore gender issues and social stereotypes at different stages of development, and to face the loss of a lifestyle built around bulimia. The intensive multimodal approach included CBT along with other types of treatment. Patients were taught cognitive restructuring that challenged the concept that weight loss was essential to happiness. Personal mastery was practiced through cosmetic change, physical exercise, and sensual awareness. Guided imagery exercises involved reliving parental conflicts about body-related issues and envisioning living through a day with a positive body image. The group engaged in experiential "acting out" work and in creative rituals to reduce sexual shame.

The Body Cathexis and Self-Cathexis Scales and the Color-a-Person Test (Wooley & Kearney-Cooke, 1986) showed significant improvement in body-image disturbance at posttreatment and 1-year follow up. Patients reported less preoccupation with appearance and greater pursuit of new life goals. The authors cautioned that any therapy focused exclusively on body image would not be as effective with bulimics as a program such as this one, which also included nutritional, interpersonal, and familial components.

Taken together these studies provide strong evidence that body-image interventions can produce rapid change. CBT seems to be a highly effective therapeutic approach, and may be enhanced further when combined with other modalities. Significant improvement occurred even with minimal treatment conducted by inexperienced counselors. Although maintenance of CBT's treatment gains for up to 2 months after treatment is encouraging, clearly longer-term follow-up assessments are needed (Butters & Cash, 1987).

A variety of cognitive–behavioral techniques were employed in these studies—including desensitization, relaxation, response initiation, physical activity, guided imagery, and cognitive restructuring. Multiple treatments make it difficult to determine which cognitive, behavioral, or experiential interventions work best, or to know how they interact. Differential effectiveness of techniques may depend on the particular problem being treated and on individual differences in response to treatment modalities. Being overweight or unattractive are psychological as well as physical variables, and, as these and other studies have indicated (Cash & Hicks, 1990), controlling for weight does not control for weight obsession. All the studies reviewed here were conducted with females, three of them with normal-weight college women. Research should be extended to include mature adult women, adolescents, clinical populations, and male and non-white subjects. With longer-term follow-up studies involving treatment comparisons and therapy component comparisons, we can determine which interventions produce the most stable results, with which problems, and with which populations.

CLINICAL APPLICATIONS

This section turns from formal outcome research to applications of CBT in a clinical setting where therapeutic interventions are often less precise but more individualized. While the following treatments have not been systematically applied or rigorously tested, they appear to be useful based on my own clinical experience. (See Freedman, 1988, for an even more detailed account.)

ASSESSMENT AND GOAL CLARIFICATION

The initial phases of assessment and diagnosis should provide insight into the specific somatic focus of the body-image disorder, its frequency, duration, and degree of intensity. How does it manifest in cognitive, affective, and behavioral terms? As Thompson, Penner, and Altabe reviewed in Chapter 2 of this volume, assessment instruments such as the Body–Self Relations Questionnaire (BSRQ) (Cash et al., 1986), the Eating Disorders Inventory (Garner & Olmsted, 1984), the Eating Attitudes Test (Garner & Garner, 1980), or the Body Shape Questionnaire (Cooper et al., 1987) can be used to pinpoint problem areas and relationships between them. When test results are reviewed with clients to articulate problems and to formulate strategies for addressing them, the assessment process itself becomes therapeutic. Negative feelings are reframed into positive goals such as "using exercise less competitively" or "eating regular meals for one day." A mutually developed list of specific goals is kept short at first, then expanded as progress occurs. Assessment helps operationalize body-image concepts and determine how the body differs from the client's ideals.

Consider the following case to illustrate this initial phase of therapy: Ellen presented with a typical complaint of body-image dysphoria focused on her 15–20 pounds of "excess" weight. The BSRQ indicated little investment in her body's health or fitness yet considerable investment in her appearance. Behavioral assessment included keeping a food diary for several weeks and monitoring her husband's remarks about her appearance. A complete personal and family weight history was taken to determine how far Ellen's current weight deviated from her natural set-point weight. For the initial phase of therapy our mutually agreed on goal was to regularize her eating habits without attempting any weight loss.

Since altering the body *is* a legitimate approach to improving body image, thorough assessment includes a review of physical features to determine whether a change of hair style, grooming, etc. is apt to be therapeutically beneficial. Which physical attributes are self-perceived and objective assets and which ones are self-perceived and objective liabilities? Makeovers are neither a salvation nor a sellout but should be explored constructively (as Cash has argued in Chapter 3, this volume). Results with surgery patients show satisfying, long-term changes so that assessment might include such possibilities. Together, client and therapist listen carefully to how the body is experienced. How are decisions made about self-presentation? (Because Ellen always wore loose, dark clothing to hide her full figure, she consequently looked drab and derived little pleasure from dressing up.) How does the client's appearance and body-image dysphoria impact on work and social life? Sentence completion exercises are one way to expose personal and social stereotypes. Responses to such stems as "Attractive people are . . ." or "Fat people should . . ." may uncover underlying assumptions that contribute to body-image problems (Freedman, 1988). When Ellen wrote "Attractive people are never overweight," we examined this response for cognitive errors and found examples to refute it.

Butters and Cash (1987) and Keeton et al. (1990) suggest a Mirror Focus Procedure for self-assessment. While nude or nearly so and in the privacy of home, the client gazes in a three-way mirror for 30 seconds at a distance of about

3 feet. The body is scanned as a whole, without fixating on any one feature. Then the client rates the comfort–discomfort level on a Subjective Units of Distress Scale (SUDS), from 0 (absolute calm) to 100 (extreme discomfort). This rating represents a baseline mirror distress level. Daily fluctuations are natural, but more stable, long-term changes in this number may reflect improvement in body-image satisfaction.

Gathering baseline data is a valuable practice to determine the magnitude of problems and to evaluate progress. A specially prepared coding sheet can facilitate systematic recording of the time, place, situation, activities, and persons present when negative thoughts or behaviors occur. Relevant baseline data might include time spent on cosmetic makeovers, food intake, use of mirrors or scales, avoidance behavior, physical activity, and automatic thoughts or self-conscious feelings. After monitoring her husband's critical remarks about her weight, Ellen discovered that they often occurred just before a social event. His comments caused heightened self-consciousness, which then prompted her to change her clothes several times before going out. A careful look at the baseline data revealed the connection between his embarrassment about her looks and her own social anxiety.

OVERMONITORING AND UNDERCONTROLLING

Baseline data may reveal chronic over- or undermonitoring and chronic over- or undercontrolling of body attributes and processes. Overmonitoring is associated with heightened self-consciousness, while overregulating may cause excessive inhibition. Undermonitoring and undercontrolling, on the other hand, often lead to addictive or impulsive behavior, such as binge eating (Beck, 1976). One common form of overmonitoring is compulsive weighing. In my survey of 200 women, nearly one-third weighed themselves more than once a week and 17% did so once a day or more (Freedman, 1988). Constant monitoring for transient weight changes magnifies their importance, triggering anxiety. Chronic weighers can gain behavioral control first by gathering baseline data about their weighing behavior, then establishing a schedule to gradually reduce scale use. By estimating weight before measuring it, they often discover that scales provide information they already know. Stimulus control involves moving the scale to a less accessible place or removing it from the house. A "scale demolition ritual" may help them "get even" with an instrument that causes so much grief.

Mirrors are another overused instrument for self-monitoring. Chronic mirror scrutiny leads to preoccupation with spots, hairs, wrinkles, etc. Normal variations get magnified into abnormalities as Ann's case exemplifies. Her presenting problem was a chronic self-consciousness that had gone on for many years. Ann's obsession with particular body parts shifted from hips to skin to hair, but her general dysphoria was consistent. Often she experienced a compulsive urge to check herself in the mirror to be sure she looked okay and to "repair" her image.

Like slot machines, mirrors invite us to take the gamble because of an occasional big payoff. When mirrors reveal problems with features such as hair or makeup, they prompt efforts at self-enhancement. Some people defensively avoid mirrors or only look "above the neck," while others like Ann become addicted to a habitual dose of mirror reflection. When stress built up, she compulsively sought her mirror to gain a sense of control of her life. Although she turned to it for reassurance, she generally wound up feeling unhappy with what she saw.

How do mirrors influence body image? First they heighten self-consciousness by drawing attention to the physical self. When self-awareness increases so does critical self-evaluation as the body becomes an object of scrutiny (Buss, 1980; Carver & Scheier, 1978). Mirrors also increase the desire to conform to stereotypic ideals of beauty. Feelings intensify when we confront the discrepancies between our real image and our ideal one. Self-reflection thus becomes a setup for self-rejection. (For an overview of mirror effects, see Fisher, 1986.) Most women report "mixed feelings" when they look in their mirrors (Freedman, 1988).

In learning to use mirrors less compulsively and more constructively, Ann began by gathering baseline data on her mirror usage: how much time was spent scrutinizing her reflection, what factors triggered the behavior, and what thoughts occurred during and after it. Whenever she turned to the mirror she tried to determine what she was looking at, what she was looking for, and what she expected or hoped the mirror would tell her. We used the triple-column technique to analyze cognitive errors and construct counterarguments. Stimulus control was practiced by removing certain mirrors from her environment and softening the lighting in her bathroom, thus toning down the mirror's messages. A schedule for mirror use was set up and slowly reduced as she progressed.

Binge eating represents a problem of undercontrol. As Monica, a typical binger observed, "Once it starts, the binge takes over. It's as if someone else gets inside my head and I'm helpless." The examples below show how behavioral interventions are used to control binge eating. They are most effective, however, when clients creatively modify them to suit their own therapeutic styles. Monica adapted the techniques this way:

1. Kept records of when and what she ate to chart her progress accurately.
2. Developed delay tactics to postpone a binge, changing into a special binge outfit that was tight fitting and then calling for a weather report to see if the urge to binge would pass during this delay period.
3. Started each binge with a mirror affirmation: "It's healthy to eat when I'm hungry. I give myself permission to eat." This conveyed a sense of control of her eating behavior.

4. Tried to binge in front of the mirror and notice the difference between eating compulsively and eating consciously.
5. Set a timer to interrupt the binge after 5 minutes and asked herself if she had enough. If not, she made a conscious decision to continue and then reset the timer once more.

INCREASING POSITIVE REINFORCEMENTS

One goal of CBT is to expand the individual's reinforcement systems so that body-related pleasures come from a variety of sources. Reinforcements in the form of self-praise have a powerful effect on body image and self-esteem, and mirrors can be used as a handy tool for prompting such praise. For example, self-compliments about appearance can be rehearsed while facing one's reflection. These "mirror affirmations" are short, positive declarations repeated with conviction while making eye contact with oneself. The goal is to practice approaching the mirror with praise statements so it becomes a stimulus cue that triggers good thoughts and feelings.

Each week Ann chose a different body part and repeated a compliment of that part whenever she turned to the mirror. ("My eyes are a lovely color.") Combining relaxation and visual imagery, she practiced relaxation in front of the mirror, focusing on problem parts. She placed reminder notes on mirrors to catch good feelings about the body, and gradually her habit of critical mirror scrutiny was replaced by conditioned self-praise. Ann also constructed a praise list that included physical dimensions of aesthetics, health, and fitness. This kind of list should be personally meaningful and extend beyond the stereotypes of attractiveness to broaden the body-image ideal. When well rehearsed, items from the praise list serve as handy defenses against habitual self-criticism.

One important advantage of group therapy is the supportive social reinforcers that naturally flow between members. In daily life, compliments can be elicited by prompting with questions ("How do you like my . . ."), by expressing pleasure ("I feel great about my . . ."), and by learning to give more compliments in order to get more in return. Although praise often enhances body image, it can also undermine it by heightening self-consciousness, by dictating a stereotypic ideal, or by invading one's privacy (e.g., intrusive comments on the street). Behavioral rehearsal helps clients learn how and when to receive or reject comments about their bodies. A good receiver graciously acknowledges wanted compliments and thereby encourages more of them, while a bad receiver reacts with indifference, embarrassment, or false modesty and thereby discourages further praise.

BROADENING THE BASIS OF BODY IMAGE

The body itself is a natural source of reinforcement. Body image is, after all, integrally connected with sensory experience. Behavioral assignments that involve moving, smelling, tasting, and touching focus attention more on how the body feels than on how it looks. They help clients to overcome deficits in identifying bodily sensations and to address their confusion and mistrust of such experiences. By playing with water, rocking to rhythm, increasing oral gratification through sucking or licking, enjoying exotic smells or scents from different body parts, the body can be experienced as more sensually satisfying.

Through techniques of sensate focus (Masters & Johnson, 1970), clients can heighten their sensual awareness by exploring body parts through self-touch. Touching the body as if it were a loving friend helps them let go of their critical judgmental view and discover body parts that may not be so lovely to look at can still feel lovely to touch. Sensual exercises (which may or may not be sexually explicit) can be combined with relaxation training and visualization of body parts. Daily meditation also directs attention away from external and toward internal sensations, establishing a "relaxation response" that unites mind and body (Borysenko, 1988).

The "body" of body image involves fitness and health as well as appearance, for attitudes about the body include what it does as well as how it looks (Cash, 1988). Physical exercise was employed as a behavioral component of CBT in several of the studies reviewed earlier. Active people rate their bodies more positively than inactive ones (Cash et al., 1986; Joesting, 1981), and 87% of a female sample reported that exercise positively affects their feelings about their body (Freedman, 1988). Those who care about fitness and health have more positive feelings about their appearance than those who are more invested in their body's looks (Cash et al., 1986). An exception to this fact, however, is found among persons with eating disorders, whose strong fitness investment is actually overcontrolled, compulsive avoidance of weight gain (Brown et al., 1989).

Strength, speed, and endurance contribute to our perceptions of physical instrumentalities. But perhaps there has been too much emphasis on exercising for fitness and health rather than for fun and fulfillment. Like eating and sleeping, physical activity is a basic form of self-nurturance that produces innate aesthetic and kinesthetic pleasures. Movement is also a way to act out body-image affect. A simple walk becomes a behavioral exercise if one repeats a phrase such as "my body feels strong," or if one visualizes oneself in motion while swimming.

Through behavioral contracting, inactive clients can be motivated to make a 1-month commitment to know and enjoy their body better through physical activity. They should start slowly and gently without any focus on fitness goals or weight loss but only on the pleasurable sensations of movement. Guilt or resistance is common among those who cannot seem to start or stick with an exercise program, which further erodes self-esteem. Sometimes I take therapy sessions onto a nearby track to help clients experiment with walking at different paces, or walking with others, or walking with music, all the while repeating body-image affirmations.

In an extensive review of the effects of fitness training on mental health, Folkins and Sime (1981) reported that physical exercise leads to improvements in mood, self-concept, and work behavior. Physiological explanations link a sense of well-being to the release of endorphins and steroids and to a general somatic relaxation effect. Cognitive explanations link affective changes to cognitive appraisal of the training effect and to the development of self-regulating strategies. Because there may be wide individual differences in the psychological benefits of fitness training, Folkins and Sime suggest that exercise may be more valuable for those who experience anxiety at the somatic level, while meditation may be a better strategy for those who experience anxiety cognitively.

CONSIDERING CULTURE AND GENDER

Negative body images are more often attributed to internal psychopathology than to external cultural imperatives. Yet social norms, when used as yardsticks for self-evaluation, can deeply affect how we see ourselves and are seen by others. Stereotypes homogenize individual differences into extremes which are then internalized as standards of human worth. Body-image disorders are partly a product of these forces interacting with biological and psychological factors. CBT can and should address the cultural pressures that shape the basic beliefs underlying these disorders (Garner, Garfinkel, & Olmsted, 1983).

For instance, communications media socialize attractiveness stereotypes by associating good looks with a glamorous life, thus creating an insidious contrast effect. After exposure to highly attractive media models, self-rating of appearance drops (Cash, Cash, & Butters, 1983), and ratings of other people's appearance declines as well (Kenrick & Gutierres, 1980). Carefully contrived advertisements compress standards of attractiveness into a young, idealized extreme that is virtually unattainable. Females are additionally victimized through the stereotyping of beautiful women as either "bimbos" (who are gorgeous but incompetent) or "bitches" (who are gorgeous but vain and manipulative). The beautiful victim is thus blamed for her assumed vanity (Cash & Duncan, 1984; Downs & Harrison, 1985; Freedman, 1986; Jurasky, 1988).

Several social trends have combined in recent years to foster an extremely thin feminine ideal, including: the women's movement which has motivated greater personal control, the weight-watching and fitness movements which have waged war on fat, and powerful media which have glorified slenderness (Garner et al., 1983; Hutchinson, 1982; Striegel-Moore, Silberstein, & Rodin, 1986). The media in particular is considered a major contributor to the body-image dysphoria that underlies eating disorders. For example, 69% of women but only 18% of men on popular TV shows were rated as being thin (Silverstein, Perdue, Peterson, & Kelly, 1986). Those women at greatest risk for eating disorders seem to have internalized most deeply the social mores equating thinness with attractiveness, so that their pursuit of thinness represents a pursuit of femininity (Wooley & Kearnery-Cooke, 1986).

Through CBT, clients can learn to identify and resist media pressures, for instance, by gathering baseline data: What programs do they commonly watch? What is being sold and what images connect physical attractiveness with glamour or goodness? How do they feel after exposure to such images? Does media avoidance make a difference in self-evaluation? A valuable exercise is simply to review the photographs in one magazine for images of full-figured women or those over fifty. In order to expand their idealized images into a broader spectrum of sizes and shapes, clients might gather photos of admirable people whose bodies are not conventional, such as Sammy Davis Jr., Margaret Mead, or Eleanor Roosevelt. By noting how these successful figures really look, clients start to recognize new choices that are more adaptive for them.

A wide range of sex differences is reported in body-image research, reflecting the centrality of the body to gender roles (Cash & Kilcullen, 1985; Jackson & Cash, 1985; Jackson, Sullivan, & Hymes, 1987). The ornamental feminine ideal demands a soft, childlike, graceful look, while the instrumental masculine ideal demands a potent, mature, aggressive look. Body images are filtered through these gender stereotypes that have important therapeutic implications (Freedman, 1986). Recall that all the studies of CBT reviewed earlier included only female subjects (partly perhaps because they are more likely to volunteer for such therapy).

The most marked sex differences occur in weight dissatisfaction. Females monitor weight more closely, diet more often, and have a narrower view of acceptable size and a greater discrepancy between their current and ideal figures (Cash et al., 1986; Fallon & Rozin, 1985; Rozin & Fallon, 1988; Streigel-Moore et al., 1986). Females also suffer greater criticism and rejection when overweight (Stake & Lauer, 1987). While men's cognitive errors tend to keep them satisfied with their weight, women's misperceptions pressure them to reduce it. Society stigmatizes obesity, causing the majority of women to misperceive and mislabel themselves as overweight when they are not (Davies & Furnham, 1986). Moreover, thinking fat seems to have as much impact as being fat. Merely *believing* that one is overweight (even if objectively one is not) is associated with low self-esteem, poor body image, increased dieting, and binging (Cash & Hicks, 1990).

Interventions for modifying misperceptions of body size include estimating weight before weighing, estimating the weight of others, reviewing trends in weight ideals, taking measurements of body parts or reinterpreting body-image misperceptions. Garner and Bemis (1982) recommend that anorexic patients be taught to reattribute faulty perceptions to their illness rather than to the body. "I can't make proper evaluations of myself because of my eating disorder. I'm like a color-blind person trying to buy a matching outfit, so I have to depend on the judgments of others since I can't trust my own."

Butters and Cash (1987) have shown that CBT is effective in reducing body-size overestimations among normal weight women. There is a real need to test cognitive–behavioral techniques in preventative programs aimed at normal women and especially at young adolescent girls. Puberty triggers a dramatic increase in overweight mislabeling and weight loss pursuits. On the day of one survey, 63% of high school girls were dieting, compared to only 16% of boys (Rosen & Gross, 1987). Since the majority of eating-disordered women report onset during adolescence, teenage dieting is not trivial but is a potentially life-threatening behavior (Freedman, 1984). Correcting body-image distortions at that crucial developmental stage can have important therapeutic value. In one study, the body cathexis scores of students rose after taking a psychology of adjustment class that included structured group activity and guided fantasy (Clance, Matthews, & Joesting, 1979). Prophylactic interventions such as this should not only sensitize young women to cultural pressures for weight loss but also teach them how to actively defend against it.

Social factors seem to have a more adverse effect on women's body image than on men's. Females are preoccupied and dissatisfied with more body parts than are males (Cash et al., 1986; Franzoi & Herzog, 1987). Females are also more concerned about their looks in general and more interested in changing their appearance (Cash et al., 1986; Jackson, Sullivan, & Hymes, 1987). The very parts that women judge most harshly are those they consider most essential to female attractiveness (Franzoi & Shields, 1984).

On the BSRQ, women are more appearance oriented, more illness oriented, more sensitive to weight issues, but less fitness oriented then men (Cash & Brown, 1989). Beyond these real differences, however, there is also an overgeneralization and exaggeration (i.e., stereotype) of the magnitude of perceived sex differences, including a disparaging assumption about the body image of women. Many therapists no doubt hold these same biased expectations, and researchers are guilty of perpetuating disfunctional stereotypes by focusing only on females in their body-image research (Cash, 1988). In the classic study by Broverman, Broverman, Clarkson, Rosencrantz, and Vogel (1970), clinicians rated healthy males and healthy people similarly on personality traits, whereas they judged mentally healthy females to be more preoccupied with appearance than is normal for a healthy person.

Playing out the feminine role can therefore be a mental-health hazard. The universality of body-image dissatisfaction in women has been described as a "normative discontent" that is epidemic (Lacey & Birtchnell, 1986; Streigel-Moore et al., 1986). Body-image conflicts are so common because it is difficult to feel like a normal woman and a normal person when these social roles are incompatible. For example, I complain that high heels hurt yet sometimes I wear them to look right. The "healthy" *person* within me says "take them off, they feel awful," while the "healthy" *woman* within me says "leave them on, they look great." I'm caught in a no-win situation. By examining their cognitions about such gender-role conflicts, clients can begin to understand how the desire for social conformity causes body-image anxiety, self-consciousness, and shame.

Since body-image problems are exacerbated by gender-role expectations, CBT can be implemented more effectively by incorporating a feminist approach. Feminist therapy shares with CBT an emphasis on the importance of social conditioning, on controlling situational variables, and on acquiring assertion skills (Freedman, 1988; Lazarus, 1974). The following components of a feminist approach are especially relevant to body-image problems:

1. Therapy rests on a basic belief that the female body and its functions are neither imperfect, deficient, or repulsive, but are normal as is. Reproductive events like menstruation and menopause are celebrated rather than hidden or denigrated. Specific questions are raised: For example, why does the female body have so much ornamental value, and why are painful aesthetic alterations needed to "normalize" it?

2. Therapy encourages assertive behavior that is competent, autonomous, and directed toward self-development rather than self-destruction. The stereotype of women as passive victims of their gender or of their bodies is challenged.

3. Therapy assumes that the personal is also political and that adjusting to prescribed gender roles just because they exist can be unhealthy. Such stereotypic images as the super woman, super mom, super sexpot, super hero make the body highly vulnerable to commercial exploitation.

4. Therapy draws on so called "feminine weaknesses" as human strengths. Traits of vulnerability, sensitivity, emotionality, patience, generosity, and social competence are used as tools to reconstruct body image.

Clinicians who are unfamiliar or uncomfortable with feminist psychology may find it expedient to refer clients to self-help resources such as Freedman (1988), Hutchinson (1985), Kano (1989), and Orbach (1978).

When working from a feminist perspective, group therapy has special value because it permits experiential techniques that challenge social stereotypes. For example, Kearney-Cooke (1989) had group members line up according to their weight. While jockeying for their position in line, they confronted the competitive aspects of the "Miss America mentality," and they considered how the goal of having a better body than other women confounds their relationships with jealousy. They were also asked to dress up like the goddess of fertility, then walk among each other throwing fertile seeds and feeling the procreative power of their maternal bodies. Afterward, one patient insightfully observed, "When I am sowing the seeds I am giving like my mother. . . but when I give, I end up alone. If I stay thin I don't have to lose myself by giving everything to others because it looks like I don't have anything 'extra' that people expect me to give."

Although it may be harder to conduct formal cognitive restructuring in groups, they do facilitate more realistic body images through interpersonal comparison. Self-disclosure by group members helps to normalize problems, and self-confrontation combines with group confrontation to break down resistance. Cognitive group therapy also provides relational support that goes beyond the therapeutic alliance.

CONCLUSION

The multiple aspects of body image beg for a multi-pronged treatment approach that includes perceptual, affective, cognitive, and behavioral components. A small but growing body of research shows consistent positive evidence that CBT reduces body-image distortion and dysphoria. Since body-image problems manifest in diverse ways, they must be approached by diverse therapeutic techniques.

Interventions based on standard cognitive–behavioral procedures must be empirically tested to determine their effects on body image. This can only be done through controlled outcome research that includes systematic trials, comparative samples, with long-term follow-up. To date, such research has been heavily focused on weight and eating disorders, especially among females. But body-image disorders include a variety of other dysmorphic complaints that are appropriate targets for CBT—concerns about stature, balding, breast size, or racial features.

Much can be gained by studying "normal" populations. For instance, what are the cognitive and behavioral factors that permit some physically unattractive people to maintain a positive body image while other very attractive people suffer from negative body image? Which of the many cognitive–behavioral techniques can influence the core personality factors and the underlying basic beliefs that help people maintain positive body-image affect over time?

Finally, clinicians have a responsibility to examine their own biases about weight or about the proper display of gender role, and to guard against expecting clients to adjust themselves to social norms that are stereotyped extremes. With regard to the body, as in other things, a good strategy seems to be one of moderation. Since perceived happiness is associated with intermediate levels of physical attractiveness, this might be emphasized as an adaptive goal. The gap between body images and ideal images can be narrowed, not only by improving cognitions about body image, but by actively challenging idealized social standards so that they become more realistic.

REFERENCES

Archer, R. P., & Cash, T. F. (1985). Physical attractiveness and maladjustment among psychiatric inpatients. *Journal of Social and Clinical Psychology*, *3*, 170–180.

Beck, A. T (1970). Role of fantasies in psychotherapy and psychopathology. *Journal of Nervous and Mental Disease, 150,* 3–17.

Beck, A. T. (1973). *The diagnosis and management of depression.* Philadelphia: University of Pennsylvania Press.

Beck, A. T. (1976). *Cognitive therapy and the emotional disorders* . New York: International Universities Press.

Beck, A. T., & Emery, G. (1979). *Cognitive therapy of anxiety and phobic disorders.* Philadelphia: Center for Cognitive Therapy.

Berscheid, E., & Walster, E. (1974). Physical attractiveness. In L. Berkowitz (Ed.), *Advances in experimental social psychology: Vol. 7* (pp. 158–216). New York: Academic Press.

Borysenko, J. (1988). *Minding the body, mending the mind.* New York: Bantam Books.

Broverman, I., Broverman, D., Clarkson, F., Rosencrantz, P., & Vogel, S. (1970). Sex role stereotypes and clinical judgments of mental health. *Journal of Consulting and Clinical Psychology, 34,* 1–7.

Brown, T. A., Cash, T. F., & Lewis, R. J. (1989). Body-image disturbances in adolescent female binge-purgers: A brief report of the results of a national survey in the U.S.A. *Journal of Child Psychology and Psychiatry, 30,* 605–613.

Bruch, H. (1973). *Eating disorders: Obesity, anorexia nervosa, and the person within.* New York: Basic Books.

Burns, D. (1980). *Feeling good: The new mood therapy.* New York: William Morrow.

Butters, J. W. (1985). *The controlled evaluation of a cognitive–behavioral treatment program for body-image dissatisfaction in college women.* Doctoral dissertation, Virginia Consortium for Professional Psychology, Norfolk, Virginia.

Butters, J. W., & Cash, T. F. (1987). Cognitive–behavioral treatment of women's body image dissatisfaction. *Journal of Consulting and Clinical Psychology, 55,* 889–897.

Buss, A. H. (1980). *Self-consciousness and social anxiety.* San Francisco: Freeman.

Carver, C. S., & Scheier, M. F. (1978). Self-focusing effects of dispositional self-consciousness, mirror presence, and audience presence. *Journal of Personality and Social Psychology, 36,* 324–332.

Cash, T. F (1985). Physical appearance and mental health. In J. A. Graham & A. Kligman (Eds.), *The psychology of cosmetic treatments* (pp. 196–216). New York: Praeger Scientific.

Cash, T. F. (1988, November). Body image and beyond. In D. Williamson (chair), *Body image or images.* Symposium conducted at the meeting of the Association for the Advancement of Behavior Therapy, New York.

Cash, T. F., & Brown, T. A. (1989). Gender and body images: Stereotypes and realities. *Sex Roles, 21,* 361–373.

Cash, T. F., Cash, D. W., & Butters, J. W. (1983). "Mirror, mirror on the wall. . . " Contrast effects and self-evaluations of physical attractiveness. *Personality and Social Psychology Bulletin, 9,* 351–358.

Cash, T. F., & Duncan, N. C. (1984). Physical attractiveness stereotyping among Black American college students. *Journal of Social Psychology, 122,* 71–77.

Cash, T. F., & Hicks, K. L. (1990). Being fat versus thinking fat: Relationships with body image, eating behaviors, and well-being. *Cognitive Therapy and Research, 14,* 327–341.

Cash, T. F., & Kilcullen, R. (1985). The eye of the beholder: Susceptibility to sexism and beautyism in evaluation of managerial applicants. *Journal of Applied Social Psychology, 15,* 591–605.

Cash, T. F., Lewis, R. J., & Keeton, P. (1987, March). *Development and validation of the Body-Image Automatic Thoughts Questionnaire: A measure of body-related cognitions.* Paper presented at the meeting of the Southeastern Psychological Association. Atlanta, Georgia.

Cash, T. F., & Smith, E. (1982). Physical attractiveness and personality among American college students. *Journal of Psychology, 111,* 183–191.

Cash, T. F., Winstead, B. W., & Janda, L. H. (1986). The great American shape up: Body image survey report. *Psychology Today, 20,* 30–37.

Clance, P. R., Matthews, T. V., & Joesting, J. (1979). Body-cathexis and self-cathexis in an interactional, awareness training class. *Perceptual and Motor Skills, 48,* 221–222.

Cooper, P. J., Taylor, M. J., Cooper, Z., & Fairburn, C. G. (1987). The development and validation of the Body Shape Questionnaire. *International Journal of Eating Disorders, 6,* 485–494.

Davies, E., & Furnham, A. (1986). The dieting and body shape concerns of adolescent females. *Journal of Child Psychology and Psychiatry, 27,* 417–428.

Dobson, K. (Ed.). (1987). *Handbook of cognitive–behavioral therapies.* New York: Guilford.

Downs, A. C., & Harrison, S. K. (1985). Embarrassing age spots or just plain ugly? Physical attractiveness stereotyping as an instrument of sexism on American television commercials. *Sex Roles, 13,* 9–19.

Dworkin, S. H., & Kerr, B. A. (1987). Comparison of interventions for women experiencing body image problems. *Journal of Counseling Psychology, 34,* 136–140.

Dykens, E. M., & Gerrard, M. (1986). Psychological profiles of purging bulimics, repeat dieters, and controls. *Journal of Consulting and Clinical Psychology, 54,* 283–288.

Ellis, A. (1962). *Reason and emotion in psychotherapy.* New York: Lyle Stuart.

Ellis, A., & Greiger, R. (1977). *Handbook of rational emotive therapy.* New York: Springer Press.

Fairburn, C. G., Cooper, Z., & Cooper, P. J. (1986). The clinical features and maintenance of bulimia nervosa. In K. D. Brownell & J. P. Foreyt (Eds.), *Handbook of eating disorders.* New York: Basic Books.

Fallon, A. E., & Rozin, P. (1985). Sex differences in perception of desirable body shape. *Journal of Abnormal Psychology, 94,* 102–105.

Fisher, S. (1986). *Development and structure of body image,* Hillsdale, NJ: Erlbaum.

Folkins, C. H., & Sime, W. E. (1981). Physical fitness training and mental health. *American Psychologist, 36,* 373–389.

Franzoi, S. L., & Shields, S. A. (1984). The body esteem scale; Multi-dimensional structure and sex differences in a college population. *Journal of Personality Assessment, 48,* 173–178.

Franzoi, S., L., & Herzog, M. E. (1987). Judging physical attractiveness: What body aspects do we use? *Personality and Social Psychology Bulletin, 13,* 19–33.

Freedman, R. J. (1984). Reflections of beauty as it relates to health in adolescent females. *Women and Health, 9,* 29–45.

Freedman, R. J. (1986). *Beauty bound.* Lexington, MA: Lexington Books.

Freedman, R. J. (1988). *Bodylove.* New York: Harper & Row.

Freeman, R. J. Beach, B., Davis, R., & Solyom, L. (1985). The prediction of relapse in bulimia nervosa. *Journal of Psychiatric Research, 19,* 349–353.

Garner, D. M., & Bemis, K. M. (1982). A cognitive–behavioral approach to anorexia nervosa. *Cognitive Therapy and Research, 6,* 213–150.

Garner, D. M., & Garfinkel, P. E. (1981). Body image in anorexia nervosa: Measurement, theory and clinical implications. *International Journal of Psychiatry in Medicine, 11,* 263–284.

Garner, D. M., Garfinkel, P. E., & Olmsted, M. P. (1983). An overview of sociocultural factors in the development of anorexia nervosa. In P. Darby (Ed.), *Anorexia nervosa: Recent developments in research* (pp. 65–82). New York: Alan R. Liss.

Garner, D. M., & Garner, P. E. (1980). The eating attitudes test: An index of the symptoms of anorexia nervosa. *Psychological Medicine, 9,* 273–279.

Garner, D. M., & Olmsted, M. P. (1984). *Eating Disorder Inventory Manual.* Odessa, Florida: Psychological Assessment Resources.

Hollon, S. D., & Beck, A. T. (1979). Cognitive therapy of depression. In P. C Kendall & S. D. Hollon (Eds.), *Cognitive–behavioral interventions: Theory, research and procedures.* New York: Academic Press.

Hutchinson, M. G. (1982). Transforming body image: Your body, friend or foe? *Women and Therapy, 1,* 59–67.

Hutchinson, M. G. (1985). *Transforming body image*. Trumansburg, New York: The Crossing Press.

Jackson, L., & Cash, T. F. (1985). Components of gender stereotypes and their implication for inferences on stereotypic and nonstereotypic dimensions. *Personality and Social Psychology Bulletin, 11*, 326–344.

Jacskon, L. A., Sullivan, L. A., & Hymes, J. S. (1987). Gender, gender role and physical appearance. *Journal of Psychology, 121*, 51–56.

Joesting, J. (1981). Comparison of students who exercise with those who do not. *Perceptual and Motor Skills, 53*, 426–428.

Jurasky, L. (1988, August). The bimbo and the bitch. In *The demand for beauty and women's mental health*. Symposium conducted at the conference of the American Psychological Association, Atlanta, Georgia.

Kano, S. (1989). *Making peace with food: A step-by-step guide to freedom from diet/weight conflict.* New York: Harper & Row.

Kaplan, S. J. (1986). *The private practice of behavior therapy*. New York: Plenum.

Katzman, M. A., & Wolchik, S. A. (1984). Bulimia and binge eating in college women: A comparison of personality and behavioral characteristics. *Journal of Consulting and Clinical Psychology, 52*, 423–428.

Kazdin, A. E., & Wilson, G. T. (1978). *Evaluation of behavior therapy: Issues, evidence and research strategies*. Lincoln: University of Nebraska Press.

Kearney-Cooke, A. (1989). Reclaiming the body: Using guided imagery in the treatment of body image disturbance among bulimic women. In L. Hornyak & E. Baker, (Eds.), *Handbook of experiential techniques in the treatment of eating disorders* (pp. 11–33). New York: Guilford Press.

Keeton, W. P., Cash, T. F., & Brown T. A (1990). Body image or body images: Comparative multidimensional assessment among college students. *Journal of Personality Assessment, 54*, 213–230.

Kendall, P. C., & Hollon, S. D. (Eds.) (1979). *Cognitive–behavioral interventions: Theory, research, and procedures*. New York: Academic Press.

Kendall, P. C., & Korgeski, G. P. (1979). Assessment and cognitive–behavioral interventions. *Cognitive Therapy and Research, 3*, 1–21.

Kenrick, D. T., & Gutierres, S. E. (1980). Contrast effects and judgments of physical attractiveness: When beauty becomes a social problem. *Journal of Personality and Social Psychology, 38*, 131–140.

Lacey, J. H., & Birtchnell, S. A. (1986). Body image and its disturbances. *Journal of Psychosomatic Research. 30*, 623–631.

Lazarus, A. (1974). Women in behavior therapy. In V. Franks & V. Burtle (Eds.), *Women in therapy* (pp. 217–229). New York: Brunner/Mazel.

Lerner, R. M., Orlos, J. B., & Knapp, J. R. (1976). Physical attractiveness, physical effectiveness and self-concept in late adolescence. *Adolescence, 11*, 313–326.

Masters, W. H., & Johnson, V. E. (1970). *Human sexual inadequacies*. Boston: Little, Brown.

Mccrea, C. W., Summerfield, A. B., & Rosen, B. (1982). Body image: A selective review of existing measurement techniques. *British Journal of Medical Psychology, 55*, 225–233.

Meichenbaum, D. H. (1977). *Cognitive behavior modification: An integrative approach*. New York: Plenum Press.

Miller, R. C., & Berman, J. S. (1983). The efficacy of cognitive behavior therapies: A quantitative review of the research evidence. *Psychological Bulletin, 94*, 39–53.

Mintz, L. B., & Betz, N. E. (1986). Sex differences in the nature, realism and correlates of body image. *Sex Roles, 15*, 185–195.

Noles, S. W., Cash, T. F., & Winstead, B. A. (1985). Body image, physical attractiveness, and depression. *Journal of Consulting and Clinical Psychology, 53*, 88-94.

Orbach, S. (1978). *Fat is a feminist issue*. New York: Berkeley Books.

Rosen, J. C., & Gross, J. (1987). Prevalence of weight reducing and weight gaining in adolescent girls and boys. *Health Psychology, 6*, 131–147.

Rosen, J. C., Saltzberg, E., & Srebnik, D. (1989). Cognitive–behavior therapy for negative body image. *Behavior Therapy, 20*, 393–404.

Rozin, P., & Fallon, A. (1988). Body image, attitudes to weight, and misperceptions of figure preference of the opposite sex: A comparison of men and women in two generations. *Journal of Abnormal Psychology, 97*, 324–345.

Sankowsky, M. (1981). *The effect of a treatment based on the use of guided visu-kinesthetic imagery on the alteration of negative body-cathexis in women.* Unpublished doctoral dissertation, Boston University, Boston.

Secord, P. F., & Jourard, S. M. (1953). The appraisal of body cathexis and the self. *Journal of Consulting Psychology, 17*, 343–347.

Silverstein, B., Perdue, L., Peterson, B., & Kelly, E. (1986). The role of the mass media in promoting a thin standard of bodily attractiveness for women. *Sex Roles, 14*, 519–532.

Stake, J., & Lauer, M. L. (1987). The consequences of being overweight: A controlled study of gender differences. *Sex Roles, 17*, 31–47.

Striegel-Moore, R. H., Silberstein, L. R., & Rodin, J. (1986). Toward an understanding of risk factors for bulimia. *American Psychologist, 41*, 246–263.

Thompson, J. K., & Thompson, C. M. (1986). Body size distortion and self-esteem in asymptomatic, normal weight males and females. *International Journal of Eating Disorders, 5*, 1061–1068.

van der Velde, C. D. (1985). Body images of one's self and of others: Developmental and clinical significance. *American Journal of Psychiatry, 142*, 527–537.

Wilson, G. T., & Franks, C. M. (Eds.). (1982). *Contemporary behavior therapy: Conceptual and empirical foundations.* New York: Guilford Press.

Wooley, S. C., & Kearney-Cooke, A. (1986). In K. D. Brownell & J. P. Foreyt (Eds.), *Handbook of eating disorders* (pp. 476–501). New York: Basic Books.

CHAPTER 14

Somatopsychic Approaches to Psychotherapy and Personal Growth

Thomas Pruzinsky

This chapter describes forms of therapy that utilize bodily interventions to facilitate personal growth or psychological body-image change. Somatopsychic approaches to human change employ bodily interventions (e.g., movement and touch) to affect psychological functioning (e.g., body image). Moreover, the somatopsychic perspective assumes that if the goal is to change an individual's perceptions of and feelings about his/her body (i.e., body image), then working *directly* with the body and bodily experience is the most efficient approach to achieve this goal. Somatopsychic techniques include body movement (e.g., Bernstein, 1980; Caplan & England, 1980; Dosamantes-Alperson, 1974; Dosamantes-Alperson & Merrill, 1980; Duggan, 1981; Feldenkrais, 1972), muscle or skin manipulation (e.g., Rolph, 1980), and body-focused techniques integrated with verbal psychotherapy. Table 14.1 provides a representative, though not exhaustive, listing of the major somatopsychic forms of psychotherapy and personal growth.

BODY IMAGE AND CHANGE IN PSYCHOTHERAPY

In most forms of psychotherapy the patient is portrayed as a disembodied entity (Pruzinsky, 1984). The role of bodily experience in personality development and change is not often emphasized. In most approaches to psychotherapeutic change, the influence of the somatic component of human experience is limited to articulating the influence of the central nervous system or other physiological activity on cognition, emotion, and behavior. While these physiological processes are critical, they lack an understanding of the "lived body" (Dillon, 1978;

296

TABLE 14.1. SOMATOPSYCHIC APPROACHES TO PSYCHOTHERAPY AND PERSONAL GROWTH

I. *Movement-oriented techniques*
   A. Dance therapy
   B. The Alexander technique
   C. Feldenkrais methods

II. *Body manipulation (touch) oriented techniques*
   A. Structural integration (Rolfing)
   B. Massage therapy

III. *Integrated techniques*

   A. Reichian theraphy

   B. Neo-Reichian theraphy

      1. Radix neo-Reichian education

      2. Medical orgonomy

   C. Bioenergetics

   D. Gestalt therapy

   E. Other approaches

      1. Lomi body work

      2. Body energy therapy

      3. Keleman somatic oriented therapy

      4. Psychomotor psychotherapy

Moss, 1978). For somatopsychic therapists, this is a serious oversight because they believe that for clinically significant and lasting psychotherapeutic change to occur there must be change in the individual's body experiences (Brown, 1973; Geller, 1978; Pesso, 1969, 1973; Pesso & Pesso, 1981; Redfearn, 1970).

Reviewing the literature on the psychological impact of body image, Fisher (1986) concluded that our behavior is significantly influenced by the way in which we have psychologically adapted to our bodily experience. Therefore, it logically follows that to facilitate human change (i.e., behavioral, cognitive, and emotional change), we must address the patient's body experiences. If an individual's relationship with his/her body (i.e., feelings about the body—beyond the dimension of feelings regarding personal attractiveness) is related to many other aspects of self, then we would be remiss in not assessing this dimension of human experience.

In articulating the therapeutic techniques of Erickson, Haley (1973, 1985) documented Erickson's belief in the importance of body image in facilitating human change. Erickson assumed that the individual's experience and perception of his/her body is essential to consider in psychotherapy because of the close relationship between body perception and self-perception (Rosen & Ross, 1968). For Erickson, assessing the patient's body image was one of his first psychotherapeutic tasks; "in brief psychotherapy one of the important considerations is the body image . . . one of the first things you do, whether it is a man or a woman, is to try to find out what their body image is" (Haley, 1985, pp. 3–4). Erickson evaluated the patient's body image by observing the patients grooming, nonverbal behavior, and their manner of making physical contact (e.g., shaking hands) (Haley, 1985). Erickson would also explicitly ask the patient about his/her feelings and beliefs about his/her body (Haley, 1985). Given Erickson's renowned ability to facilitate human change, we should heed his recognition of the importance of body image in psychotherapy.

SOMATOPSYCHIC APPROACHES TO HUMAN CHANGE: BASIC ASSUMPTIONS

The somatopsychic approaches to psychotherapy implicitly or explicitly share basic assumptions about human nature. Most importantly, they share an emphasis on the interrelatedness of physical and psychological functioning (Brown, 1973; Geller, 1978; Hanna, 1970, 1973, 1979, 1980; Keleman, 1975, 1979; Rolf, 1977). They also share other basic assumptions, three of which are articulated below:

Assumption 1

The first assumption is that development of *the sense of "self" is based on the experience of being embodied*. We are born with bodies, but we are not born with a sense of self. The sense of self, of being distinct and having an existence independent of inanimate objects and other people, is based on our experience of being embodied (Dillon, 1978; Mahler & McDevitt, 1982). On the basis of bodily experience, that is on the basis of a difference between "in here" and "out there," a basic sense of sense of self develops (Fisher, 1986). Fenichel (1945) makes this point clear:

> In the development of reality the conception of one's own body plays a very special role. . . . At first, there is only the perception of tension, that is, of "inside something." Later, with an awareness that an object exists to quiet this tension, we have an "outside something." Due to the simultaneous occurrence of both outer tactile and inner sensory data one's own body becomes something apart from the rest of the world and thus the discerning of the *self from the non-self* is made possible. The sum total of the mental representations of the body and its organs, the so-called body-image, constitutes the idea of "I" and is of basic importance for the further formation of the ego. (Fenichel, 1945, pp. 35–36)

The infant's "psychological birth" occurs through the separation–individuation process—a process mediated primarily through bodily experience

(Mahler & McDevitt, 1982). Separation refers to the infant's emergence from symbiotic fusion with the mother. Individuation refers to the child's assumption of his/her own individual characteristics (Mahler, Pine, & Bergmann, 1975). Two critical influences on the separation–individuation process are touch (mediated through the skin) and movement (mediated through kinesthesis and proprioception).

Touch

The initial interactions between the mother and infant occur through skin contact. *In utero*, the child is physically symbiotic with the mother. After birth, the child is held, fed, cleaned, protected, and nurtured in close contact with the mother's skin. A great deal of emotion and communication is expressed in the tactile contact between mother and child (Montague, 1978). In the child's early months and years, communication is largely through touch.

The conduit for this communication is the skin. The nature and quality of this physical contact is critical in the child's development (Montague, 1978). Perhaps most importantly, the skin provides the basis for defining what is "self" and what is not "self" (Mahler & McDevitt, 1982). Through communication via touch (e.g., through body care) the mother can convey loving acceptance, caring, and a sense of safety, or can convey the opposite. Additionally, Harlow and his colleagues (e.g., Harlow & Zimmerman, 1958, cited in Montague, 1978) demonstrated that primates have a need for tactile stimulation that can be more powerful than the need for food.

From the earliest moments, the emotional quality of the tactile experience of the child begins to influence his/her development of identity, including the all-important development of a boundary between the self and the world. This boundary development provides the psychological foundation for the sense of self (Mahler & McDevitt, 1982). Fisher (1986) summarizes the empirical support for the influence of the body-image boundary on many psychological variables. Thus, the psychological separation between the world and the individual, the creation of the body-image boundary, is mediated by tactile experience. The role of touch, and the sensations and emotions associated with the skin, have yet to be fully realized (Montague, 1978; Pruzinsky, 1984).

Movement

The sense of self and the boundary between the self and the world solidify as the child begins to *move* away (psychologically and physically) from the mother. The separation–individuation process is partly mediated by movement and associated kinesthetic and proprioceptive cues (Mahler & McDevitt, 1982; Stark, 1982). Mahler and McDevitt (1982) underscore the importance of proprioception in the separation–individuation process. "What we want to stress . . . is that the available observational evidence points to the conclusion that at this very earliest stage of development, proprioception . . . conveys the first glimmerings of a primitive core of a body self" (Mahler & McDevitt, 1982, p. 829). Schilder (1935) also emphasized the importance of movement and proprioception in his "postural model" of body image.

Assumption 2

The second basic assumption of the somatopsychic therapies is that all experience takes place in the context of bodily experience, in particular, against a constant background of kinesthetic and proprioceptive cues. Whatever our emotional, interpersonal, cognitive, or behavioral experience, there is an ever-present (albeit tacit) experience of being embodied (Dillon, 1978). How we experience our bodies may not only serve as constant background for all experience but *may* also influence perception and memory.

Perception

Perception refers to the way in which we construct our world from an infinite range of available stimuli. The importance of visual and auditory perceptual information is obvious. However, the influence of proprioceptive and kinesthetic senses on perception have not been emphasized in contemporary theories of perception, though these influences have been noted by important psychological theorists in previous eras (e.g., the sensory-tonic theory of perception) (Wapner & Werner, 1965; Witkin, Lewis, Hertzman, Meissner, Machover, & Wapner, 1954). The critical role of kinesthesis in perception was made by a leading theorist of structuralism—Titchner.

> In Titchner's view there is one special type of sensation that is paramount as a contextual meaning providing process, namely, kinaesthesis. As the organism faces the situation it adopts an attitude toward it, and the kinaesthetic sensations resulting from this attitude (assuming it to be muscular tension or reaction) give the context and meaning of the object to which the organism is reacting. (Allport, 1955; quoted in Fisher & Cleveland, 1968, p. 41)

Examples of empirical research may help clarify these points. For example, Pope (1978) demonstrated that postural changes influence individuals' reports of the perception of their internal as well as external environments; in other words, focus of attention was influenced by posture. Kroth (1970) demonstrated a similar influence of posture on reports of cognitive and emotional processes. Therefore, it may be that, in a manner not yet understood nor fully explored, bodily experience, via kinesthetic cues, influences the manner in which we perceive the world (e.g., Beigel, 1953; Deutsch, 1952; Gellhorn, 1964; Guze, 1953; Pasquarelli & Bull, 1951).

Memory

An assumption of many of somatopsychic therapies is that a relationship exists between kinesthesis, proprioception, and memory. The general idea, odd as it may seem, is that memory can be "stored in muscle." Particular muscular patterns (experienced as kinesthetic sensations) are believed to represent particular forms of memory (see Geller, 1978). That is, particular forms of holding one's self can be "stored" in the body image and, therefore, provide cues for the release of particular memories.

This point is made with respect to dance therapy. "The connection that develops between physical action and inner feeling state results from *muscular memory* associated with the feeling" (Stark, 1982, p. 311; emphasis added). This relationship between muscle and memory may not seem so far-fetched when one considers the very close relationship between facial expression (mediated by muscles) and emotion. Ekman and his colleagues (Ekman, Levenson, & Friesen, 1983) have documented the role of facial expression on emotional experience; particular patterns of contraction and relaxation of muscles are directly associated with particular emotional experiences.

An interesting example of memory being associated with particular bodily states is an empirical investigation by Rand and Wapner (1967). These investigators studied the role of postural positioning in memory storage and retrieval. In this study, subjects who learned nonsense syllables while standing were better able to recall those same syllables while standing, than while sitting. Other studies have produced similar findings (e.g., Berdach & Bakan, 1967). One rationale for why body position may influence memory is that posture and the general pattern of muscle tonus, and the subsequent kinesthetic and proprioceptive sensations provide a tacit context for learning and memory. Contextual knowledge is more easily retained and recalled than acontextual knowledge (Jenkins, 1971).

Assumption 3

The third assumption of somatopsychic forms of therapy is that effective change in human functioning must address both the physical and psychological levels of human existence. Habitual patterns of perception, memory, experiencing emotion, and processing information are assumed to be important in defining the self and the focus of psychotherapy. In verbally oriented psychotherapy, we assume that changes need to be made in ingrained patterns of perception, memory, cognition, emotional experience, physiological arousal, and behavior.

Somatopsychic therapies additionally assume that habitual patterns of experiencing the body and habitual patterns of muscle tension also need to be changed. Just as there are habitual patterns of cognitive and emotional response, there also habitual body-focused responses. For example, on the basis of past experiences, we may have a habitual pattern of motorically responding when we are touched. When in a new situation, we may habitually respond in a similar manner, even though there is no necessary reason to do so. The important point is that we all learn ways of coping with the world. These coping strategies are cognitive, emotional, and *bodily*. Fight, flight, and frightful immobility are indeed bodily expressions and experiences. Long after the need to cope in such a manner is gone we continue to employ the same defensive mechanisms in order to protect ourselves. These defense mechanisms are repeatedly employed, internalized, and become unconscious (tacit). Evaluating and changing these bodily mechanisms is a major focus of the somatopsychic forms of therapy.

Enhanced Body Awareness

The first step toward any type of change is awareness of the problematic patterns of adaptation and reaction. For example, for the cognitive–behavioral behavior therapist, one of the first therapeutic tasks is to instruct the patient in self-monitoring of behavior and cognition. Patients are taught to discern the patterns of thoughts and behaviors associated with particular interpersonal and emotional situations. Similarly, to promote psychological change via bodily oriented interventions, one must become more in tune with the messages the body provides and the influence of bodily experience on our thoughts, feelings, and personalities (Stark, 1982). There must be self-monitoring of bodily experience.

Becoming more aware of bodily experience is a challenging task. Many proponents of somatopsychic therapies assume that our cultural experience has led us to be out of touch with the "lived experience" of our bodies (Geller, 1978). While we attempt to maximize bodily pleasure, and emphasize the importance of appearance, hygiene, and fitness, little education is provided regarding appreciating the experience of embodiedment; an ignorance, some would argue, borne out of existential concerns and a denial of death (Becker, 1973). Wilbur (1980) makes these points clear:

> As it turns out, few of us have lost our minds, but most of us have long ago lost our bodies, and I'm afraid that we must take that literally. It seems, in fact, that "I" am almost sitting on my body as if I were a horseman riding on a horse. I beat it or praise it, I feed, clean and nurse it when necessary. I urge it on without consulting it and I hold it back against its will. When my body-horse is well-behaved I generally ignore it, but when it gets unruly— which is all to often—I pull our the whip to be beat it back into reasonable submission.
>   Indeed, my body just seems to dangle along under me. I no longer approach the world *with* my body but *on* my body. I'm up here, it's down there and I'm basically uneasy about just what it is that *is* down there. My consciousness is almost exclusively head consciousness—I *am* my head, but I *own* my body. Thus a split is created; a boundary, a split, a fissure, or in the words of Lowen a *block*. (Wilbur, 1979, pp. 106-107)

This theme regarding the need for greater awareness of being embodied unifies the somatopsychic therapies. Awareness of the body requires time and energy to develop. Such awareness is a skill that needs to be learned and practiced. The type of awareness that needs to be developed is described by Brown (1973):

> The special kind of perceptual awareness we have to cultivate before we can truly identify with our bodies has to remain unfocused and diffused; an essentially undifferentiated mode of perception in which there is the capacity to receive simultaneously in awareness an undefinable number of different kinaesthetic and proprioceptive stimuli from different parts of the body. (Brown, 1973, p. 101)

Each form of therapy devoted to work with the body has its own methods of developing body awareness.

Change

The body-oriented approaches to therapy " . . . are based on the principle that is becoming more obvious to researchers on this level, a principal that can be loosely stated as follows: *"For every mental 'problem' or 'knot,' there is a corresponding bodily 'knot,' and vice-versa* since, in fact, the body and the mind are not two" (Wilbur, 1977, pp. 244–245). This premise is summarized by dance therapist Trudi Schoop (1971). While she uses dance therapy as an example, the essence of what she has to say has broader thematic significance:

> If I am correct in assuming that the mind and the body are interactive, I feel a problem of mental disturbance can be influenced from either side. When psychoanalysis brings about change in the mental attitude, there should be a corresponding physical change. And when dance therapy brings about a change in the body behavior, there should be a corresponding change in the mind. (Schoop, 1971, p. 5; quoted in Geller, 1978, p. 349)

By improving one system of human functioning (e.g., the body), other systems are improved (e.g., cognition and emotion). In contrast to verbal psychotherapy, somatopsychic therapies work with body structure and movement and the general experience of being embodied.

BODY-THERAPY TECHNIQUES

Systems of psychotherapy and personal growth that focus on body manipulation increased in popularity during the development of the human potential movement (Corsini, 1981; Green, 1981). They share certain philosophical similarities and assumptions. While sharing a focus on bodily experience in human functioning, they nevertheless differ in terms of vocabulary, specific techniques, as well as their theories of psychopathology and of human change processes (Geller, 1978).

The following section describes somatopsychic approaches to human growth and change, focusing on those utilizing primarily movement or touch techniques and those integrating verbal and somatopsychic techniques.[1] No attempt is made to comprehensively describe this voluminous and sometimes esoteric literature. Detailed descriptions of the techniques are available in the primary sources and comparisons among the major therapies are available (e.g., Brown, 1973; Lowen, 1975).

BODY-MOVEMENT TECHNIQUES

Most forms of verbal psychotherapy assume that all participants are seated in chairs. Little or no attention is paid to the meaning of body movement or the use of body movement to facilitate therapeutic change. For these verbally oriented therapies, body movement is important only in terms of evaluating nonverbal communication (Steere, 1982). For somatopsychic therapies, however, an individual's style of movement or posture is assumed to be an important personality component (e.g., Alexander, 1958, 1974; Feldenkrais, 1973; Geller, 1978; Kepner, 1987, Minton, 1989; North, 1972). Therefore, adjustments in habitual patterns of movement are considered essential for facilitating change in human functioning and experience.

Dance-Movement Therapy

Many therapeutic approaches use movement to promote human change (e.g., Alexander, 1974; Feldenkrais, 1973; Pesso, 1969, 1973, 1980). Dance-movement therapy is a particularly well-known form of somatopsychic therapy. It is utilized primarily as an adjunctive treatment for a range of psychological problems, including learning disabilities, mental retardation, autism, and schizophrenia (Chace, 1953; Duggan, 1981; Espernak, 1981; Frick, 1982), as well eating disorders (Kaslow & Eicher, 1988; Krueger & Schofield, 1987; Rice, Hardenbergh, & Hornyak, 1989; Stark, Aronow, & McGeehan, 1989).

The Process of Dance-Movement Therapy

Although the techniques and theoretical background of dance-movement therapies differ from traditional verbal psychotherapies, there are many impor-

---

[1]Separating the techniques into movement, touch, and "integrated" approaches is somewhat artificial. Most somatopsychic therapies use movement *and* touch *and* integrate the focus on bodily processes into the person's total experience. However, some approaches emphasize either movement *or* touch and some therapeutic approaches more comprehensively integrate verbal psychotherapeutic techniques with bodily approaches.

tant similarities between them. For example, both approaches require a correct match between the type of therapy employed and the patient's particular problems (Stark, 1982). Additionally, the nature of the therapist patient relationship is critical (Dosamontes-Alperson, 1987), and the therapeutic goal for both approaches is the healthier functioning of the individual (Bernstein, 1986; Stark, 1982).

> In dance-movement therapy, by working with muscular patterns and focusing on the interrelationship between psychological and physiological processes, clients are helped to experience, identify, and express feelings and conflicts. From this kinaesthetic level, individuals and groups are led to further discovery of emotional material through symbolic representations, images, memories, and personal meanings of their life experiences. Through movement interaction, the dance-movement therapist helps clients to develop their self-awareness, work through emotional blocks, explore alternative modes of behavior, gain a clear perception of themselves and others, and effect behavioral changes that will lead to healthier functioning. (Stark, 1982, p. 308)

Dance-movement therapy utilizes diverse techniques, including movement exaggeration, tension discharge exercises, and the use of rhythmic movement for emotional expression (Stark, 1982). Very often these are conducted in a group therapy format. Verbal integration of the body-focused experience is employed (Stark & Lohn, 1989). The theoretical interpretation of the movement and psychological themes depends on the therapist's theoretical perspective (e.g., Jungian, Gestalt, Transpersonal; Bernstein, 1986).

Dance-movement therapies have three major goals, including changes in self-awareness, body experience and functioning, and interpersonal functioning (Stark, 1982).

Changes in Self-Awareness

The first step in facilitating psychological change is developing self-awareness. For the dance-movement therapist, an awareness of the relationship between bodily experience and emotional experience is primary:

> Intrinsic to dance-movement therapy practice is the belief that one must be aware of bodily experiences and their meanings (sensory and kinaesthetic experiences and emotional states) for self-understanding. . . .
> The most direct experience that one can have with one's self is through one's body. The physical experience of one's muscular actions and kinaesthetic sense provides an immediate way of knowing and experiencing one's self. (Stark, 1982, pp. 315–316)

Changes in Body Experience and Functioning

Through dance-movement therapy, patients develop new ways of experiencing and using their bodies. Patients become aware of the relationships between their current habitual patterns of movement, associated kinesthetic and proprioceptive sensations, and related inter- or intrapersonal conflicts or concerns. Patients learn to express and release emotions and tensions associated with intrapersonal and interpersonal concerns by using movement. Patients can explore their range of choices with respect to body movement and explore as well as develop new movement patterns while learning how to communicate through body movement (Stark, 1982). These changes in the use of the body are intended to result in "a sense of bodily integration and coordination, and . . . a realistic body image" (Stark, 1982, p. 314).

Changes in Interpersonal Functioning

Changes in interpersonal functioning in dance-movement therapy occur partially as a result of interacting with other group members or through the interaction between the dance therapist and patient. In the course of therapy, patients become aware of the their habits of movement and posture with respect to interpersonal interactions. For example, a patient may tend to move away from authoritative or dominant individuals. Within the context of therapy, attempts to change this behavior are explored. Patients may be requested to physically "reach out" and "make contact" with the therapist or group members and to explore the nature of their physical movement toward or away from others. In this manner, the goals of self-awareness and body-awareness are integrated with influential processes of interpersonal functioning.

The combination of self-awareness of movement, changes in body experience and body functioning, and exploring the relationship between movement and interpersonal relationships may facilitate body-image change. According to Stark (1982); "Movement evokes changes in body image. Articulation of body parts, recognition of bodily sensations such as breathing, or awareness of muscular activity, are just a few examples of how kinesthetic sensations can contribute to the recognition and development of body image" (p. 312). In the process of dance-movement therapy, patients are encouraged to act out in movement feelings of body-image distortion, as well as alternative patterns of movement to facilitate a change in body-image (Chace, 1975; Stark, 1982).

The Alexander Technique and Feldenkrais Methods

Another system of human change primarily utilizing body movement and position is the *Alexander Technique*. This approach is designed to improve body functioning by facilitating awareness of one's movement habits, and by promoting postural realignment and muscle coordination (Alexander, 1958, 1974; Barker, 1978; Caplan & Englard, 1980; Jones, 1976). Change is achieved by the individual giving "largely passive mental directions (for example, "Let the back lengthen and widen") to his own body while the teacher uses his hands to guide the student into an improved kinesthetic experience" (Caplan & Englard, 1980,

p. 24). The Alexander Technique focuses on the manner in which the head rests on the spine, the use of the neck, and spinal cord function (Frager, 1980). While not strictly a form of psychotherapy, it "constitutes a significant psychotherapeutic tool or orientation to life. Its approach is holistic, furthering positive change and self-awareness through mind–body integration" (Caplan & England, 1980, p. 25) and is employed as an adjunct to verbal psychotherapy (Caplan & England, 1980).

The Alexander Technique has been extensively researched, utilizing experimental methodologies, in a programmatic series of studies documenting the positive effects of the technique (Jones, 1976). Additionally, a great deal of "testimonial" support, from prominent individuals in human behavior, including John Dewey and Fritz Perls (Barker, 1978; Caplan & England, 1980; Jones, 1976; Tengwall, 1981), exists for the technique's effectiveness.

The work of Moshe Feldenkrais is similarly focused on promoting increased awareness and efficiency of body functioning (Feldenkrais, 1972; Rywerant, 1983). Feldenkrais's work is based on his awareness of the relationship between body experience and self-image (Feldenkrais, 1972; Frager, 1980). Feldenkrais's techniques for promoting self-change are separated into two approaches: awareness through movement and functional integration (Frager, 1980).

"Awareness through movement" is composed of a series of exercises, most often conducted in groups. In his book illustrating awareness through movement, Feldenkrais describes a series of "twelve practical lessons." For example, in a lesson on "perfecting the self-image," Feldenkrais gives exercises and instructions for attending to body awareness, stating that in this particular 1-hour lesson: "You will learn the effect of movements of the head on muscular tension, the effect of imagined movement on real movement, and to inhibit verbalization in imagined movement—all of which leads to completion of the body image" (Feldenkrais, 1972, p. 130).

The functional integration component of Feldenkrais's system employs individual sessions between the patient and therapist, focusing on developing awareness of bodily sensations and the "natural readjustment of posture, muscle tension, and body image . . . " (Frager, 1980, p. 220). Functional integration is undertaken to develop a broader range of fully experienced and coordinated body movement (Frager, 1980).

SOMATOPSYCHIC TECHNIQUES EMPLOYING TOUCH

As noted earlier, our experience of touch forms an important foundation for our sense of self. Touch facilitates the development of body boundaries and body image (Mahler & McDevitt, 1982). Proponents of somatopsychic therapies believe that a change in one's sense of self may be facilitated through therapeutic touch.

Emotional and Ethical Issues

Touch is an extremely powerful mode of communication. Many emotions are associated with touching, ranging from sexual to religious feelings (e.g., the laying on of hands in the healing process) (Riscalla, 1975). These emotional issues, along with the possibility of sexual violations occurring within psychotherapy (Bouhoutsos, 1985; Gartrell, Herman, Olarte, Feldstein, & Loalio, 1986) have fostered ignorance regarding the potential therapeutic power of touch in psychotherapy.

The ethical use of touch in therapy requires a highly refined sense of clinical discretion. Clinical discretion is critical in terms of timing and manner of touch, as well as with whom the touching is taking place (Goodman & Teicher, 1988; Willis, 1987). In the hands of clinicians who do not have the best interests of the patient in mind, the use of touch can be devastatingly harmful. However, in the hands of clinicians with a highly refined sense of clinical discretion, touch can be a powerful therapeutic intervention (Kepner, 1987).

Goals of Using Touch in Psychotherapy

Touch in psychotherapy can be used as an end in itself (Kepner, 1987)—for example, to convey emotional support. Empathic and compassionate touch in the course of therapy is used at the end of emotional sessions or at particularly emotional points within a session to convey support and reassurance. The therapist's empathic expression is natural, and the therapist knows that it will be experienced as such by the patient (Kepner, 1987).

Touch can also be used as a means to an end (Kepner, 1987). For example, by utilizing touch the "therapist can directly demonstrate the existence of bodily tension, position the client's posture to illustrate new possibilities, . . . assist movement and so on" (Kepner, 1987, p. 72). "The skilled use of touch [can] deeply affect the client's bodily being and sense of self; the recall of body memory, the release of long withheld emotions, the reorganization of body structure and resulting change in the client's relationship to life" (Kepner, 1987, p. 72).

Structural Integration

A somatopsychic approach to human change that primarily uses touch is structural integration (often referred to as "Rolfing" after the developer of the technique, Ida Rolf) (Rolf, 1977, 1980). The focus is on realigning bodily structure by employing very deep muscle and fascia massage (Rolf, 1977, 1980). Structural realignment is deemed necessary because chronic patterns of posture and movement, and past emotional and physical trauma, have disturbed the original, efficient, and orderly pattern of body structure (Rolf, 1977, 1980).

Structural integration requires ten sessions wherein the rolfing therapist "through directed pressure brings deviant myofascial connective tissue components toward their normal position" (Rolf, 1980, p. 639). Directed pressure refers to using "deep tissue massage, mainly through stretching the fascial tissue to reestablish balance, muscle movement, and flexibility. Most of the rolfing work involves lengthening and stretching tissues that have grown together or become unnaturally thickened as a result of past trauma and poor postural and movement habits" (Frager, 1980, pp. 217–218).

Structural integration does not integrate the cognitive and emotional aspects of the rolfing with the structural (bodily) changes. Rolf states that structural integration ". . . is not primarily a psychotherapeutic approach to the problems of humans, but the effect it has had on the human psyche has been so noteworthy that many people insist on so regarding it" (Rolf, 1980, p. 639). "The psychological effect of rolfing is far greater than one would expect to induce in this brief encounter. . . " (p. 640). Some empirical work documenting the positive physical and psychological impact of structural integration has been conducted (Frager, 1980).

INTEGRATED APPROACHES

Somatopsychic therapies sometimes fail to integrate the somatic experience with cognitive, emotional, and interpersonal experiences:

> It is not uncommon for individuals who have been through various body therapies to have shown little corresponding change in their emotional life. Frequently they are unable to maintain their postural and muscular organization changes because they have not examined the place of these physical aspects in their emotional lives. (Kepner, 1987, p. 35)

Forms of psychotherapy integrating physical and psychological processes (e.g., Reichian, Neo-Reichian, bioenergetics) address this issue.

Reichian Therapy

The originator of psychotherapy integrating psychological and physical processes is Wilhelm Reich. Reich was trained in traditional psychoanalysis and made important contributions to the study of character analysis (Reich, 1945). An individual's character structure describes the person's consistent and automatic pattern of responding to emotional and interpersonal situations. Reich later proposed that each of the character types he described (e.g., the oral character, anal character, etc.) manifested very specific patterns of muscular tension (i.e., muscular "armoring") and bodily experience. Reich would physically work with these patterns of "muscle armoring" (e.g., by using massage) in the context of verbally oriented psychotherapy. Reich believed that by addressing both the psychological and physical aspects of the individual he could enhance the therapeutic process.

The specific techniques employed in Reichian therapy include deep breathing (used to produce changes in body sensation and emotional release), deep massage, and manipulation of facial expressions (Hoff, 1978). These physical processes facilitate emotional experience (Kepner, 1987). The focus of Reichian therapy is on the interaction between physical and psychological processes. The clinical literature has described Reichian therapy as having a powerful potential for facilitating profound personality changes (Green, 1981; Lowen, 1975).

Reichian therapy had a significant number of devoted followers (Lowen, 1975), though Reich's work has not found its way into mainstream psychotherapy (Lowen, 1975). However, many body-oriented psychotherapies have been developed. These are often technical and theoretical variants of the basic Reichian position (e.g., Baker, 1967, 1980; Baker & Nelson, 1981; Kelley & Wright, 1980; Schaler & Royak-Schaler, 1980; Warburton, 1981). Of particular importance is bioenergetics, developed by Lowen (Lowen, 1958, 1967, 1972), a student of Reich. Lowen's technical innovations and writings have facilitated the wider dissemination of "body work" into mainstream psychotherapy (e.g., the use of such cathartic methods as hitting a pillow).

Nevertheless, there is still limited clinical and empirical knowledge regarding the effectiveness of these body-oriented techniques. There is also limited knowledge regarding the manner in which the techniques involving work with the body can be effectively integrated into the practice of traditional verbally oriented psychotherapy (Norcross, 1986, 1987). For example, movement-related tasks can be integrated into the process of therapy (Kepner, 1987; Lowen & Lowen, 1977). Gestalt therapists may ask the client to simply become aware of or exaggerate a particular movement (Kepner, 1987). We can also conduct very simple "movement experiments" within the context of verbally oriented psychotherapy. For example, we can ask unassertive or "defeated" patients to change their body position (e.g., to not slouch) when talking about their lack of ability to positively effect change in their lives. The patient can be directed to become aware of the manner in which he/she is sitting or breathing, and to experiment with different ways of moving when planning or rehearsing the changes that he/she would like to make in his/her life (Jette, 1981). Another method is to simply integrate the use of exercise as one component in a treatment program (e.g., Johnsgard, 1989).

A similar approach to integrating touch into verbally oriented psychotherapy can also be helpful. For example, the use of touch to express support is something that many therapists are comfortable with. Further steps to incorporate touch can also be taken.

Work with touch can, like body-oriented work in general, be thought of on a continuum. Just as I can use attention to body process . . . without doing any major experiment such as movement or vigorous exercise, so too I can use touch in a brief and unobtrusive way that does not involve extensive hands-on application. For example, in observing a characteristic facial tension, I may say, "I am noticing that you hold your facial muscles in particular way. May I show you where I mean?" If the client assents, I may get up from my chair, gently and briefly use my hands to demonstrate what I am seeing, and then sit down again. This simple and unintrusive work gradually makes more extensive use of touch possible by making it familiar in a safe and graded way. (Kepner, 1987, p. 85)

This gradual approach may be helpful for both patients and therapists to become more aware of the powerful impact of touch in the process of psychotherapy.

SUMMARY AND CONCLUSIONS

This chapter draws our attention to the importance of bodily experience in the development and change of human functioning. Somatopsychic approaches to therapy emphasize the central role that bodily experience plays in the developments of the self, in providing a constant background (or foundation) for all psychological experience, and in influencing the processes of perception and memory. Additionally, the somatopsychic approaches to therapy emphasize direct work with the body and body experience as one method of facilitating body-image change. The most frequently employed technical interventions are the use of body awareness, body movement, and touch.

The anecdotal and clinical literature on the use of body-oriented psychotherapies emphasizes the powerful positive effect of these techniques on psychological functioning (e.g, Duggan, 1981; Green, 1981; Lowen, 1975). Fisher (1986) states: "Although such systems had been widely applied, little is known empirically about their effectiveness or in what ways, if any, they alter the body image. In fact, the scientific literature dealing with relationships between therapy and body image is relatively sparse" (Fisher, 1986, pp. 302–303).

However, Fisher (1986) does review the extant literature on the psychological impact of a range of body-oriented interventions, including the impact of dance therapy on schizophrenics (e.g., Goertzel, May, Salkin, & Schoop, 1965; May, Wexler, Salkin, & Schoop, 1963; Salkin & May, 1967), experiential movement therapy for nonpsychotic patients (Dosamantes-Alperson & Merrill, 1980), bioenergetic training for drug addicts, neo-Reichian bodywork workshops, and the psychological impact of rolfing. While the empirical evidence is not consistent, there is a general trend in Fisher's (1986) review to support the position that body-oriented interventions have a potential for a positive effect on psychological functioning. As is often true with research on mainstream forms of therapy, there has not yet been enough research conducted to specify which of the many body-oriented techniques are effective for which types of patients. However, there is very compelling clinical rationale for continued exploration of the effectiveness of these forms of human change process.

REFERENCES

Alexander, F. M. (1958). *Physical dynamics of character structure: Bodily form and movement in analytical therapy.* New York: Grune & Stratton.

Alexander, F. M. (1974). *The resurrection of the body.* New York: Delta.

Allport, G. (1955). *Theories of perception and the concept of structure.* New York: Wiley.

Baker, E. F. (1967). *Man in the trap.* New York: Collier Books.

Baker, E. F. (1980). Medical orgonomy. In R. Herink (Ed.), *The psychotherapy handbook* (pp. 448–452). New York: New American Library.

Baker, E. F., & Nelson, A. (1981). Orgone therapy. In R. J. Corsini (Ed.), *Handbook of Innovative Psychotherapies* (pp. 599–612). New York: Wiley.

Barker, S. (1978). *The Alexander technique: The revolutionary way to use your body for total energy.* New York: Bantam Books

Becker, E. (1973). *The denial of death.* New York: The Free Press.

Beigel, H. G. (1952). The influence of body position on mental processes. *Journal of Clinical Psychology, 8,* 193–199.

Berdach, E., & Bakan, P. (1967). Body position and the free recall of early memories. *Psychotherapy: Theory, Research and Practice, 4,* 101–102.

Bernstein, P. L. (1980). Dance therapy. In R. Herink (Ed.), *The psychotherapy handbook* (pp. 142–145). New York: New American Library.

Bernstein, P. L. (Ed.). (1986). *Theoretical approaches in dance-movement therapy* (Vol. 1). Dubuque, Iowa: Kendall/Hunt Publishing.

Bouhoutsos, J. (1985). Therapist–client sexual involvement: A challenge for mental health professionals and educators. *American Journal of Orthopsychiatry, 55,* 177–182.

Brown, M. (1973). The new body psychotherapies. *Psychotherapy: Theory, Research and Practice, 10,* 98–116.

Caplan, D., & England, F. (1980). The Alexander technique. In R. Herink (Ed.), *The psychotherapy handbook* (pp. 23–26). New York: New American Library.

Chace, M. (1953). Dance therapy as an adjunctive therapy with hospitalized mental patients. *Bulletin of the Menninger Clinic, 17,* 14–19.

Corsini, R. J. (Ed.). (1981). *Handbook of innovative psychotherapies* (pp. 599–612). New York: Wiley.

Deutsch, F. (1952). Analytic posturology. *Psychoanalytic Quarterly, 21,* 196–214.

Dillon, M. C. (1978). Merleau-Ponty and the psychogenesis of the self. *Journal of Phenomenological Psychology, 9,* 84–98.

Dosamantes-Alperson, E. (1974). Carrying experiencing forward through authentic body movement. *Psychotherapy: Theory, Research and Practice, 11,* 211–214.

Dosamantes-Alperson, E. (1987). Transference and countertransference issues in movement psychotherapy. *The Arts in Psychotherapy, 14,* 209–214.

Dosamantes-Alperson, E., & Merrill, N. (1980). Growth effects of experiential movement psychotherapy. *Psychotherapy: Theory, Research and Practice, 17,* 63–68.

Duggan, D. (1981). Dance therapy. In R. J. Corsini (Ed.), *Handbook of innovative psychotherapies* (pp. 229–240). New York: Wiley.

Ekman, P., Levenson, R. W., & Friesen, W. V. (1983). Autonomic nervous system activity distinguishes among emotions. *Science, 221,* 1208–1210.

Espernak, L. (1981). *Dance therapy: Therapy and application*. Springfield, Illinois: Charles C. Thomas.

Feldenkrais, M. (1972). *Awareness through movement*. New York: Harper & Row.

Fisher, S. (1986). *Development and structure of the body image*. Hillsdale, NJ: Erlbaum.

Frager, S. (1980). Touch: Working with the body. In A. C. Hastings, J. Fadiman, & J. S. Gordon (Eds.), *Health for the whole person* (pp. 215–232). New York: Bantam Books.

Frick, R. M. (1982). The ego and the vestibular system: Some theoretical perspectives. *Psychoanalytic Quarterly, 2*, 93–122.

Gartrell, N., Herman, J., Olarte, S., Feldstein, M., & Loalio, R. (1986). Psychiatrist–patient sexual contact: Results of a national survey. *American Journal of Psychiatry, 143*, 1126–1131.

Geller, J. D. (1978). The body, expressive movement, and physical contact in therapy. In J. L. Singer & K. S. Pope (Eds.), *The power of human imagination: New methods in psychotherapy* (pp. 347–379). New York: Plenum Press.

Gellhorn, E. (1964). Motion and emotion: The role of proprioception in the physiology and pathology of the emotions. *Psychological Review, 71*, 457–472.

Goertzel, V., May, P. R. A., Salkin, J., & Schoop, T. (1965). Body-ego techniques: An approach to the schizophrenic patient. *Journal of Nervous and Mental Disease, 141*, 53–60.

Goodman, M., & Teicher, A. (1988). To touch or not to touch. *Psychotherapy, 25*, 492–500.

Green, B. (1981). Body therapies. In R. J. Corsini (Ed.), *Handbook of innovative psychotherapies* (pp. 95–106). New York: Wiley.

Guze, H. (1953). Postural redintegration and hypnotherapy. *Journal of Clinical and Experimental Hypnosis, 1*, 76–82.

Haley, J. (1973). *Uncommon therapy*. New York: Grunne & Stratton.

Haley, J. (1985). *Conversations with Milton Erickson, M.D.: Volume 1. Changing individuals*. New York: Triangle Press.

Hanna, T. (1970). *Bodies in revolt: A primer in somatic thinking*. New York: Holt, Rinehart & Winston.

Hanna, T. (1973). The project of somatology. *Journal of Humanistic Psychology, 13*, 3–14.

Hanna, T. H. (Ed.). (1979). *Explorers of humankind*. New York: Harper & Row.

Hanna, T. (1980). *The life of the body*. New York: Random House.

Harlow, H. F., & Zimmerman, R. R. (1958). The development of affectional responses in infant monkeys. *Proceedings, American Philosophical Society, 102*, 501–509.

Hoff, R. (1978). Overview of Reichian therapy. In E. Bauman, A. I. Brint, L. Piper, & P. A. Wright (Eds.), *The Holistic Health Handbook* (pp. 205–211). Berkely, CA: And/Or Press.

Jenkins, J. J. (1971). Remember that old theory of memory? Well forget it. In R. Shaw & J. Bransford (Eds.), *Perceiving, Acting and Knowing* (pp. 413–429). Hillsdale, NJ: Erlbaum.

Jette, N. (1981). *Assertive training through movement*. Springfield, Illinois: Charles C. Thomas.

Jongsgärd, K. W. (1989). *The exercise prescription for depression and anxiety*. New York: Plenum.

Jones, F. P. (1976). *The Alexander technique: Body awareness in action*. New York: Schoer Books.

Kaslow, N. J., & Eicher, V. W. (1988). Body image therapy: A combined creative arts therapy and verbal psychotherapy approach. *The Arts in Psychotherapy, 15*, 177–188.

Keleman, S. (1975). *Your body speaks its mind*. New York: Simon & Schuster.

Keleman, S. (1979). *Somatic reality*. Berkeley, California: Center Press.

Kelley, C. R., & Wright, J. (1980). Radix neo-Reichian education. In R. Herink (Ed.), *The psychotherapy handbook* (pp. 540–542). New York: New American Library.

Kepner, J. I. (1987). *Body process: A Gestalt approach to working with the body in psychotherapy*. New York: Gestalt Institute of Cleveland Press.

Kroth, J. A. (1970). The analytic couch and response to free association. *Psychotherapy: Theory, Research and Practice, 7*, 206–208.

Krueger, D., & Schofield, E. (1987). Dance/movement therapy of eating disordered patients: A model. *Arts in Psychotherapy, 13*, 323–331.

Lowen, A. (1958). *The language of the body*. New York: Collier.

Lowen, A. (1967). *The betrayal of the body*. New York: Collier.

Lowen, A. (1972). *Depression and the body*. Baltimore: Penguin.

Lowen, A. (1975). *Bioenergetics*. New York: Penguin.

Mahler, M. S., & McDevitt, J. B. (1982). Thoughts on the emergence of self, with particular reference to the body self. *Journal of the American Psychoanalytic Association, 32*, 827–848.

Mahler, M. S., Pine, F., & Bergmann, S. (1975). *The psychological birth of the human infant*. New York: Basic Books.

May, P. R. A., Wexler, M., Salkin, J., & Schoop, T. (1963). Non-verbal techniques in the re-establishment of body image and self-identity—A preliminary report. *Psychiatric Research Reports, 16*, 68–82.

Minton, S. C. (1989). *Body and self: Partners in movement*. Champaign, Illinois: Human Kinetics.

Montague, A. (1978). *Touching: The human significance of the skin* (2nd ed.). New York: Perennial Library.

Moss, D. (1978). Brain, body, and world: Perspectives on body-image. In R. S. Valle & M. King (Eds.), *Existential-phenomenological alternatives in psychology* (pp. 73–93). New York: University Press.

Norcross, J. C. (Ed.). (1986). *Handbook of eclectic psychotherapy*. New York: Brunner/Mazel.

Norcross, J. C. (Ed.). (1987). *Casebook of eclectic psychotherapy*. New York: Brunner/Mazel.

North, M. (1972). *Personality assessment through movement*. London: MacDonald & Evans.

Pasquarelli, B., & Bull, N. (1951). Experimental investigations of the body–mind continuum in affective states. *Journal of Nervous and Mental Disease, 113*, 512–521.

Pesso, A. (1969). *Movement in psychotherapy: Psychomotor techniques and training*. New York: University Press.

Pesso, A. (1973). *Experience in action: A psychomotor psychology*. New York: University Press.

Pesso, A., & Pesso, D. (1980). Psychomotor psychotherapy. In R. Herink (Ed.), *The psychotherapy handbook* (pp. 524–526). New York: New American Library.

Pope, K. (1978). How gender, solitude and posture influence the stream of consciousness. In K. S. Pope & J. L. Singer (Eds.), *The stream of consciousness: Scientific investigations into the flow of human experience* (pp. 259–299). New York: Plenum Press.

Prestera, H. A. (1980). Body energy therapy. In R. Herink (Ed.), *The psychotherapy handbook* (pp. 69–70). New York: New American Library.

Pruzinsky, T. (1984). *The role of the body in the development and change of the self*. Unpublished manuscript, The Pennsylvania State University, University Park.

Rand, G., & Wapner, S. (1967). Postural status as a factor in memory. *Journal of Visual Learning and Verbal Behavior, 6*, 268–271.

Redfearn, J. W. T. (1970). Bodily experience in psychotherapy. *British Journal of Medical Psychology, 43*, 310–312.

Reich, W. (1945). *Character analysis*. New York: Simon & Schuster.

Rice, J. B., Hardenbergh, M., & Hornyak, L. M. (1989). Disturbed body image in anorexia nervosa: Dance/Movement therapy interventions. In L. M. Hornyak & E. K. Baker (Eds.), *Experiential therapies for eating disorders* (pp. 252–278). New York: Guilford Press.

Riscalla, L. (1975). Healing by laying on of hands: Myth or fact. *Ethics in Science and Medicine, 2*, 167–171.

Rolf, I. P. (1977). *Rolfing: The integration of human structures*. New York: Harper & Row.

Rolf, I. P. (1980). Structural integration. In R. Herink (Ed.), *The psychotherapy handbook* (pp. 639–640). New York: New American Library.

Rosen, G. M., & Ross, A. O. (1968). Relationship of body image to self-concept. *Journal of Consulting and Clinical Psychology, 32*, 100.

Rywerant, J. (1983). *The Feldenkrais method: Teaching by handling*. San Francisco: Harper & Row.

Salkin, J., & May, P. R. A. (1967). Body ego technique. *Journal of Special Education, 1*, 375–386.

Schaler, J. A., & Royak-Schaler, R. (1980). Lomi body work. In R. Herink (Ed.), *The psychotherapy handbook* (pp. 354–356). New York: New American Library.

Schilder, P. M. (1935). *The image and appearance of the human body: The constructive energies of the psyche*. New York: International Universities Press.

Schoop, T. (1971). Philosophy and practice. *American Dance Therapy Newsletter, 5,* 3–5.

Stark, A. (1982). Dance-movement therapy. In L. E. Abt & I. R. Stuart (Eds.), *The newer therapies: A sourcebook* (pp. 308–325). New York: Van Nostrand Reinhold.

Stark, A., Aronow, S., & McGeehan, T. (1989). Dance/movement therapy with bulimic patients. In L. M. Hornyak & E. K. Baker (Eds.), *Experiential therapies for eating disorders* (pp. 121–143). New York: Guilford Press.

Stark, A., & Lohn, A. F. (1989). The use of verbalization in dance/movement therapy. *The Arts in Psychotherapy, 16,* 105–113.

Steere, D. A. (1982). *Bodily expressions in psychotherapy*. New York: Brunner/Mazel.

Tengwall, R. (1981). A note on the influence of F. M. Alexander on the development of Gestalt therapy. *Journal of the History of the Behavioral Sciences, 17,* 126–130.

Wapner, S., & Werner, H. (Eds.). (1965). *The body percept*. New York: Random House.

Warburton, E. (1981). Radix neo-Reichian education. In R. J. Corsini (Ed.), *Handbook of innovative psychotherapies* (pp. 736–746). New York: Wiley.

Wilbur, K. (1977). *The spectrum of consciousness*. London: The Theosophical Publishing House.

Wilbur, K. (1979). *No boundary: Eastern and western approaches to personal growth*. Los Angeles: Center Publications.

Willis, C. (1987). Legal and ethical issues of touch in dance/movement therapy. *American Journal of Dance Therapy, 10,* 41–53.

Wilson, J. M. (1982). The value of touch in psychotherapy. *American Journal of Psychotherapy, 52,* 65–72.

Witkin, H. A., Lewis, H. B., Hertzman, M., Meissner, P., Machover, K., & Wapner, S. (1954). *Personality through perception*. New York: Harper and Brothers.

CHAPTER 15

Psychotherapy and the Body in the Mind

Michael J. Mahoney

Psychology and psychotherapy have now entered their second century as recognized professions, and recent conceptual developments suggest that their theories, research, and practice are likely to be dramatically different in the decades to come. The nature of those developments and their possible sequelae are beyond the scope of this chapter, and I therefore defer a full discussion of them to other sources (Altman, 1987; Fiske & Schweder, 1986; Ford, 1987; Hilgard, 1987; Mahoney, 1990; National Research Council, 1988). One of those developments, however, is particularly relevant to this volume and bears significant implications for our conceptualization and practice of psychotherapy. Tersely stated, that development is the (belated) "embodiment" of mind, knowing, and all human experience, and the corresponding invitation to move beyond traditional "talking heads" versions of psychological services. In this chapter, I shall first contextualize that development by brief reference to other developments in and well beyond psychology. I shall then discuss some of the practical issues that are raised by some of these views as they bear on our research into and treatment of "body-image" disorders. My coverage of this topic must be somewhat cursory, but resources for further reading are suggested.

CONCEPTUAL SHIFTS IN MODERN PSYCHOLOGY

To contextualize the importance of the "embodiment of mind" in contemporary psycholological theory and research, it is worth briefly noting some of the other conceptual developments that have paralleled this important development. Although there are differences as to how some of these developments have been described and interpreted by various observers, there seems to be general consensus that some sweeping shifts are transforming the face, form, and functions of modern psychology and psychotherapy. At the risk of capsulization, these shifts include the following:

1. There has been a decline in "justificational" (authority-based) theories of knowing (including positivism and logical empiricism), with an increasing reliance on "nonjustificational" theories based in the power of criticism and the simultaneous evaluation of multiple competing perspectives. Although this development is among the most difficult to describe without getting into obtuse technicalities, it boils down to the (often grudging) acknowledgment that scientific research does not have some privileged guarantee of its own validity. This acknowledgment may seem less than earth-shaking for those who have always viewed science as tentative and open-ended. Its conceptual wallop stems from the fact that it dilutes the half-conscious and widespread illusion that there is, in fact, an ultimate, absolutely-objective arbiter that can decide scientific disputes (whether that arbiter be logic, path analysis, a Master's theory, or whatever). Not surprisingly, this development is also associated with the decline in naive "objectivism" and with recent critiques of the dogmatic self-righteousness termed "scientism" (Mahoney, 1989).

2. There has been a decline in the popularity of "classical rationalism" as the most adequate and appropriate metatheory from which to view psychological phenomena. Formally inaugurated by Pythagoras, classical rationalism has long argued that "thought is superior to sense," and that mathematics is the purest and most powerful form of thought. The consequences and implicit constraints on human inquiry that stem from this bold claim are only now being recognized. Suffice it to say that conscious, explicit, and communicable forms of knowing now appear to be not only a portion, but a relatively small portion, of what constitutes the *in vivo* expression of (comprehensively critical) "rationality" (Mahoney, 1976; Weimer, 1979).

3. The recent resurgence of attacks on classical realism, combined with the growing popularity of J. J. Gibson's "ecological realism," emphasize the persistence of longstanding issues regarding the relationship between knowing and the known. Indeed, developments in understanding the psychosocial impact of human appearance have been made from this perspective (see Alley, 1988). In the decline of objectivist epistemologies, solipsistic subjectivism is not the only alternative. "Constructivist" theories have offered some promising integrations of organism–medium exchanges and their possible complexities throughout a dynamic and enduring "coupling." In constructivist analyses, knowing and experience are always actively participatory and predominantly anticipatory (Mahoney, 1988a, 1988b).

4. Reductionist causal analyses have come under increasing attack during the past few decades, in part reflecting the decline in simple, linear ("billiard ball") determinism. Interactive dynamics and reciprocity models have been proposed as preferable alternatives (see Lerner & Jovanovic, Chapter 5, this

volume), with a corresponding appreciation that psychological phenomena involve complex systems of interdependent phenomena.

5. Growing interest in evolutionary studies and their relevance for human psychological development has refocused and reformulated many traditional questions in psychological theory. The operation of "variation" and "selective retention" mechanisms, for example, is apparent well beyond the level of genetics, and the activities of the organism have come to be appreciated as fundamentally "embodied" (whether the activities are observable or not).

6. The doctrine of "cerebral primacy" has fallen on its metaphorical face. A conceptual relative of classical rationalism, cerebral primacy has been the doctrine (predominantly developed by evolutionary biologists) that brain development precedes, potentiates, and regulates body development. Hence, the century-old myth that human bipedalism was made possible by a rapid increase in the relative size of the neocortex. That myth was effectively demolished by a small woman (the Australopithecine fossil named "Lucy"). It is now recognized that body and brain have exhibited a synergistic co-evolution, with neither totally separated from nor dominant over the other.

7. In a somewhat parallel conceptual move, the "control structure of the mind" has recently been the target of serious reappraisal. Traditional models of "the Victorian brain" (espoused by Meynert, Freud, and others) have assumed that the most-recently-evolved parts have also been the "highest" and most powerful. Computer science, artificial intelligence, and information processing models later lent encouragement to this notion, suggesting that "executive programs" constitute the centralized control structures that coordinate the complex activities of brain and body. From a variety of research sources, it now appears that bodybrain control is not centralized, and that decentralized (coalitional) control offers a more adequate portrayal of coordinated activity. (This point becomes technical, but it has dramatic implications for conceptualizations of practice.) In essence, the control models now considered most viable are those proposing a complex "heterarchy" (system of nested hierarchies) in which "centers" of bodybrain activity may move dynamically with the momentary parameters of the task or activity involved.

8. There has been a shift in the rated importance of emotionality and emotional processes in psychological functioning (including that traditionally termed cognitive) and a reappraisal of the relationships among cognition, affect, and behavior. "Prime mover" arguments are now considered oversimplifying (i.e., where behavior, cognition, or affect are seen as the "first" or most important dimension to change, with the other two tagging along obediently).

9. Relevant to this last shift, there has been an increasing interest in the potential role of disorder, disequilibrium, and dynamic "essential tensions" in the life-span development of living systems. Some of this interest has stemmed from developmental psychology, some from the "sciences of complexity," and some from work on nonequilibrium thermodynamics. All point to the limitations of mechanistic Newtonian views of a static equilibrium, and recent research

has begun to explore the extent to which episodes of systemic disorganization may be important in the emergence of new and more viable dynamic equilibria. These dynamics are themselves uniquely patterned, and the self-organizing properties of living systems have lent additional momentum to the belated recognition of the power of subsystems that protect and attempt to preserve "system integrity," expressed from the levels of basic biological survival to those of abstract dimensions of the self.

10. Traditional models of mental representation have recently been criticized for their oversimplifying assumptions. There seems to be little debate that the living system attempts to order its experience by constructing private (and predominantly tacit) theories of the world (and, in socialized humans, the "self"), but the nature of such theories and their representation "in the head" is now a hot topic in the cognitive sciences. It seems clear, for example, that "copy" theories and "computational" theories—two of the traditionally most popular—are untenable. Indeed—and this is where I shall make my transition to body-image disorders and their conceptualization—the currently most viable models invoke an "embodiment" of mentation that integrates bodybrain activity in a way that (finally) transcends the mind–body dualisms enshrined by Plato and Descartes (M. Johnson, 1987; Mahoney, 1990).

PSYCHOLOGICAL SERVICES AND THE HUMAN BODY

Each of the foregoing developments has important implications for the conceptual directions and service refinements being explored by mental health researchers and practitioners, not to mention, those for much broader issues in science and the humanities. I focus here on psychological approaches to the body as the "assumptive world" out of which have emerged most theories and therapies of body image and its disorders.

Historical Acknowledgments

All attempts to understand current conceptualizations of the body and body image are themselves embedded in a history of such attempts, and many modern scholars admit that they have just begun to appreciate the extensive embeddedness of our embodiment in the full range of historical documents (Berman, 1989; Feher, Naddaff, & Tazi, 1989). In other words, human writings have generously appealed to concepts and experiences that are based in the everyday life of the body, including its nervous system. This is not a reiteration of classical empiricism (the doctrine that all knowledge is based in experience) but is an acknowledgment that the conceptual leaps made possible by the emergence of formal symbol systems (such as language and mathematics) were not magically extricated from their own progenitors. Although modern cultures may view animal learning as crude, "more primitive," and "less powerful" than our "higher" forms of knowing, there is substantial evidence to the contrary. Moreover, as David Hume enjoyed reminding us, even the most polished of scientific formulations amounts to little more than "mere animal belief" when its logical assumptions are examined closely.

That the body and its image have long been the objects of personal and public evaluations is readily illustrated, as is the idea that their "objectification" was dramatically amplified following the Renaissance, the scientific revolution, and the continuing advancement of medical technology (Duby, 1988; Goldberg, 1985; Nuland, 1988; Starr, 1982). In fact, at least part of the regrettable hostilities between the professions of psychiatry and psychology has its base in assumptions and traditions regarding the domain of the body and its treatment (Buie, 1989; Wright & Spielberger, 1989). As alternatives to allopathic medicine have gained in popularity, conflicts have arisen over the professional competencies and responsibilities attendant upon the treatment of a client's body. Not surprisingly, those conflicts have been more intense when the body has been treated directly and explicitly without recognized professional supervision (such as in the case of some of the so-called "body therapies") than when a professional health-care team has collaborated on the treatment (Bliss, 1985; Feiss, 1979; Hill, 1978; Matarazzo, Weiss, Herd, Miller, & Weiss, 1984; Weil, 1983). I shall have more to say about these body therapies in the next section. For the moment, suffice it to say that we are likely to encounter continuing conflicts over the "proper" and "exclusive" rights of the many health sciences and their service components. At least one positive outcome of these conflicts to date has been a multidisciplinary convergence on the need to clarify and emphasize clients' rights and responsibilities in their own health care.

Body Image and Its Treatment

As other contributors to this volume have made clear, the concept of body image is anything but simple, and the treatment of body-image disorders touches upon issues that cover the full spectrum of theory and practice in psychotherapy. Body-image issues cannot, for example, be separated from cultural, ethnic, and gender issues, nor can they be optimally addressed in treatment without an appreciation for some of the variables that may serve as obstacles or aids to change (Anderson & Zinsser, 1988; Freedman, 1988; Hartman & Blankstein, 1986; Hsu, 1989; Neal & Wilson, 1989). Moreover, the mental health professional must consider the many possible and most probable sequelae to a variety of intervention strategies. Is the client's distress and functioning likely to be positively or adversely influenced by a change in body appearance, no matter how the latter is achieved? When body appearance is, in fact, targeted for change, what health risks and individual issues bear on how such a change is accomplished (e.g., via surgery, diet, and/or exercise)? How does one assess changes in body image, and when should more emphasis be placed on the "image" than on the body? I do not pretend to be privy to any guaranteed answers to questions like these, but I do admit to a continuing struggle with them on a case-to-case basis.

The most emphatic statement I care to make in this domain is that *an adequate understanding of body-image disorders and their treatment requires a fundamental appreciation of developmental issues in identity ("self") formation and change.* Not surprisingly, this statement reflects my current conceptual "base camp" for understanding human change processes and their facilitation (Mahoney, 1990, in press). Nor is this the first or most elegant expression of the necessary relationship between body image and various aspects of the self-system (Frick, 1982; Guidano, 1987; Pruzinsky, 1984). What it does emphasize, however, is something that researchers and therapists specializing in body-image disturbances have long recognized: namely, that the therapeutic "solution" usually involves much more than strategic adjustments in the body or in the client's perception and evaluation of it. There is much more to body image than the visual and aesthetic, and there is much more complexity to professional services in this area than a "corrective" alignment of beliefs and social realities.

Given present limitations of space, I shall illustrate the above assertions via two brief excursions into ongoing research. The first has to do with our continuing studies of personal development (both inside and outside formal psychological services), and the second deals with developmental issues in the experience of self (bodily and otherwise).

Preliminary Studies of Self-Appraisal

"Self-system" variables have become important considerations in the understanding and treatment of a variety of clinical problems (Hartman & Blankstein, 1986; Nurius, Lovell, & Edgar, 1988; Nurius & Majerus, 1988). Now that the self has (re)gained the interest and respect of psychological researchers and practitioners, however, some challenging issues have emerged. Definitions and methodologies abound, and there are wide-ranging differences in assumptions about the nature of the self and its psychological operations (Baumeister, 1987; Broughton, 1986; Doi, 1985; Guidano, 1987; Harre, 1984; Harter, 1983; F. Johnson, 1985; Kegan, 1982; Rosenberg, 1979; Sanford, 1966; Young-Eisendrath & Hall, 1987). Without belaboring that range and those differences, it is noteworthy that the meaning and experience of "self" varies across cultures, ages, and ideologies, and that evaluations of self-attributes are often related to various forms of stereotyping (Cota & Fekken, 1988; Doi, 1985; Marsella, Devos, & Hsu, 1985; Smith, 1985; White & Kirkpatrick, 1985).

The internal consistency or integration of the self is an issue that deserves comment. Until relatively recently, significant deviations from a sense of "unity" within the self were considered to be signs of possible psychopathology or impaired "ego development." In the last decade, however, there has been growing tolerance and even some enthusiasm for the notion of "multiplicity" or "diversity" within individual self systems. Besides providing additional grist for some philosophers' mills, the "multiplicity-of-self" notion has stimulated reconceptualizations of clinical theories and therapies (Elster, 1985; Mahoney, 1990; Rosenberg & Gara, 1985; Sampson, 1985). Thus, the "multiple-selves" concept has dovetailed with "possible-selves" concepts and their invitations to appreciate both the complexity and the developmental dynamics of changing and unchanging aspects of the individual (Linville, 1985, 1987; Markus & Nurius, 1986; Sampson, 1985).

There is a conceptual paradox here that is related to this last complexity. How does one conceptualize and counsel in the face of unchanging continuities and never-ending challenges to change? I have elsewhere argued that there is a significant relationship between the experience of self and "resistance" to change (Mahoney, 1990). Briefly put, I endorse what might be called a "self-protective theory of resistance" in that behavioral stereotypy and avoidance of unfamiliar or challenging experiences are predictable outcomes when an individual is asked or demanded to change "too much, too soon." According to this view, the personal ordering of experience—the ongoing construction and experience of "personal realities" throughout life-span identity development—is inherently related to the self-organizing processes that characterize humans as living systems (Brandtstadter, 1989; Ford, 1987; Greenwald, 1980; Guidano, 1987; Hermans, 1987, 1989; Hoelter, 1985; Miller, 1988; Piolat, 1988). When life challenges (or trauma) force the individual too far beyond familiar experiences of self, world, and their relationships, the person often reacts in patterns that may appear resistant. My point is that these reactions are not unnatural or necessarily unhealthy; in fact, they reflect the living system's attempts to preserve and protect its faltering organizational integrity.

Some of our studies of resistance and the experience of change have involved pilot investigations of exercises designed to evaluate various dimensions of individuals' "relationships with themselves." In an ongoing project in our laboratory, for example, individuals are invited to participate in a series of experiences aimed at developing self-awareness and enhancing self-esteem. These experiences include the following:

1. Personal journal work, in which the individual keeps a diary of moods, events, and reflections.
2. Life review project, in which the individual records memories of and associations with each year of their life and then reflects on the patterns they see, feel, and remember in the process.
3. Guided meditation, involving introductory exercises in both focal and mindful (fluid) concentration.
4. Stream of consciousness, in which the individual reports the spontaneous flow of their thoughts, images, sensations, and so on.
5. Mirror time, in which the individual spends time in front of a mirror, describing the experience spontaneously and/or responding to standardized questions.

6. Restricted environmental stimulation technique (REST), which facilitates imagery, accentuates self-generative processes, and affords different experiences of the stream of consciousness.

Measures of self-concept, self-esteem, mood, social bonding, and health are thus collected, in addition to the performance of some physiological monitoring. A preliminary finding that emerged from a study that included physiological measures is pertinent to this discussion (Blanco, Guidano, Mahoney, & Reda, 1986).

In a collaborative research project with Drs. Blanco, Guidano, and Reda of Italy, psychotherapy clients were interviewed and physiologically monitored during a 5-minute baseline and a 15-minute session of "mirror time." Four clinical groupings were studied: phobic ($n = 16$), depressive ($n = 12$), obsessive–compulsive ($n = 13$), and eating-disordered ($n = 19$); a nonclinical

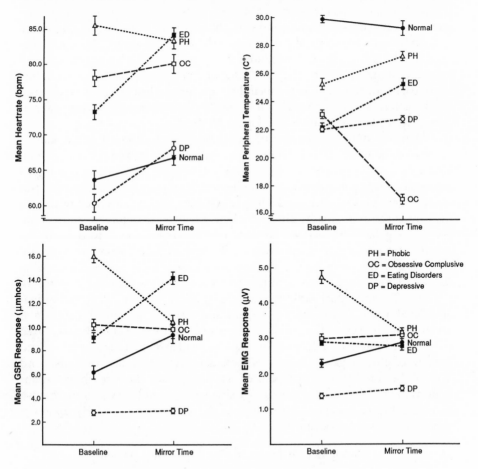

FIGURE 15.1. Mean physiological responses during baseline and mirror time. Copyright 1989 by M.J. Mahoney. Reprinted by permission.

comparison group of 23 volunteers went through the same procedure. One of the purposes of this study was to examine individual and diagnostically grouped patterns of bodily experience and physiolgical self-regulation. Because of our beliefs about the central role of "selfhood processes" in psychological adjustment (Guidano, 1987; Mahoney, 1990; Reda, 1986), the mirror-time procedure was thought to be a particularly appropriate exercise that might clarify patterns of self-organization.

There were, indeed, substantial differences among the groups in both baseline and experimental-phase responding (see Figure 15.1). Even more interesting than these differences, however, were the data collected on physiological organization within subjects. Common measures of physiological responsivity are usually correlated with one another at least moderately and in a direction that reflects some degree of whole-system coherence. Thus, stress-induced increases in heart rate are generally associated with reductions in peripheral skin temperature, increased muscle tension, and so forth. Even with allowances for individual differences and the temporal "desynchrony" of some systems, the nonclinical control subjects in our study exhibited these expected patterns of physiological coherence during baseline. They lost some of that dynamic coordination during the initial stages of the challenge (their first exposure to their image in the mirror), and their autonomic responses then gradually returned toward the original pattern of systemic coordination (see Figure 15.2).

Markedly different patterns of responsivity were observed in the clinical subgroups, however. Depressed psychotherapy clients showed reduced physiological coherence (relative to the nonclinical sample), and their physiological organization was not as dramatically influenced by the experimental task. In this study, highly anxious individuals showed a pattern that was inverted relative to nonclinical controls. That is, the physiological coherence of phobic subjects was poor during baseline, *improved* at mirror-image onset, and subsequently declined. Metaphorically, it appeared as if they exhibited more physiological coherence at the onset of the stressor—something like an initial "organizing alarm reaction"—and then gradually returned to their baseline patterns of response. The individual patterns exhibited by obsessive–compulsive and eating-disordered clients were more complex and are not presented here. It is noteworthy, however, that subjects diagnosed with eating disorders reported the poorest awareness of their bodily responses and exhibited the least integrated patterns of physiological coherence. These data are preliminary, of course, and have not been independently replicated. However, they illustrate a novel means of measuring and displaying physiological coherence, and they suggest that we have just begun to appreciate some of the complexities and dynamics of individual self-system organization.

Developmental Issues in the Experience of Self

A second illustration of the relevance of self-system variables to the conceptualization and treatment of body-image disturbances comes from the literatures on

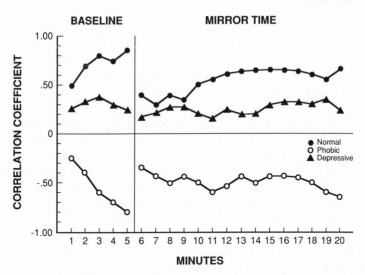

FIGURE 15.2. Patterns of physiological coherence before and during mirror time. Copyright 1989 by M.J. Mahoney. Reprinted by permission.

identity and emotional development. Those literatures are extensive, and their growth appears to be accelerating. My brief comments will be focused on John Bowlby's attachment theory and some of its clinical implications (Belsky & Nezworski, 1987; Bowlby, 1988; Guidano, 1987). Extensive research, including longitudinal studies, have corroborated Bowlby's insight that emotional self-organization and identity development are intimately related to the quality and availability of attachment relationships. Although the individual's earliest attachments may have particularly powerful impact on psychological development, the influence of human relationships on his/her quality of life extends across the life span (Evoy, 1981; Parkes & Stevenson-Hinde, 1982; Wachs & Gruen, 1982; Winnicott, 1965). Moreover, and most pertinent to the present volume, the individual's experience of self as a capable and lovable person is significantly related to these early and ongoing human relationships. As specialists in the eating disorders have noted, for example, a person's experiences and evaluations of his/her body are clearly developmental in origin (Burn, 1987; Garner & Garfinkel, 1985; Hornyak & Baker, 1989).

This last point was dramatically illustrated to me in the treatment of an individual whose presenting complaint was chronic and severe depression (Mahoney, in press). "David" was referred by a psychiatrist who had supervised his most recent hospitalization for bulimarexia. An additional diagnosis of obsessive–compulsive personality disorder was noted in his medical records, which also indicated that he had been in virtually continuous intensive therapy for 22 years with seven different therapists. Aside from being male, David's developmental history reflected many commonalities with that of the "typical" anorectic and bulimic. He was, for example, the only child of professional parents, an excellent student, and prone to episodes of poor impulse control. Although his bulimarexia did not fully manifest until early adulthood, he had been preoccupied with his body since early childhood.

In the course of our work together, we interviewed his parents by phone and learned about several experiences that had not been noted in David's most recent medical records. His mother reported, for example, that he had been born with an undescended testicle and that David had suffered through corrective surgery when he was only a few weeks old. The undescended testicle was retrieved and stitched to the inside of his thigh. She reported that he cried almost constantly for days thereafter and that the stitches became badly infected. The testicle had to be surgically removed, and David's scrotum remained intermittently inflamed and infected for months. With the best of intentions, his parents had been meticulously attentive to David and his body, an attentiveness that was later expressed as overprotectiveness. For example, David's earliest memory (at about 3 years of age) involved walking across a playground with his parents. When he saw some children climbing on a play structure, David tried to free himself from his parents (each was holding a hand) in order to join the children. He remembers both parents conveying a loud and clear message to him: "No! *David* can't do it." David reported that in later-life challenges—many of which he avoided—he remembered the clarity and gravity of that early warning. His body was not like that of his peers, and he believed he had to make adjustments for his implied handicap(s).

In his adult life, David became obsessed with his body and appearance. He made weekly trips to a dermatologist, usually for reassurance or for treatment of scars he had created in his private attempts to remove a blemish. He was grossly underweight, but reported that he was less frightened of being fat than he was of having food somehow "get stuck" inside him. During periods of severe stress, he would spend as much as 3 hours per evening binging, purging, and trying to defecate. He compulsively checked his vomitus for tiny food particles, inspected his rectum and colon for stool fragments, and so forth. As David put it, "I don't trust my body to do anything right, least of all handle food." Our therapeutic work together lasted more than 3 years and was focused primarily on his awareness, experience, and evaluation of himself. Although the quality of his life improved greatly (our latest contact was at 5 years posttreatment), he is still prone to eating binges and obsessive–compulsive patterns when stressed. I should perhaps add that one of the components of our work was "mirror time," a procedure that we developed together.

Besides illustrating the developmental aspects of the experience of self, David's case history emphasizes a point that has been overshadowed by the recent popularization of "brief psychotherapy." This is a controversial point, and one that is not resolved by extant research on psychotherapy outcome: namely, that *significant changes in "core" psychological dimensions are rarely easy, simple, or rapid.* In other words, dramatic shifts in an individual's experience of such core dimensions as (1) self (identity), (2) reality (meaning, order), (3) values, and (4) power (competence, control) are often difficult to facilitate and take long periods of time (Mahoney, 1990, in press). Thus, although important steps toward healthier functioning can be made in 10–12 sessions, the timeline for *enduring* changes in identity and body image, in my opinion, extend across a scale of years.

THE BODY IN PSYCHOTHERAPY: CONCLUDING REMARKS

I shall conclude this chapter with a brief reference to the somatic or "body therapies" that have become increasingly popular in the last few decades. The literature on those therapies is scattered across many disciplines, and it is predominantly descriptive and promotional rather than scientifically evaluative (Feder & Feder, 1981; Feiss, 1979; Hill, 1978; Keleman, 1979). Given this state of the art, my remarks are necessarily conjectural.

Let me begin by saying that I am a cautious supporter of the use of exercise, dance, movement meditation, and professional massage as adjuncts to psychotherapy, particularly with individuals who have suffered physical or sexual abuse or who struggle with their experience and appraisal of their body. I emphasize the word "cautious" because of my concerns about serious lapses of professionalism and violations of clients' welfare in some of the more evangelical somatic treatments. It is, in fact, out of those concerns that I applaud recent efforts to clarify ethical issues and articulate codes of professional practice standards by experts in these areas (King, 1989; Willis, 1987).

Although I am oversimplifying, the array of body therapies can be conceptualized in terms of two basic emphases—(a) touch and (b) movement—with the addendum that the client attend to and integrate their experience of these with their ongoing endeavors in personal development. There is, of course, good reason to believe that some forms of touch may be therapeutic, although the mechanisms for its benefits are poorly understood (Barnes, 1988; Montagu, 1971; Pattison, 1973; Whitcher & Fisher, 1979; Willison & Masson, 1986). One of the major problems here is that touch is also culturally stereotyped and associated with sexuality. Given that psychotherapy already involves a special (nonsexual) form of intimacy, indiscriminate touch may actually harm rather than help a client (Goodman & Teicher, 1988). On the other hand, a therapist who is meticulously avoidant of all human contact—including handshakes, shoulder pats, and affectionate hugs—may also create obstacles for some clients. The bottom line here, I believe, is good professional judgment and clear communication with the client.

There is also an extensive and growing literature on the benefits of exercise and physical activity in health and psychological well-being (Berger & Owen, 1988; Crews & Landers, 1987; Mitchell, 1987; Morgan, 1985a, 1985b). In fact, in a recent national survey of American clinical psychologists, there was strong transtheoretical consensus that optimal psychotherapy should include the recommendation of exercise or physical activity as an adjunct to psychological treatment (Mahoney, Norcross, Prochaska, & Missar, 1989). This is noteworthy in part because it was an issue of consensus among behaviorists, psychoanalysts, humanists, cognitivists, and eclectic practitioners. One of the unresolved issues is what kind of movement should be prescribed for which clients, and under whose supervision.

This last point is one worthy of brief elaboration because it raises the important issue of competence in professional practice. The signs are clear that physical and body-based forms of intervention are being incorporated into the "standard practice" of psychotherapy, and that their incorporation brings complex ethical and legal issues (Jansen & Barron, 1988; Kilburg, 1988; Willis, 1987). But many (if not most) psychologists have not been trained in physical and somatic forms of interventions, and there are extensive ambiguities about what constitutes professional competence and its boundaries in these domains. Must a psychotherapist be "board certified" in kinesiology, for example, in order to instruct a client in walking with an awareness of their center of gravity (Minton, 1989)? This is, perhaps, an exaggerated example, but it illustrates some of the complexities facing health-care professionals who want to work with an integrated model of bodybrain activity.

Before closing, let me disclose my personal preferences (and practices) with regard to the use of techniques that go beyond "the talking cure" in psychotherapy. As a clinical sport psychologist (Mahoney, 1989), I am particularly attuned to bodybrain issues and I often recommend that clients explore various types of physical activities and massage as part of their overall program of personal development and self-care. With some clients I will demonstrate techniques aimed at enhancing sensory or movement awareness, and (thanks to some candid clients years ago) I am comfortable with affectionate hugs and occasional hand holding in sessions. However, for clients who might benefit from exploring massage or other forms of touch and movement, I routinely refer them to colleagues in those specializations. Just as I nurture working relationships with local physicians, I try to acquaint myself with professionals in the community who specialize in physical therapy, dance, massage, movement meditation, and the like. What I find particularly important in such collaborations is that we be able to communicate clearly, and that we agree that the client will be best served by confining our respective services to our individual competencies. This requirement does limit potential collaborations, but I have found it more practical and ethical than its alternatives. Finally, one of the ways I evaluate a body/movement therapist's competencies is by observing or partaking of their professional services, either through a class or individual session. Besides learning about the range of somatic practices and practitioners that are attracting clients, I have found this to be a rich experience in learning about myself and my own embodiment.

I close, then, with a capsule summary. Both within and beyond the confines of scientific psychology and psychotherapy, we are in the midst of some sweeping conceptual developments that are transforming our ideas about ourselves and our worlds. Within psychology, there has been an increasing acknowledgment of the importance of emotionality, identity, and experiential (embodiment) issues in personal development. With the exception of the somatic and body/movement therapies and some of the behavior therapies, mainstream psychotherapy has continued to live up to its original portrayal as "the talking cure." Among others, researchers and therapists specializing in body-image disturbances have helped to pioneer an interface between therapeutic dialogue and experiential exercises (e.g., Hornyak & Baker, 1989). A host of ethical and legal issues are invoked, not to mention the ideological "turf battle" over the rights to treat the human, body and all. From the "developmental constructivist" position from which I currently view personality development and psychotherapy, body-image disturbances cannot be adequately understood or optimally treated without an appreciation of their developmental, interpersonal, and self-system dimensions. I briefly illustrated this point with a clinical study of "mirror time," a technique inspired by my work with a somatically preoccupied client named David. Finally, I endorsed the idea that constructive collaborations can and should be developed among medical, mental health, exercise, dance, massage, and other professional specialists. Indeed, I hope that such collaborations will not only afford improved services to clients and better professional relations, but also help respond to the hubris of those "information scientists" who have recently declared the human body "obsolete" (Carstensen & Kadrey, 1989).

REFERENCES

Alley, T. R. (1988). *Social and applied aspects of perceiving faces*. Hillsdale, NJ: Erlbaum.

Altman, I. (1987). Centripetal and centrifugal trends in psychology. *American Psychologist, 42,* 1053–1069.

Anderson, B. S., & Zinsser, J. P. (1988). *A history of their own: Women in Europe from prehistory to the present* (Vol. 1). New York: Harper & Row.

Barnes, D. M. (1988). Meeting on the mind. *Science, 239,* 142–144.

Baumeister, R. F. (1987). How the self became a problem: A psychological review of historical research. *Journal of Personality and Social Psychology, 52,* 163–176.

Belsky, J., & Nezworski, M. T. (Eds.). (1987). *Clinical implications of attachment theory*. Hillsdale, NJ: Erlbaum.

Berger, B. G., & Owen, D. R. (1988). Stress reduction and mood enhancement in four exercise modes: Swimming, body conditioning, hatha yoga, and fencing. *Research Quarterly for Exercise and Sport, 59*, 148–159.

Berman, M. (1989). *Coming to our senses: Body and spirit in the hidden history of the west*. New York: Simon & Schuster.

Blanco, S., Guidano, V. F., Mahoney, M. J., & Reda, M. A. (1986, October). *The experimental use of mirror time in cognitive psychotherapy*. Paper presented at the annual meeting of the Italian Psychological Society, Milano.

Bliss, S. (Ed.). (1985). *The new holistic health handbook*. Lexington, MA: Stephen Greene Press.

Bowlby, J. (1988). *A secure base: Parent–child attachment and healthy human development*. New York: Basic Books.

Brandtstadter, J. (1989). Personal self-regulation of development: Cross-sectional analyses of development-related control beliefs and emotions. *Developmental Psychology, 25*, 96–108.

Broughton, J. M. (1986). The psychology, history, and ideology of the self. In K. S. Larsen (Ed.), *Dialectics and ideology in psychology* (pp. 128–164). Norwood, NJ: Ablex.

Buie, J. (1989). Turf battle heats up on many fronts. *APA Monitor, 20*, 15–16.

Burn, H. (1987). The movement behavior of anorectics: The control issue. *American Journal of Dance Therapy, 10*, 54–76

Carstensen, J., & Kadrey, R. (Summer, 1989). Is the body obsolete? *Whole Earth Review, 63*, 2–69.

Cota, A. A., & Fekken, G. C. (1988). Dimensionality of the personal attributes questionnaire: An empirical replication. *Journal of Social Behavior and Personality, 3*, 135–140.

Crews, D. J., & Landers, D. M. (1987). A meta-analytic review of aerobic fitness and reactivity to psychosocial stressors. *Medicine and Science in Sports and Exercise, 19*, S114–S120.

Doi, T. (1985). *The anatomy of self: The individual versus society*. Tokyo: Kodansha.

Duby, G. (Ed.). (1988). *A history of private life: Revelations of the medieval world*. Cambridge: Harvard University Press.

Elster, J. (Ed.). (1985). *The multiple self*. Cambridge: Cambridge University Press.

Evoy, J. J. (1981). *The rejected: Psychological consequences of parental rejection*. University Park, PA: Pennsylvania State University Press.

Feder, E., & Feder, B. (1981). *The expressive arts therapies: Art, music, and dance as psychotherapy*. Englewood Cliffs, NJ: Prentice-Hall.

Feher, M., Naddaff, R., & Tazi, N. (Eds.). (1989). *Fragments for a history of the body* (Vols. 1, 2, and 3). Cambridge, MA: MIT Press.

Feiss, G. J. (1979). *Mind therapies body therapies*. Millbrae, CA: Celestial Arts.

Fiske, D. W., & Schweder, R. A (Eds.). (1986). *Metatheory in social science: Pluralisms and subjectivities*. Chicago: University of Chicago Press.

Ford, D. H. (1987). *Humans as self-constructing living systems: A developmental perspective on behavior and personality*. Hillsdale, NJ: Erlbaum.

Freedman, R. (1988). *Bodylove*. New York: Harper & Row.

Frick, R. B. (1982). The ego and the vestibulocerebellar system: Some theoretical perspectives. *Psychoanalytic Quarterly, 51*, 93–122.

Garner, D. M., & Garfinkel, P. E. (Eds.). (1985). *Handbook of psychotherapy for anorexia nervosa and bulimia*. New York: Guilford.

Goldberg, B. (1985). *The mirror and man*. Charlottesville, VA: University Press of Virginia.

Goodman M., & Teicher, A. (1988). To touch or not to touch. *Psychotherapy, 25*, 492–500.

Greenwald, A. G. (1980). The totalitarian ego: Fabrication and revision of personal history. *American Psychologist, 35*, 603–618

Guidano, V. F. (1987). *Complexity of the self*. New York: Guilford.

Harre, R. (1984). *Personal being: A theory for individual psychology*. Cambridge: Harvard University Press.

Harter, S. (1983). Developmental perspectives on the self-system. In E. M Hetherington (Ed.), *Handbook of child psychology: Socialization, personality, and social development* (Vol. 4, pp. 275–386). New York: Wiley.

Hartman, L. M., & Blankstein, K. R. (Eds.). (1986). *Perception of self in emotional disorder and psychotherapy.* New York: Plenum.

Hermans, H. J. M. (1987). Self as an organized system of valuations: Toward a dialogue with the person. *Journal of Counseling Psychology, 34,* 10–19.

Hermans, H. J. M (1989). The meaning of life as an organized process. *Psychotherapy, 26,* 11–22.

Hilgard, E. R. (1987). *Psychology in America: A historical survey.* New York: Harcourt Brace Jovanovich.

Hill, A. (Ed.). (1987). *A visual encyclopedia of unconventional medicine.* New York: Crown Publishers.

Hoelter, J. W (1985). The structure of self-conception: Conceptualization and measurement. *Journal of Personality and Social Psychology, 49,* 1392–1407.

Hornyak, L. M. , & Baker, E. K. (Eds.). (1989). *Experiential therapies for eating disorders.* New York: Guilford.

Hsu, L. K. G. (1989). The gender gap in eating disorders: Why are the eating disorders more common among women? *Clinical Psychology Review, 9,* 393–407.

Jansen, M., & Barron, J. (1988). Introduction and overview: Psychologists' use of physical interventions. *Psychotherapy, 25,* 487–491.

Johnson, F. (1985). The western concept of self. In A. J. Marsella, G. Devos, & F. L. K. Hsu (Eds.), *Culture and self: Asian and western perspectives.* (pp. 91–138). London: Tavistock.

Johnson, M. (1987). *The body in the mind.* Chicago: University of Chicago Press.

Kegan, R. (1982). *The evolving self: Problem and process in human development.* Cambridge, MA: Harvard University Press.

Keleman, S. (1979). *Somatic reality.* Berkeley, CA: Center Press.

Kilburg, R. R. (1988). Psychologists' and physical interventions: Ethics, standards, and legal implications. *Psychotherapy, 25,* 516–531.

King. R. K. (1989). An emerging profession. *Massage Therapy Journal, 28,* 5–6.

Linville, P. W. (1985). Self-complexity and affective extremity: Don't put all of your eggs in one cognitive basket. *Social Cognition, 3,* 94–120.

Linville, P. W. (1987). Self-complexity as a cognitive buffer against stress-related illness and depression. *Journal of Personality and Social Psychology, 52,* 663–676.

Mahoney, M. J. (1976). *Scientist as subject: The psychological imperative.* Goleta, CA: Health Science Systems.

Mahoney, M. J. (1988a). Constructive metatheory: I. Basic features and historical foundations. *International Journal of Personal Construct Psychology, 1,* 1–35.

Mahoney, M. J. (1988b). Constructivist metatheory: II. Implications for psychotherapy. *International Journal of Personal Construct Psychology, 1,* 229–315.

Mahoney, M. J. (1989). Sport psychology. In V. P Makosky (Ed.), *The G. Stanley Hall lecture series* (Vol. 9). Washington, DC: American Psychological Association.

Mahoney, M. J. (1990). *Human change processes.* New York: Basic Books.

Mahoney, M. J. (in press). *Personal change: Selected exercises and experiences.* New York: Basic Books.

Mahoney, M. J., Norcross, J. C., Prochaska, J. O., & Missar, C. D. (1989). Psychological development and optimal psychotherapy: Converging perspectives among clinical psychologists. *Journal of Integrative and Eclectic Psychotherapy, 8,* 251–263.

Markus, H., & Nurius, P. (1986). Possible selves. *American Psychologist, 41,* 954–969.

Marsella, A. J., Devos, G., & Hsu, F. L. K. (Eds.). (1985). *Culture and self: Asian and western perspectives.* London: Tavistock.

Matarazzo, J. D., Weiss, S. M., Herd, J. A., Miller, N. E., & Weiss, S. M. (Eds.). (1985).

Behavioral health: A handbook of health enhancement and disease prevention. New York: Wiley.

Miller, A. (1988). Toward a typology of personality styles. *Canadian Psychology, 29,* 263–283.

Minton, S. C. (1989). *Body and self: Partners in movement.* Champaign, IL: Human Kinetics.

Mitchell, J. D. (1987). Dance/movement therapy in a changing health care system. *American Journal of Dance Therapy, 10,* 4–10.

Montagu, A. (1971). *Touching: The human significance of the skin.* New York: Harper & Row.

Morgan, W. P. (1985a). Affective beneficence of vigorous physical activity. *Medicine and Science in Sports and Exercise, 17,* 94–100.

Morgan, W. P. (1985b). Psychogenic factors and exercise metabolism: A review. *Medicine and Science in Sports and Exercise, 17,* 309–316.

National Research Council. (1988). *The behavioral and social sciences: Achievements and opportunities.* Washington, DC: National Academy Press.

Neal, A. M., & Wilson, M. L. (1989). The role of skin color and features in the black community: Implications for black women and therapy. *Clinical Psychology Review, 9,* 323–333.

Nuland, S. B. (1988). *Doctors: The biography of medicine.* New York: Random House.

Nurius, P. S., Lovell, M., & Edgar, M. (1988). Self-appraisals of abusive parents. *Journal of Interpersonal Violence, 3,* 458–467.

Nurius, P.ß., & Majerus, D. (1988). Rethinking the self in self-talk: A theoretical note and case example. *Journal of Social and Clinical Psychology, 6,* 335–345.

Parkes, C. M., & Stevenson-Hinde, J. (Eds.). (1982). *The place of attachment in human behavior.* New York: Basic Books.

Pattison, J. E. (1973). Effects of touch on self-exploration and the therapeutic relationship. *Journal of Consulting and Clinical Psychology, 40,* 170–175.

Piolat, M. (1988). Estimation of self-change by adults: Effect of temporal reference point and self-image comparison mode. *European Bulletin of Cognitive Psychology, 8,* 281–292.

Pruzinsky, T. (1984). *The influence of the body in the development and change of the self.* Unpublished manuscript, University of Virginia Health Sciences Center, Charlottesville.

Reda, M. A. (1986). *Complex cognitive systems and psychotherapy.* Rome: Nuova Italia Scientifica.

Rosenberg, S. (1979). *Conceiving the self.* New York: Basic Books.

Rosenberg, S., & Gara, M. A. (1985). The multiplicity of personal identity. In P. Shaver (Ed.), *Review of personality and social psychology* (Vol. 6, pp. 87–113). Beverly Hills, CA: Sage.

Sampson, E. E. (1985). The decentralization of identity: Toward a revised concept of personal and social order. *American Psychologist, 40,* 1203–1211.

Sanford, N. (1966). *Self and society: Social change and individual development.* New York: Atherton Press.

Smith, M. B. (1985). The metaphorical basis of selfhood. In A. J Marsella, G. Devos, & L. K. Hsu (Eds.), *Culture and self: Asian and western perspectives* (pp. 56–88). London: Tavistock.

Starr, P. (1982). *The social transformation of American medicine.* New York: Basic Books.

Wachs, T. D., & Gruen, G. E. (1982). *Early experience and human development.* New York: Plenum.

Weil, A. (1983). *Health and healing: Understanding conventional and alternative medicine.* Boston: Houghton Mifflin.

Weimer, W. B. (1979). *Notes on the methodology of scientific research.* Hillsdale, NJ: Erlbaum.

Whitcher, S. J., & Fisher, J. D. (1979). Multidimensional reaction to therapeutic touch in a hospital setting. *Journal of Personality and Social Psychology, 37,* 87–96.

White, G. M., & Kirkpatrick, J. (Eds.). (1985). *Person, self, and experience: Exploring Pacific ethnopsychologies.* Berkeley, CA: University of California Press.

Willis, C. (1987). Legal and ethical issues of touch in dance/movement therapy. *American Journal of Dance Therapy, 10,* 41–53.

Willison, B. G., & Masson, R. L. (1986). The role of touch in therapy: An adjunct to communication. *Journal of Counseling and Development*, *64*, 497–500.

Winnicott, D. W. (1965). *The family and individual development*. London: Tavistock.

Wright, R., & Spielberger, C. D. (1989). *Psychiatry declares war on psychology*. Washington, DC: Association for the Advancement of Psychology.

Young-Eisendrath, P., & Hall, J. A. (Eds.). (1987). *The book of the self: Person, pretext, and process*. New York: New York University Press.

PART VI

SUMMARY AND CONCLUSIONS

CHAPTER 16

Integrative Themes in Body-Image Development, Deviance, and Change

Thomas Pruzinsky
Thomas F. Cash

This volume covers many diverse perspectives on body image. Our contributing authors reviewed the historical (Fisher), cultural (Fallon), and psychometric (Thompson et al.) perspectives on the body-image construct. Body–image development was described from contextual (Lerner & Jovanovic), psychodynamic (Krueger), and social–clinical psychological perspectives (Cash). Body-image phenomena were examined in relation to physical deviance resulting from trauma (Bernstein), congenital deformity (Shontz, Pertschuk), and psychopathologies (Cash, Rosen, Pruzinsky). Body-image change was described with respect to the medical interventions of reconstructive surgery (Pertschuk) and cosmetic surgery (Pruzinsky & Edgerton), and the psychological interventions derived from cognitive–behavioral (Freedman), psychodynamic (Krueger), developmental constructivist (Mahoney), and somatopsychic (Pruzinsky) viewpoints. Despite the diversity of perspectives in this volume, we wish to articulate seven integrative themes that we believe have emerged.

THEME 1. BODY IMAGES REFER TO PERCEPTIONS, THOUGHTS, AND FEELINGS ABOUT THE BODY AND BODILY EXPERIENCE

We have many percepts, thoughts, and feelings about our body—its overall appearance, specific features or parts, age, ethnicity, strength, body functions, sexuality, etc. Perceptually, we construct images and appraisals of the size and shape of various aspects of our body. Our cognitive body image includes attentional body-focus and related self-statements, as well as beliefs about our bodies and bodily experience (Buss, 1980; Butters & Cash, 1987; Freedman, 1988). The emotional component includes our experiences of comfort or discomfort, satisfaction or dissatisfaction associated with our appearance as well as with many other aspects of body experience (e.g., Cash & Brown, 1987; Fisher, 1986, 1989; Thompson, 1990).

A central aspect of this theme is that body image is a highly personalized or *subjective* experience. There is no necessary correlation between subjective experience and "objective" reality. Thus, the individual's subjective impression or experience of the body is not necessarily congruent with the physical reality of the individual's body. This conclusion is evident in the review of individuals' evaluation of personal appearance (Cash), the experience of physical disability (Shontz), eating disorders (Fallon, Rosen, Krueger, Freedman) and other forms of psychopathology (Pruzinsky), and the experiences of those individuals requesting reconstructive (Pertschuk) or cosmetic surgery (Pruzinsky & Edgerton). In the majority of these instances there is a self-disparaging distortion of body image. That is, the person's subjective experience is more negative than the objective reality would imply—as we find in eating disorders, depression, dysmorphophobia, and so forth. On the other hand, there are also instances in which the "reality" of the person's physical attributes appears more negative than the individual's subjective evaluation—as Shontz points out with regard to some physical disabilities. With apology for the cliché, we maintain that you can't judge a book (body image) by looking at its cover (the "reality" of physical appearance).

THEME 2. BODY IMAGES ARE MULTIFACETED

Implicit in the first theme is the second—that body image is multifaceted (Cash & Brown, 1987; Fisher, 1986; Keeton, Cash, & Brown, 1990; Schilder, 1935). For example, in this volume and elsewhere, Shontz (1974) describes seven functions performed by the body-image construct (a sensory register, an instrument for action, a source of drives, a stimulus to the self, a stimulus to others, a private world, and an expressive instrument). Additionally, as Fisher concludes in Chapter 1 of this volume, there is really no such singular term "the body image." Extant research clearly indicates that body experience encompasses the perception of and attitude toward appearance, body size, body spatial position, body boundaries, body competence, and the gender-related aspects of one's body. An individual's attention can move from one of these components to another, or simultaneously be at one or more levels (Fisher, Chapter 1, this volume).

In Chapter 2, Thompson and his colleagues provide a detailed, useful description of the many body-image assessment procedures. Clearly, the zeit-geist reflects a division of body-image instruments and indices into those that are perceptual and those that are attitudinal. In contrast with the attitudinal body-image measures, the perceptual, size accuracy/distortion measures are less interchangeable and, as Rosen reveals in Chapter 9, do not always differentiate eating-disordered and nondisordered groups (see also Ben-Tovim, Walker, Murray, & Chin, 1990; Cash & Brown, 1987; Keeton et al., 1990). The perceptual methods tap either whole-body or body-part percepts and range from simple silhouette selection to "higher tech" instrumentation involving video adjustments of subjects' photographic images. However technologically ap-pealing the elaborate "whistles-and-bells" methods, simple assessment strategies may have as much reliability and validity.

Our view is that assessment of body-image percepts should consider more than just accuracy of judging overall body size. Body-shape judgments, in which perceivers appraise body-area *proportionalities*, should be measured. For example, Schlundt's computerized Body Image Testing System (BITS) (Schlundt & Johnson, 1990) holds promise, as it is both simple and capable of tapping perceived proportionalities of body parts. Recent research further confirms the importance of assessing *ideal* (desired) body-size and body-shape percepts and their discrepancies from self-percepts (see Barrios, Ruff, & York, 1989; Keeton et al., 1990; Schlundt & Johnson, 1990; Thompson, 1990; Thompson et al., Chapter 2, this volume; Williamson, 1990). Clearly, perceptual methods focus on the torso not on judgments about the relative size or positioning of other physical attributes, such as facial features. Perhaps the video imaging technology used clinically by some plastic and maxillofacial surgeons can be extended to quantify perceptual body experiences of these dimensions.

Although the various attitudinal indices of body image are more intercor-related, they are certainly not isomorphic (see Brown, Cash, & Mikulka, in press; Cash, 1989; Cash & Brown, 1987; Keeton et al., 1990). From the traditional social psychological perspective, an attitude consists of affective, cognitive, and behavioral facets. Consideration of each facet in relation to attitudes toward one's body represents a more fine-tuned approach to body-image assessment. Of particular contemporary interest are conceptual models of attitudinal body image that consider cognitive or schematic processing of body-related information (Barrios et al., 1989; Buss, 1980; Butters & Cash, 1987; Cash & Hicks, 1990; Cash, Lewis, & Keeton, 1987; Eldredge, Wilson, & Whaley, 1990; Schlundt & Johnson, 1990; Striegel-Moore, McAvay, & Rodin, 1986). Moreover, a person's body experience is not limited to the domain of body appearance/aesthetics but includes experiences of bodily sensation, function, fitness, and health/illness as well (see Brown et al., in press; Cash, Chapter 3, this volume; Cash et al., 1986; Fisher, Chapter 1, this volume; Franzoi & Shields, 1984; Shontz, Chapter 7, this volume).

Experiences regarding the body can occur at conscious, preconscious, and unconscious levels of awareness (see Krueger, Chapter 12, this volume). For example, an individual may consciously report disliking certain body features and negative thoughts and evaluations of that body part as well as associated dysphoric affect. The individual may also be dimly aware that this particular physical feature is similar to a parent's physical feature (preconscious awareness). With assistance, some individuals can verbalize these preconscious thoughts and feelings. However, people cannot tell us about their unconscious experiences. For example, patients may have feelings about their parents that have come to be symbolized in the physical features that they share with their parents (Druss, 1953; Jacobson, Meyer, & Edgerton, 1961; Meerloo, 1956). Previous experiences, such as childhood teasing about appearance (Cash et al., 1986; Thompson, 1990) or a former overweight condition (Cash, Counts, & Huffine, in press; Stunkard & Mendelsohn, 1967), may continue to influence body experiences long after the causes have subsided. Thus, there are many components and layers to body image (Horowitz, 1966).

Pathological body-image experiences can occur at many levels. For example, body-image problems can be the result of neurological or physiological malfunctioning (Fisher, Chapter 1, this volume; Shontz, Chapter 7, this volume). Body-image pathology can also be the result of dysfunctional cognitive, perceptual, behavioral, or affective factors, as well as interactions among these factors. Furthermore, body-image difficulties occur in a particular sociocultural context—against the backdrop of standards related to culture, gender, age, ethnicity, etc.

Similarly, body-image change can occur along many dimensions. Facilitating change in body experience can focus on actual physical alteration (e.g., through weight loss or gain, or cosmetic and reconstructive surgery), change in body experience (e.g., change in the proprioceptive feedback; see Pruzinsky, Chapter 8, this volume), change in emotional reactions to the body (Krueger, Chapter 12, this volume), or change in the cognitive and behavioral aspects of body image (Freedman, Chapter 13, this volume), or a combination of these approaches.

THEME 3. BODY-IMAGE EXPERIENCES ARE INTERTWINED WITH FEELINGS ABOUT THE SELF

This theme emerged in practically every chapter of this book (see also Fisher, 1986; Krueger, 1989). How we perceive and experience our bodies significantly relates to how we perceive ourselves. Our most fundamental sense of ourselves is as a body (Mahler & McDevitt, 1982). The sense of self is based on the experience that one is embodied and differentiated from the outside world and from others. This initial sense of self is based on the experience of tactile and kinesthetic sensations (Pruzinsky, Chapter 8, this volume). The emergence of self-awareness among certain higher primates, including most humans by the age of 2, is evident in their ability to recognize bodily self in a mirror (Amsterdam, 1972; Gallup, 1977; Schulman & Kaplowitz, 1977).

For many people, body schemata are central cognitive structures within the self system. The activation of these body schemata will color perceptions of other aspects of the self (Markus, 1977; Streigel-Moore et al., 1986). For example, contextual cues concerning food, body size, or physical attractiveness may trigger negative body schemata (e.g., Cash, Cash, & Butters, 1983) that, in turn, engender disparaging judgments about personal competence (e.g., Del-Rosario, Brines, & Coleman, 1984). Thus, if one has negative body-image attitudes, then one is vulnerable to negative experiences of the self as a whole (Cash, Chapter 3, this volume). Conversely, it is also the case that persons sometimes project blame onto the body for perceived deficiencies in other aspects of the self.

THEME 4. BODY IMAGES ARE SOCIALLY DETERMINED

The development of body image is based on interactions with our primary caretakers (Krueger, 1989; Mahler & McDevitt, 1982). The initial years with our parents almost exclusively involve interacting in terms of bodily functions. How these bodily functions are handled can set an important emotional tone for our incipient experiences of our bodies and ourselves (Fisher, 1986). Thus, if our parents are responsive, empathic, and not intrusive regarding our bodily needs and functions, we can more easily develop a well-integrated sense of bodily self and, therefore, a more integrated sense of self as a whole (Krueger, 1989). The nature of the early relationships with our care providers is revealed in the eating disorders (Rosen, Chapter 9, this volume), in hypochondria and self-mutilation (Pruzinsky, Chapter 8, this volume), and in other forms of body-related disturbance (Krueger, Chapter 12, this volume).

The social influences on body image continue throughout life. For example, as we develop, others react to our appearance in terms of our attractiveness, gender appropriateness, physical strength, ethnicity, etc. As Cash reviews in Chapter 3 of this volume, caretakers' feelings and reactions to children's physical attributes, as early as infancy, may affect attachment processes. Such reactions powerfully influence how we come to think and feel about ourselves (Alley & Hildebrandt, 1988; Cash, Chapter 3, this volume; Lerner & Jovanovic, Chapter 5, this volume). Despite notions that "beauty is in the eye of the beholder," clear social standards for physical attractiveness exist (Bull & Rumsey, 1988). In this book's chapters by Fallon, Rosen, and Freedman, the cultural standards for thinness are implicated in the development of the eating disorders. The social standards for beauty and the stigma associated with being "different" especially come to the fore with individuals who have profound facial deformity (Bernstein, Chapter 6, this volume; Bull & Rumsey, 1988;

Pertschuk, Chapter 11, this volume) or significant obesity (Cash, Chapter 3, this volume).

The social impact of cultural definitions of attractiveness and body experience appears to differentially impact females and males. Fisher (1986) compiled many of these body-image-related gender differences. Overall, females appear to be more critical of their appearance than males, especially with regard to being overweight. However, females are generally more comfortable with bodily changes than males. Additionally, females are much more likely to experience eating disorders (see the Fallon, Rosen, Freedman chapters in this volume), more likely to experience somatization disorders (American Psychiatric Association, 1987), and are much more likely to undergo cosmetic plastic surgery than males (Pruzinsky & Edgerton, Chapter 10, this volume). However, as Cash points out in Chapter 3, as scientists, clinicians, or just ordinary human beings, we risk exaggeration of these gender differences, proceeding as if women are "body-image basket cases" and as if men have no body-image concerns at all. Such gender-based biases must be avoided by researchers and clinicians in their attempts to understand or enhance persons' body images.

THEME 5. BODY IMAGES ARE NOT ENTIRELY FIXED OR STATIC

Aspects of our body experience are constantly changing. On an *attentional-focus* level as minutes pass we may be more or less aware of certain body parts or aspects of our bodies. For example, a television advertisement may "prime" persons to think about their weight, their attractiveness, or the appearance of their hair or makeup. Furthermore, different moods may affect our evaluation of our appearance. For example, when we are in a positive mood, our evaluation of our weight or other physical features may be significantly more positive than when we are in a negative mood (Freedman, Chapter 13, this volume). Moreover, we may enhance our body-image affect by aesthetic self-management—adorning our bodies with favorite clothes, jewelry, cosmetics, fragrances, and so forth (Cash, Chapter 3, this volume).

As argued previously (Cash, Chapter 3, this volume), many theorists and researchers have taken a "trait perspective" on body image (as well as objective appearance attributes like physical attractiveness), examining the construct exclusively in terms of a stable and cross-situationally consistent personality characteristic. We urge a shift in this paradigm to a person-by-situation, interactional paradigm in which body-image *states* are examined in relation to the dynamic interplay of person variables (e.g., body-image attitudes and orientations, attentional focus and self-monitoring, physical attractiveness, personality factors, etc.) *and* contextual stimuli (i.e., body-related cues and stimuli of the social environment). Similarly, Williamson (1990) has articulated a two-pronged model of body-image disturbance in relation to eating disorders. The model includes both *stable* body-image disturbances and *reactive* disturbances that occur in response to environmental challenges to the fear of weight gain.

All body-image experiences must be understood from a *developmental* perspective (Lerner & Jovanovic, Chapter 5, this volume; Mahoney, Chapter 15, this volume). Our bodies change as we grow and age, and each developmental stage has its associated body-image markers (Fisher, 1986). These physical attributes often have salient cultural meanings that entail standards for social evaluation and for internalized self-evaluation. Childhood brings about dramatic changes in size and strength. Adolescence brings about many physical changes that facilitate the development of sexual functioning (Lerner & Jovanovic, Chapter 5, this volume). Middle and old age bring along a decline in physical stamina, as well as appearance changes (Adams, 1985; Butler, 1967; Colarusso & Nemiroff, 1981; Janelli, 1986; Johnson, 1985; Nemiroff & Colarusso, 1985).

These later stages of life have not been the subject of a great deal of research despite the observation that " . . . preoccupation with changes in the body in the second half of life are universal phenomena . . . " (Nemiroff & Colarusso, 1985, p. 307), or as these authors further elucidated:

> In the course of midlife development, there is a normative conflict between wishes to deny the aging process and acceptance of the loss of a youthful body (Colarusso & Nemiroff, 1981). The resolution of this conflict leads to a reshaping of the body image and a more realistic appraisal of the middle-aged body. (p. 308)

There are also different *trajectories* of body-image change. For example, there are both gradual and abrupt changes in the body and body images. The rate of change in body image does not always keep pace with the rate of change in the body. Who among us has not stood before a mirror after a new haircut or hairstyle or shaven-off beard and felt some concern or a vague sense of depersonalization because of the perceived disparity and the search for the "the new me."

As a rule, gradual changes in the body are more easy to psychologically accommodate than abrupt changes. Despite a negative evaluation of changes associated with aging, most individuals are able to come to terms with them. However, if an individual is *suddenly* confronted with an awareness of age-related changes in appearance, the psychological reaction can be much more disruptive (e.g, individuals who have regained their vision after extended periods of blindness can have dramatic reactions to their realization of body changes) (see Stone, Oldenkamp, & Fritz, 1983; Sutherland & Karlinsky, 1989, for further discussion of this subject).

Similar observations regarding trajectories of body-image change are made with respect to the type and degree of physical change brought about by cosmetic plastic surgery (Pruzinsky & Edgerton, Chapter 10, this volume). Too much surgical change, even if it makes the individual more attractive, can be psychologically disruptive. Another example of body-image trajectories are the observations of Cash and colleagues (Cash et al., in press) regarding vestigial body images in formerly overweight individuals. Some individuals who lose a great deal of weight retain an image of themselves as overweight—the phenomenon of "phantom fat."

The trajectories of body-image change are also evident in clinical observations of the differential emotional impact of traumatic versus congenital facial deformity. As a rule, traumatic deformity is more psychologically disruptive than a congenital facial deformity (Pertschuk, Chapter 11, this volume). The individual with the acquired deformity not only has to cope with the severe problems that all facially deviant individuals must cope with, but must also mourn the loss of a formerly intact facial appearance (Bernstein, Chapter 6, this volume).

The issue of the trajectories of body-image change raises the question: What is the role of body and what is the role of "mind" in the processes of body-image change? This is a question that cannot currently be answered. However, certain physical and psychological approaches to body-image change are known to be effective. Currently, cognitive–behavioral forms of therapy are the most well-documented (Butters & Cash, 1987; Freedman, Chapter 13, this volume; Rosen, Chapter 9, this volume). However, more studies, with longer-term follow-up, are of critical importance as are comparisons with other forms of psychotherapeutic intervention (e.g., psychodynamically-oriented interventions or experiential forms of intervention). As Mahoney (Chapter 15, this volume) suggests, combined forms of treatment (i.e., physical *and* psychological) likely hold the greatest promise for promoting the most profound and lasting body-image change because they would directly address the multidimensionality of body image. As the multimodal therapist Arnold Lazarus (1985) asserts, the treatment of complex human problems requires that we "leave no stone unturned."

THEME 6. BODY IMAGES INFLUENCE INFORMATION PROCESSING

How we feel and think about our body influences the way that we perceive the world (Markus & Smith, 1981; Schlundt & Johnson, 1990). In his comprehensive review of body-image research, Fisher (1986) concluded that:

> [W]e have discovered that body attitudes are woven into practically every aspect of behavior. The full range of their involvement cannot be overstated . . . Body attitudes consistently reveal themselves whenever persons interpret unstructured stimuli . . . body attitudes have an impact on the broad process of *perceptual tuning*. They can apparently affect the acceptance or rejection of multiple types of information. (p. 625; emphasis added)

One simple example of this process is the cosmetic surgery patient who is concerned about his nasal appearance. This individual is more likely to pay attention to his nasal appearance and to compare his nose with other noses in a constant search for differences and similarities ("Mine isn't as bad as that one" or "I wish I had a nose like that"). To a great extent he sees the world in terms of noses. Similarly, balding men focus on their hair loss more and notice other balding men more (Cash, 1987). Persons with elaborate body-size schemata are quick in processing information about food and body shape (Markus, Hamil, & Sentis, 1987).

Bodily self-conscious persons allocate large portions of their daily attention to this one aspect of their existence. Furthermore, social events that may not be related to the person's appearance are interpreted in terms of the individual's appearance. For example, a person who is self-conscious about his or her nose and who is slighted in a social situation is more likely to interpret this social slight in terms of the faulty nose as opposed to seeing it as the result of his or her own behavior, or the personality or emotional state of the other person. Thus, the self-conscious person infers "I was treated rudely because I am not attractive" instead of "I was treated rudely because that person was having a bad day." This process was demonstrated in a creative experiment by Kleck and Strenta (1980). Using theatrical makeup, the researchers constructed a facial scar on women prior to their interaction with a stranger. Unbeknownst to the women, however, the "scar" was removed before the face-to-face conversation occurred and the stranger was really a confederate of the study. Relative to the control group, those women who *believed* that they had a disfigurement reported more discomfort and alterations of gazing behavior *in the partner* during the interaction. Thus, our body images can alter our information processing and cause us to "see" what we expect to see.

THEME 7. BODY IMAGES INFLUENCE BEHAVIOR

An individual's conscious, preconscious, and unconscious body images influence behavior (Fisher, 1986), particularly interpersonal relationships (Fisher, 1989). For example, not only do physically attractive persons have advantages in their social worlds that may foster the development of real social competencies, but having the *belief* that one is attractive (i.e., positive body-image attitudes) also fosters social confidence and skill (Cash, Chapter 3, this volume; Pruzinsky & Cash, 1990).

On the other hand, individuals who are homely or who have a facial deformity are more likely to be socially withdrawn and inhibited (Bernstein, Chapter 6, this volume; Cash, Chapter 3, this volume; Clifford, 1987; Pertschuk, Chapter 11, this volume). Patients seeking cosmetic plastic surgery often develop defensive strategies for managing their self-consciousness (Harris, 1982). These defense mechanisms are those behaviors that self-conscious individuals employ to hide the bodily feature of concern (Harris, 1982). The strain of hiding their deformity (e.g., not appearing in bright light, never allowing a profile view) can lead to social withdrawal and a constriction of social interaction. When these individuals do interact socially, they are likely to speak less frequently and less forcefully. In turn, such processes can exert a subsequent, adverse impact on the overall self-concept (Pruzinsky & Cash, 1990).

Other behavioral processes in response to body-image perceptions and attitudes are evident. For example, females with hypertrophic breast development may gain weight, perhaps unconsciously, to camouflage their breast size (Goin & Goin, 1981). Similarly, cosmetics use as well as other grooming behaviors are, in part, motivated efforts to cope with or compensate for specific disliked body features (see Cash, Chapter 3, this volume). The behavioral impact of body image in the eating disorders has also been documented (Rosen, Chapter 9, this volume). In fact, Rosen has developed a "behavioral" body-image measure to assess the adjustive behaviors engaged in for the sake of avoidance of negative body-image affect and concealment of weight-related body features. Additionally, the range of behaviors that women engage in to meet cultural standards for beauty are well documented by Fallon (Chapter 4, this volume). Yet, with the liberalization of sex roles in recent years, men are becoming more concerned and active in their own appearance management (Adler, Michael, & Greenberg, 1986; American Society for Plastic and Reconstructive Surgery, 1989; Cash, Chapter 3, this volume; Cash et al., 1986).

A FINAL WORD

Despite its long history, the concept of body image has remained rather elusive, in part because it has meant different things to different scientists and practitioners. Although the contributors to this volume have tried to be specific about the particular referents and meanings whenever they used the singular term "body image," they have not always done so. The difficulty has less to do with the "body" than with the "image" part of the term. The word "image" connotes a "picture in the head, " and such mental representations fail to fully capture the complexity and multidimensionality of the concept (Anderson, 1985). Perhaps we should insist on its plural usage or should do away with "body image(s)" altogether, replacing it with a more generic, nonconnotative term such as *body experience* (see Lipowski, 1977). But alas, old habits are hard to break, and we suspect "body image" is here to stay.

If we have achieved no more here than an expansion of the intellectual horizons of the reader, we are content. Our aim was to assemble interdisciplinary perspectives on the psychology of body experience. No doubt there are gaps in the content of our coverage. There is always more that could be included. Our further hope is that the heuristic impetus of this work will create more knowledge that can be included . . . next time.

The future of scientific understanding and clinical applications derived from a "psychology" of body experience requires that it not exclusively belong to psychology. Fruitful inquiry and practice must entail true interdisciplinary interest and ownership. This enterprise cannot thrive within a parochial clinical psychology, but requires the contributions of other psychological specialties (e.g., perception, cognitive, developmental, social, health, sport, rehabilitation, and neurophysiological psychologies), in addition to those from the fields of biology, ethology, sociology, anthropology, endocrinology, dermatology, orthopedics, orthodontic dentistry, and plastic and reconstructive surgery. Through our collective and collaborative efforts we must strive to understand the "normal" and the anomalous variations in human appearance and body experience. These efforts, we hope, can serve us all by improving the quality of embodied life.

REFERENCES

Adams, G. R. (1985). Attractiveness through the ages: Implications of facial attractiveness over the life cycle. In J. A. Graham & A. M. Kligman (Eds.), *The psychology of cosmetic treatment* (pp. 131–151). New York: Praeger Scientific.

Adler, J., Michael, R., & Greenberg, N. F. (1986, April 14). You're so vain. *Newsweek*, pp. 48–55.

Alley, T. R., & Hildebrandt, K. A. (1988). Determinants and consequences of facial aesthetics. In T. R. Alley (Ed.), *Social and applied aspects of perceiving faces* (pp. 101–140). Hillsdale, NJ: Erlbaum.

American Psychiatric Association. (1987). *Diagnostic and Statistical Manual for Mental Disorders* (3rd ed., rev.). Washington, DC: Author.

American Society for Plastic and Reconstructive Surgery. (1989). *Report of surgical procedures conducted by Board Certified Plastic and Reconstructive Surgeons*. Chicago, IL: Director of Communications Executive Office. Unpublished report.

Amsterdam, B. (1972). Mirror self-image reactions before the age of two. *Developmental Psychology*, 5, 297–305.

Anderson, J. (1985). *Cognitive psychology and its implications*. New York: W. H. Freeman.

Barrios, B. A., Ruff, G., & York, C. (1989). Bulimia and body image: Assessment and explication of a promising construct. In W. G. Johnson (Ed.), *Advances in eating disorders* (Vol. 2, pp. 67–89). New York: JAI Press.

Ben-Tovim, D., Walker, M. K., Murray, H., & Chin, G. (1990). Body-size estimates: Body image or body attitude measures? *International Journal of Eating Disorders*, 9, 57–67.

Brown, T. A., Cash, T. F., & Mikulka, P. J. (in press). Attitudinal body-image assessment: Factor analysis of the Body-Self Relations Questionnaire. *Journal of Personality Assessment*.

Bull, R., & Rumsey, N. (1988). *The social psychology of facial appearance*. New York: Springer-Verlag.

Buss, A. H. (1980). *Self-consciousness and social anxiety*. San Francisco: Freeman.

Butler, R. N. (1967). Research and clinical observations on the psychologic reactions to physical changes with age. *Mayo Clinic Proceedings*, 42, 596–619.

Butters, J. W., & Cash, T. F. (1987). Cognitive–behavioral treatment of women's body-image dissatisfaction. *Journal of Consulting and Clinical Psychology*, 55, 889–897.

Cash, T. F. (1987). *The psychosocial effects of male pattern balding: A scientific study*. Technical report for The Upjohn Company submitted to Manning, Selvage, & Lee, New York.

Cash, T. F. (1989). Body-image affect: Gestalt versus summing the parts. *Perceptual & Motor Skills, 69,* 17–18.

Cash, T. F., & Brown, T. A. (1987). Body image in anorexia nervosa and bulimia nervosa: A review of the literature. *Behavior Modification, 11,* 487–521.

Cash, T. F., Cash, D. W., & Butters, J. (1983). "Mirror, mirror on the wall. . . ?": Contrast effects and self-evaluations of physical attractiveness. *Personality and Social Psychology Bulletin, 9,* 351–358.

Cash, T. F., Counts, B., & Huffine, C. E. (in press). Current and vestigial effects of overweight among women: Fear of fat, attitudinal body image, and eating behavior. *Journal of Psychopathology and Behavioral Assessment.*

Cash, T. F., & Hicks, K. L. (1990). Being fat versus thinking fat: Relationships with body image, eating behaviors, and well-being. *Cognitive Therapy and Research, 14,* 327–341.

Cash, T. F., Lewis, R. J., & Keeton, P. (1987, March). *Development and validation of the Body-Image Automatic Thoughts Questionnaire: A measure of body-related cognitions.* Paper presented at the meeting of the Southeastern Psychological Association, Atlanta.

Cash, T. F., Winstead, B. A., & Janda, L. H. (1986). The great American shape-up: Body image survey report. *Psychology Today, 20(4),* 30–37.

Clifford, E. (1987). *The cleft palate experience: New perspectives on management.* Springfield, IL: Charles C. Thomas.

Colarusso, C. A., & Nemiroff, R. A. (1981). *Adult development: A new dimension in psychodynamic theory and practice.* New York: Plenum Press.

DelRosario, M. W., Brines, J. L., & Coleman, W. R. (1984). Emotional response patterns to body-weight related cues: Influence of body weight image. *Personality and Social Psychology Bulletin, 10,* 369–375.

Druss, R. G. (1953). Changes in body image following augmentation breast surgery. *International Journal of Psychoanalytic Psychotherapy, 2,* 248–256.

Eldredge, K., Wilson, G. T., & Whaley, A. (1990). Failure, self-evaluation, and feeling fat in women. *International Journal of Eating Disorders, 9,* 37–50.

Fisher, S. (1986). *Development and structure of the body image* (Vols. 1 & 2). Hillsdale, NJ: Erlbaum.

Fisher, S. (1989). *Sexual image of the self: The psychology of erotic sensations and illusions.* Hillsdale, NJ: Erlbaum.

Franzoi, S. L., & Shields, S. A. (1984). The Body Esteem Scale: Multidimensional structure and sex differences in a college population. *Journal of Personality Assessment, 48,* 173–178.

Freedman, R. J. (1988). *Bodylove.* New York: Harper & Row.

Gallup, G. G., Jr. (1977). Self-recognition in primates: A comparative approach to the bidirectional properties of consciousness. *American Psychologist, 32,* 329–338.

Goin, J. M., & Goin, M. K. (1981). *Changing the body: Psychological effects of plastic surgery.* Baltimore: Williams & Wilkins.

Harris, D. L. (1982). The symptomatology of abnormal appearance—an anecdotal survey. *British Journal of Plastic Surgery, 35,* 312–323.

Horowitz, M. J. (1966). Body image. *Archives of General Psychiatry, 14,* 456–460.

Jacobson, W. E., Meyer, E., & Edgerton, M. T. (1961). Psychiatric contributions to the clinical management of plastic-surgery patients. *Postgraduate Medicine, 29,* 513–521.

Janelli, L. M. (1986). Body image in older adults: A review of the literature. *Rehabilitation Nursing, 11,* 6–8.

Johnson, D. F. (1985). Appearance and the elderly. In J. A. Graham & A. M. Kligman (Eds.), *The psychology of cosmetic treatments* (pp. 152–160). New York: Praeger Scientific.

Keeton, W. P., Cash, T. F., & Brown, T. A. (1990). Body image or body images? Comparative, multidimensional assessment among college students. *Journal of Personality Assessment, 54,* 213–230.

Kleck, R. E., & Strenta, A. (1980). Perceptions of the impact of negatively valued physical characteristics on social interaction. *Journal of Personality and Social Psychology, 39*, 861–873.

Krueger, D. (1989). *Body self and psychological self: Developmental and clinical integration in disorders of the self.* New York: Brunner/Mazel.

Lazarus, A. A. (1985). *Casebook of multimodal therapy.* New York: Guilford.

Lipowski, Z. J. (1977). The importance of body experience for psychiatry. *Comprehensive Psychiatry, 18*, 473–479.

Markus, H. (1977). Self-schemata and processing information about the self. *Journal of Personality and Social Psychology, 35*, 63–78.

Markus, H., Hamil, R., & Sentis, K. P. (1987). Thinking fat: Self schemas for body weight and the processing of weight relevant information. *Journal of Applied Social Psychology, 17*, 50–71.

Markus, H., & Smith, J. (1981). The influence of self-schemata on the perception of others. In N. Cantor & J. Kihlstrom (Eds.), *Personality, cognition, and social interaction.* Hillsdale, NJ: Erlbaum.

Mahler, M. S., & McDevitt, J. B. (1982). Thoughts on the emergence of self, with particular reference to the body self. *Journal of the American Psychoanalytic Association, 32*, 827–848.

Meerloo, J. A. M. (1956). The fate of one's face. *Psychiatric Quarterly, 30*, 31–43.

Nemiroff, R. A., & Colarusso, C. A. (1985). Issues and strategies for psychotherapy and psychoanalysis in the second half of life. In R. A. Nemiroff & C. A. Colarusso (Eds.), *The race against time: Psychotherapy and psychoanalysis in the second half of life* (pp. 303–329). New York: Plenum Press.

Pruzinsky, T., & Cash, T. F. (1990). Medical interventions for the enhancement of physical appearance. In T. P. Gullotta (Ed.), *The promotion of social competence in adolescence.* Beverly Hills, CA: Sage.

Schilder, P. (1935). *The image and appearance of the human body.* London: Kegan, Paul, Trench, Trubner & Co.

Schlundt, D. G., & Johnson, W. G. (1990). *Eating disorders: Assessment and treatment.* Boston: Allyn & Bacon.

Schulman, A. H., & Kaplowitz, C. (1977). Mirror-image responses during the first two years of life. *Developmental Psychobiology, 10*, 133–142.

Shontz, F. C. (1974). Body image and its disorders. *International Journal of Psychiatry in Medicine, 5*, 461–471.

Stone, L. S., Oldenkamp, S. M., & Fritz, K. J. (1983). Behavioral disturbance following intraocular lens implantation. *Annals of Ophthalmology, 15*, 946.

Striegel-Moore, R., McAvay, G., & Rodin, J. (1986). Psychological and behavioral correlates of feeling fat in women. *International Journal of Eating Disorders, 5*, 935–947.

Stunkard, A. J., & Mendelsohn, M. (1967). Obesity and body image: I. Characteristics of disturbances in the body image of some obese persons. *American Journal of Psychiatry, 123*, 1296–1300.

Sutherland, A., & Karlinsky, H. (1989). Abrupt recognition of age-related physical changes in appearance following cataract surgery. *Journal of the American Geriatric Association, 37*, 447–449.

Thompson, J. K. (1990). *Body image disturbance: Assessment and treatment.* New York: Pergamon Press.

Williamson, D. A. (1990). *Assessment of eating disorders: Obesity, anorexia, and bulimia nervosa.* New York: Pergamon Press.

Index